RELIGION, POPULISM, AND MODERNITY

CONTENDING MODERNITIES

Series editors: Ebrahim Moosa, Atalia Omer, and Scott Appleby

As a collaboration between the Contending Modernities initiative and the University of Notre Dame Press, the Contending Modernities series seeks, through publications engaging multiple disciplines, to generate new knowledge and greater understanding of the ways in which religious traditions and secular actors encounter and engage each other in the modern world. Books in this series may include monographs, co-authored volumes, and tightly themed edited collections.

The series will include works that frame such encounters through the lens of "modernity." The range of themes treated in the series might include war, peace, human rights, nationalism, refugees and migrants, development practice, pluralism, religious literacy, political theology, ethics, multi- and intercultural dynamics, sexual politics, gender justice, and postcolonial and decolonial studies.

RELIGION, POPULISM, AND MODERNITY

Confronting White Christian Nationalism and Racism

Edited by
ATALIA OMER
AND
JOSHUA LUPO

University of Notre Dame Press
Notre Dame, Indiana

University of Notre Dame Press
Notre Dame, Indiana 46556
undpress.nd.edu
Copyright © 2023 by the University of Notre Dame

All Rights Reserved

Published in the United States of America

Library of Congress Control Number: 2023937444

ISBN: 978-0-268-20581-2 (Hardback)
ISBN: 978-0-268-20582-9 (Paperback)
ISBN: 978-0-268-20583-6 (WebPDF)
ISBN: 978-0-268-20580-5 (Epub)

CONTENTS

Introduction: The Cultural Logic of White
Christian Nationalisms   1
ATALIA OMER AND JOSHUA LUPO

CHAPTER 1. Religious Nationalism and Right-Wing Populism:
Trumpism and Beyond   21
PHILIP GORSKI

CHAPTER 2. Zombie Nationalism: The Sexual Politics of White
Evangelical Christian Nihilism   51
JASON A. SPRINGS

CHAPTER 3. Renarrating the Past: The Case of "Modern"
"White" "American" Catholics   100
R. SCOTT APPLEBY

CHAPTER 4. Constructing "Religion," Performing "The People":
Political Theology and the Paradox of Popular
Sovereignty   130
RICHARD AMESBURY

CHAPTER 5. Anti/Philosemitism, Religion, and the Logic of
Ethnic Nationalism in Poland   159
GENEVIÈVE ZUBRZYCKI

CHAPTER 6. The Pull to the Right of the Right, Religion, and
the Ecological Crisis: Evaluating a Religio-Secular
Perspective through a Reading of Bruno Latour's
Late Work   182
YOLANDE JANSEN AND JASMIJN LEEUWENKAMP

| CHAPTER 7. | Which Populism, Which Christianity?
SINDRE BANGSTAD | 223 |
| CHAPTER 8. | Going Rogue on Islam: Derrida's Muslim Hauntology and Nationalism's Specters
EBRAHIM MOOSA | 245 |

List of Contributors 281

Index 285

INTRODUCTION

The Cultural Logic of White Christian Nationalisms

ATALIA OMER AND JOSHUA LUPO

During the first two decades of the twenty-first century, the international norms and institutions that defined the modern world following the devastation of two world wars in the previous century began to falter. The Global War on Terror has significantly affected norms of political sovereignty and autonomy, and Euro-American flavors of anti-Muslim racism have spread across continents. In addition, and relatedly, over the past two decades we have also witnessed the erosion of democratic norms and accompanying virtues. It is important to note here that some marginalized communities claim that these democratic norms were never as enacted as proponents of this system have claimed. The decay of these democratic institutions made space for ethnoreligious-centric accounts of national and civilizational belonging, fascistic rhetoric, and raw racism. Such developments compel us to revisit the basic questions that anchor the study of religion and politics in the modern age. This book is specifically about religion and violent and exclusionary populist nationalisms. It is not about a religion writ large, but about a specific variety of racialized Christianity whose followers are populist chauvinist actors who draw exclusionary boundaries that mark who does and does not belong to the community.

1

This is the second volume emerging from a working group on theory and religion convened by the Contending Modernities (CM) global research initiative. Based at the Kroc Institute for International Peace Studies at the University of Notre Dame, CM has initiated four global working groups of scholars. The first focuses on religion and the human person, the second on migration and the new cosmopolitanism, the third on the themes of authority, community, and identity in sub-Saharan Africa and Indonesia, and the fourth on reexamining religion in modernities. The earlier phases of this initiative focused on enhancing anthropological, sociological, and theological understandings of how "modernities" inform and are constituted by lived experience, religious ethics, sociopolitical agency, and struggles for pluralistic forms of life. Both the quantity and quality of scholarship that these initial working groups generated have enhanced and deepened the scope of the study of religion, particularly in its emphasis on Islam, Catholicism, and the secular as discursive traditions, and Muslims and Catholics as meaning-making agents.

In June 2018, we convened an interdisciplinary group of scholars, all of whom have done extensive work in the study of religion in multiple capacities, with an understanding that the next phase of CM will focus more robustly on the secular as a discursive tradition constitutive of "religion" as a category of analysis and theory. Our intention was to think constructively about ways to intervene in conversations on secularization and stretch scholarship on religion and modernity beyond the inhibiting critical turn. Animating this objective is the concern that critical and genealogical studies of "religion" that treat it solely as a comparative category implicated in Euro- and Christian-centric visions of social and political life constrain constructive engagements with "religion" from their potentially emancipatory, prophetic, and subversive capacities. They also tend to view innovations in subjects' creative reimagining of religion and the elasticity of the concept such reimagining indicates as nothing but the domestication of religion. Feminist religiosity and interpretive lenses[1] seem to disrupt ahistoric and romantic impositions of un-freedom that are part and parcel to religiosity. However, for these critics, they often bestow conservative, patriarchal, and heteronormative interpreters with hermeneutical authenticity and give their approaches epistemological priority. We wish to retain the insights of genealogical accounts of the secular and the religious, while nonetheless push beyond them by also giving attention to the dynamic way in which persons reinterpret these categories in particular social and political contexts.

Beyond Genealogy:
A Framework for Analyzing Religion and Populism

This book's focus on nationalism, and especially White Christian populist and supremacist rhetoric that traffics in an exclusionary conception of peoplehood, foregrounds the relevance of hermeneutic creativity and innovation that animates both the exclusionary discourse of authenticity (the "real nation") and expansive and inclusive discourse. The genealogical study of the secular exposes the "nation," even in its secular self-representation, as infused with a theopolitics,[2] or a theopolitical settlement,[3] within which "religion" is defined, governed, and diffused.[4] The relationship between "religion" and "state," however, is not unidirectional, and the reliance of the institution of the state on the "nation" as its authorizing discourse explains the fallacy of the tired and provincial "ethnic versus liberal" typology of nationalism. This is not to say that there is not a difference between less exclusive and more exclusive citizenship discourses. Rather it is to underscore that the focus on the "nation" and "nationalism," particularly in its contemporary exclusionary trends, sharpens our understanding of religion in modernity.

This is especially the case with the genealogical approach to the analysis of modern nationalism. By this we mean an intellectual excavation that seeks to uncover the underlying antisemitic and anti-Muslim grammars of modernity, and their complex intersections with patterns of racialization.[5] When one scratches the surface, this excavation uncovers Euro- and Christian-centricity that manifests itself in a variety of ways in supremacist and nationalist discourses across Euro-America.[6] This genealogical approach contrasts with efforts to resuscitate political theology as a scholarly interpretive space.[7] The latter is preoccupied with how religious narratives authorize state-sanctioned violence and power, and vice versa. This preoccupation relieves it from addressing its own roots in Christian theology, White supremacy, and Nazi ideology, or, more precisely, the legacy of the conservative German Nazi legal scholar Carl Schmitt.[8] For example, a perusal of journal articles dedicated to the study of political theology reveals repeated investigations of settler colonialisms and White supremacy, expositions of religiously sanctioned violent regimes, and attempts to unmask the theology undergirding pretenses to secularity. This form of unmasking allows for scholars to persist in foregrounding

Christian categories and histories, even if this is done so critically, for the purpose of annotating the theological substance supposedly underpinning the infrastructure of state power and coloniality. This line of exposition and demystification of what is "really there" under multiple liberal façades exposes the subfield as fixated nonetheless on Euro-Christian hegemony and its White supremacist architecture.[9] This is the answer to what is really there and what subsequently needs to be dismantled.

It is not always clear, however, if the dismantling is meant to recover the "real" that underpins the political projects of modernity or if it is meant to aid in imagining new, historically located, trajectories for political justice. Indeed, the way that political theology approaches and genealogical approaches converge with one another precludes an analysis of the complex ways in which modernity's institutions produce new communal, sociopolitical, cultural, and religious meanings. The genealogical and expository (resuscitated political theology) reveals a great deal about the ongoing manifestations of Euro- and Christian-centricity today but, because of its inwardly directed gaze, very little about new ways of imagining political life outside these boundaries. Instead, we more often find an inward romantic harkening to a precolonial social and political imaginary of tradition. The limits reside precisely in the power-reductionist abstract and general schemes that persistently affirm that the only true agents in this story are Euro-American empires and their midwife, White colonial Christianity. Here we agree with Sindre Bangstad (chapter 7), who offers a response to some of the contributions in this volume, that an alternative approach would not do away with genealogical lenses, but lead us to think more capaciously about what can be accomplished by them.

Through an analysis of case studies and theoretical work on modernity that has been carried out by thinkers such as Max Weber, Friedrich Nietzsche, Bruno Latour, and Jacques Derrida, this volume grapples, in specific and grounded terms, with the cultural logic of White Christian nationalisms both in their global interconnectedness and in their specific histories. Indeed, as Geneviève Zubrzycki's (chapter 5) examination of Polish nationalism shows, Christianity is deployed in decidedly different ways by exclusionary Polish nationalists as opposed to White nationalists in the United States. This difference matters when it comes to thinking and acting constructively and transformatively in ways that are historically grounded and critically complex, rather than reductive and reactionary. It is in this space of difference that we hope these theoretical interventions can facilitate a move away from a radically purist form of deconstruction. Such deconstruction is rarely oriented by the empirical realities of the people who inhabit the ideological realities of modern nationalisms and their shifting contours. These contours are an outcome not only of ideas but also political practices, social mechanisms, and institutional designs and constraints. In other words, understanding how antisemitism and philosemitism promote various forms of Polish nationalism, as Zubrzycki does in this volume, requires more interpretive and sociological specificity than just an abstract critique of modernity as a Euro- and Christian-centric project whose afterlife continues to endure in the present. Indeed, as Ebrahim Moosa shows in his essay (chapter 8), Derrida, the "father" of deconstruction, himself fell prey to the false binary between Europe and Islam that buttressed rather than deconstructed myths of Euro-supremacy. In pointing to the limits of Derrida's philosophy, Moosa pushes us to imagine discursive alternatives beyond the European framework.

The undeniable ascendance of right-wing populism—a term we intend to highlight as a common denominator in the exclusionary and antiequality stances of multiple nationalisms across Euro-America—is consistent with modernity's project of displacement, elimination, slavery, and capitalist exploitation. Those who adhere to the mythology of liberal pluralism may decry this characterization. But the turn to a variety of exclusionary nationalisms does not constitute a departure from this legacy, just as the early variety of European fascism and Nazism likewise did not.[10] In the regimes of right-wing populists, one can identify shrinking democratic spaces and the consolidation, in some instances, of "traditional morality" as a trump card to suppress the principle of equality and antibigotry while all along entrenching neoliberal rationality and antidemocratic proclivities.[11] Neoliberal ideology, in this instance, refers to the combination of economic, social, and political policies that emphasize individual responsibility for sociopolitical ills, such as poverty, while ignoring the structural features—deregulation, mass incarceration, redlining, among many others—that give rise to them. Such an ideology inhibits the ability of all citizens to participate equally in democratic processes and promotes an oligarchic form of governance that often relies on racist, heteronormative, and misogynistic currencies in its attempt to shore up political power. Each instance of right-wing populism deploys religion as a marker, a boundary. This very deployment is modernist and reflects a form of religious innovation as well as theological poverty and even illiteracy.[12] People may self-report that religion qua their sense of national identity is deeply important to them, and that both expressions of patriotism and religiosity are held "sincerely." But, in reality, they often have very little facility with the history of interpretations, methodologies of learning, and fluency in liturgy and practice of the traditions to which they adhere. Actual religious knowledge or literacy seems to be irrelevant to the realities shaped through ethnoreligious nationalist discourses.[13] This is a paradox that the following chapters on religion, nationalism, and populism clarify. Such an intervention is necessary because louder and more masculine and militant interpreters of religion do not have a monopoly on what counts as religious knowledge. Indeed, such interpreters often display a poverty of such knowledge. When we train our focus on the religious and political agency of feminist and non-militant interpreters of religious traditions—who, often because of their positionality, are required to steep themselves deeply in religious literacy—new avenues of interpretation open up.

Likewise, we recognize a need to connect social scientific scholarship that studies religion as a self-evident variable that influences, if it is not imbricated with, sociopolitical outcomes with genealogical and decolonial work that unsettles religion's analytic stability in narratives of modernity. We, therefore, operate with an understanding of modernity as an ideological and political project that relates in complex ways to the legacies of colonialism and neocolonialism. Hence, as scholars of coloniality and other critics of modernity have exposed, modernity comes with a dark side.[14] They have demystified modernity's claims of progress with evidence of patterns of racialization, dehumanization, exploitation, displacement, and genocide. Scholarship in religious studies that has begun to cross-fertilize with decoloniality scholarship has highlighted the constitutive relations between race and religion, rooted prototypically in 1492.[15] Other key decolonial interventions bring gender and race further into the conversation in their detailing of the economic logic of coloniality.[16] Others caution against the pitfalls of romantic ahistoricity because of the disservice such accounts do to contemporary Indigenous struggles.[17] Still others draw our attention to the overfixation among academics on epistemological undoing at the expense of decolonial sociological imagination and politics.[18] Decoloniality also orients some theological reflections that identify positive ethical religiosity outside power reductionist accounts that attribute modernity and empire to western Christianity's universalizing cosmology, in both its theological and secularized modalities. Decolonial theologies, together with a decolonial intersectional approach, offer opportunities for double critique, hermeneutical fluidity, and constructive and agentic interruption into the matrixes of domination and exploitation.[19] Theory in religion and modernity can no longer afford bracketing the decolonial analytic prism because colonial presences permeate exclusionary nationalist rhetoric and practice in Euro-America, and also in former European colonies, such as India, the Philippines, and Sri Lanka. Constructions of nation and peoplehood constitute the main sites of analysis for the present volume.

Defining Terms: The Nation and Populism in Modernity

Our working group included scholars who seek to foreground the prism of coloniality in order to offer fresh insights for the study of religion and modernity as it plays out in contemporary political moments, assemblages, and ideologies. Such scholars, whose contributions are also included in two other books in the CM's series on religion and modernity, offer critical analytic and genealogical tools to demystify narratives of progress as inherent to modernity. They do so by reframing modernity through multiple idioms, from mission to modernization, to democratization and development. Among our interlocutors in this volume are also included scholars working within more bounded categories and with an empirical focus on "religion" as a social fact that has theological content, an institutional presence, and sociopolitical causality. As these and other authors show, this understanding of religion plays out in complex ways in nation-states constituted within modernist frameworks.

The centrality of the nation to the story of modernity is not new to theorists of nationalism and religion. Benedict Anderson, Anthony D. Smith, Anthony Marx, Talal Asad, and Saba Mahmood have all made connections between the nation and modernity. In particular, Asad, Mahmood, and other critical scholars of the "secular" have demystified modernity's pretenses to having created a "secular" sphere free of religion. Instead, the modern liberal nation-state and its secular idioms operate myopically to conceal its deep historical, philosophical, and theological parochialism and grammars despite its universalizing scope and implementation. By focusing on contestations over the "nation" in Euro-America, the contributions to this volume reveal the ongoing and elastic relevance of nationalism to the analysis of religion and modernity. Populist trends, at the time of this writing, span the globe, but a focus on White Christian manifestations of the nation invites decolonizing and intersectional analytic tools precisely because of the puzzling ways in which the vernacular of White populist nationalists connects across national boundaries. This is clear in how multiple groups across different national contexts use civilizational language and practice xenophobia, Islamophobia, antisemitism, sexism, and other forms of bigotry and racism. These hatreds are interconnected and reveal long histories of racializing certain religious communities. Since these issues are deeply related to the constitution of religion and modernity, it is not a coincidence that the authors in this volume grapple with these enduring legacies.

Let us now devote some space to gaining clarity on the meaning of populism that is operative in this book. Populism is a complex phenomenon that defies a simple definition and is not associated with one political outlook. In this volume, we focus on right-wing populism because in it we see the unique coalescing of the modernist forces of White supremacy, nationalism, misogyny, and Islamophobia.[20] Daniele Albertazzi and Duncan McDonnell define "right-wing populism" of the kind mushrooming and consolidating around the world in the early decades of the twenty-first century as "a thin-centered ideology which pits a virtuous and homogeneous people against a set of elites and dangerous 'others' who are together depicted as depriving (or attempting to deprive) the sovereign people of their rights, values, prosperity, identity, and voice."[21] Although each instance of right-wing populism is unique, a general anti-Muslim and Islamophobic trend is self-evident in countries such as France, England, Germany, Hungary, Sweden, the Netherlands, and the United States, among others.[22] The right-wing exclusionary populist imaginary frequently promulgates fears of "invasion, infiltration, contagion, conspiracy, replacement and impending irreversible crisis."[23] Such rhetoric often targets Muslims and other minorities. Two of the mechanisms for such targeting play out in the retrieval of orientalist tropes concerning fears of sexual violations of White women by Brown and Black men,[24] and in the emphasis on sexual liberation as a constitutive value of western (European) civilization. That latter is wielded as an exclusionary threshold preventing political belonging.²⁵

The right-wing populist moment, however, also manifests itself in the desire for increased control over women's bodies, reproductive rights, and freedoms, and also in assaults on the rights of LGBTQI communities. This is hardly shocking since in one context after another the strengthening of right-wing forces involves coalitions of conservative Christian forces and reactionary toxic masculinity. Xenophobic national discourses, in other words, also exhibit toxic masculinity. This connection illuminates the gendered dimensions of nationalisms regardless of whether antiwomen and/or anti-LGBTQI sentiments are explicitly or implicitly utilized in rhetorical constructions of belonging and nonbelonging. For example, neoliberal White feminists partake in what Sara Farris coined "femonationalism." Using this term, she analyzes the convergence of "right-wing parties and neoliberals to advance xenophobic and racist politics through the touting of gender equality" at the same time that "various well-known and quite visible feminists and femocrats . . . [frame] Islam as a quintessentially misogynistic religion and culture."²⁶ The dynamics of sexual politics differ from one case to another, but the point is that it remains—whether in its progressive pretenses or in conservative actions through courts, legislation, or executive decrees—an important site to gauge populist, exclusionary, sociopolitical shifts, which, as Farris notes, also entail gendered economic exploitation of migrant and other minority women in the service industries.²⁷ Jason A. Springs's contribution (chapter 2) in this volume takes up the logic of sexual politics in perpetuating White evangelicals' political exclusionary project in the United States, thus connecting, in a manner keeping with intersectional analysis, the categories of race, gender, and sexuality.

However, the common anti-Muslim racism trend threaded throughout the multiple instances of right-wing populism also betrays another commonality: right-wing populist political parties thrive on rearticulated forms of antisemitism and, at the same time, support Israeli policies concerning the occupation of Palestinian lands and people. In doing so, they embody the (perhaps surprising) lack of contradiction between Zionism and antisemitism. Israeli Jewish politicians and lobbyists who were associated with Netanyahu's government did not protest—indeed, they condoned—so-called strong men, from Victor Orbán to Donald Trump, regardless of their active employment and retweeting of antisemitic tropes or their inclusion of known Nazis in their cabinets.[28] Indeed, this marriage of populist demagogues across seemingly contradictory political ideologies reveals the assimilation of Israel into a civilizational discourse and the relatively recent construction of Jews as "White" and part of the supersessionist construct of the Judeo-Christian.[29]

CRITICAL VISIONS FOR THE FUTURE: CHAPTER SUMMARIES

Despite this grim picture, the phenomenon of right-wing populism in the current moment offers an opportunity for constructive conversation that can take critical work seriously. Doing so, however, requires a shift away from pure abstraction, and from the methodological nationalism that hermetically bounds the cultural logic of a single instance of nationalism, to a deeper decolonial analysis of the kind that Santiago Slabodsky argues for in another contribution in this book series.[30] The specific case studies in the United States, Germany, Poland, and France ground the study in the vernacular nationalist discourses of a given society, but do not lose track of the importance of theory as they do so. Hence, some of the case studies offer resources to expose the specific and general ways in which antisemitism and anti-Muslim racism intersect with the populist moment of right-wing Christian nationalism. Others emphasize the persistent relevance of gendered conceptions of race to the imagining of peoplehood and the religio-ethnic thresholds of exclusion and inclusion. The essays reveal how this intersection exposes the enduring legacies of western Christian colonialism. Because such legacies manifest differently in different contexts, examining their varieties requires specialized historical and cultural knowledge. For example, drawing on Bruno Latour's philosophical oeuvre, Yolande Jansen and Jasmijn Leeuwenkamp (chapter 6) connect the often undertheorized role of the ecological emergency to a broader analysis of the tide of right-wing populist discourses throughout Europe. They underscore that understanding the cultural logic of contemporary right-wing Christian nationalistic expressions demands a deep historical lens and decolonial prism. Meanwhile, Zubrzycki focuses on how philosemitism functions in a discourse about Polishness to convey progressive and inclusive (or cosmopolitan) visions of the nation. This deployment of philosemitism seemingly contrasts with how antisemitism is likewise deployed as a symbolic foil promoting exclusionary or "ethnic" (Catholic) Polishness. Both antisemitism and philosemitism operate within the absences of actual Jews whose presence had already been eradicated. Hence, this case of philosemitism without Jews, which involves multiple practices of cultural appropriation, exemplifies why it is necessary to critically engage with modernity as a narrative of barbarity—by treating its dark sides of genocides and slavery as parts of its very definition rather than perversions of an otherwise enlightened intellectual and political project—and with its legacies of erasures and dehumanization.[31] The figure of the Jew in the contestation of the thresholds of Polishness shows a particularly Polish expression of a long legacy of labeling and accusing people of secret Jewish identities. This reveals the modernist understanding of Jewishness as inscribed in blood. Such a modernist understanding of identity is reflected, as Zubrzycki notes, in the impossibility of identity in Poland outside of racial and/or ethnic categories. The cosmopolitan mobilization of philosemitism also goes hand in hand with anti-Muslim practices because antisemitism is weaponized globally to secure Zionism and Islamophobia. The consolidation of the Judeo-Christian as a civilizational and orientalist discourse bifurcates these two "others" of Europe.

Indeed, without foregrounding the intricate relationship between Europe's "Jewish question" and "Muslim question," the enduring role of Christianity's complicity with coloniality remains invisible. In a related fashion, understanding Christian modernity not only in terms of the double and interwoven othering of Muslims and Jews, but also as the result of the intra-Christian reinvention of the community of Christians as "a community of blood" in the fifteenth century's *limpieza de sangre*, is necessary. This development anticipates modern nationalism and clarifies the continuities between Christian political theology and modern racism. It also clarifies the aforementioned deeper roots of the modernist interlinking of "race" and "nation." The labor of decoloniality, however, is not merely to engage in discursive critique but also semiotic intervention. To decolonize this discourse means to make Europe visible as a theopolitical project and to illuminate the ways that right-wing populisms continue to rely on Europe's story line while intersectional modes of imaginations and solidarity disrupt its logic. In their closing essays in this volume, Ebrahim Moosa (chapter 7) and Sindre Bangstad (chapter 8), in particular, begin to help us imagine these ways forward.

Beyond this crosscutting analysis of the theopolitics of modernity at the intersection of Islamophobia and antisemitism, a decolonial prism further demands that we weave into our analysis a concern with how gender, race, and economic variables intersect with these concerns. Doing so exposes not only the Christian cultural logic, rhetoric, and demagoguery but also an underlying global exploitative logic of neoliberalism.[32] Indeed, sexual politics is an essential feature of right-wing populism that usually comes with toxic masculine flavors.[33] Bracketing it as unrelated to how religion fits into right-wing populist rhetoric is analytically problematic. Some of the meditations in this volume focus on one facet or another of this analytic grid, but they all contribute building blocks for a more robust decolonial engagement with religion and modernity as they unfold in and within the contestations of peoplehood, citizenship, and nation. The specificities of the case studies offer contextually layered, hermeneutically open, and intersectionally attuned accounts of modern nationalism and religion as coimbricated and constitutive of a modernist discourse of authenticity upon which populist and conservative religiosity thrives.

In his chapter, Springs outlines what he calls the practices of evangelical nihilism to explicate the anatomy of right-wing exclusionary nationalist discourses in the United States. In doing so he is attuned to the concerns of both intersectional analysis and hermeneutic openness we described in the previous paragraph. He practices an intersectionally attuned form of analysis by exposing how enduring patterns of racialization, the ontologization of marriage, and racialized norms are inscribed into a gender-producing nihilistic hermeneutics. He contrasts the latter with a coherent theology of same-sex marriage that does not theorize theological imaginations out of existence or render them poetic and thus domesticated into liberal frames. Instead, a double critique and hermeneutical openness grounded in postliberal theology allows for Springs to engage tradition using its own tools. Doing so deconstructs its heteropatriarchy and points to a new, egalitarian vision of the tradition. On the other side of modernity as a site of religious innovation and hermeneutic creativity, Springs uses "Nietzschean tools" to show how the nation-state as a site for religious innovation is inextricably linked to the racializing and gendering of religious and political expressions. Yet, nihilistic hermeneutics is only a part of the story. A layered account of the nation as a site of religious innovation challenges totalizing and pessimistic accounts of modernity. This account also gestures toward the crucial decolonial task of critiquing the theopolitics of liberal political discourse and its foundational analytic categories.

If Springs interprets the nation as a site of multidirectional reconfiguration of religion and nation (through the complex mediation of institutions and legal mechanisms), Richard Amesbury (chapter 4) argues that peoplehood, the site of popular sovereignty, constitutes a performative regress whose logic eventually leads to an authorized people. Christianity, for him, is up for grabs by populists who offer an alternative interpretation to inclusive and liberal hermeneutics. Of course, both the exclusionary and inclusionary modes of Christianity's relation to the thresholds of belonging or nonbelonging to the "nation" in the United States or Germany (the two foci of Amesbury's argument) are as equally modernist as the hermeneutically expansive and conservative approaches to marriage and sexuality. This brings to the fore an overlap between Springs and Amesbury. If Springs focuses on the racialized and gendered exclusionary patterns of nihilistic Christian hermeneutics, then Amesbury identifies the structural mechanics of sovereignty that enable such a variety of Christianity to permeate what it means to belong to the "nation." Amesbury echoes Benedict Anderson's important observation that modern nationalism is philosophically unsound while nonetheless potent as a political force. It is this paradox that partly explains the performative logic of peoplehood. Still, and here Amesbury connects to the genealogical line of inquiry (as do all of our contributors), the appeals to Christianity or Christianism (in Rogers Brubaker's formulation) in European contexts illuminate not only the specific mechanics of peoplehood in Germany but also the broader political and theological underpinnings rooted in coloniality. For in Germany, it is not only the nation that is at stake in grounding who the sovereign is, but it is also Christian/European civilization that is at stake. As Amesbury shows in his analysis of the AfD party, what is sought after in identifying who the people embody is not simply a crude vision of German peoplehood, but a vision of the people as inextricably secular, Christian, and in need of defense from those it identifies as not sharing in those identities, namely, Muslims. Of course, this "defense" takes on forms of sexual and gendered politics and rhetorical maneuvers. Amesbury does not discuss these, but when read alongside

Springs's contribution, they can nonetheless be seen. By foregrounding the White Christian "nation" as an analytic site, both Springs and Amesbury significantly expand our understanding of religion and modernity in a way that moves beyond abstractions and generic reductive explanatory accounts and into historically located sites of hermeneutic creativity and the mechanics of governmentality.

Certainly, the appeals to a Christian civilizational identity are never generic but always mediated through the glorification of peoplehood itself. Philip Gorski (chapter 1) shows that conceptions of peoplehood share elective affinities with religious meanings, symbols, narratives, and, most foundationally, conceptions of chosenness, which are grounded in biblical prototypes. Gorski, as do the other contributors herein, offers a cultural analysis that identifies the relationship between religious conservatism and right-wing populism in the United States (with some comparative references to other cases around the world). Gorski focuses his analysis on identifying a cultural logic that links race, religion, and nation and its deployment in Trumpism. For Gorski, both the modern nation and religion are intricately grounded in Christian readings of Hebrew scriptures. This fact explains the volcanic capacity of "religion" to erupt through the discourse of nationalism, and vice versa. He views Trumpism as a secularized White Christian nationalism, one that is also gendered. By exposing the constitutive relations of Whiteness, Christianity, and gender, Gorski takes on the challenge of analyzing religion and modernity intersectionally, exposing the "nation" once again as a site both particular and theory-producing. In conversation with Gorski and Springs, in his response R. Scott Appleby (chapter 3) reflects on both the overlaps and disjunctures between the White evangelical experience in the United States and the Catholic experience. He is particularly attuned to how White nationalism has become imbricated in more recent articulations of Catholic theology and the challenges of overcoming it in the present.

These chapters on White Christian nationalisms, therefore, reveal the intricately constitutive relation of religion and race or ethnicity, the religious dimensions of the ecological crisis and its denialism in Trumpism, the persistence (even if transmogrified) of antisemitism and anti-Muslim racism in constructing contemporary visions of the nation as a "golden age," the operation of sexual politics in exclusionary practices used to authorize state violence, and the global circulation and exchanges among

White nationalists across various locales. Of course, Zionist antisemitism finds even a deeper cultural logic in, and elective affinities with, Christian restorationist theologies that interpret the return of all Jews to Zion as a key stage in an end-time narrative. This Christian Zionism has illuminated for centuries now, but especially since the nineteenth century, the intimate relation between anti- and philosemitism and Zionism, understood as the restoration and/or "return" to Zion of the Jewish people. Why does this complex interdependence matter for the contemporary moment of antisemitic Zionism? It matters if we are to understand the contemporary reemergence of antisemitism in its deeper cultural, theological, and political roots, and if we are to understand the degree to which these roots have laid the foundation for the local contestation of nationalist discourses, whether in Poland, Hungry, France, Norway, or the United States. Such interdependence is also necessary if we are to make sense of the neoliberal shrinking of these countries' democratic spaces and how they intersect with or diverge from anti-Muslim narratives.

Indeed, empirical evidence shows that antisemitism correlates positively with high levels of anti-Muslim racism—that is increasingly codified in law—in contexts where right-wing populists surge.[34] The co-occurrence of anti-Muslim racism and antisemitism is only surprising if one succumbs to the discursive dichotomization of Muslims and Jews, with "Muslims" often being used interchangeably (and erroneously) with "Arabs." The concurrence of Zionism with antisemitism unsettles the post–World War II apparent assimilation of Jews into secularized White Christian political spaces and narratives of belonging. The protection of whatever "virtuous community" against "infiltrators" and "foreigners" (regardless of whether they are actual citizens) is articulated specifically through appeals to a particular retrieval of "historical" racialized accounts of the nation when it was "pure" or "great."

This rhetorical maneuver exposes the interlinking of Whiteness and Christianity so central to coloniality, where the latter is understood as a concept that captures the constitutive and enduring relations between modernity and colonialism.[35] Within the academic study of religion, this relation plays out in the construction and deployment of the comparative categories of "religion" and "race" in the service of empire and control.[36] Along with class and political economy, various nationalisms filtered through political liberal discourses of citizenship undertheorize and/or myopically conceal "race" and racialized religion's participation in the construction of their "natural" boundaries and thresholds of belonging and nonbelonging. A thick and layered description of nationalisms, as the contributors here provide, concretize the analysis of the intersection of race and religion and clarify why an examination of the cultural logic of nationalism paves the way for constructive and hermeneutic creativity with both nation and religion.[37]

Within European national discourses—whose boundaries are defined through appeals to conceptions of the "people" rooted, to varying degrees, in Christianity as a source of belonging (peoplehood), values, tradition, cultural inheritance, heritage, and other labels that exclude multiple others—the presence of Jews and the assimilation of some Jews into White Christianity comes under scrutiny. Indeed "White Christianity" is not generic but is manifested in multiple specific stories that are uniquely Italian, Dutch, French, Hungarian, Polish, Serb, American, and so forth. Yet a deep historical analysis that centralizes a critique of coloniality and the semiotic circuits of racialization and cultural exchange foregrounds a more discursive account that sees the architecture and/or grammar beyond and beneath the particular variation when articulating an overarching account of political secularism and its underpinning religio-political imagination.

The chapters in this book focus on the specifics of the cultural logic of French *laïcité*, Polishness, the AfD party, and White nationalism in the United States. These studies illuminate the importance of exposing and explaining the cultural logic of nationalism, scrutinize the layered ways in which religiosity is co-constituted with nationality, and show how the nation remains a site for redemptive aspirations and religious fulfillment, one that often traffics in the language of authenticity, purity, and chosenness and/or exceptionalism. The intersectional lens we all deploy helps unpack the mechanics and contents of such exclusionary constructions and exposes their uniquely modern construction. The nationalisms examined here are not only Christian but also White, and their Whiteness presses upon us the importance of theory on religion and modernity that is intersectional and decolonial in its sensitivity. And yet, the sociological specificity of the case studies challenges reactionary and reductive accounts of colonial afterlives or how colonial rationalities continue to manifest through different mechanisms and sociopolitical and religious formations. Hence, the essays in this book illuminate the productive difference between a critical analysis of the genealogy of modernity and its enduring operation in ethnoreligious nationalist exclusionary discourses and the hermeneutical breadth and historical and sociological intricacies of nationalism that cannot be subsumed into simplistic narratives about religion and empire.

NOTES

1. For examples of such challenges, see Aysha A. Hidayatullah, *Feminist Edges of the Qur'an* (Oxford: Oxford University Press, 2014); Ziba Mir-Hosseini, *Men in Charge? Rethinking Authority in Muslim Legal Tradition* (London: Oneworld Academic, 2015).

2. For example, Talal Asad, *Formations of the Secular: Christianity, Islam, Modernity* (Stanford, CA: Stanford University Press, 2003).

3. For example, Elizabeth Shakman Hurd, *The Politics of Secularism in International Relations* (Princeton, NJ: Princeton University Press, 2008).

4. See Saba Mahmood, *Religious Difference in a Secular Age: A Minority Report* (Princeton, NJ: Princeton University Press, 2015); Winnifred Fallers Sullivan, *The Impossibility of Religious Freedom* (Princeton, NJ: Princeton University Press, 2005); Hussein Ali Agrama, *Questioning Secularism: Islam, Sovereignty, and the Rule of Law in Modern Egypt* (Chicago: University of Chicago Press, 2012).

5. See Anya Topolski, "The Dangerous Discourse of the 'Judeo-Christian' Myth: Masking the Race-Religion Constellation in Europe," *Patterns of Prejudice* 54, no. 1–2 (2020): 71–90. See also Yolande Jansen and Nasar Meer, "Genealogies of 'Jews' and 'Muslims': Social Imaginaries in the Race-Religion Nexus," *Patterns of Prejudice* 54, no. 1–2 (2020): 1–14.

6. See also Atalia Omer, "Nationalism, Religion, Ideology," in *Routledge Handbook of Religion and Ideology*, ed. Jeff Haynes (New York: Routledge, 2022), 51–64.

7. See Ulrich Schmiedel and Joshua Ralston, eds., *The Spirit of Populism: Political Theologies in Polarized Times* (Leiden: Brill, 2022).

8. Not all varieties of political theology trace their conceptual roots to Schmitt, but his theoretical framework and its state-centricity has nonetheless come to dominate the field as it is imagined in the journal *Political Theology* and in the wider field of religious studies.

9. See, for instance, the special issue of the *Political Theology* (Summer 2020) dedicated to the thought of Jean Bodin (1529/30–1596), a French intellectual whose thought participated in authorizing European colonialism and its practices of displacement.

10. Hannah Arendt, *Imperialism: Part Two of "The Origins of Totalitarianism"* (New York: Harcourt Brace Jovanovich, 1968); Achille Mbembe, "Necropolitics," *Public Culture* 15, no. 1 (2003): 11–40.

11. See Wendy Brown, *In the Ruins of Neoliberalism: The Rise of Antidemocratic Politics in the West* (New York: Columbia University Press, 2019), esp. chap. 4.

12. The concept of religious literacy is deployed in a variety of ways. We follow Diane Moore's critical and theoretical definition of religious literacy, which, deploying Donna Haraway's concept of "situated knowledges," means not only facility with the actual contours of traditions but also a willingness to subject interpretations and practices to critical, historicist, and epistemological approaches from the margins. See Moore, "Overcoming Religious Illiteracy: A Cultural Studies Approach," *Religious Education* 109, no. 4 (2014): 379–89.

13. See also Olivier Roy, *Holy Ignorance: When Religion and Culture Part Ways* (Oxford: Oxford University Press, 2010).

14. The concept of "coloniality" was first articulated by Aníbal Quijano, "Coloniality of Power, Eurocentrism, and Latin America," *Nepantla: Views from South* 1, no. 3 (2000): 533–80; see also Enrique Dussel, "Eurocentrism and Modernity (Introduction to the Frankfurt Lectures)," *Boundary 2* 20, no. 3 (1993): 65–76. Ella Shohat stresses the multiplicity and multidirectionality of 1492, illuminating that coloniality is not a unitary story line. See Shohat, "Taboo Memories, Diasporic Visions: Columbus, Palestine, and Arab-Jews," in *Taboo Memories, Diasporic Visions* (Durham, NC: Duke University Press, 2006), 201–32; see also Walter Mignolo, *The Darker Side of Western Modernity: Global Futures, Decolonial Options* (Durham, NC: Duke University Press, 2011).

15. Nelson Maldonado-Torres, "On the Coloniality of Being: Contributions to the Development of a Concept," *Cultural Studies* 21, no. 2–3 (2007): 240–70; Nelson Maldonado-Torres, "AAR Centennial Roundtable: Religion, Conquest, and Race in the Foundations of the Modern/Colonial World," *Journal of the American Academy of Religion* 82, no. 3 (2014): 636–65; An Yountae, "A Decolonial Theory of Religion: Race, Coloniality, and Secularity in the Americas," *Journal of the American Academy of Religion* 88, no. 4 (2020): 947–80; Gil Anidjar, *Blood: A Critique of Christianity* (New York: Columbia University Press, 2014).

16. Sylvia Wynter, "Unsettling the Coloniality of Being/Power/Truth/Freedom: Towards the Human, After Man, Its Overrepresentation—An Argument," *New Centennial Review* 3, no. 3 (2003): 257–337; Maria Lugones, "Heterosexualism and the Colonial/Modern Gender System," *Hypatia* 22, no. 1 (2007): 186–209.

17. Silvia Rivera Cusicanqui, "Ch'ixinakax utxiwa: A Reflection on the Practices and Discourses of Decolonization," *South Atlantic Quarterly* 111, no. 1 (2012): 95–109.

18. Martin Savransky, "A Decolonial Imagination: Sociology, Anthropology and the Politics of Reality," *Sociology* 51, no. 1 (2017): 11–26.

19. For example, Santiago Slabodsky, "Christian Hegemonies: Evolutionism, Analectics, and the Question of Interreligiosity in a Decolonial Philosophy of Religion" (lecture, Colloquium on Coloniality, Race, and Philosophy of Religion, Harvard Divinity School, Cambridge, MA, November 30, 2018). For the employment of the double critique in the burgeoning field of critical Muslim studies, see Critical Muslim Studies, "Cape Town: Decolonial Struggles and Liberation Theologies," https://criticalmuslimstudies.co.uk. For related lines of engagement in South Africa (a leading example of efforts to decolonize knowledge production), see Savo Heleta, "Decolonizing Knowledge in South Africa: Dismantling the 'Pedagogy of Big Lies,'" *Ufahamu: A Journal of African Studies* 40, no. 2 (2018): 47–65. See also Farid Esack, *Qur'an, Liberation and Pluralism: An Islamic Perspective of Interreligious Solidarity against Oppression* (Oxford: Oneworld, 1997).

20. Variations of left-wing populism have no doubt also engaged in these forms of discrimination, but they have in general been less centered on them, and thus do not as strongly bring into relief these features of modernity that threaten the lives of so many.

21. Cited in Nadia Marzouki and Duncan McDonnell, "Populism and Religion," in *Saving the People: How Populists Hijack Religion*, ed. Nadia Marzouki, Duncan McDonnell, and Olivier Roy (Oxford: Oxford University Press, 2016), 1–12, at 3.

22. Through the Preventing Violent Extremism discourse and the focus on securitizing religion, Islamophobia and anti-Muslim sentiments are also exported to and codified throughout the global South.

23. Marzouki and McDonnell, "Populism and Religion," 5.

24. Ibid., 6.

25. Judith Butler, "Sexual Politics, Torture, and Secular Time," in *Frames of War: When Is Life Grievable?* (London: Verso, 2016), 101–36; Joan Wallach Scott, *Sex and Secularism* (Princeton, NJ: Princeton University Press, 2018).

26. Sara R. Farris, *In the Name of Women's Rights: The Rise of Femonationalism* (Durham, NC: Duke University Press, 2017), 4. For similar analytic approaches, see also Jasbir Puar, *Terrorist Assemblages: Homonationalism in Queer Times* (Durham, NC: Duke University Press, 2007).

27. For an analysis of erotic nationalism and the centrality of the control of women's bodies to religious nationalism, see Roger Friedland, "Money, Sex, and God: The Erotic Logic of Religious Nationalism," *Sociological Theory* 20, no. 3 (2002): 381–425.

28. For example, Trump employed Sebastian Gorka, a Hungarian with known Nazi ties. See Masha Gessen, "The Weaponization of National Belonging, from Nazi Germany to Trump," *The New Yorker,* July 21, 2019, https://www.newyorker.com/news/our-columnists/the-weaponization-of-national-belonging-from-nazi-germany-to-trump.

29. See Santiago Slabodsky, *Decolonial Judaism: Triumphal Failures of Barbaric Thinking* (New York: Palgrave Macmillan, 2014).

30. Santiago Slabodsky, "Seeing the Old in the New: The Coloniality of the Liberal-Populist Marriage," in *Religion, Modernity, and Colonialism*, ed. Atalia Omer and Joshua Lupo (forthcoming, University of Notre Dame Press).

31. For key examples, see Walter Benjamin, "On the Concept of History," in *Illuminations*, ed. Hannah Arendt, trans. Harry Zohn (New York: Harcourt, Brace & World, 1968), 255–66; Max Horkheimer and Theodor W. Adorno, *Dialectic of Enlightenment: Philosophical Fragments*, ed. Gunzelin Schmid Noerr, trans. Edmund Jephcott (Stanford, CA: Stanford University Press, 2002 [1947]).

32. Farris, *In the Name of Women's Rights*.

33. Puar, *Terrorist Assemblages*; Scott, *Sex and Secularism*; Friedland, "Money, Sex, and God."

34. For an examination of this issue, see Peter Gottschalk, "Hate Crimes Associated with Both Islamophobia and Anti-Semitism Have a Long History in America's Past," *The Conversation*, June 3, 2019, https://theconversation.com/hate-crimes-associated-with-both-islamophobia-and-anti-semitism-have-a-long-history-in-americas-past-116255; see also, FBI, "2017 Hate Crime Statistics," https://ucr.fbi.gov/hate-crime/2017/topic-pages/tables/table-1.xls.

35. For example, Anibal Quijano, "Coloniality and Modernity/Rationality," *Cultural Studies* 21, no. 2–3 (2007): 168–78; Mignolo, *Darker Side of Western Modernity*; Lugones, "Methodological Notes toward a Decolonial Feminism," in *Decolonizing Epistemologies: Latina/o Theology and Philosophy*, ed. Ada Isasi-Diaz and Eduardo Mendieta (New York: Fordham University Press, 2012), 68–86.

36. David Chidester, *Empire of Religion: Imperialism and Comparative Religion* (Chicago: University of Chicago Press, 2014).

37. For an exposition of the methodology of the hermeneutics of citizenship, see Atalia Omer, *When Peace Is Not Enough: How the Israeli Peace Camp Thinks about Religion, Nationalism, and Justice* (Chicago: University of Chicago Press, 2013).

CHAPTER 1

Religious Nationalism and Right-Wing Populism

Trumpism and Beyond

PHILIP GORSKI

Abstract

An enduring puzzle around Donald Trump's 2016 electoral success was his ability to mobilize an extraordinarily high level of support among White Christian voters, White evangelical voters in particular. This chapter offers a new conceptual framework for understanding Trump's enduring evangelical support: White Christian nationalism. White Christian nationalism might be viewed as part of a broader global trend of religious nationalism cultivated by right-wing populist leaders. However, White Christian nationalism also proves unique in its ability to connect specific constructions of race, religion, and nation through narrative themes, including blood tropes, apocalyptic narratives, persecution/victimization narratives, and messianic expectations. Understanding how Trumpism effectively secularized the metaphors at the heart of White Christian nationalism offers key insights into Trump's success among White evangelical Christians, and for understanding contemporary right-populist politics and political theology.

One of the great puzzles of the 2016 presidential election in the United States was the extraordinary support that Donald Trump received from White evangelicals. Roughly 40 percent voted for Trump during the GOP primaries and more than 80 percent ultimately voted for him in the general election.[1] Nor was this enthusiasm specific to White *evangelicals*. On the contrary, it was shared by White Christians more generally, albeit to a lesser degree. But it was specific to *White* evangelicals. The majority of non-White evangelicals voted for other candidates.

One of the great puzzles of the four years of the Trump administration was the remarkable stability of Trump's approval ratings among White evangelicals. In postelection opinion polls, 70–80 percent still supported him.[2] In 2020, 83 percent of White evangelicals again cast their ballots for Trump, more than in 2016. The same trend can be observed among White Christians more generally, including Catholics:[3] they, too, seem to have set aside whatever misgivings they may have had about Trump. Non-White Christians have not; they disapprove of Trump's performance more strongly than ever.

Nor is this a uniquely American puzzle, or one that will fade away now that Trump has left office. The affinity between religious conservativism and right-wing populism is a phenomenon that long antedates Trump and extends to many parts of the world, including Orbán's Hungary, Modi's India, Bolsonaro's Brazil, and Duterte's Philippines. The affinity is perhaps less obvious and also less important in western Europe, but even there neo-populists, such as Matteo Salvini, Marine Le Pen, and Geert Wilders, have frequently positioned themselves as defenders of "Christian civilization."[4]

Of course, not all religious conservatives feel attracted to the populist message. In the United States, for instance, the ranks of the #never-Trumpers include a good number of conservative Christian intellectuals, Protestant and Catholic. One thinks of the *New York Times* columnists Peter Wehner and Ross Douthat, for example. In western Europe, meanwhile, many of the official representatives of the Christian churches have publicly denounced conservative populism.

The question, then, is which religious conservatives support the populists and why? The general answer I propose here is "religious nationalists."[5] And in the case of the United States, "White Christian nationalists."[6] This chapter has three interrelated aims: (1) to unpack the cultural logic that connects race, religion, and nation in contemporary US politics—and US religious history, more generally;[7] (2) to show how Trump has mobilized it; and (3) to ask whether similar logics are at work in other cases.

Nor is that the only seeming oxymoron in the following analysis. I will also argue that Trumpism is best understood as a secularized version of White Christian nationalism. By this, I mean a version that has been evacuated of scriptural references and theological content. On the one hand, Trumpism mobilized the central metaphors and tropes of White Christian nationalism, specifically blood metaphors and apocalyptic tropes. That is what is old about it. This is why Trumpism still resonates with evangelicals, without being obviously evangelical. On the other hand, it is not bound by Christian ethics or political theology. This is what makes it new, and also dangerous: it cannot be held accountable to any higher standard.

"Religious Nationalism"?

At first glance, the relationship between religion and nationalism may appear more contradictory than complementary. Isn't religion universalistic and nationalism particularistic? Isn't religion traditional and nationalism modern? A certain narrative of western modernity might lead one to think so. But this narrative is mistaken, because religion and nationalism as we now understand them have a common, historical root. Both are derived from a certain (Christian) reading of the Hebrew scriptures. This means that there are hidden links between religion and nation that can always be reactivated, even if they have lain dormant for a time.

Until recently, most social scientists would have dismissed the very concept of religious nationalism as an oxymoron. Some still do. Nationalism was long assumed to be a wholly "modern" phenomenon.[8] Some even regarded it as an ersatz religion for a secular modernity, the cultural stuff used to plug up the God-shaped hole left behind by a *deus absconditus*.[9] Today, however, many scholars understand religious nationalism as a distinctive variant of modern nationalism, one that makes religious identity the litmus test of national belonging.[10]

In the United States, for example, religious nationalists have long argued that only a "good Christian" can be a "real American," and vice versa.[11] Just a century ago, however, just being a good Christian was not enough; real Americans were *Protestant* Christians. Today, one can also be a Catholic (so long as one is antiabortion) or even (!) a Jew (so long as one is strongly "pro-Israel"). Nor are such claims about the link between religious and national identity peculiar to the United States. As Geneviève Zubrzycki argues elsewhere in this volume (chapter 5), one hears similar rhetoric about Polish-ness and Catholicism.[12] And, one might add, about Hindu-ness and Indian-ness or Sunni-ness and Turkish-ness, too.[13]

One could still argue that religious nationalism is a specifically modern phenomenon, of course, and for two reasons. First, because religious nationalism emerges as a specific type only in opposition to a secular nationalism, that is, to a form of nationalism based on ideas of civic belonging or ethnic origins. These conceptions first arise during the democratic revolutions of the late eighteenth century and the romantic movements of the late nineteenth century, respectively. And second, because the category of religion as we now understand it arguably first emerges during this same period as a means of conceptualizing the relationship of Christianity to other traditions, and its superiority to them.[14] The idea that there are multiple species of religion that are members of the same genus did not really begin to take shape in the west until the early modern era, when overseas exploration brought western Christians into sustained contact with "Oriental" religion and did not fully take hold until western colonialism sparked claims of religio-cultural superiority vis-à-vis non-Christian others.[15]

Still, these arguments should not be overstated either, and for similar reasons. Ethnic identities have long been intertwined with religious identities.[16] They still are. Sometimes in obvious ways, as in the opposition between Catholic Ireland and Protestant England. But also in subtle ways, as in the Protestant influence on the civic culture of the United States, with its emphasis on personal beliefs and individual rights, or in the Catholic influence on the civic culture of France, with its emphasis on public space and sartorial conformity.[17] Religion and national identity, it appears, are not so easily disentangled.

Nor is this entanglement an accident of history. Western nationalism itself has religious roots. The common root is the Hebrew scriptures or, rather, a certain Christian appropriation of them. The definitional triptych of the nation—"people, land, and state"—is already prefigured in the Pentateuch, after all, which speaks of a chosen people, a holy land, and a Jewish polity.[18] And most western nationalisms originally arose out of Christian claims to supersede the ancient Israelites as God's chosen people.[19] Virtually every nation in Europe advanced claims of this sort at some point in its history.

Americans were hardly alone in their claims of chosenness.[20] On the contrary, claims of national chosenness were so ubiquitous in the history of western Europe and its settler colonies as to be practically commonplace. They were the rule rather than the exception. The Dutch and the English both envisioned themselves as "New Israels" during the Reformation Era, for example.[21] That, in fact, is the historical origin of the American conceit. Nor were they anything like the first to do so. The Hebraic analogy had already made earlier appearances in medieval France and seventh-century England, too.[22] American religious historians have long been aware of the role that such claims have played in the development of American national consciousness. The New England Puritans already cast themselves in the role of the "New Israel" in the early seventeenth century. And when the Puritan settlers were subsequently cast as the founding grandfathers of the United States, and their Thanksgiving was proclaimed the nation's second national holiday after the Fourth of July, the claim of chosenness was effectively extended to the nation as a whole.[23]

Claims of national chosenness are still alive even today in the semisecular ideology of "American Exceptionalism," which insists that the United States is a "nation like no other" upon which a special "mission" has been conferred, a "crusade" to defend freedom. The crusader variant of religious nationalism is not new either. It made its first appearance during the Puritans' wars with the native peoples during the late seventeenth century. Since then, it has reappeared in many different guises in the nation's many different wars: as Anglo-Protestant nationalism in the French and Indian War, for example, as WASP nationalism in the colonial conquests of the fin de siècle, as "Judeo-Christian" nationalism in the Cold War against "godless Communism," and, more recently, against "radical Islam."

No one should be surprised to discover an additional link between race and nation. After all, the Latin word for "nation" is the root word for "birth," and the "birth of a nation" often has overtones of race, especially in the United States. But what do Whiteness and Christianity have to do with one another? In recent years, critical social scientists have argued that we need to think "intersectionally" about race, class, and gender.[24] Recently, some scholars have proposed that we think about religion intersectionally, too.[25] Certainly, that is warranted in the American case.

For in the United States, religious nationalism has always been entangled with White supremacism. It has always been *White* Christian nationalism. All too often, blood conquest and blood purity have gone hand in hand. On the frontier and in the colonies, "uncivilized" and "heathen" peoples—red, brown, and yellow—were to be subjugated, and then civilized, or, failing that, simply destroyed, or, more politely, allowed to "disappear."[26] The racial logic of the "Indian wars"—White claims on a promised land in the hands of colored "Canaanites"—was simply extended westward and southward in the repression of Asian immigrants and the seizure of Mexican territory.[27] After all, productive land could not be left in the hands of unproductive people, the argument went! On the plantation, meanwhile, the subjugation of Black slaves helped to create and then reinforce an enduring culture of White violence.[28] The honor of White men, it seemed, could only be effectively sustained through periodic assaults on Black bodies.

Nor is this all. Christian nationalism of the crusading sort has also led to a militaristic understanding of the American state.[29] For blood conquest and blood purity inevitably go together with blood sacrifice and military might. If the United States was to Christianize the world and rid it of evil, if that was its mission, then military might was necessarily one of the means.

Academic analysts have often remarked on the quasi-religious character of modern nationalism. Some have explained this in functional terms. On this account, nationalism is a "political religion" that fills the "God-shaped hole" left by secularization.[30] Others have explained it in instrumental terms.[31] From this perspective, nationalist politicians cynically invoke religious language to galvanize their followers. The genealogical account suggests a different perspective: modern nationalism has a religious "unconscious" that can always be summoned back to the surface again. And often is. Not least in the United States.

Christian Nationalism in American History

As should be clear by now, Christian nationalism is nothing new in the United States. On the contrary, it is very, very old—almost as old as New England, which is, in fact, where it first began. But for much of US history, White Christian nationalism has also lain dormant and has mostly reared its head during wartime. Why? Because Christian nationalism was a useful tool for wartime mobilization. It raised the stakes of a conflict by turning profane wars into holy wars.[32] It was also a soothing balm for uneasy consciences and mourning survivors.[33] It drew a clear line between us and them, and aligned it with the line between good and evil. It also lent meaning to the casualties of war by turning death in battle into martyrdom for the faith, a blood sacrifice on the altar of a righteous nation.[34] In all these ways, religious nationalism made it possible to override the moral universalism of the Christian Gospels, with their clear proscriptions on violence and killing.

Once a wartime tool, White Christian nationalism has lately become a fixed feature of the American cultural landscape, even during peacetime. Why? One reason is geopolitical. For most of their history, Americans were highly suspicious of standing armies. This is an old suspicion that derives from the political tradition known as civic republicanism.[35] Civic republicans have always seen standing armies as seedbeds of tyranny. And this is one reason why US armies were always demobilized so rapidly in peacetime. The Cold War put an end to this. Americans were taught to love the military and to associate fighting with freedom.[36] They were taught that "freedom isn't free": it must be bought with blood.

There is also another important reason for the recent growth of religious nationalism: a theological shift within American Protestantism itself. For most of US history, the vast majority of Protestant theologians espoused a "postmillennialist" understanding of Christian eschatology.[37] On this reading of biblical prophecy, the second coming of Christ will occur after his followers have established the Kingdom of God for a thousand years, that is, after the millennium. For postmillennialists, the violent struggles between supernatural beings depicted in the book of Revelation are to be understood metaphorically, as spiritual struggles within the individual believer's heart. The other reading of biblical prophecy is "premillennialist." Premillennialists believe that the second coming of Christ will initiate the Kingdom of God. That is, it will precede the millennium. Premillennialists understand Revelation as a literal depiction of the final conflict between the forces of good and evil. Premillennialism has become increasingly influential among American Protestants over the last century.[38] Today, it is the hegemonic view, at least among evangelical Christians.

And not only among them. By now, apocalypticism has seeped deep into the country's secular, pop culture.[39] Consider the "left behind" novels by Tim La Haye and Jerry Jenkins. They are part Tom Clancy mystery and part end-times theology. They have sold tens of millions of copies. Or, in a still more secular vein, consider books such as Cormac McCarthy's *The Road* or films such as *X-Men: Apocalypse*. They are part of the burgeoning genre of "postapocalyptic" works. In this way, key elements of Christian nationalism have become a core part of secular culture. They supply Americans with some of their most potent cultural tropes and political frames.

Apocalypticism is one key component of Christian nationalism, American style.[40] Blood rhetoric is the second. Blood serves as a kind of linguistic binding agent. It is the metaphorical glue that holds together three key elements of Christian nationalism: blood conquest, blood sacrifice, and blood belonging. The promised land must be taken by force, as it was in the backwoods of New England, the prairies of the Midwest, and the deserts of the Southwest. With the "closing of the frontier" in the late nineteenth century, the crusading impulse was directed outward into the American Empire.[41] It still is. White Christian nationalists like to say that the United States has always been a force for good in the world. And by force, they understand military force. For them, the US military is the human arm of divine justice.

Of course, war brings death, which is interpreted as blood sacrifice. Though here, too, there has been a change. Old-time Christian nationalism transfigured battle death into Christian martyrdom.[42] Even so measured a politician as Abraham Lincoln spoke of hallowed ground consecrated by the blood of fallen soldiers in the text of his Gettysburg Address. Today, politicians more often speak the watered-down language of "ultimate sacrifice." But the theological undertones of such talk are clear enough for those with ears to hear them.

What about blood belonging? American identity cannot be grounded in a myth of shared descent in the way that many other national identities can. Apart from the native peoples, Americans are all from someplace else. Christian nationalists have usually defined American identity in terms of some ethnoreligious other. In Puritan New England, Native Americans and Protestant sectarians were usually cast in this role.[43] In the southern colonies, of course, it was African slaves who were the racial *and* religious other.[44] By the mid-nineteenth century, Irish and Italian Catholics were regarded as the chief threat to a Protestant America.[45] During the late nineteenth century, Jews from Central and Eastern Europe were costarring with them in this role. Nowadays, of course, it is Muslim Americans, Latino immigrants, and secular progressives who are portrayed as mortal threats to a Judeo-Christian United States. In each period, religion and race have been intertwined with each other.

RELIGIOUS NATIONALISM AND RACE

From the start, the Whiteness of White Christian nationalism was opposed to Blackness, to Redness, and to color more generally. Until well into the nineteenth century, many American Whites believed that their Black slaves had no souls to save.[46] To be Black was to be irredeemable. The reverse was also true. To be unredeemed was to be "Black." Until well into the twentieth century, the Irish and Italian Catholics and Central and East European Jews who immigrated to the United States were regarded not only as religious others but also—and therefore—as racial others.[47] Italians, Irish, and Jews were widely understood as not quite White. Their whitening was only gradual. The whitening of Mexican Americans, meanwhile, was halting at best, that of Asian Americans more halting still.[48]

The racial segregation of American churches is well known—and enduring.[49] But the effects of Whiteness on evangelical Christianity were both theological and sociological. Consider biblical literalism. Its origins are usually traced to the reception in the United States of German "historical-criticism" during the late nineteenth century and the eruption of the "fundamentalist/modernist" controversy during the early twentieth century.[50] But as the religious historian Mark Noll has persuasively shown, biblical literalism initially emerged a half century earlier—as a means of defending slavery.[51] Whereas abolitionists appealed to the "spirit" of the Bible, pro-slavery theologians fastened onto the "letter"—onto specific passages that mentioned slavery in an approving fashion. Many conservative Protestants were already inclined to biblical literalism long before the Social Gospel and the Scopes Trial turned them against political and theological liberalism.

Or consider the evangelical reading of Christian ethics in terms of "personal accountability" rather than "social justice." As the political scientist Michael Lienesch and other scholars have shown, it was propagated by Gilded Age business elites as a means of opposing the Social Gospel and providing theological cover for laissez-faire economics.[52] And as the American historian Kevin Kruse and others have shown, it was repropagated by Cold War business elites for similar purposes.[53] Conservative Christians were taught that their faith was about saving individual souls, not pursuing the common good. But the ethics of personal accountability had as much to do with race as with economics. As sociologists Christian Smith and Michael Emerson have demonstrated, personal accountability talk has also become a means of stripping inequality of its social context—a means, that is, of blaming the poor, and especially poor Blacks, for their own poverty, for a lack of wealth that is demonstrably better understood in structural and historical terms.[54]

Finally, consider evangelical theologians' newfound love for the subtleties of the Holy Trinity. For decades, evangelical preachers have urged their followers to establish a "personal relationship with Jesus." So "Christ-centered" was their theology that God the Father sometimes seemed to fade into the background. As for the Holy Spirit, that was for the "Holy Rollers" of a Pentecostal persuasion. No more. As "radical Islam" has replaced "Godless communism" as the other for religious conservatives, evangelical theologians have rediscovered the Triune God.[55] For Trinitarian doctrine makes it possible to draw a sharp line between Christianity and Islam, which insists on the one-ness of God. It allows evangelical theologians to argue that Christian and Muslims do not worship the same God. That this dividing line also runs between Christianity and Judaism, or that the doctrine of the Trinity is not explicitly mentioned in scripture is evidently of no account. The theology must be bent to fit the politics. The racial tail is wagging the theological dog, and not for the first time in the history of evangelicalism.

Contemporary White Christian Nationalism: The Four Key Elements

The original recipe for American religious nationalism had two ingredients: apocalypticism and blood rhetoric. Today's new and improved recipe contains two additional ones: messianism and victimization narratives. Messianism had relatively little purchase in the high-church WASP version of American religious nationalism that was predominant until the early twentieth century. On the contrary, there was widespread distrust of the charismatic preachers and faith healers who have long been stock figures of revivalist and sectarian movements within American Protestantism. But messianic leaders are absolutely central within the low-church milieu that now dominates American Protestantism. The lineage is long: itinerant preachers were gradually followed by urban revivalists, who were followed in turn by the radio and TV preachers and now by the celebrity pastors of the country's gigachurches. Given this history, it is hardly surprising that conservative evangelicals would be drawn to messianic leaders.

A similar dynamic can be observed with respect to victimization narratives. The high-church American Protestants of the nineteenth century often hailed from the well-heeled classes.[56] Or at least aspired to them. They were more apt to understand themselves as conquerors than as victims. Not so their low-church, sectarian brethren. The collective memory and everyday experience of Baptists and Pentecostals was and is rife with a sense of victimization. This is one reason why most evangelicals now believe—truly and fervently believe—that Christians are the single "most persecuted group in America."[57]

The American version of religious nationalism now has at least four key elements:

1. *Blood tropes.* Talk of blood is the red thread that runs through both the Jewish and Christian scriptures. There is talk of blood sacrifice, blood conquest, blood purity, and blood atonement, among other things. Blood is the solvent that rinses out the universalistic aspirations of Christianity. It is also the cement that binds it to the particularistic (and racialized) vision of the nation. In short, blood rhetoric is what makes it possible to nationalize (and racialize) Christianity. It is what makes the ideal of the (White) Christian nation possible.
2. *Apocalyptic narratives.* The histories of Judaism and Christianity are both replete with apocalyptic discourse. For most of these histories, however, literalist interpretations of the apocalyptic texts (e.g., Daniel, Revelation) were confined to fringe movements. Over the last century, however, they have become a core element of evangelical Christianity. And not only of evangelical Christianity. Apocalyptic tropes now

pervade the popular culture of the United States too. Apocalyptic story lines are a recurring feature of contemporary film and literature. In this way, biblical literalism has seeped deep into "secular" culture and laid the groundwork for a seeming contradiction: secularized versions of White Christian nationalism.

3. *Persecution/victimization narratives.* The "pariah" status of the ancient Jews and Roman persecution of the Jesus movement left a deep imprint in the collective memories of both traditions. It is especially deep among present-day American evangelicals. This is understandable. After all, evangelicals are the scions of "low-church" sects and movements (e.g., Baptists and Methodists) that were objects of high-brow contempt and sometimes also subjects of political persecution both in the Old World and the New. Over the last half century, White evangelicals have become increasingly prosperous and powerful. At the same time, however, the non-White and non-Christian populations have grown rapidly, especially over the last two decades. These twin developments—economic and demographic—explain why many evangelicals feel persecuted, and also why such claims seem preposterous to many nonevangelicals. For what is really at issue is not so much (Christian) persecution as (White) privilege. Wedding cakes are not the moral equivalent of lynching trees.

4. *Messianic expectations.* Full-blown messianic movements have probably been somewhat more common in modern Judaism, but modern Christianity has certainly had its share (e.g., David Koresh) and the history of American Protestantism is replete with charismatic preachers (e.g., George Whitefield) who claimed quasi-messianic powers. If anything, messianism is even more pronounced in contemporary American evangelicalism. There are various reasons for this. Perhaps the most important is that modern media—radio, television, and social media—have spawned a new breed of celebrity pastors with mass followings. With their professional staffs and high-tech sanctuaries, contemporary megachurches have generated a new, spectatorial form of religiosity that centers around CEO pastors who control sprawling empires of satellite congregations and parachurch organizations. As the congregants become more passive, "gifted" pastors become ever more important. Messianism is hoped for, even expected.

Trumpism as White Christian Nationalism

With this four-point definition in hand, it becomes much easier to understand why Trumpism resonated so strongly with some American evangelicals.[58] There was to begin with Trump's catastrophizing rhetoric. To be sure, it was not explicitly apocalyptic. Trump does not allude to the end-times in the way that some Republican politicians have been wont to do. Indeed, given his meager knowledge of Christian scripture, it is not clear that he would be capable of doing so. But Trump certainly does espy disaster and conflict most everywhere he looks. "Disaster" is one of his favorite words. And for him, recent US history has been a long litany of disasters. Provoking conflict, meanwhile, is one of his favorite tactics. For him, American life—indeed all life—is ultimately a struggle between "us" ("very good people") and "them" ("very bad people").

Then, there is Trump's morbid fascination with blood, particularly women's blood. Recall his bizarre remarks about the female TV news anchors Megyn Kelly and Mika Brzezinski during the 2016 campaign—about "blood coming out of [Kelly's] whatever" or "blood streaming down [Brzezinski's] face."[59] A more chilling example concerns an apocryphal story concerning General John Pershing that Trump frequently recounted in his campaign speeches, often to raucous applause.[60] During the Philippine-American War, so the story goes, Pershing captured fifty "Muslim terrorists." He then had fifty bullets dipped in pig's blood. Forty-nine of the bullets were used to execute forty-nine of the prisoners. The fiftieth bullet was then given to the fiftieth soldier, who was instructed to return to "his people" and warn them not to engage in terrorism. And they did not—for thirty years! Or so the story goes. For Trump, blood is full of danger and power; it can pollute, especially when it is women's blood. But it can also purify, especially when it is men's blood. White Christian nationalists are equally fascinated with blood.

What about messianism? It goes without saying that Trump views himself in messianic terms. In his 2016 speech accepting the Republican nomination for president, for example, he claimed that "I am your voice" and "I alone can fix it." During the 2019 trade war with China, he glanced heavenward and announced that "I am the chosen one."[61] More surprising perhaps is how quick some were to embrace Trump's conceits and how willing they have been to defend them. Some evangelicals immediately compared Trump to messianic leaders from the Hebrew Bible, such as King David. More saw in him a modern-day King Cyrus, the Persian emperor who freed the Jews from their Babylonian captivity.[62] They hoped that he would deliver them from the Kenyan captivity under Barack Obama and restore them to their rightful place in the American Jerusalem: Washington, DC.

Which brings us to the fourth and final area of overlap between Trumpism and evangelicalism: the discourse of victimization.[63] Despite his supposedly messianic powers, Trump constantly complains that he and his allies are being treated "unfairly" and persecuted by their enemies. During his presidential campaigns, for example, he warned that the electoral system was "rigged" against him. After the 2016 election, he claimed that he had lost the popular vote only because "millions" of people had voted "illegally." He then denounced the Mueller investigation as "rigged," a "hoax," and a "witch hunt." Then came the "Big Lie" following his defeat in the 2020 presidential election. Trump surely regards himself as a "winner," but he also feels like a victim. Despite his (supposedly) enormous business successes, he feels himself wrongly excluded from the upper echelons of New York City society, which won him the sympathy of evangelicals, who also feel rejected by "cultural elites." To the secular observer, these claims of persecution may seem overstated. But there is no doubt that they are sincerely felt nonetheless.

Thus far, I have argued that the connection between Trumpism and evangelicalism is White Christian nationalism. Which is to say that White evangelicals supported Trump if and insofar as they are also White Christian nationalists. There is also solid statistical evidence to support this argument. Sociologist Sam Perry and political scientist Andrew Whitehead constructed a measure of White Christian nationalism, based on six questions taken from the 2007 wave of the Baylor Religion Survey.[64]

So, what does this scale have to do with race? As it turns out, a lot. The higher your score on the Christian nationalism scale, for example, the more likely you are to oppose interracial marriage, especially between Whites and Blacks.[65] You are also more likely to support restrictions on immigration on the grounds that Latino immigrants contribute to crime and live off welfare. Indeed, once you control for Christian nationalism, the correlation between evangelicalism and racism simply disappears.

How about violence? In a follow-up study, Perry and Whitehead have shown that there is a strong statistical relationship between support for Christian nationalism and opposition to gun control.[66] It is also well established that evangelicalism is strongly correlated with various measures of patriotism and militarism.[67] One suspects that this relationship would also disappear if one controlled for White Christian nationalism.

Where does the apocalypse fit into this, though? As it turns out, apocalyptic beliefs are strongly correlated with Christian nationalism, too.[68]

In sum, the historical and cultural analysis and the statistical and quantitative analysis corroborate one another. My analysis of Trumpism and evangelicalism and Perry and Whitehead's analysis of Christian nationalism and racism are clearly complementary.

There is good news and bad news in these findings. The good news is that evangelicalism per se is not associated with racism, xenophobia, and militarism.[69] The bad news is that many evangelicals are White Christian nationalists, as are quite a number of conservative Protestants more generally.

But most observers of the Trump phenomenon have interpreted it as a form of right-wing populism. What if anything does right-wing populism have to do with White Christian nationalism and with religious nationalism more generally?

RIGHT-WING POPULISM AND RELIGIOUS NATIONALISM

There is widespread scholarly agreement that populism is not an "ideology," at least not in the sense that, say, liberalism or communism are ideologies.[70] Populism does not have a Mill or a Marx, a treatise or a manifesto. Nor does it have a program of reform or revolution, such as the expansion of individual rights or the abolition of private property. And yet, though it may lack the intellectual systematicity of these nineteenth-century ideologies, it is not without a certain coherence.

Some analysts have proposed that populism is best understood as a political discourse centered around the notion of the "sovereign people" and related notions such as "popular will" and "popular unity."[71] This is why populist rhetoric so often has a democratic ring. However, as proponents of this interpretation are quick to point out, right-wing populists also reject core elements of *liberal* democracy, such as the rule of law, minority rights, and formal procedure. On this reading, right-wing populism aspires to *il*liberal democracy. Appeals to "popular sovereignty" are used to delegitimate and override liberal principles. They also hint at the violence inherent in any nation's founding and warn of its possible return.

But there is more to populist discourse than claims to popular sovereignty. Populist discourse also has a narrative dimension and a conceptual one. How so? In *Strangers in Their Own Land*, her widely read ethnography of White conservatives in the rural South, Arlie Hochschild concluded that her subjects interpreted the world through the frame of a "deep story," a narrative that they themselves were not always readily able to articulate, but which they still immediately recognized and affirmed as "theirs" as soon she articulated it for them.[72]

The central event in the populist story is "line-cutting." Hochschild's subjects imagine themselves to be waiting patiently in a long queue that leads to the "American dream" of material prosperity. But the line is standing still. In fact, it hasn't moved in years, decades even. Why? Up ahead, her subjects notice, other people are cutting in line, immigrants and minorities who just recently arrived. Not only that, agents of the US federal government are actually escorting them to the front of the line. This, they feel, is deeply unjust. The unspoken premise is that "we the people"—the ones at the front of the line, who were always already "here first" regardless of when we actually arrived—are White people. Right-wing populism contains hints of violence, then, but also demands for justice, but an unequal justice that privileges Whiteness.

Hochschild's analysis can be generalized. The deep story she discovers in the South is actually just one variant of a more generic narrative that underlies right-wing populism throughout the world. This story features four actors: a pure people, a corrupt elite, an undeserving other, and a messianic leader. The people have been betrayed by the elite, which is allied with the other, and the leader promises to expel the infiltrators and restore the people to its birthright. Of course, different actors can be cast in these roles. That is what makes the narrative generic.

Are the people "pure" because they are religious? And, if so, which religion—Protestant, Catholic, Muslim, Hindu, Buddhist, Shinto? Or are they pure because they are "secular," which is to say, not Muslim, as in present-day western Europe? And who is the corrupt other? Politicians?

Intellectuals? Journalists? Bureaucrats? What about the undeserving other? Most every religion has been cast in this role somewhere at some time, including Christianity. Finally, what has been lost and is now being reclaimed? Purity? Prosperity? Honor? As with other fairy tales, the possible variations of the populist narrative are locally variable and virtually endless. Vagueness is a feature of this narrative, rather than a bug: "the people" is an empty signifier that can be filled with varied contents, not only by populist demagogues but also by their followers.

One question that has long bedeviled scholars of populism is whether it is progressive, conservative, or protean. Focusing on narrative allows us to resolve this issue. For there is also a left-wing version of populism's deep story. It features three actors rather than four: an oppressed people, a corrupt elite, and a social movement. In this account, the people are being exploited by the elite and have joined together in a movement of liberation. Bernie Sanders's two campaigns for the presidency are paradigmatic examples of the left-wing variant of populism. It pits the 99 percent against the 1 percent, and its slogan is a "political revolution" in the name of "not me, but us."

Note that the two variants of populism overlap on two points: their elevation of the common people and their condemnation of a corrupt elite. This explains the shape-shifting character of populist politics. It is why populist politicians and/or their followers sometimes shift from one end of the political spectrum, as with the "Bernie to Trump" voters in 2016.[73] But the two populisms do also diverge in two key respects: there is no ethnocultural other in the progressive version, and the focus is on the movement rather than the leader. In general, class rather than culture is the cleavage that matters most in progressive versions of populism. And the corrupt elites are economic rather than cultural elites.

In my present analysis, though, the focus is on right-wing populism. These movements have at least two other common, if not universal, features. The first—and the most important for our purposes—is a charismatic leader. Because the populist goal of popular unity can never really be achieved, it must be performed. In left-wing populist movements, the unity of the people is usually embodied in "the movement." Left-wing populist movements do of course have leaders (e.g., Juan and Eva Perón, William Jennings Bryan). But they point away from themselves and toward the movement or the people in their rhetoric and their performances. In right-wing populist movements, by contrast, popular unity and power is more often incorporated in a leader who promises power and salvation, not to mention retribution and revenge. Recall Trump's speech at the Republican National Convention in 2016: "I am your voice" and "I alone can fix it."

A second common, if not universal, feature of right-wing populist movements (sometimes found in the left-wing variant, too) is the performance of "bad manners," above all by the leader, but also by his (or, occasionally, her) followers.[74] Following Benjamin Moffitt, by "bad manners" I understand ongoing violations of social norms of polite speech and sometimes also of proper dress and grooming. The speech of populist leaders is often impolite and profane. In a rambling monologue before the Conservative Political Action Committee in March 2019, for instance, Trump described charges of Russian collusion as "bullshit," a word never before uttered by a sitting president in a public address. Venezuela's Hugo Chavez was also renowned for his profanity and invective, as is the Philippines' former president Rodrigo Duterte. This symbolic violence against social norms sets the stage for and sometimes devolves into verbal or physical violence against cultural others, as in the mass shooting in El Paso, Texas, which targeted Latinos. In both instances, the violence is a demonstration of sovereignty, in which the power of the people supersedes laws and institutions.

Perhaps the most peculiar aspects of populist performance are its stylistic aspects. The personal appearance of right-wing populist leaders is often unconventional or even bizarre. Many of today's populist leaders sport highly eccentric coiffures (e.g., Trump, Wilders, and Boris Johnson). Others adopt peculiar habiliments (e.g., Chavez's iconic track suits, Modi's equally iconic *chaiwala* outfits, Trump's overlong red ties). But this eccentricity has its own logic. Bad manners and strange dress serve two important purposes: they distance the leader from the elite and thereby signal his or her closeness to the people, even as they also distance the leader from "ordinary" people who cannot afford to defy convention. The populist leader is both a man of the people and a man beyond the people, human and superhuman at the same time.

Having enumerated some important characteristics of both religious nationalism and right-wing populism, it is now possible to identify some of the elective affinities between them.

The Elective Affinities

The "elective affinities" concept was first introduced into historical social science by the German sociologist Max Weber, but he had borrowed the phrase from Goethe, who had himself borrowed it from chemistry. Goethe's novel *Die Wahlverwandtschaften* (*Elective Affinities*) featured two aristocratic couples that split apart and then recombined into one new couple and two abandoned spouses. In chemistry, the phrase describes chemical reactions in which two compounds form a new compound and various precipitates when combined. Elective affinity, then, is not just a poetic phrase for a "causal relationship," as is sometimes claimed. It describes the process whereby two existing elements give way to a new historical compound.

The relationship between conservative religion and right-wing populism is also one of elective affinity. Each contains elements that are strongly attracted to one another. But each also contains elements that are not so easily bonded together. When the two are combined, they form a new compound and generate certain precipitates. The new compound is religious nationalism; the precipitates include religious universalism and political conservatism. The result of the reaction is a metamorphosis: universalistic religion is particularized, and political conservatism is radicalized.

Consider the affinity from the standpoint of conservatism. Religious conservatives are attracted to right-wing populist movements and parties if and insofar as they do the following:

1. Invoke notions of blood sacrifice, blood conquest, blood purity, and, more generally, attribute mystical powers to human blood.
2. Paint the contemporary world in Manichaean and apocalyptic terms, as a cosmic struggle between good and evil that is hurtling toward its final and violent denouement.
3. Portray the dominant ethnocultural majority as a persecuted, religious minority, in particular, a minority persecuted on account of its faith.
4. Are headed by a charismatic leader who makes messianic promises and claims magical powers.

Let us call these four features the *religious nationalist quadrilateral* (RNQ).

It is important to emphasize that this affinity obtains, not only for conservative Christians, but for religious conservatives in many traditions, not only ones that centrally feature the RNQ (e.g., evangelical Protestantism or Shia Islam) but even in ones that do not. Hindu nationalists in India and Buddhist nationalists in Sri Lanka have rummaged through their own traditions in search of a textual basis for the RNQ—and they have not come up empty-handed. For blood, they have substituted soil, as in "Mother India" or Sri Lanka's "sons of the soil."[75] For the linear eschatology of the Abrahamic faiths, they have substituted a cyclical eschatology of cataclysmic renewal with violent "karpas." They, too, have found their others in Muslims and secularists. And they have often found their messianic leaders in political gurus, rather than in messiah figures. Where the RNQ did not exist, then, something analogous had to be invented.

The affinity is not one-sided but mutual. Right-wing populists are drawn to religious nationalism insofar as it does the following:

1. *Emphasizes the moral purity of the common people.* For secular populists, religion serves mainly as a marker of cultural authenticity, rather than as a mark of divine salvation. In the American South, for instance, the "evangelical" label sometimes functions as an ethnic identity, rather than a religious one, and in South Asia, secular nationalists often claim to be "Hindus" on ethnocultural grounds. In Europe, meanwhile, right-wing populists often style themselves as defenders of "Christian civilization" even though they themselves are not practicing Christians, while in Turkey right-wing populists portray themselves as stewards of "Ottoman civilization," thereby aligning themselves with the last caliphate.
2. *Blames national decline on cultural elites, and especially on secular intellectuals.* By tacitly defining "the corrupt elite" in cultural terms and focusing especially on humanist intellectuals, right-wing populists are able to deflect attention from the economic elites and religious intellectuals who typically serve as their financial backers and public apologists. Ironically, insofar as economic inequality and regional decline are key drivers of populist resentments, "culture wars" tactics of this sort not only mask but exacerbate the socioeconomic causes of the populist backlash, all while justifying policies that benefit the privileged. Hindu nationalist attacks on set-aside programs for lower castes

and other underprivileged groups are but one example of such a dynamic.
3. *Clearly identifies moral and/or religious others who can never become full members of the people.* This, too, forms a general pattern that goes together with national variations. In the United States, western Europe, and also in much of South Asia, the Muslim has become the paradigmatic other, who is doubly unassimilable, both because Muslims are not members of the "national religion" but also because they are supposedly incapable of becoming fully secular. Why? Because secularity is rooted in Christianity—or so goes the claim. This dynamic is not specific to Christianity, however. Indeed, in other contexts, such as Nepal or the Persian Gulf countries, it is the Christian who is doubly unassimilable, both as a *de facto* agent of western imperialism and an apostate from the national religion(s). This exclusionary dynamic is inherent to religious nationalism whatever its roots.
4. *Sanctifies the charismatic leader, despite or even because of his or her bad manners.* Secular conservatives often prefer strong leaders, not because they believe in political messiahs, but rather because they believe in hierarchy. They often cathect with unruly leaders, despite their penchant for order, not because it signals superhuman powers, but because it signals masculine bravado, a willingness to flout the "pussified" and "feminine" norms of polite society. From this perspective, bad manners are simply one tactic in a broader repertoire of dominance politics, where the aim is not to achieve agreement but to compel submission. Populist leaders vary a great deal in their manners, with some displaying great decorum (e.g., Modi and Erdogan), but they are quite uniform in their displays of hypermasculinity (e.g., physical strength, sexual prowess, athletic ability, etc.).

To reiterate, this new compound generates at least two precipitates: ethical universalism and political conservatism. Most religions embrace some form of ethical universalism. They command their followers to ignore differences of race and even of religion in their moral dealings with other people. When conservative religion joins with populist politics to form religious nationalism, however, ethical universalism must be abandoned in favor of ethical particularism: only conationals cum coreligionists have full moral worth; all others merit moral indifference at best. This moral alchemy often requires a certain measure of pseudo-theological labor. In justifying Trump's harsh immigration policies in the face of the Christian ethics of hospitality, for example, Mike Huckabee enlisted St. Paul's teachings on obedience to political authority. In his telling, would-be Central American refugees became de facto "lawbreakers" rather than modern day Samaritans.

At least since Edmund Burke, political conservatives have styled themselves the defenders of cultural tradition and local community and resisted top-down, state-led reforms on the grounds that they unsettle the extant moral and social order. Neoliberals could still pretend that they were conservatives by espousing "family values" and "religious tradition" while turning a blind eye to the social and cultural effects of market fundamentalism. At first glance, populists might seem to be pursuing a similar strategy insofar as they portray themselves as the defenders of cultural identity and national community, even as they launch a frontal attack on political norms and minority communities. But right-wing populism is better understood as reactionary and even radical. Reactionary, insofar as it seeks to reclaim rather than preserve, as in "Make America Great *Again.*" And radical, insofar as it does not hesitate to use the violence of the state in pursuit of their ends.

Conclusion

So, why did so many evangelicals vote for Donald Trump, not once but twice? Again, it's important to emphasize that many of them did not. Non-White evangelicals mostly voted for Hillary Clinton and Joe Biden. Also, a number of evangelical intellectuals publicly opposed Trump, as did a number of female pastors and youth leaders. But most White evangelicals did vote for him in the end. More devout evangelicals seem to have voted for him because of their opposition to abortion and gay marriage. Less devout evangelicals have voted for him because they are White Christian nationalists. What's more, the devout seem to have overcome their initial reservations about Trump and now enthusiastically support him, perhaps because he helped realize their long-cherished goal of overturning *Roe v. Wade* or perhaps simply because they have become die-hard political partisans.

What many White evangelicals seem not to realize is just how costly this victory was. For the alliance between evangelical Christianity and political conservatism has a price, two prices, to be exact. The first is the rapid growth of "religious nones" in the younger generation. Young people who might have had a lukewarm relationship to organized religion and might even have returned to the church as they grew older are now rejecting religion in growing numbers and on political grounds. This should worry evangelicals given their concern with saving souls. The second price is growing fissures within the evangelical fold itself. Some have already left the fold. They are still Christians. But not evangelicals. Others are pushing back against the aging White men who still claim to speak for the evangelical faithful, at least until recently, men such as Franklin Graham and Jerry Falwell Jr. This should also worry evangelicals, given their history of schism.

What, finally, does all of this portend for the future of American religion and democracy? In *Democracy in America*, Tocqueville observed that religion and republicanism had always gone hand in hand in the United States, and to the benefit of both. Not because church and state were merged or because the clergy meddled in politics but precisely because they weren't and didn't. There was no established religion, and the clergy maintained a respectful distance from politics. Still, religion provided a powerful buttress to republican government. The churches schooled Americans in the practice of voluntary association while the clergy gently instilled respect for the nation's laws. Not always, of course, but in their better moments at least.

In France, on the other hand, religion and republicanism were increasingly at odds with each other, and to the detriment of both. The rupture between religion and republicanism during the French Revolution was succeeded by a bad marriage between religion and empire consecrated by Napoleon. There was an official religion, and the clergy were politically vocal. In this ill-fated union between throne and altar, the Catholic Church supported the French monarchy, while the clergy preached obedience to authority, and republicans therefore opposed both. This same dynamic played out across all of Latin Europe. In these countries, it was politics rather than science that really drove people out of the churches.

Having discerned the likely outcome of these dynamics early on, Tocqueville issued this warning: "Religion by uniting with different political powers, can . . . form only burdensome alliances. It has no need of their help to survive and may die, if it serves them."[76]

The religious Right in Trump's America would do well to heed Tocqueville's advice. Since the late 1970s it has embraced the Republican Party ever more tightly, alienating increasing numbers from Christianity. For a time, the adverse effects of the evangelical–Republican alliance on Christianity were concealed by high birth rates among religious conservatives. But then, three years ago, a number of evangelical leaders made a Faustian bargain with Trump: their moral credibility in exchange for promises of political protection. As a result, the day of reckoning is coming, and coming soon.

NOTES

1. Sarah Pullman Bailey, "White Evangelicals Voted Overwhelmingly for Donald Trump, Exit Polls Show," *Washington Post,* November 9, 2016, https://www.washingtonpost.com/news/acts-of-faith/wp/2016/11/09/exit-polls-show-white-evangelicals-voted-overwhelmingly-for-donald-trump/.

2. Philip Schwadel and Gregory A. Smith, "Evangelical Support of Trump Remains High," *Pew Research Center,* March 18, 2019, https://www.pewresearch.org/fact-tank/2019/03/18/evangelical-approval-of-trump-remains-high-but-other-religious-groups-are-less-supportive/.

3. Matthew Bunson, "Finding the Catholic Vote," *National Catholic Register,* February 24, 2020, https://www.ncregister.com/news/ewtn-news-realclear-opinion-research-poll-no-2-finding-the-catholic-vote.

4. Rogers Brubaker, "Between Nationalism and Civilizationism: The European Populist Moment in Comparative Perspective," *Ethnic and Racial Studies* 40, no. 8 (2017): 1191–1226.

5. Philip Gorski and Gülay Türkmen-Dervişoğlu, "Religion, Nationalism, and Violence: An Integrated Approach," *Annual Review of Sociology* 39, no. 1 (2013): 193–210.

6. Philip Gorski, *American Covenant: A History of Civil Religion from the Puritans to the Present* (Princeton, NJ: Princeton University Press, 2017); Philip Gorski, *American Babylon: Democracy and Christianity before and after Trump* (London: Routledge, 2020).

7. Philip Gorski, "Why Evangelicals Voted for Trump: A Critical Cultural Sociology," in *Politics of Meaning/Meaning of Politics: Cultural Sociology of the 2016 Presidential Election,* ed. Jason L. Mast and Jeffrey C. Alexander (Cham: Palgrave Macmillan, 2019), 165–83.

8. E. J. Hobsbawm, *Nations and Nationalism since 1780: Programme, Myth, Reality* (New York: Cambridge University Press, 1992); Ernest Gellner, *Nations and Nationalism* (Ithaca, NY: Cornell University Press, 1983).

9. Benedict Anderson, *Imagined Communities* (London: Verso, 1991).

10. Peter Van der Veer, *Religious Nationalism: Hindus and Muslims in India* (Berkeley: University of California Press, 1994); Mark Juergensmeyer, *The New Cold War? Religious Nationalism Confronts the Secular State* (Berkeley: University of California Press, 1993); Roger Friedland, "Religious Nationalism and the Problem of Collective Representation," *Annual Review of Sociology* 27 (2001): 125–52.

11. Gorski, *American Babylon*; Gorski, *American Covenant*.

12. See also Geneviève Zubrzycki, *The Crosses of Auschwitz: Nationalism and Religion in Post-Communist Poland* (Chicago: University of Chicago Press, 2006).

13. Jyotirmaya Sharma, *Terrifying Vision: MS Golwalkar, the RSS, and India* (New Delhi: Penguin Books India, 2007); Jyotirmaya Sharma, *Hindutva: Exploring the Idea of Hindu Nationalism* (New Delhi: Penguin Books India, 2011); Jyotirmaya Sharma, *A Restatement of Religion: Swami Vivekananda and the Making of Hindu Nationalism* (New Haven, CT: Yale University Press, 2013); Sam Kaplan, "'Religious Nationalism': A Textbook Case from Turkey," *Comparative Studies of South Asia, Africa and the Middle East* 25, no. 3 (2005): 665–76.

14. Jonathan Z. Smith, *Relating Religion: Essays in the Study of Religion* (Chicago: University of Chicago Press, 2004); Talal Asad, *Genealogies of Religion: Discipline and Reasons of Power in Christianity and Islam* (Baltimore, MD: Johns Hopkins University Press, 1993); Tomoko Masuzawa, *The Invention of World Religions: Or, How European Universalism was Preserved in the Language of Pluralism* (Chicago: University of Chicago Press, 2005); Brent Nongbri, *Before Religion: A History of a Modern Concept* (New Haven, CT: Yale University Press, 2013).

15. Bryan S. Rennie and Phillip L. Tite, *Religion, Terror and Violence: Religious Studies Perspectives* (New York: Routledge, 2008).

16. Steven Grosby, "Religion, Ethnicity and Nationalism: The Uncertain Perennialism of Adrian Hastings," *Nations & Nationalism* 9, no. 1 (2003): 7–13; Adrian Hastings, *The Construction of Nationhood: Ethnicity, Religion, and Nationalism* (New York: Cambridge University Press, 1997).

17. John R. Bowen, *Why the French Don't Like Headscarves: Islam, the State, and Public Space* (Princeton, NJ: Princeton University Press, 2007); Conor C. O'Brien, *Godland: Reflections on Religion and Nationalism* (Cambridge, MA: Harvard University Press, 1988).

18. Anthony D. Smith, *Chosen Peoples: Sacred Sources of National Identity* (New York: Oxford University Press, 2004).

19. William R. Hutchison and Hartmut Lehmann, *Many Are Chosen: Divine Election and Western Nationalism* (Minneapolis, MN: Fortress Press, 1994).

20. Conrad Cherry, *God's New Israel: Religious Interpretations of American Destiny* (Chapel Hill: University of North Carolina Press, 1998).

21. Philip Gorski, "The Mosaic Moment: An Early Modernist Critique of Modernist Theories of Nationalism," *American Journal of Sociology* 105, no. 5 (2000): 1428–68.

22. Colette Beaune and Frederic Cheyette, *The Birth of an Ideology: Myths and Symbols of Nation in Late-Medieval France* (Berkeley: University of California Press, 1991); Philip Gorski, "Premodern Nationalism: An Oxymoron? The Evidence from England," in *The SAGE Handbook of Nations and Nationalism*, ed. Gerard Delanty and Krishan Kumar (London: SAGE Publications, 2006), 143–56.

23. George McKenna, *The Puritan Origins of American Patriotism* (New Haven, CT: Yale University Press, 2007).

24. Kimberlé Crenshaw, "Mapping the Margins: Intersectionality, Identity Politics, and Violence Against Women of Color," *Stanford Law Review* 43, no. 6 (1991): 1241–99.

25. Melissa Wilde and Lindsay Glassman, "How Complex Religion Can Improve Our Understanding of American Politics," *Annual Review of Sociology* 42 (2016): 407–25.

26. Jean M. O'Brien, *Firsting and Lasting: Writing Indians Out of Existence in New England* (Minneapolis: University of Minnesota Press, 2010).

27. Laura E. Gómez, *Manifest Destinies: The Making of the Mexican American Race* (New York: New York University Press, 2018); Beth Lew-Williams, *The Chinese Must Go: Violence, Exclusion, and the Making of the Alien in America* (Cambridge, MA: Harvard University Press, 2018).

28. Stephanie McCurry, *Masters of Small Worlds: Yeoman Households, Gender Relations, and the Political Culture of the Antebellum South Carolina Low Country* (New York: Oxford University Press, 1997).

29. Fred Anderson and Andrew Cayton, *The Dominion of War: Empire and Liberty in North America, 1500–2000* (New York: Viking, 2005); Walter A. McDougall, *The Tragedy of US Foreign Policy: How America's Civil Religion Betrayed the National Interest* (New Haven, CT: Yale University Press, 2018); Nicholas Guyatt, *Providence and the Invention of the United States, 1607–1876* (Cambridge: Cambridge University Press, 2007).

30. Emilio Gentile, *Politics as Religion* (Princeton, NJ: Princeton University Press, 2006).

31. Paul R. Brass, *Theft of an Idol: Text and Context in the Representation of Collective Violence* (Princeton, NJ: Princeton University Press, 1997).

32. Philip Smith, *Why War? The Cultural Logic of Iraq, the Gulf War, and Suez* (Chicago: University of Chicago Press, 2005).

33. Drew Gilpin Faust, *This Republic of Suffering: Death and the American Civil War* (New York: Vintage, 2009).

34. Harry S. Stout, *Upon the Altar of the Nation: A Moral History of the American Civil War* (New York: Viking, 2006).

35. Martin Van Gelderen and Quentin Skinner, *Republicanism: A Shared European Heritage*, Vol. 1, *Republicanism and Constitutionalism in Early Modern Europe* (New York: Cambridge University Press, 2002).

36. Jonathan P. Herzog, *The Spiritual-Industrial Complex: America's Religious Battle against Communism in the Early Cold War* (New York: Oxford University Press, 2011); Thomas Jeremy Gunn, *Spiritual Weapons: The Cold War and the Forging of an American National Religion* (Westport, CT: Praeger, 2009); Angela M. Lahr, *Millennial Dreams and Apocalyptic Nightmares: The Cold War Origins of Political Evangelicalism* (New York: Oxford University Press, 2007).

37. James H. Moorhead, "The Erosion of Postmillennialism in American Religious Thought, 1865–1925," *Church History* 53, no. 1 (1984): 61–77; James H. Moorhead, *World without End: Mainstream American Protestant Visions of the Last Things, 1880–1925* (Bloomington: Indiana University Press, 1999).

38. Paul Boyer, *When Time Shall Be No More: Prophecy Belief in Modern American Culture* (Cambridge, MA: Harvard University Press, 1992); Matthew Avery Sutton, *American Apocalypse: A History of Modern Evangelicalism* (Cambridge, MA: Harvard University Press, 2014).

39. Richard Kyle, "The End of the World as We Know It: Faith, Fatalism, and Apocalypse in America," *Journal of American History* 85, no. 3 (1998): 1172; Amy Johnson Frykholm, *Rapture Culture: Left Behind in Evangelical America* (New York: Oxford University Press, 2004).

40. Gorski, *American Covenant*; Gorski, *American Babylon*.

41. Clifford Putney, *Muscular Christianity: Manhood and Sports in Protestant America, 1880–1920* (Cambridge, MA: Harvard University Press, 2009); Daniel Immerwahr, *How to Hide an Empire: A Short History of the Greater United States* (New York: Farrar, Straus and Giroux, 2019); Greg Grandin, *The End of the Myth: From the Frontier to the Border Wall in the Mind of America* (New York: Metropolitan Books, 2019).

42. Stout, *Upon the Altar of the Nation*; Matthew Patrick Rowley, *"Godly Violence: Military Providentialism in the Puritan Atlantic World"* (DPhil thesis, University of Leicester 2018), 1636–76.

43. Jill Lepore, *The Name of War: King Philip's War and the Origins of American Identity* (New York: Vintage Books, 1999); Nancy Shoemaker, *A Strange Likeness: Becoming Red and White in Eighteenth-Century North America* (New York: Oxford University Press, 2006); James A. Warren, *God, War, and Providence: The Epic Struggle of Roger Williams and the Narragansett Indians against the Puritans of New England* (New York: Scribner, 2018).

44. Katharine Gerbner, *Christian Slavery: Conversion and Race in the Protestant Atlantic World* (Philadelphia: University of Pennsylvania Press, 2018).

45. John Higham, *Strangers in the Land: Patterns of American Nativism, 1860–1925* (New York: Atheneum, 1965).

46. Winthrop D. Jordan, *White over Black: American Attitudes toward the Negro, 1550–1812* (Chapel Hill: University of North Carolina Press, 2013).

47. Eric L. Goldstein, *The Price of Whiteness: Jews, Race, and American Identity* (Princeton, NJ: Princeton University Press, 2019); Karen Brodkin, *How Jews Became White Folks and What That Says about Race in America* (New Brunswick, NJ: Rutgers University Press, 1998); Matthew Frye Jacobson, *Whiteness of a Different Color: European Immigrants and the Alchemy of Race* (Cambridge, MA: Harvard University Press, 1999); David R. Roediger, *The Wages of Whiteness: Race and the Making of the American Working Class* (London: Verso, 1991); Thomas A. Guglielmo, *White on Arrival: Italians, Race, Color, and Power in Chicago, 1890–1945* (New York: Oxford University Press, 2003); Noel Ignatiev, *How the Irish Became White* (London: Routledge, 2009); Gary Gerstle, *American Crucible: Race and Nation in the Twentieth Century* (Princeton, NJ: Princeton University Press, 2017).

48. Neil Foley, *The White Scourge: Mexicans, Blacks, and Poor Whites in Texas Cotton Culture* (Berkeley: University of California Press, 2018); William Deverell, *Whitewashed Adobe: The Rise of Los Angeles and the Remaking of Its Mexican Past* (Berkeley: University of California Press, 2004); Evelyn Nakano Glenn, *Unequal Freedom: How Race and Gender Shaped American Citizenship and Labor* (Cambridge, MA: Harvard University Press, 2009); Cybelle Fox, *Three Worlds of Relief: Race, Immigration, and the American Welfare State from the Progressive Era to the New Deal* (Princeton, NJ: Princeton University Press, 2012).

49. Kevin D. Dougherty, "How Monochromatic Is Church Membership? Racial-Ethnic Diversity in Religious Community," *Sociology of Religion* 64, no. 1 (2003): 65–85; C. Kirk Hadaway, David G. Hackett, and James Fogle Miller, "The Most Segregated Institution: Correlates of Interracial Church Participation," *Review of Religious Research* 25, no. 3 (1984): 204–19.

50. George Marsden, *Fundamentalism and American Culture* (New York: Oxford University Press, 2006).

51. Mark A. Noll, *The Civil War as a Theological Crisis* (Chapel Hill: University of North Carolina Press, 2006).

52. Michael Lienesch, *Redeeming America: Piety and Politics in the New Christian Right* (Chapel Hill: University of North Carolina Press, 1993); Sarah Ruth Hammond and Darren Dochuk, *God's Businessmen: Entrepreneurial Evangelicals in Depression and War* (Chicago: University of Chicago Press, 2017); Darren E. Grem, *The Blessings of Business: How Corporations Shaped Conservative Christianity* (New York: Oxford University Press, 2016).

53. Kevin M. Kruse, *One Nation under God: How Corporate America Invented Christian America* (New York: Basic Books, 2015); Wendy Wall, *Inventing the "American Way": The Politics of Consensus from the New Deal to the Civil*

Rights Movement (New York: Oxford University Press, 2009); Jason W. Stevens, *God-Fearing and Free: A Spiritual History of America's Cold War* (Cambridge, MA: Harvard University Press, 2010).

54. Michael O. Emerson and Christian Smith, *Divided by Faith: Evangelical Religion and the Problem of Race in America* (New York: Oxford University Press, 2001).

55. Ruth Graham, "The Professor Suspended for Saying Muslims and Christians Worship One God," *The Atlantic,* December 17, 2015, https://www.theatlantic.com/politics/archive/2015/12/christian-college-suspend-professor/421029/; John Patrick Hartley, *Religious Exclusivists Taking Inclusive Action? Theorizing Exclusivist Practice in Muslim-Christian Relations* (New Haven, CT: Yale University ProQuest Dissertations Publishing, 2016).

56. H. Richard Niebuhr, *The Social Sources of Denominationalism* (New York: Henry Holt and Co., 1929); Jerry Z. Park and Samuel H. Reimer, "Revisiting the Social Sources of American Christianity, 1972–1998," *Journal for the Scientific Study of Religion* 41, no. 4 (2002): 733–46.

57. Daniel Cox, Rachel Lienesch, and Robert Paul Jones, "Who Sees Discrimination? Attitudes on Sexual Orientation, Gender Identity, Race, and Immigration Status," in *American Values Atlas* (Washington, DC: Pew Religious Research Institute, 2017), https://www.prri.org/research/americans-views-discrimination-immigrants-blacks-lgbt-sex-marriage-immigration-reform/.

58. Gorski, "Why Evangelicals Voted for Trump"; Gorski, *American Covenant.*

59. Glenn Thrush and Maggie Haberman, "Trump Mocks Mika Brzezinski; Says She was 'Bleeding Badly from a Face-Lift,'" *New York Times*, June 29, 2017, https://www.nytimes.com/2017/06/29/business/media/trump-mika-brzezinski-facelift.html; Philip Rucker, "Trump Says Fox's Megyn Kelly Had 'Blood Coming out of Her Wherever,'" *Washington Post*, August 8, 2015, https://www.washingtonpost.com/news/post-politics/wp/2015/08/07/trump-says-foxs-megyn-kelly-had-blood-coming-out-of-her-wherever/.

60. Linda Qiu, "Study Pershing, Trump Said. But the Story Doesn't Add Up," *New York Times*, August 17, 2017, https://www.nytimes.com/2017/08/17/us/politics/trump-tweet-pershing-fact-check.html.

61. Harriet Sherwood, "The Chosen One? The New Film That Claims Trump Election Was an Act of God," *The Guardian*, October 3, 2018, https://www.theguardian.com/us-news/2018/oct/03/the-trump-prophecy-film-god-election-mark-taylor.

62. Katherine Stewart, "Why Trump Reigns as King Cyrus," *New York Times*, December 31, 2018, https://www.nytimes.com/2018/12/31/opinion/trump-evangelicals-cyrus-king.html.

63. John Fea, *Believe Me: The Evangelical Road to Donald Trump* (Grand Rapids, MI: Wm. B. Eerdmans, 2018); Angela Denker, *Red State Christians: Understanding the Voters Who Elected Donald Trump* (Minneapolis, MN: Fortress Press, 2019).

64. Andrew Whitehead and Samuel Perry, *Taking America Back for God: Christian Nationalism in the United States* (New York: Oxford University Press, 2020).

65. Samuel L. Perry and Andrew L. Whitehead, "Christian Nationalism and White Racial Boundaries: Examining Whites' Opposition to Interracial Marriage," *Ethnic and Racial Studies* 38, no. 10 (2015): 1671–89.

66. Andrew L. Whitehead, Landon Schnabel, and Samuel L. Perry, "Gun Control in the Crosshairs: Christian Nationalism and Opposition to Stricter Gun Laws," *Socius* 4 (2018): 1–13.

67. Andrew M. Greeley and Michael Hout, *The Truth about Conservative Christians: What They Think and What They Believe* (Chicago: University of Chicago Press, 2006).

68. Samuel L. Perry, *Addicted to Lust: Pornography in the Lives of Conservative Protestants* (New York: Oxford University Press, 2019).

69. Janelle Wong, *Immigrants, Evangelicals, and Politics in an Era of Demographic Change* (New York: Russell Sage Foundation, 2018).

70. Cas Mudde and Cristóbal Rovira Kaltwasser, *Populism: A Very Short Introduction* (New York: Oxford University Press, 2017); Jan-Werner Müller, *What Is Populism?* (Philadelphia: University of Pennsylvania Press, 2016); Kirk A. Hawkins, *Venezuela's Chavismo and Populism in Comparative Perspective* (New York: Cambridge University Press, 2010); Benjamin Moffitt, *The Global Rise of Populism: Performance, Political Style, and Representation* (Stanford, CA: Stanford University Press, 2016).

71. Müller, *What Is Populism?*

72. Arlie Hochschild, *Strangers in Their Own Land: Anger and Mourning on the American Right* (New York: The New Press, 2016).

73. Joshua J. Dyck, Shanna Pearson-Merkowitz, and Michael Coates, "Primary Distrust: Political Distrust and Support for the Insurgent Candidacies of Donald Trump and Bernie Sanders in the 2016 Primary," *PS: Political Science & Politics*, 51, no. 2 (2018): 351–57.

74. Moffitt, *The Global Rise of Populism*.

75. Sharma, *Hindutva*; Stanley J. Tambiah, *Buddhism Betrayed? Religion, Politics, and Violence in Sri Lanka* (Chicago: University of Chicago Press, 1992).

76. Alexis de Tocqueville, *Democracy in America*, trans. Gerald E. Bevan (London: Penguin, 2003), 348.

CHAPTER 2

Zombie Nationalism

The Sexual Politics of White Evangelical Christian Nihilism

JASON A. SPRINGS

Abstract

Despite their purported demographic and institutional decline, White evangelical voters were instrumental in the election of Donald Trump in 2016, and even more so in his 2020 loss. The story of Trump's electoral successes among Christian voters in the last two elections is in large part the story of religious nationalism—and White Christian nationalism in particular—because Trump personifies the convergence of nationalism-infused forms of messianism and apocalypticism intrinsic to White evangelicalism, which culminate in QAnon cultic ideology. However, these same ethnoreligious/nationalist patterns and logics extend much further back than Trump's insurgent candidacy. This chapter traces the recurring, resurgent patterns of "zombie nationalism" among White evangelical Christians in the United States over the last half century that emerged in response to periods of significant societal change and certain recurring sociopolitical issues. In particular, alongside established elective affinities around ethnicity (Whiteness) and religion (Christianity), this chapter makes the case for incorporating

> *gender and sexual politics as key factors in the articulation and legitimation of religious nationalism in the United States. White Christian nationalism tends to reemerge as a salient political force during periods of rapid social change and diversification, driven by racialized religious grievances symptomatic of Nietzsche's concept of ressentiment, or the paradoxical internalization and reprojection of a person's or group's perceived endangerment, victimhood, and/or suffering, in order to gain power. Drawing on examples of marriage equality and reproductive rights, this chapter demonstrates how an understanding of sexual politics is key to both apprehending and breaking the cyclical reanimation of White Christian nationalism. Escaping the nihilistic impulses driving these cycles will require White evangelicals to develop new hermeneutical tools capable of transforming the exclusionary patterns of racism, ethnocentrism, heteronormativity, and patriarchy that fuel the engine of ressentiment animating zombie nationalism.*

Reports of the death of White Christian America have been greatly exaggerated. Amid numerous predictions of its impending demise in the second decade of the twenty-first century, White Christian America has resurged again politically and culturally. If not as bombastic as the emergent Moral Majority of the early 1980s, nor as institutionally consolidated as the Christian Coalition of the 1990s, the latest self-assertion of White Christian America is more concentrated and immediately politically influential than either earlier episode.

White Christian political mobilization was a central driver that delivered Donald Trump to victory in the 2016 U.S. presidential election. White Christians self-identifying as "evangelical"—26 percent of voters in the 2016 election[1]—marshaled their votes for Trump in greater numbers than for any single candidate in the previous four presidential elections, a rate of 81 percent.[2] White Catholics followed closely, voting for Trump at a rate of 60 percent.[3] Nor was the 2016 election a momentary forced "choice of a lesser evil" for White evangelicals. A broad plurality of White evangelicals supported Trump throughout the primaries leading up to the general election, despite having a slate of alternative candidates from which to choose.[4] More significantly, White evangelicals increased their support for Trump and his policies throughout his presidency. They supported his constricting immigration and walled border policies (including separating children from their asylum seeking parents),[5] his prohibition of immigrants from various Muslim-majority countries (upheld by the Supreme Court in June 2018), and his deploying federal troops to violently quell peaceful protests in the Black Lives Matter uprisings of 2020.[6] By the end of Trump's presidency, the more frequently a White evangelical attended church, the stronger his or her support for the Trump agenda was likely to be.[7] In full awareness of what a Trump presidency would be like, White evangelical Christian support trended further upward for Trump's attempted reelection in 2020 (84 percent).[8]

Religious nationalism accounts for much of the upsurge of White evangelical voting in the 2016 and 2020 elections.[9] And yet, elements of nationalism do not merely explain the backlash voting patterns in two elections. Rather, they illuminate an animating—and *re*animating—impulse, pattern, and logic that has surged and resurged for more than a half century in White Christian America.

In this chapter I demonstrate how tracing the multiple, interwoven threads of religious nationalism in White evangelical Christian America illuminates the complex reasons why it is far from its death throes. The nationalism of White evangelicals in the Trump era is not a new phenomenon. It is one that reanimates past—and recurring—logics and patterns of ethnoreligious nationalism in the United States.[10] This dynamic is manifest in encounters with (allegedly) threatening societal change. It persists by self-protectively morphing and resurging sociopolitically, at distinctive points in time, and by reigniting in response to specific issues. I describe this persistently recurring dynamic and pattern as "zombie nationalism."

Whiteness and Christianity have long endured as legitimating forms of American nationalism.[11] And yet, focus upon Whiteness and Christianity alone leaves multiple dynamics of the ethnoreligious nationalism of White evangelicals obscured from view. Attending to gender norms and sexual politics as drivers of ethnoreligious nationalism is equally indispensable.[12] Indeed, I argue that White Christian sexual politics uniquely illuminate the elective affinities between ethnicity, religion, and nationalism in this case, as they are inextricably interwoven with the normative ideals of White evangelical Christianity. Sexual politics, I will show, infuse the sociopolitical processes by which zombie nationalism asserts and reasserts itself—time and again—in a rapidly changing context.

Nationalist dynamics sometimes camouflage themselves. They may persevere through seemingly transformational processes where the rhetoric and surface appearance changes, but the purposes and effects are re-created, rescripted, and reinforced in new ways. In my second section, I argue that, in the case of White evangelical Christians in the United States, this process of preservation through transformation is propelled by a dynamic that Friedrich Nietzsche termed *ressentiment*, an attitude toward the world that animates the "zombie nationalism" White evangelical Christians have exemplified for sixty years. In short, by illuminating the recurrent patterns of sexual politics propelling zombie nationalism, I demonstrate that the beating heart of much contemporary, White evangelical Christianity is, in fact, Nietzschean nihilism.

In the third section, I explicate the reasons that the zombie nationalism of White Christian evangelicals cannot be reduced without remainder to the interlacing, elective affinities of ethnicity, religion, and nationality. I examine in detail the ways that *sexual politics* operates as a distinct driver of zombie nationalism, and how the nihilism associated with Nietzsche's account of *ressentiment* facilitates this. The most recent resurrection of White evangelical nationalism bears patterns of refusal, resistance, political reanimation, and resurgence that recur in new form, yet distinctly replicate earlier episodes of refusal and resistance, specifically regarding earlier bans on interracial sex, marriage, and procreation. In the concluding section, I explore what it might mean theologically and hermeneutically for White evangelical Christians to engage transformatively, rather than reacting protectively and oppositionally, in the face of the changes that characterize the present context.

THE ZOMBIFICATION OF WHITE CHRISTIAN NATIONALISM

Recent studies indicate that White Christian America is rapidly aging and diminishing in population, its institutions are receding, and its influence waning. If demography is destiny, the argument runs, the relevant demographic trends indicate that White Christian America is dying.[13]

Amid these projected realities, Robert Jones warns of the emergence of a White evangelical Christian "Frankenstein's monster," an entity stitched together from the remnant fragments of formerly hegemonic cultural and institutional bodies. Though long decaying, they become reanimated and propelled by the surging currents and organizing shocks of mobilizing for specific political and culture war causes. Frankenstein's monster thus stands in as a metaphor for the kind of aggressive, concentrated culture war resurgence that White evangelicalism has taken on in the face of its demographic decline, and that it has opted for in its political resurgence under Trump, and in successive waves of Trump*ism* (which has surged beyond the Trump presidency itself).[14] And yet, careful inspection of Mary Shelley's classic narrative shows that Jones's analogy breaks down in ways that are detrimental to the point he seeks to convey with it. Exploring the analogy further reveals that there is a more descriptively and analytically illuminating comparison available.

Throughout the modern and late modern world, one finds many expressions of fascination with monsters. Mary Shelley perhaps most famously and influentially portrayed monstrosity in the modern world through her creation of Dr. Frankenstein's monster. Shelley infused her creation with acute self-awareness, hyper-self-reflexivity, and (ironically) compassion as an essential feature of natural life. The creature's desire for empathetic relationship, yet acute recognition of his loneliness and power—a beautiful soul enshrouded within the body of stitched-together corpse fragments and inspirited by the overreaching genius of modern medical materialism—could only be hated and shunned for the monstrosity of its external appearance.

At one level, Shelley's monster was a model of true humanity—vulnerable, compassionate, and, because of that, suffering a life brought into being out of death. It was the marginalization of the creature's humanity, interspliced by his desperate search for empathetic, charitable companionship, that drove him to terrorize, but ultimately mourn the death of his creator, Victor Frankenstein.[15] Paradoxically, in virtue of their revulsion at the unnaturalness of his external features, the humans he encountered could only perceive the unalloyed humanity of Dr. Frankenstein's creation as a form of repulsive monstrosity. Their perception of a monstrous creature was, in effect, a mirror image of the destructive monstrosity incipient in the heart of modern humanity.

In contrast to Jones's analogy of a White evangelical "Frankenstein's monster," the ethnoreligious nationalism that animates contemporary U.S. White evangelicalism is fashioned much more in the image of the zombies of George Romero's film *Dawn of the Dead* (1978). Like Romero's zombies (and in diametric contrast to Shelley's creation), this mutation of nationalism has demonstrated little capacity for the kind of self-discovery, hyper-self-reflexivity, critical-reflectiveness, compassion for the living, and desire for an evolving relationship conveyed in the tragic vulnerability of Victor Frankenstein's monster.[16] In the Romero original, the zombies emerge slowly. They traverse the terrain with seemingly infinitesimal motions. Their power is in the ways they pursue their objectives in mindless, lockstep conformity, and with undeterrable resolve. So it is for the social and ideological patterns that inspirit the latest resurrection of White evangelical Christian political resurgence. This pattern is reflected in dynamics of re-animation born of motivating commitments and beliefs ("worldview") that are not amenable to contrary evidence.[17] Such recurring dynamics are fueled by U.S. White evangelical Christians conceptualizing themselves as an increasingly marginalized remnant in a society that (putatively) originally did, and (allegedly) should still, reflect their central identity and values.[18] They perceive themselves to be perennially persecuted victims of an aggressively anti-Christian "secular" society.[19] For White evangelicals, these grievances infuse (and further propagate themselves through) pop-culture variations on spiritual warfare, end-time apocalypticism, and messianism. This renders White evangelicals susceptible to extreme forms of cognitive dissonance, and radicalization.[20] As a result, many Trump-era evangelical Christians are primed to embrace "end-time" and messianism-inflected conspiracy theories dressed in the garb of Trump-driven, Republican politics. From this ensues a proclivity to position their political and cultural opponents on the far side of a Manichaean divide, and to infuse contemporary politics with cosmic urgency.

During the Trump presidency, for example, White evangelical Christians were recruited in ever-increasing numbers into QAnon conspiracy ideology.[21] Some evangelical thinkers have sounded the alarm about this trend among White evangelicals. They see the evangelical embrace of QAnon as a departure from true evangelicalism into an altogether different, heretical religious movement.[22] And yet, this makes evangelical denial of its relation to QAnon too easy and un-self-critical. Clearly, not all evangelicals are QAnon followers. And not all QAnon followers are evangelicals. However, in fact, many White evangelicals are primed to embrace QAnon ideology for reasons intrinsic to twentieth- and twenty-first-century White evangelicalism. Indeed, ethnoreligious nationalism—and the distinctive form of zombie nationalism I describe here—is one form of connective tissue creating the symbiosis between much White evangelicalism and QAnon conspiracy ideology.

QAnon and White Evangelical Nationalism

QAnon theories, and internet "drop" events associated with them, emerged in the second year of Trump's presidency and quickly evolved into an increasingly mainstream religio-political movement promoted by Trump (via Twitter).[23] They portray him as a messianic figure who is a bulwark for U.S. White evangelicals and other putatively "patriotic" populations against assaults upon Christian culture. "Q" is a clandestine (that is, "anonymous," hence, "QAnon") internet presence whose viral posts and YouTube videos—frequently sprinkled with quotations from Christian scripture (e.g., 2 Chronicles 7:14) and soliciting prayer from his/her followers—purport to expose the insidious inner workings of the "deep state," and the intrinsic deceptiveness of "mainstream media." "Q" purports to reveal how the struggles against these are infused with apocalyptic significance, cohere with end-time biblical prophecy, and aim at the retrieval and defense of the United States' true identity as a Christian nation.[24]

In its most acute form, QAnon conspiracy ideology alleges that the Democratic Party is controlled by a cabal of global elite ("globalist") and "deep state" anti-Christian and anti-Trump actors (specifically naming the Rothschilds, George Soros, Bill and Hillary Clinton, Bill Gates, and "Hollywood" figures, among others). It further alleges that this cabal engages in pedophilia, child sex-trafficking, ritual cannibalism of children, and worships Satan.[25] This ideology amplifies Trump's baseless claims that he won the 2020 presidential election, and that that election was stolen from him and his followers.[26] Though they seem so ridiculous as to be dismissed out of hand, in fact, White evangelicals in the United States embrace these claims at astonishing rates, rates far higher than their nonevangelical, Republican counterparts.[27]

Examined in terms of their religio-cultural structures, these conspiracy-fueled patterns of demonization and scapegoating of opponents are neither novel nor especially unusual. They reanimate distinct features of widely circulated antisemitic conspiracy theories, such as the Protocols of the Elders of Zion, an early twentieth-century Russian czarist fabricated account of a Jewish economic and political elite allegedly controlling global politics and economics. QAnon crosses various "Protocols" tropes with the recurrent "blood libel" accusations that inspired numerous Christian pogroms against European Jews, namely, that Jews kidnapped Christian children and used their blood in ritual observance. QAnon demonizes and scapegoats its targets in similar ways, and similarly inspires violence.[28] The antisemitic contours of QAnon ideology make it especially attractive to White supremacists and White nationalists (e.g., the Proud Boys). Its ethnonationalist elements, intermingling with its religious dimensions, create an intoxicating elixir for White evangelicals who may think of themselves as sharing little in common with avowed White nationalists or card-carrying White supremacists. Yet, their elective affinities, as Philip Gorski also examines in his contribution to this volume (chapter 1), converge in the connective tissue of ethnoreligious nationalism.[29]

Trump-era White evangelicals have widely adopted various messianic interpretations of Trump. Many of these feed directly into QAnon claims that Trump is an "end-time" defender of U.S. Christian culture.[30] American evangelical culture amplifies these claims and dynamics exponentially. QAnon is, in effect, one part Frank Peretti spiritual warfare,[31] one part *Left Behind* series apocalypticism,[32] one-part Elders of Zion antisemitic conspiracy theory, and one part *Celebrity Apprentice*.

End-time, apocalyptic, messianic drivers of White evangelical Christian nationalism are not new. They have a long history among White U.S. evangelicals. The best-selling, end-time prophecy publishing industry of the 1970s and 80s, launched by Hal Lindsey's *The Late Great Planet Earth* (1970), and its influence on evangelical political engagement in the 1980s, is one prior example of the various entanglement of strands that reemerge in evangelical Christian enmeshment in QAnon ideology. The 1970s and 80s end-time prophecy and apocalypticism shaped White evangelical attitudes toward U.S. national identity in the Cold War. It informed their views toward political policy, for example, regarding the prospects of nuclear war, which many evangelicals viewed as the form that biblically prophesied apocalypse might take. Indeed, Lindsey claimed, it was the Antichrist that would "delude the world with promises of peace."[33] Ronald Reagan catered to his evangelical base by occasionally entertaining their apocalypticism at various points throughout his presidency.[34] This occurred again with the release of the *Left Behind* book series during the 1990s. Selling about 80 million copies altogether, this series shaped evangelical views about the State of Israel, and especially fueled Christian Zionism.[35]

QAnon ideology symbiotically feeds upon the impulses toward apocalypticism and messianism that are intrinsic to White evangelicalism. It infuses these with Republican politics, retrieving and synergistically reanimating prior patterns of religious nationalism. These occur, for example, in reemergent concepts of the Christian nation (peoplehood) as a victimized-yet-faithful and long-suffering remnant, that conception's interwovenness with embattled Christian identity and culture (a myth of origin), and the exceptional role of the United States in God's providential plan within world history (the exceptionalism of a "new Israel"), and especially the return of the Christian messiah (messianism). The cyclical resurgence of these dynamics exemplifies "zombie nationalism."[36]

Rather than the demise prognosticated by social scientists, the case of "the end of White Christian America" is an example by which to examine how forms of religious authority and identity navigate conflicts precipitated by rapid change, relativized significance in a diversifying context, and might vie for constructive transformation—or retrenchment through insidious radicalization—in the shifting contexts of modernity. Particularly illuminating are the ways that White evangelicals innovate—or degenerate—using modern discourse on religion, law, and nationalism to consolidate and reassert their positions, rather than reject or modify those. Equally instructive are the ways they innovate—or degenerate—using their own religious self-understandings and scriptural practices in these circumstances.

Any hope for constructive transformation will entail grappling with changes in registers that have emerged in U.S. society more broadly, registers of race, ethnicity, gender, and sexuality. At the same time, responding intelligently and intentionally requires that White Christians, in a spirit of teachability, come to terms with past—and recurring—patterns of racism, ethnocentrism, heteronormativity, and patriarchy that remain extant (if at times sublimated or camouflaged). The extent to which they persist in the future in various forms will depend on whether White evangelical Christians deal with these, and how. It is here that the distinct terms of nationalism discourse are currently limited, but hold great promise, to illuminate the nature and character of the problems.

Limitations of the Standard Terms: Race, Religion, Nationalism

"Nationalism" can be a blunt category left without qualification. For my purposes here, I situate that concept in a line of thinking indebted to Max Weber. On this account, it is an analytical concept that is intrinsically multifocal because of, in part, its elective affinities with other modes of constructing, justifying, and legitimating group identity and cohesion. Some define "nationalism" as an intrinsically religious category in the sense that it entails an idolatrous worship of the nation and the nation's manifestation in the machinations of statecraft.[37] In contrast to this, the Weberian categories admit of more nuance and flexibility.[38]

The term "ethnic" indicates "origin by birth or descent." And, in fact, Weber influentially defined "ethnicity" as a "subjective belief in common descent." According to this definition, whether common descent is based on objective realities is largely beside the point. A fluid list of features is frequently invoked as material bases for shared ethnic identities (e.g., language, manners and mores, shared origin stories, among others). The key for Weber is the commonly held *belief* in, or basic perception and embodied sense of, the "naturalness"—frequently conceived as inherited or received—of shared membership in the group, and the community's common origin and ensuing destiny. In the United States, being "White" is a category that has been fluid enough to gradually encompass differentiating identities that were initially mutually exclusive (Irish, Italian, Polish, and even Ashkenazi Jews, among others).

In sum, then, both nationality and ethnicity are historically produced or constructed. Both occur in a group's unifying account of, and belief in, its "common descent" and constituent features of shared identity.[39] The concepts of nation and ethnicity differ in that nations and national identities tend to be intricately linked to concerns for legitimation of themselves in sociopolitical contexts and purposes. These pertain to political autonomy, authentication and justification of the state with which that people administers its nationhood (i.e., nation-state), or to the demarcation and preservation of a group's boundaries and identity in a diverse national context.[40]

Methodologically, the multifocal Weberian lens has the virtue of deploying distinctions, instead of presuming dichotomies, which illuminate elective affinities—as opposed to identical (or dichotomously defined) essences—between religion, nationalism, and ethnicity.[41] This lens highlights how both ethnicity and religion (fluidly conceptualized as they may be) can interweave and become mutually reinforcing (and often tend or gravitate toward one another) for the purposes of demarcating and legitimating a political entity, claims for autonomy or political influence, or for cultural prestige, defense, and/or identity preservation. Identifications and justifications demonstrating such an elective affinity would be "ethnoreligious," and reflect the elective affinities between ethnicity and religion for such purposes, on Weber's account. In such an example, with a shared belief both in a common descent and in shared, identifying cultural features (ethnos), a group generates even greater practical and institutional cohesion by interweaving these with the practices, understandings, and institutions of a religious tradition. Or, if elective affinities did not occur in formal interconnection between ethnicity and religious elements of a historical religious tradition, the affinity might occur through "selective retrieval" of elements from proximal religious traditions and practices, deployed for purposes of interpreting the meaning and amplifying a sense of transcendent or world-historical significance of the bonds that bind (*religare/religio*) that group together. Generally, such ethnoreligious justification would relate to nationalism insofar as its purposes in demarcating the group also served purposes of generating and amplifying the shared belief in, cohesion, and legitimation of that group for sociopolitical purposes, historical significance, and cultural prestige.[42]

To take one example, ethnoreligious nationalist identification would construe White Protestant Christians as distinctive inheritors of the legacy of Anglo-Protestant Christian values. It would base this understanding in the conceptions, symbols, cultural meanings, manners, and mores considered to be distinctive of the American nation in its founding along Anglo-Protestant lines. It might invoke a claim of "origins" to justify its understanding of the nature, character, and identity that the nation-state was intended, and/or ought, to reflect in perpetuity. Such claims would maintain, for example, that the United States is a nation founded upon "Christian" or "Judeo-Christian" values. It would find these encapsulated in, say, the Ten Commandments, and also in values of religious freedom, individual liberty, and the belief that it is a nation "chosen" by God and designated a vessel to spread those values throughout the world. This would reflect an example of "ethno-religious nationalism."[43]

As a matter of fact, the above reflects many of the self-understandings of White Protestant Christians through the nineteenth- to the mid-twentieth-century United States. Indeed, ethnoreligious nationalism fitting such a description was at the heart of Protestant, anti-Catholic xenophobia throughout the nineteenth century and twentieth century. The hierarchy and authority structure of the Catholic Church (derided as antithetical to the Protestant doctrine of "the priesthood of all believers" and more democratic church polities) was deemed inimical to religious liberty. Allegiance to the pope and Vatican, and Catholic Churches that reflected distinctive ethnonational cultures (e.g., Irish-Catholic, Polish-Catholic, Lithuanian-Catholic, and so forth) were portrayed as "dual," "multiple," or "conflicting allegiances," and as antidemocratic, rendering questionable the sincerity of Catholics' loyalty to the United States.[44]

Of course, many White Christian Americans (including White Catholics) now hold similar views of Muslim Americans through the first decades of the early twenty-first century. Indeed, it was the anti-Muslim rhetoric and policies characterizing Trump's presidency that elicited the support of many White Christians.[45] Pew Research Center surveyed White evangelical laypeople regarding which issues were "very important" to them in deciding how to vote in 2016. Contrary to many presumptions that typical "culture war" issues (antiabortion, most conspicuously) drove their voting, threats of terrorism (89%) and the economy (87%) far outpaced concern for Supreme Court appointments (70%) and abortion (52%). Moreover, the results for evangelical laypeople diverged starkly from the reasons reported by evangelical religious leaders. For the leadership, Supreme Court appointments and antiabortion topped the list. Most White evangelical Christians (74%) reported sustained support for Trump's ban on immigration from seven Muslim majority countries (though Iraq was later exempted from the ban). Roughly the same percentage remained concerned about the likelihood of religious extremist acts committed in the name of Islam around the world, and in the United States.[46]

Conceptualizing Race

Why and how to focus on *Whiteness* in recent evangelical political activism, and in regard to Trumpian populism more generally? Indeed, some argue that, although Christian nationalism is profoundly influential in recent

U.S. politics, culture, and society more broadly, "being White," or "White evangelical"—even the "religiousness" of such nationalism—has very little to do with the deeper, motivating interests and purposes of Christian nationalism. On the one hand, they argue, Christian nationalism frequently underwrites and fuels political support and organizing for specific issues associated with, for example, pro "law and order" policies, against gun control, and anti-same-sex marriage policies, among others. Yet, they argue, what *really* motivates and fuels their activism is the desire for power. On this account, "Christian nationalism" is the means by which conservative Americans of whatever race, ethnicity, or socioeconomic class desire to "institutionalize conservative Christian cultural preferences in America's policies and self-identity."[47] This account reduces Christian nationalism to a multipurpose tool by which conservative-minded Americans pursue power and political and cultural influence. They do so by baptizing their political aims in religious language and moral signifiers. Race is not entirely irrelevant on this account, of course. At bottom, however, this is about the pursuit of power by the already privileged to "defend against shifts in the culture toward equality for groups that have historically lacked the access to levers of power—women and sexual, racial, ethnic, and religious minorities."[48]

Rather than enhancing the precision with which we might understand and treat the nature, character, and influence of "Christian nationalism" in contemporary public discussion and debate, this account actually dulls it. It occludes the ways that, in the United States, pursuit and protection of political power and cultural influence continue to be a discourse intrinsically inscribed by racial and ethnic valences, identities, and differences.[49]

Of course, thinkers and social critics charge that scholars, academics, and social commentators of all sorts are eager to uncover and impute charges of racism to conservative and religious members of U.S. society where (they claim) racism does not really exist. However, such objections deploy exceedingly narrow concepts of "race" and "racism." "Racism" easily becomes a sanitized term that obscures more than it illuminates. It is sanitized insofar as it purports to name intentional and explicit attitudes associated with discrimination and bigotry that an individual holds toward a person or group based upon their racial identity or characteristics the person shares with a racialized group. Without important qualifications, such a conception elides structural causes and conditions (structural forms) of racism. It obscures the ways that cultural practices, conceptions, and implicit and unrecognized biases camouflage participation in structural forms of racism or make them feel and appear "not wrong."[50]

So understood, race has always inscribed religious practices and religious discourse in the United States. These intersect and inextricably interweave with ethnicity, gender, and class. By diminishing the racial dimensions of this history, and its effect upon the present—by treating it as, at most, secondary and dependent in significance—this account detaches the power and longtime prevalence of Christian ethnoreligious nationalism from historical specificity. It erases the specific, radical changes to which White evangelical and Catholic Christians are reacting in their embrace of Trumpism. It thus leaves the concept of religious nationalism to hover in the realm of the generic and abstract, as an instrument of generically "conservative Americans." Similarly, it uproots the structural and cultural nature and character of "race" and "racism," a dynamic that reflects White American Christians' broad refusal to recognize racism as a structural and cultural phenomenon (rather than a matter of personal attitude and explicit belief, from which most White people easily excuse themselves).[51]

As we will see in the next section, it is the withering away and feared loss of phenomena such as racially inflected advantage (however tacit) and protection of what Weber identifies as a central driver of ethnonationalism, that is, "cultural prestige" and influence, that currently mobilize White evangelical Christians in mass patterns of behavior and voting trends that reveal a degree of uniformity (and amplification of previous logics and behaviors) not seen heretofore. At the same time, these also reflect patterns and logics of in-group protection, survival, and political reassertion that have been evident before.

Beyond reduction to a group's "pursuit of power," how do racial, ethnic, and religious identities intersect to influence the distinctly oppositional and conflictual appeals to nationalism in the context of the Trump presidency? What is at stake? Again, Weber's account of elective affinities between ethnicity, religion, and nationalism permits a more fluid and nonreductionistic, multifocal conceptualization—one in which ethnicity and race interweave with and infuse a conception of religious identities and practices—making that identity, in part, distinctly what it is. To put it in terms from Gorski's chapter, what results is a compound. These two interact synergistically, further, with all the religious and ethnic/racialized features that constitute U.S. nationalism (Christian and Jewish myths, symbols, origin stories, and exceptionalist claims for the nation's special favor, duties, and world-historical significance in relation to the Judeo-Christian God). The result, again, is the more flexible analytical category of ethnoreligious nationalism. Redescribed philosophically, the animating process bears striking resemblance to the nihilistic innovation that occurs by way of spiritual defensiveness and retaliation described by Nietzsche in *The Genealogy of Morals*.

"Evil Be Thou My Good":
White Evangelical Ressentiment as Ethnoreligious Nationalism

Diversification by non-European immigrant groups has been occurring at an increasingly rapid pace in the United States over the past half century. This has occurred especially in the wake of amplified Asian and Latin American immigration since passage of the Hart–Celler Immigration and Nationality Act of 1965.[52] Numerous studies indicate that increasingly rapid societal diversification—accompanied by experience and/or fear that one's majority status is diminishing, and that such reorientation is a necessary part of the increasing justness of a society—triggers identity defensiveness.[53] Not surprisingly, then, White people in the United States now widely report that they perceive discrimination against White people to be as significant a problem as discrimination against Blacks and other minorities.[54] Such surveys correlate with the upsurge of White entitlement, White fragility, and increasingly reactionary and virulent forms of White supremacy in recent decades, and especially in the 2016 and 2020 elections.[55] These are circumstances ripe for exploitation by appeals to White identity and grievance politics, which characterize much of the conflict and divisiveness in contemporary U.S. society.

White evangelical Christian perceptions of discrimination track closely with the reported grievance trends of White Americans generally. Eighty percent of White evangelicals report "perceived in-group embattlement," alleging that "discrimination against Christians is as big a problem as discrimination against other groups in America."[56] A majority of White evangelical Christians claim that "American culture and way of life" have worsened since the 1950s.⁵⁷ Hence White evangelicals' widespread attunement to the invitation to "make America great again." White evangelical Christianity interweaves with conservative politics in the United States. Indeed, White evangelical Christians demonstrate marked uniformity in their political affiliations—predominantly Republican.⁵⁸

Evangelical Christian members of minority racial and ethnic groups diverge greatly from White evangelicals in their political views and voting practices.⁵⁹ Non-White evangelicals are less politically conservative on numerous social and political issues, and generally less aligned with Republican Party affiliation, than White evangelicals. They diverge on issues such as immigration policy and militant enforcement of national borders, the realities of climate change, progressive taxation of the rich, the government's role in providing health care, support for the Black Lives Matter movement, and the present-day effect of the legacy of slavery in the United States.⁶⁰ Janelle Wong makes the case that, on the one hand, these divergences are owing to non-White evangelicals' experiences as members of racial or ethnic minority groups—their experiences of varying degrees and forms of nonmajority standing, and often, struggles against forms of marginalization related to immigration and immigrant status—in the United States. On the other hand, even more importantly, Wong's work indicates a difference in minority and immigrant evangelicals in virtue of what they lack. Namely, they do not harbor a similar sense of "grievance" and perception that they have "lost" a culture and society that once was (putatively) rightfully theirs. White evangelicals, by contrast, perceive themselves becoming an increasingly embattled, politically less influential, culturally marginal, discriminated against, and soon to be minority group.⁶¹ The temptation is for White evangelical politics to become—insofar as it is not already—inspirited and driven by a perception of its own endangerment, and a spirit of victimhood, turned inward upon itself, exemplifying what Nietzsche called *ressentiment*.⁶²

As Nietzsche had it, *ressentiment* is a process by which a person or group responds to its own perceived endangerment, victimhood, and/or suffering by internalizing its angst and frustrating and festering desire for revenge, then projecting it outward as means by which to assert itself. It wields its alleged victimization as a covert means of conjuring and asserting power—even dominance—in the form of retribution against what it perceives (and claims) to be the source of its precarity. *Ressentiment* is self-deceiving in that the source of the group's power—its amplification of its own alleged victimization—produces an inability to accurately perceive the true cause of its perception of self-suffering.[63] *Ressentiment* transvalues (revalues) values in order to locate meaningfulness in the group's perception of its marginalization and suffering. They claim that this is their pursuit of true justice, not revenge. The group then repurposes that putative suffering and alleged endangerment as a weapon. The transvaluation of values becomes a means of a form of spiritualized self-protection and reprisal.[64]

For example, a group might reposition the diminishment (or relativization) of its own prior cultural power and significance as its having become, allegedly, a culture perennially under attack. The group may do this, for example, by construing some emergent, newly established recognition and equality for a previously unrecognized and marginalized group that it opposes as discrimination against its sacred beliefs, and an infringement upon its rights of belief and practice to continue treating that previously "deviant" group as inferior. In such a case it reacts by transvaluing values and concepts. For example, political and legal recognition, and just treatment, of the previously excluded group now constitutes the formerly hegemonic group's victimization and infringement upon its rights. It does this rather than recognizing and adjusting, adapting, and transforming itself in the face of new realities, and a more precise and encompassing account of justice.[65] What they claim to be "justice" for them (in this case protection of their right to religious freedom) is, in fact, their transvaluation of values of justice and equality in a defensive and retaliatory reaction born of *ressentiment*.

In its general contours, *ressentiment* becomes a source of power because it is creative. It invents by transposing the meaning of values, and the orientation of actions that ensue therefrom, in virtue of the group's self-deceived conviction that its members are the people who are *truly* endangered, and in pursuit of true justice. In this way, even "the highest values devalue themselves," despite the stated intentions of those who might promulgate those values as absolute or nonnegotiable.[66] This value transvaluation—and thereby, in the process, group self-invention and assertion—reveals how the treasured beliefs and alleged inviolable truths of the group are, in fact, symptomatic of a western mythos (a dynamic Nietzsche described as indicative of nihilism).[67] In the present case, the mythos manifests in the outworking of a particular form of ethnoreligious nationalism. This process of transvaluation and self-invention fits Nietzsche's description of nihilism (even if tacitly so and/or unintended by the group in question).

Held up to the recent history of White evangelical Christians, *ressentiment* describes an animating dynamic for the ways that ethnoreligious nationalist logics exemplify recurrent patterns of self-preservation through transformation, reanimation, and resurgence that constitute the zombie nationalism at the heart of White evangelical, culture war Christianity. This pattern of *ressentiment* among White Christians occurs nowhere more dramatically than in White evangelical and White Catholic Christians' present-day, and previous, discourses on sexual politics.

THE SEXUAL POLITICS OF ETHNORELIGIOUS NATIONALISM

One example of sexual politics that triggers the *ressentiment* of White U.S. evangelicals is marriage equality for LGBTQ people. Indeed, until very recently, homosexuality in U.S. society was treated as exemplifying a kind of monstrosity, or moral abomination. Same-sex attraction was alleged to be perverse behavior originating from an internal deviant impetus. It was with the advent of behavioral psychology in the mid-twentieth century that this deviance was believed to be alterable by "scientific" means. Psychologists thought they could behaviorally restructure the homosexual person's desires. This rendered obsolete the traditional methods of treating homosexual tendencies through bodily and psychiatric incapacitation (e.g., chemical castration and ice pick lobotomy). The cutting edges of mid-twentieth-century behavioral psychology claimed to restructure the deviant channels of homosexual desires through "behavior modification" and "operant conditioning." Throughout the 1950s and 60s, homosexuality was treated increasingly with "aversion therapy"—in the case of gay men, electrical shocks to the genitals and vomit-inducing drugs coupled with forced viewing of images of naked men. Subjects would then be sent on romantic outings with women. Such "behavior modification" treatments failed spectacularly. They left their subjects traumatized, scarred, and suicidal. Homosexuality entered the DSM-II (1968) as a mental disorder and reclassified as a "sexual orientation disorder" because of the emergence of

Zombie Nationalism   69

a discipline-wide consensus in 1973. It was dropped from the DSM in 1988, and from the World Health Organization (ICD-10) in 1992.

U.S. culture and law now recognize same-sex marriage and include it with respect to equality before the law. These historically invisible, marginalized, persecuted, and stigmatized people are recognized as fully human—recognized legally and socially in their full humanity—rather than as people beholden to the monstrous miscreation or medicalized sicknesses of mental illnesses, such as "sexual orientation disturbance"[68] or spiritual perversion and depravity. Gays and lesbians thus became recognized as bearers of the rights of full citizenship as such (e.g., marital rights, parental rights of child adoption, and so forth). Yet these developments transgress the evangelical conviction that same-sex and family relationships are abominations in that they transgress putatively natural and divinely sanctioned norms (i.e., contravene their, putatively, biblical understanding of marriage between one man and one woman).

Ressentiment takes forms of spiritual and psychological retaliation in response to one's self-diagnosed oppression and victimhood. The legalization of marriage equality makes same-sex marriage something that evangelical Christians must live with, accommodate, even stand alongside in equality before the law. In principle, they must serve same-sex couples as customers in their businesses that serve the public. They must extend marital benefits to same-sex spouses in institutions that receive tax-exempt status from the state. And yet, same-sex marriage remains, to many evangelical Christians, a moral abomination.[69]

Many White evangelical Christians respond by claiming that forcing them to recognize same-sex marriage as marriage, and to treat it equally with heterosexual marriage, renders them victims of the latest phase in the sexual revolution initiated a few decades ago as the most recent sexual fad or latest "sexual orthodoxy." Marriage equality encroaches upon their "sincerely held belief" that same-sex relations are abominations, and, as a matter of (putative) ontological fact, cannot be marriages at all. They thus invoke their right to religious freedom. This is their right to freely adhere to their sincerely held belief, and to live in accord with that belief, namely, that they must never act in ways that either facilitate or endorse even tacitly these abominations (same-sex marriage, adoption by same-sex couples, and so forth).[70] Indeed, those evangelical Christians who hold out the prospect for treating spiritually—even "curing"—the conditions of same-sex desire and love claim the mantle of rights for their cause. Though the most famous interdenominational Christian (predominantly evangelical Protestant) "gay conversion" organization, Exodus International, renounced conversion therapy, closed its doors, and issued an apology for the suffering it caused, many of its network members continue to operate. Other evangelical organizations persist in variations of "conversion therapy," or psycho-social and spiritual treatment for "homosexual urges."[71]

Here again we see this group's creative innovation with—transvaluation of—legal norms for religious purposes that are both defensive (motivated by their putative victimhood), but also obliquely retaliatory (textbook features of Nietzschean *ressentiment*). Evangelical organizations such as James Dobson's Focus on the Family now justify their persistence in "gay conversion therapy" as the "right of the patient" to seek the form of therapy that they desire, including "sexual orientation change efforts," however harmful that "treatment" has proven to be.[72] In fact, "conversion therapy" has been not only discredited as a form of treatment by countless studies among psychologists and medical researchers, but it has also been shown to be damaging to the people to whom it is applied (in clear contravention of the Hippocratic Oath). It has, as a result, been legally banned in many places across the United States. And yet, in 2019 a conservative Christian advocacy organization filed suit against the New York City Council's ban on conversion therapy. They claimed that such a ban violates the rights to the free speech of doctors and patients (i.e., doctors who might counsel patients in favor of "sexual orientation conversion therapy," or patients who might seek it). The City Council preemptively reversed its ban on conversion therapy as a result. They reasoned that, were the challenge appealed to the U.S. Supreme Court (now with three justices nominated by Trump), the ban might be overturned under the auspices of "free speech" or "religious freedom," and perhaps result in the compulsory reversal of any such similar ordinances across the United States.[73]

In sum, then, contra the self-perception of themselves as a persecuted group that seeks to merely be legally accommodated in order to faithfully observe their religious beliefs against same-sex marriage, in fact, some White evangelicals continue to seek out and "cure" LGBTQ people. This is not a passive appeal to accommodation. Rather, it is an active deployment of culture war sexual politics. How does it reveal the pivotal role of sexual politics in racialized ethnoreligious nationalism? As I make evident in the next subsection, this sexual politics drives the recurring logic and dynamics that resurrect White evangelical Christian ethnoreligious nationalism time and again—animating zombie nationalism.

A New Name for Some Old Forms of Bigotry:
"Religious Freedom" as Ressentiment

The 2013 Supreme Court decision *United States v. Windsor* declared unconstitutional the Defense of Marriage Act of 1996, which had defined marriage as a union between one man and one woman in federal law, and which had granted the states the right to deny the marriage of same-sex couples. *Obergefell v. Hodges* (2015) further required the federal government, and all states, to recognize and respect same-sex marriage equality, and to confer all the rights and protections attendant to such recognition. On the night that the Supreme Court handed down its decision in *Obergefell*, President Barack Obama illuminated the White House in rainbow-colored lights—the colors symbolizing Gay Pride since the inception of the gay rights movement (and the constituent colors of the Gay Pride flag). For many evangelical Christian Americans, this action taken by the first African American president was nothing less than a culture war broadside against evangelical Christian identity and marked the rapid dissolution of Christian culture in the United States.

Statistically, approval of same-sex marriage has increased throughout U.S. society in recent decades. It has slightly improved even among some younger, White evangelical Christians. And yet, as evangelical historian John Fea recounts, it is difficult to overestimate the influence that the establishment of same-sex marriage equality exerted in amplifying a sense of grievance and igniting "righteous anger" (and ensuing "passion for justice"—a hallmark of *ressentiment*) among White evangelicals. Such self-righteousness further fueled support for Trump. White evangelicals took *Obergefell* to exemplify the marginalization—indeed, the endangerment—of White, evangelical Christian America. "When LGBT activists claimed that Obama was on 'the right side of history' in his support of gay marriage, the message to evangelicals was clear: they were on the wrong side," Fea writes.[74] "As the presidential election cycle began, evangelicals felt marginalized and even threatened by the social progressivism they witnessed under Obama's administration. The traditional institutions they deemed essential to a healthy society—the society that was at the core of their childhood and upbringing—was crumbling around them, and they were terrified."[75]

Fea is far from alone in attributing White evangelicals' embrace of Trump as backlash to their self-declared endangerment by the previous president, and to a societal shift toward same-sex marriage equality that occurred "too quickly for many Americans."[76] And yet, such a focus neglects the deep history and subterranean—yet episodically resurgent—dynamics that made their path to Trump predictable, if not inevitable.

When viewed through the lenses of ethnoreligious nationalism I have discussed, by contrast, the deep history of evangelical sexual politics, and the logic by which it drives a resurrection of ethnoreligious nationalism—zombie nationalism—comes into view. In fact, White evangelicals have been at a juncture of obstinate opposition previously regarding their views of the "sanctity of marriage" as between one man and one woman. The sincerely held belief in 2016 that same-sex marriage (and all homosexual sexual relations) is a moral and spiritual abomination, and thus contradicts the true meaning of "marriage," claims that it contravenes putatively ontological differences between men and women. Further, this belief appeals to "civilizational normativity," frequently based on the putative dictates of natural law. And this belief claims, namely, that "for more than two millennia, the belief that marriage is a union between a man and a woman served as a bedrock of Western civilization."[77] These claims replicate earlier evangelical opposition to interracial sex and marriage. In fact, they resurrect and reanimate identical logics and sexual politics of the earlier case. Both cases spurred upsurges in evangelical Christian ethnoreligious nationalism.

In popular perception, evangelical Christians awakened politically in the 1970s, primarily in response to the Supreme Court ruling that abortion was a constitutional right (*Roe v. Wade*, 1973).[78] This court case purports to mark a point of political awakening and mobilization through moral outrage that quickly consolidated religious activism in the antiabortion movement. In fact, this narrative obscures more than it illuminates, and is based on a highly revisionist account of religious history of the twentieth- and twenty-first-century United States.

In the years immediately following the *Roe v. Wade* ruling in 1973, numerous White Christian evangelical groups supported the legalization of abortion. In fact, it took several years for abortion to be recruited as a political and cultural wedge that could divide religiously self-identified voters from those they saw as their opposition—feminists, liberal Democrats, and so-called secular activists of all types.[79] The logics and structural features that fueled White Christian political, cultural, and social aggressiveness toward such putative abominations also find stark recurrence in recent examples of culture war activism and political populism.

Long before abortion was recruited as a wedge controversy, other "moral abominations" led White evangelical Christians to engineer protective legal and political formations in defense against the putative onslaught against their religion and culture. "Interracial mixing," "interracial marriage," and "interracial procreation" stand out as such antecedent abominations; interracial sexual relations were rejected by conservative Christians as "miscegenation" because they transgressed ontological racial differences. White Americans' intimacy with African Americans was a religious prohibition—a taboo.[80] Countless documented lynchings were related to (perceived or real) interracial intimacy, sexual relations, or "flirting." The power of this taboo was exacerbated, and became more aggressively enforced, in virtue of the putative monstrosity that would result in the amalgamation of the distinct races.

Many evangelicals argue that the parallel is not valid. Most have long since renounced explicit racism. They argue that "race mixing" and "miscegenation," though clearly taboo and sincerely believed to be moral abominations at the time, differed, nonetheless, in that the coupling in question fell within the realm of biological complementarity of particular sexual reproductive organs. Transgressing this conception of sexual complementarity, as same-sex coupling does, violates "natural" (putatively ontological) forms of differentiation in ways that "miscegenation" and "amalgamism" of interracial sex and relationships never did.[81]

And yet, this objection is based on revision of the justifications recognized as self-evident and theologically justified at the time. The view that interracial sex, marriage, and procreation were biological, moral, and spiritual abominations, and thus ought to be legally banned, was held by White evangelical Christians in ways similar to their current opposition to same-sex marriage through the latter part of the twentieth century. They deemed the racialized differences just as ontological, and grounded in natural law, as the differences in personhood and status that existed between Whites and Blacks.[82] For Protestants, this took the form of a theological basis for separate races.[83] Alleged biological complementarity of interracial sexual relations and marriage was considered a violation of ontological conditions, as same-sex sexual relations and marriage are considered by most White evangelicals today.

Similarly, appeals to the logic of putative "ontological difference" between races, and claims that sexual separation of the races was a "civilizational norm," served as bases for excluding certain people from legal marriage. They also drove Christian evangelical ethnoreligious nationalism in the earlier case of interracial sex and marriage. For example, in prohibiting marriage between any "person of African descent," and "any person not of African descent," the terms of Oklahoma's 1908 antimiscegenation law attempted to make the ontological and civilizational bases of such statutes clear. In a similar way that the putative abomination of same-sex marriage (or any same-sex sexual relations) is for most White evangelicals and White Catholics today, interracial sex and marriage were claimed to be a violation of God's law and of the essential natures of White and Black manhood and womanhood. They allegedly defied "civilizational norms."[84] They contravened the sanctity of marriage, per se. Moreover, the fact that instances of miscegenation could result in procreation spurred expansive legal innovation—laws that would cover the distinct class of cases in which interracial sex resulted in "mixed-race" offspring.[85]

For example, two years after the Civil War, the Pennsylvania Supreme Court ruled in favor of segregated railway cars, arguing that "the natural law which forbids [interracial marriage] and that social amalgamation which leads to a corruption of races, is as clearly divine as that which imparted to [the races] different natures."[86] Indiana, Alabama, and Virginia soon followed by citing God's divinely sanctioned, natural law to uphold the illegality of racial intermarriage, invoking the "theology of separate races" to underwrite human law. And even though no *federal* antimiscegenation law was passed, state antimiscegenation laws were not challenged until 1948. Indeed, Christian theological beliefs and religious invocations of "natural law" have animated twinned aversions and political responses—equally vehement—toward Supreme Court rulings: the ruling that legalized interracial marriage (*Loving v. Virginia* [1967]) and a half century later the ruling that legalized same-sex marriage (*Obergefell*).

There are important differences between the two episodes, of course. Earlier appeals were to racialized sexual ontology (Blacks and Whites as separate races, the intermixing of which contravened their respective racial natures). The later claim is based in gendered biosexual ontology (the putative complementarity by which to "insert Tab A into Slot B"). Even so, the same logic of ontology as bases for (and ensuing appeal to) "civilizational norms" and "natural law" reanimates the ethnoreligious nationalism of White evangelicals in their embrace of Trump in their repudiation of legalization of same-sex marriage equality. In short, the sexual politics of White, evangelical Christians inspirits the latest resurrection of zombie nationalism.

To the purview of the vast majority of White evangelical Christians, the legalization of same-sex marriage cannot be seen as a long occluded, despised, marginalized, and persecuted group finally achieving recognition and equality before the law. From their vantage point, same-sex marriage equality cannot appear as an instance of the arc of the moral universe bending toward justice. Any such claim or description is transvalued into the secular state's, and secular culture's, legal vindication of the latest "sexual orthodoxy" in the wake of the revolution for sexual libertinism of the 1960s and 70s, a putative "sexual orthodoxy" appearing roughly "two minutes ago on the clock of history" and now imposed upon them. Of course, by this logic, civil rights for African Americans and suffrage and rights for women fall roughly 2.5 and 3 minutes prior on the clock of civilizational history, respectively.[87] Progressive Christians fought for these earlier changes (and many did so in recent years for same-sex marriage equality), but conservative Christians fought against each of them.[88]

White evangelicals protest that they are the victims of an antireligious, militantly secular state and nihilistic culture. This culture, they allege, marginalizes them by requiring that they legally recognize and provide services in businesses (or in government, universities, or other organizations that serve the public and/or have tax-exempt status), accommodate, and/or provide benefits for same-sex married couples. Such recognition of same-sex marriage is portrayed as compelled endorsement of sin, transgression of natural law, and, as such, as an infringement on persons' religious freedom to believe and treat same-sex marriage as an abomination in God's eyes and therefore as inauthentic marriage. This becomes the victimization of "polite persecution," much like White Christians who were forced to recognize, first, laws overturning Jim Crow segregation and then gradually interracial marriage, sex, procreation, adoption, and child-rearing.[89]

Deploying religious claims and teachings of a religious tradition in ways that invert the values of equality and freedom effects a "transvaluation of values."[90] The right to refuse services to same-sex partners seeking to legally marry is resituated as a "freedom" that is essential to witnessing to, and enacting, the love of Jesus. Persisting in this refusal—albeit, preferably in loving tone and style—becomes a (putative) witness of faithfulness to the love and truth of Christ. At least one of the alleged "lies" they resist, presumably, is that same-sex marriage is anything other than perversion.[91]

Again, this illuminates sexual politics as a driver of zombie nationalism. What appears on its face to be merely a backlash over sexual politics at a recent point in time occurs in a context in which the aggrieved opposition (White evangelical Christians), in fact, has a deep history and longtime presence of deploying such a logic of ressentiment. White Christians in the United States have been politically mobilized for decades. Centuries before that—as early as the first and second Great Awakenings in the United States—White Christians worked to spiritually and culturally evangelize the United States through an integrative vision of the nation as a sacred, chosen nation.[92] White Christians in the United States are a long-established culturally hegemonic group. In this context, what might appear to be an isolated episode in sexual politics (i.e., rearguard defense against newly legalized same-sex marriage) is, when placed in historical context, one surgent moment in a longtime contest over the identity and character of the society. White evangelical Christians resist this change, portraying it as aggressive encroachment by a secular state in a rapidly secularizing culture and society, a society they claim is increasingly hostile to evangelical Christian beliefs and to the free practice of religion more generally.

The claims of their oppression—"soft tyranny" and "polite persecution"—occur not merely in the secular state's putative infringement upon allegedly sincerely held commitments of a religious worldview. This is the secular state's supposed violation of one's basic right to religious freedom. This position construes religious freedom both as a distinctive "first freedom" as inscribed in the First Amendment and a civilizational value that is intrinsic to the Judeo-Christian ethos of the U.S. founding. Allegedly, it is the fact that the nation-state has become aggressively secular that has contorted the original meaning of the basic principles of religious liberty and civilizational ethos. On this reading, the state was meant to embody this ethos, and should continue to do so in the present. Thus, their own fight for the "soul" (identity and character) of American society is infused by Christian nationalism.

This response reflects the ways that this group is grappling with allegedly sudden, seemingly drastic elements of modernization. These forms of modernization are present in epistemic, cultural, and legal changes that have followed from increasing moral and religious diversification, and from social and cultural transformation. These result from a movement for equal legal standing by marginalized—and genuinely persecuted—minorities and previously excluded communities.[93] The evangelical Christian response is not a retreat into a simple enclave mentality and existence, as some evangelicals did in order to practice their segregationist Christian commitments when the mores and laws prohibiting racial segregation and racial intermarriage changed.[94] The response, rather, reflects an attempt to contest these effects of modernization in U.S. society by using modern moral and legal terms (that is, vindication of rights of religious freedom as those are conceived by and for evangelical Christians, especially in contrast to Muslims and atheists),[95] and by using legal-rational and bureaucratic processes. They deploy these tactics to preserve beliefs they consider to be nonnegotiable but that have become recognized as dehumanizing and damaging to others (e.g., protecting rights to defend and promote "conversion therapy") and thus have been legally changed. This creativity with modern legal and moral norms and concepts also leads to innovation and creativity with the religious dimensions of national identity, and the societal and legal implications that flow therefrom. This creativity is not the innovation of working within the normative constraints of a living and well-ordered tradition. It is the kind of creativity that Nietzsche described as emerging from the nihilism that underpins *ressentiment*. It exemplifies the resourcefulness and self-vindication of the transvaluation of values.

The patterns of ethnoreligious nationalism inscribed in White Christian resistance to interracial sex and marriage, and, later, resistance to same-sex sexual relations and marriage, evince markedly similar logic and dynamics. The key insight this connection illuminates is that, to identify and unlearn these patterns of ethnoreligious nationalism—to escape the cycles of zombie nationalism—White evangelicals (along with White Americans more generally) will have to learn what it means to be, and to have been all along,

White, cis-hetero-normative, and patriarchal (as interwoven identities) in a context that bears the stamp of the distinctive racial history, history of sexual politics, and hegemony of White Christianity, as pertains in the United States. The group will have to reconceptualize its role in a changed and changing context. How might this be possible working from within the Christian tradition itself?

A Mess of Pottage:
The Hermeneutics of White Evangelical Nihilism

At the outset of this chapter, I posed a question: Can White evangelical Christians in the United States engage intentionally and instructively in the constructive transformation of their tradition in the face of inevitable changes? Or, are they condemned to assume a defensive, rearguard preservationism that camouflages the culture war and political activism that has led them to embrace Trumpian populism and claim Trump as a messianic figure for them? Some—perhaps many—can answer this question only by an appeal to faithfulness. They can only respond to the changes brought on by an increasingly diverse, expanded account of justice and ensuing changes in society and culture according to what they believe to be the dictates of Christian faith. I have argued that what may appear to them to be the dictates of Christian faith can, in fact, be—and we have very strong reasons to claim that, for many White evangelical Christians, already are—nihilistic *ressentiment* precisely of the kind that Nietzsche diagnosed as a tendency and temptation in certain forms of perceived self-embattlement and alleged experience of suffering.

Some evangelicals will ask, rightly, "Must we simply adjust our religious understandings, beliefs, and practices to accord with the alterations in the culture around us?" The wisest among them will ask, alternatively, "Are there reasons internal to our tradition—scriptural and theological reasons—that motivate and underwrite constructive transformation regarding same-sex marriage, much as they did the eventual (at times, very slow) transformation of White evangelical views toward slavery, women's rights, and racial segregation?" Such questions might contain the antidote to the recurrent patterns that constitute zombie nationalism.

As laws and culture changed around them, the evangelical opposition to interracial marriage and procreation gradually waned. There have been holdouts, of course, and racism has a way of preserving itself through transformation in this regard, even after it has become impolitic or impermissible in public, polite company.[96] However, for the most part, White Christians no longer view interracial relations, sex, marriage, and procreation as abominations on biblical grounds, as many once did. Indeed, for some, that position now seems unthinkable. Can a comparable pattern of adaptation occur over the question of same-sex marriage?

Transformation on the question of race relations occurred, in part, in response to—by listening to—the testimonies of African American theologians and activists on these issues. Can the same happen if Christians listen to the voices of Christian theologians and ethicists who speak from within the commitments of the tradition but to and from the experiences of LGBTQ Christians? In the final section, I examine one such example. Specifically, I explore how the hermeneutics (the interpretive practices of their scripture) can either reflect the nihilist *ressentiment* or give rise to the constructive, intentional transformation of the tradition itself through "faith seeking understanding."

Dionysius versus the Crucified

It may appear natural to attribute White evangelical embrace of Trump populism and politics to cynical utilitarianism oriented by sexual politics. From this perspective, the value of certain political ends believed to follow from an evangelical worldview (e.g., curtailing LGBTQ rights, cementing a conservative supermajority on the Supreme Court, overturning *Roe v. Wade*, among others) overrides the obvious contradictions presented by a political representative who was vocally "pro-choice" until his late switch to Republican Party politics, a serial philanderer (and accused sexual predator by multiple women) who contravenes all the appeals to "character" and "virtue" heralded as nonnegotiable by evangelical Christian "value voters" through the 1990s and 2000s (he is a serial liar, which is only one of his vices).[97] In such a utilitarian calculus, the political end justifies the religiously idolatrous means. Yet such ascription reduces evangelical political attitudes to the mechanics of a calculus. Upon closer inspection, there is far greater religious self-invention on the part of White evangelical Christians than a cynical utilitarian equation could ever admit (paralleling their innovation with rights language and legal norms on the sociopolitical sides).

There are elective affinities that bind White evangelicals to Trump.[98] And yet, rather than fix either evangelicals or Trumpian populism into broad typologies, we must admit that they are already enmeshed in ways that elude the simple disaggregation of them into separate categories.[99]

In 1995, after much lobbying by White evangelical Christians, the U.S. Congress passed the Jerusalem Embassy Act, which recognized Jerusalem as the capital of Israel and a unified city. It also claimed that the U.S. embassy should be moved there. Many White Christian evangelicals (some of them self-ascribed "Christian Zionists") lobbied for decades for the United States to recognize Jerusalem as wholly in the possession of Israel and as its capital. It expresses powerful symbolism in terms of religious and nationalist politics. To some it also has meaning in terms of evangelical eschatology, according to which recognition of Jerusalem is deemed an indicator of the fulfillment of Christian prophecy, and the immanent return of the Christian messiah.[100] Others saw it as a vindication of U.S. support for a democratic nation and state founded upon the same basic values.[101] Still others saw it as finally honoring and fully recognizing the land "where Jesus walked."[102]

The controversial nature of the law spurred the U.S. Congress to include an escape clause in the legislation. U.S. policy would default to recognizing Jerusalem unless the president enacts a waiver, requiring renewal every six months. After twenty years of renewals, in December 2017, President Donald Trump formally recognized Jerusalem as the capital of Israel. "I want to tell you that the Jewish people have a long memory," Israeli prime minister Benjamin Netanyahu declared in response, "so we remember the proclamation of the great king, Cyrus the Great, Persian king 2,500 years ago. He proclaimed that the Jewish exiles in Babylon could come back and rebuild our Temple in Jerusalem."[103]

The reference to Cyrus was a direct appeal to many evangelical Christians throughout the United States. White evangelicals, especially, had been making the comparison between Trump and the Persian ruler as early as the presidential primaries.[104] Just as God used this Persian emperor as an instrument in reversing the Babylonian captivity, and allowed the orthodox Yahwists to return to the promised land and rebuild the Temple, so God, they claimed, was using Trump as a vessel by which to reclaim the place and role of White evangelical Christians—and White Christian evangelicalism—in American society.[105] This interpretive move has manifest widely among the White evangelical community in the United States.[106] Interpretively, it purports to absorb the present-day world into the world of Christian scripture through a hermeneutic of figural interpretation. However, in fact, this diametrically opposes—indeed, reverses—the interpretive direction that occurred through the long Christian tradition of figural (or typological) interpretation.[107]

As a tradition of Christian scriptural interpretation, figural interpretation oriented the historical world by the scriptural world, rather than situating the Bible and its contents as simple artifacts within human history. It thus required a scripturally oriented heuristic approach. Otherwise, it would become crude historical proof-texting, in which figures and developments of the present day are selectively assigned biblical analogues—and theological, world-historical meaning—but, ultimately, as dictated by the interests and purposes of the interpreter. In the latter case, historical and political events and figures become, in effect, selectively baptized with biblical meaning according to the interpretive preferences of the interpreter. Contemporary sociopolitical events get dressed up in the garb of biblical events and circumstances to imbue them with transcendent and world-historical meaning (another dynamic of zombie nationalism, e.g., the putative end-time and messianic significance of the State of Israel). The latter interpretive approach, in which human history determines the interpretive significance of Christian scripture, is symptomatic of distinctly eighteenth- and nineteenth-century developments in practices of scriptural interpretation.[108]

In the long history of Christian figural interpretation, by contrast, interpretation had to be anchored in, and oriented by, the center point of the biblical witness, namely, the life, death, and resurrection of Jesus. By this standard of Christian interpretive tradition, the figuring of Trump as a present-day Cyrus flies free of any Christological anchor and orientation. It exemplifies hermeneutical proof-texting driven by transvaluative response to the driving concerns of the day. It is symptomatic of the Nietzschean nihilism (driven by *ressentiment*) that is the beating heart of much contemporary White evangelical Christianity.

Ironically, examples of the intratraditional adjustment and transformation through the deep tradition of Christocentric biblical interpretation demonstrate how same-sex marital unions are wholly consistent with a Trinitarian God's election and transfiguration of embodied human personhood. They are, in fact, one particular instance of a long tradition of God having agapeically transformed human persons and relationships, first and orientationally, in the life, death, and resurrection of Jesus.[109]

By the Christian tradition's own best lights, overemphasis on the putative iron-clad dictates of human interpretations of natural law risk becoming idolatrous. It "hog ties" God with what humans understand to be the dictates of "nature." One ethicist explains:

> Natural law is an important Christian idea . . . but an ethics of natural law always runs the risk of treating untransformed nature as normative for Christians, whereas the whole point of the Church, the body of Christ, is to transform the natural. The Christian norm for sexuality is not natural law; it is rather human nature transformed, eros swept up into agape. When Christian ethicists condemn same-sex coupling as unnatural, they are underestimating God's capacity to transfigure it, to make it mean something agapeic, by incorporating it into God's triune life. . . . [I]t is an offense to God's freedom and sovereignty to suggest that God is incapable of transfiguring the fidelity of a same-sex couple into whatever he wants it to mean. . . . [T]he biblical evidence strongly suggests that God is himself prepared to act "contrary to nature" for his own salvific purposes.[110]

In short, to retrieve the biblical groundedness they purport to espouse, White Evangelical Christians must begin again to learn how to read their scriptures. Such a Christocentric reorientation is a necessary first step in excising the *ressentiment*-infused sexual politics that have been for so long, and are again today, the beating heart of the zombie nationalism that is resurrecting White evangelical Christianity. Otherwise, far from the "born-again" evangelicalism of Jimmy Carter they long ago rejected, in their undeviating orbit around Trump messianism and Republican Party politics, White evangelicals will increasingly resemble the walking dead.

NOTES

1. As determined by National Election Pool exit polls, cited in Jason Husser, "Why Trump Is Reliant on White Evangelicals," The Brookings Institution, April 6, 2020, https://www.brookings.edu/blog/fixgov/2020/04/06/why-trump-is-reliant-on-white-evangelicals/.

2. Self-identified evangelical Christians constitute 25 percent of the U.S. electorate. Seventy-six percent of self-identified evangelicals are White. See David Masci and Gregory A. Smith, "5 Facts about U.S. Evangelical Protestants," Fact Tank: News in the Numbers, Pew Research Center, March 1, 2018, https://www.pewresearch.org/fact-tank/2018/03/01/5-facts-about-u-s-evangelical-protestants/.

3. Daniel Cox and Robert P. Jones, "The High Correlation between Percentage of White Christians, Support for Trump in Key States," Public Religion Research Institute (PRRI), November 17, 2016, https://www.prri.org/spotlight/trump-triumphed-white-christian-states/. "Representing more than one in every four voters, and with 81 percent supporting the Republican candidate in 2016 (up from a very solid 78 percent in 2012 and 74 percent in 2008), white evangelicals are undoubtedly among the most powerful voting blocs in U.S. politics today"; see Janelle S. Wong, *Immigrants, Evangelicals, and Politics in an Era of Demographic Change* (New York: Russell Sage, 2018), 2.

4. Philip Gorski, "Why Evangelicals Voted for Trump: A Critical Cultural Sociology," *American Journal of Cultural Sociology* 5, no. 3 (2017): 338–54.

5. "In a January [2018] Washington Post-ABC poll, 75 percent of white evangelical Christians rated 'the federal crackdown on undocumented immigrants' as positive, compared with 46 percent of U.S. adults overall, and 25 percent of nonwhite Christians"; see Michelle Boorstein and Julie Zauzmer, "Why Many White Evangelicals Are Not Protesting Family Separations on the U.S. Border," *Washington Post,* June 18, 2018, https://www.washingtonpost.com/news/acts-of-faith/wp/2018/06/18/why-many-white-evangelical-christians-are-not-protesting-family-separations-on-the-u-s-border/; see also Chrissy Stroop, "White Evangelicals Have Turned on Refugees," *Foreign Policy,* October 29, 2018, https://foreignpolicy.com/2018/10/29/white-evangelicals-have-turned-on-refugees/; and Gregory Smith, "Most White Evangelicals Approve of Trump Travel Prohibition and Express Concerns about Extremism," Pew Research Center, February 27, 2017, https://www.pewresearch.org/fact-tank/2017/02/27/most-white-evangelicals-approve-of-trump-travel-prohibition-and-express-concerns-about-extremism/.

6. McCay Coppins, "Christians Who Loved Trump's Stunt," *The Atlantic,* June 2, 2020, https://www.theatlantic.com/politics/archive/2020/06/trumps-biblical-spectacle-outside-st-johns-church/612529/?fbclid=IwAR3tMKaltgMB5iJ_ZPlw9_c79LITJrGIJv0_jWoWDVDqjxY1AFhbHU2K_vg; Andrew Whitehead and Samuel Perry, *Taking America Back for God: Christian Nationalism in the United States* (New York: Oxford University Press, 2020), 110–17.

7. "White evangelicals make up a staunchly and increasingly Republican group that generally backs Trump and his policies. In the January 2019 survey, for instance, nearly three-quarters of white evangelicals expressed support for substantially expanding the wall along the U.S. border with Mexico. White evangelical Protestants who regularly attend church (that is, once a week or more) approve of

Trump at rates matching or exceeding those of white evangelicals who attend church less often. Indeed, in the first few months of Trump's presidency, white evangelicals who attended church at least weekly were significantly more likely than less-frequent churchgoers to approve of Trump's performance (79% vs. 71%). In the most recent period analyzed—from July 2018 to January 2019—70% of white evangelicals who attend church at least once a week approve of Trump, as do 65% of those who attend religious services less often"; see Philip Schwadel and Gregory Smith, "Evangelical Approval of Trump Remains High, but Other Religious Groups Are Less Supportive," Pew Research Center, March 18, 2019, https://www.pewresearch.org/fact-tank/2019/03/18/evangelical-approval-of-trump-remains-high-but-other-religious-groups-are-less-supportive/.

8. Ruth Igielnik, Scott Keeter and Hannah Hartig, "Behind Biden's 2020 Victory," Pew Research Center, June 30, 2021, https://www.pewresearch.org/politics/2021/06/30/behind-bidens-2020-victory/. In the early months of 2020 White evangelicals approved of Trump and his policies at levels matching the rates at which they voted for him in the 2016 (81%) and 2020 elections (75%). "When asked if Trump was performing well as president, 77 percent of white evangelicals approved of him in a March 22–25 [2020] Washington Post-ABC national poll, compared with 74 percent in February, and a record high of 81 percent mark in January"; see Sarah Pulliam Bailey, "Prominent Southern Baptist Albert Mohler Opposed Trump in 2016. Now, He Says He Will Vote for the President," *Washington Post*, April 16, 2020, https://www.washingtonpost.com/religion/2020/04/16/souther-baptist-albert-mohler-to-vote-trump/.

9. Gorski, "Why Evangelicals Voted for Trump," 338–54.

10. In this way, my chapter differs from Gorski's contribution to this volume (chapter 1).

11. Richard Amesbury develops a similar point in chapter 4 herein.

12. Indeed, Roger Friedland argues powerfully that erotics of religious nationalism are fundamental across context and cases (in the U.S., and in India as Hindu nationalism, among others). See Friedland, "Money, Sex, and God: The Erotic Logic of Religious Nationalism," *Sociological Theory* 20, no. 3 (2002): 381–425, esp. 399–401.

13. See Robert P. Jones, *The End of White Christian America* (New York: Simon and Schuster, 2016), chap. 2. "For the first time in our history, the United States ceased to be a majority white Christian country; white Christians were 54 percent of the population in 2008 but only 47 percent in 2014. Since [2016], those trends have continued unabated. According to data from the Public Religion Research Institute (PRRI) . . . only 43 percent of the country identified as white and Christian by the 2016 election, and this number drops again to 41 percent in the most recent 2018 data. Notably, the white evangelical Protestant subgroup, the group that threw 80 percent of its votes behind Trump in 2016, has experienced a similar decline. White evangelical Protestants dropped from 21 percent of the

population in 2008 down to 17 percent in 2016 and further to 15 percent by 2018, according to PRRI studies"; see Robert P. Jones, "The Electoral Time Machine That Could Elect Trump," PRRI, October 11, 2019, https://www.prri.org/spotlight/the-electoral-time-machine-that-could-elect-trump/. For earlier articulations of this demographic decline, see Robert P. Jones, "Southern Evangelicals: Dwindling—and Taking the GOP Edge with Them," *The Atlantic*, Oct 17, 2014, https://www.theatlantic.com/politics/archive/2014/10/the-shriking-evangelical-voter-pool/381560/.

14. Jones, *The End of White Christian America*, 231.

15. "Shall I respect man when he contemns me? Let him live with me in the interchange of kindness, and instead of injury I would bestow every benefit upon him with tears of gratitude at his acceptance. But that cannot be; the human senses are insurmountable barriers to our union," the Creature declares in chapter 17 of the novel. On these themes, see Harold Bloom, "Introduction," in *Mary Shelley's "Frankenstein"* (New York: Chelsea House, 2007), 1–11.

16. David Gushee is an example of an effort to critically awaken many of his fellow evangelicals (to no avail) to their idolatry and abdication of their witness to Jesus in following Trump. Gushee was compelled to disavow evangelicalism after his persistent efforts to raise critical awareness on these matters was rejected outright by evangelical leaders and—as evidenced in the persistence of broad-based voting, polling, and behavior patterns—of the evangelical laity themselves. See David Gushee, *Still Christian: Following Jesus out of American Evangelicalism* (Louisville, KY: Westminster John Knox, 2017), 146; see also Gushee, *The Future of Faith in American Politics: The Public Witness of the Evangelical Center* (Waco, TX: Baylor University Press, 2008), 6; and Gushee, "2018 AAR Presidential Address: In the Ruins of White Evangelicalism: Interpreting a Compromised Christian Tradition through the Witness of African American Literature," *Journal of the American Academy of Religion* 87, no. 1 (2019): 1–17. A few other evangelical scholars and writers have attempted to raise similar critical reflectiveness, See Ronald Sider, ed., *The Spiritual Danger of Donald Trump: 30 Evangelicals on Justice, Truth, and Moral Integrity* (Eugene, OR: Cascade, 2020).

17. For example, evidence that U.S. society is not essentially a nation founded upon—and thus to be oriented in perpetuity—by Christian, or "Judeo-Christian," values. The attempt to challenge this belief (a belief shared broadly by evangelical reading audiences) by one evangelical scholar of American religious history meets with decidedly mixed results. See John Fea, *Was America Founded as a Christian Nation?* (Louisville, KY: Westminster John Knox, 2017); for an example of an evangelical scholar's attempt to persuade U.S. evangelicals that their embrace of Christian nationalism as a mode of allegiance to early twenty-first-century Republican politics is a Faustian bargain, see Charles Marsh, "Wayward Christian Soldiers," *New York Times*, January 20, 2006, https://www.nytimes.com/2006/01/20/opinion/wayward-christian-soldiers.html; for a more extensive analysis and

critique, see Marsh, *Wayward Christian Soldiers* (New York: Oxford University Press, 2007).

18. Andrew L. Whitehead, Joseph O. Baker, and Samuel L. Perry, "Despite Porn Stars and Playboy Models, White Evangelicals Aren't Rejecting Trump. This Is Why," *Washington Post*, March 26, 2018, https://www.washingtonpost.com/news/monkey-cage/wp/2018/03/26/despite-porn-stars-and-playboy-models-white-evangelicals-arent-rejecting-trump-this-is-why/.

19. For a self-identified evangelical scholar who warns U.S. evangelical Christians against embracing a sense of persecution under attack by an allegedly aggressively secular U.S. society, see Alan Noble, "The Evangelical Persecution Complex: The Theological and Cultural Roots of a Damaging Attitude in the Christian Community," *The Atlantic*, August 4, 2014, https://www.theatlantic.com/national/archive/2014/08/the-evangelical-persecution-complex/375506/.

20. Edward G. Simmons, David C. Ludden, and J. Colin Harris, "Setting Your Own Rules and Cognitive Dissonance: The Case of Donald Trump and Conservative Christian Evangelicals," in Sider, ed., *The Spiritual Danger of Donald Trump*, 139–50.

21. For an overview of the emergence of QAnon, see Adrienne LaFrance, "The Prophecies of Q," *The Atlantic*, June 2020, https://www.theatlantic.com/magazine/archive/2020/06/qanon-nothing-can-stop-what-is-coming/610567/; on the rapid expansion and distinct susceptibility of evangelical Christians to QAnon conspiracy theories, see Katelyn Beaty, "QAnon: The Alternative Religion That's Coming to Your Church," *Religion News Service*, August 17, 2020, https://religionnews.com/2020/08/17/qanon-the-alternative-religion-thats-coming-to-your-church/; see also Daniel Burke, "How QAnon Uses Religion to Lure Unsuspecting Christians," CNN, October 15, 2020, https://www.cnn.com/2020/10/15/us/qanon-religion-churches/index.html.

22. For evangelical Christian analysis of QAnon's rapidly expanding influence upon their own churches and membership, see Morgan Lee, "Why Someone You Love Might Join QAnon: For Christians Broaching Conversations with Those Persuaded by an Increasingly Popular Conspiracy Theory," *Christianity Today*, September 19, 2020, https://www.christianitytoday.com/ct/2020/september-web-only/qanon-evangelicals-global-conspiracy-theory.html.

23. On the rapid expansion of QAnon's presence across social media, and its gradual mainstreaming in congressional politics, see Marc-Andre Argentino, "QAnon Conspiracy Theory Followers Step out of the Shadows and May Be Headed to Congress," *The Conversation*, July 8, 2020, https://theconversation.com/qanon-conspiracy-theory-followers-step-out-of-the-shadows-and-may-be-headed-to-congress-141581.

24. For exposition and analysis of the deeper dynamics, and their relation to deep evangelical fixation with "spiritual warfare," see S. Jonathan O'Donnell, "QAnon, Spiritual Warfare, and the Orthotaxies of America," *Fordham University*

Press Blog, November 25, 2020, https://www.fordhampress.com/2020/11/25/qanon-spiritual-warfare-and-the-orthotaxies-of-america/.

25. See LaFrance, "The Prophecies of Q."

26. "69 percent of evangelical Republicans say the claim that there was widespread fraud in the 2020 election is either mostly or completely accurate. In contrast, Republicans who are not evangelical are far less likely to believe this claim is accurate—40 percent say it is mostly or completely accurate. . . . Only 27 percent of evangelical Republicans say that Joe Biden's election win was legitimate, compared to more than half (51 percent) of nonevangelical Republicans. Nearly three-quarters (72 percent) of evangelical Christian Republicans say Biden was not legitimately elected. . . . Despite the well-documented evidence showing that Trump supporters broke into the U.S. Capitol, a majority (56 percent) of evangelical Republicans believe the claim that the attack was carried out by antifa. Only about one-third (36 percent) of Republicans who are not evangelical Christian believe it was antifa who attacked the Capitol"; see Daniel A. Cox, "Rise of Conspiracies Reveals an Evangelical Divide in the GOP," American Enterprise Institute, February 12, 2021, https://www.americansurveycenter.org/rise-of-conspiracies-reveal-an-evangelical-divide-in-the-gop/#_edn1; Reuters Staff, "Fact Check: Men Who Stormed Capitol Identified by Reuters Are Not Undercover Antifa as Posts Claim," *Reuters*, January 9, 2021, https://www.reuters.com/article/uk-factcheck-capitol-mob-antifa-undercov/fact-check-men-who-stormed-capitol-identified-by-reuters-are-not-undercover-antifa-as-posts-claim-idUSKBN29E0QO.

27. A December 2020 poll of a representative sample of 1,115 U.S. adults found that "fewer than half (47%) are able to correctly identify that this statement is false: 'A group of Satan-worshipping elites who run a child sex ring are trying to control our politics and media.' Thirty-seven percent are unsure whether this theory backed by QAnon is true or false, and 17% believe it to be true. . . . Thirty-nine percent of Americans agree there is a deep state working to undermine President Trump—another tenet of QAnon. This belief is driven primarily by Republicans and FOX News viewers (a majority of both groups agree with this), though nearly half of white men and rural residents (49% each) agree as well"; see Mallory Newall "More Than 1 in 3 Americans Believe a 'Deep State' Is Working to Undermine Trump," Ipsos, December 30, 2020, https://www.ipsos.com/en-us/news-polls/npr-misinformation-123020. A 2018 poll conducted by the Wheaton College Billy Graham Center Research Institute found that 46 percent of self-identified evangelicals and 52 percent of those whose beliefs tag them as evangelical "strongly believe[s] the mainstream media produces fake news," another tenet of QAnon. Indeed, the more active respondents were in their church, the more mistrusting of news media they were. This, along with their widespread embrace of Trump, renders them especially susceptible to the central claims of QAnon theories. See Ed Stetzer, "Evangelicals Need to Address the QAnoners in Our Midst," *USA*

Today, September 4, 2020, https://www.usatoday.com/story/opinion/2020/09/04/qanon-and-evangelicals-its-time-address-qanoners-column/3446756001/; see also Robert K. Vischer, "Eric Metaxes and the Losing of the Evangelical Mind," *Religion News Service*, December 20, 2020, https://religionnews.com/2020/12/01/eric-metaxas-and-the-losing-of-the-evangelical-mind/.

28. Lois Beckett, "QAnon: A Timeline of Violence Linked to the Conspiracy Theory," *The Guardian*, October 16, 2020, https://www.theguardian.com/us-news/2020/oct/15/qanon-violence-crimes-timeline.

29. Hence the convergence of large groups of White supremacists and White evangelicals in the January 6, 2021, storming of the U.S. Capitol. See Elizabeth Dias and Ruth Graham, "How White Evangelicals Fused with Trump Extremism," *New York Times*, January 11, 2021, https://www.nytimes.com/2021/01/11/us/how-white-evangelical-christians-fused-with-trump-extremism.html?action=click&module=Top%20Stories&pgtype=Homepage.

30. I unpack a specific, and influential, example of this in the penultimate section of this chapter. See, for example, Daniel Block, "Is Trump Our Cyrus? The Old Testament Case for Yes and No," *Christianity Today*, October 29, 2018, https://www.christianitytoday.com/ct/2018/october-web-only/donald-trump-cyrus-prophecy-old-testament.html.

31. For the character and influence of Frank Peretti's best-selling spiritual warfare Christian fiction, *This Present Darkness* (1986) and *Piercing the Darkness* (1988), see Sara Diamond, *Not by Politics Alone: The Enduring Influence of the Christian Right* (New York: Guilford Press, 1998), 213–15; see also Robert Geulich, "Spiritual Warfare: Jesus, Paul and Peretti," *Pneuma* 13, no. 1 (1991): 33–64.

32. Matthew Avery Sutton, *America Apocalypse: A History of Modern Evangelicalism* (Cambridge, MA: Harvard University Press, 2014), chap. 11, esp. 364–66.

33. See Paul Boyer, *When Time Shall Be No More: Prophecy Belief in Modern American Culture* (Cambridge, MA: Harvard University Press, 1992), 144, and see esp. 144–51; and Sutton, *America Apocalypse*, chap. 11, esp. 363–66.

34. Ibid.

35. Melani McAlister, "Prophecy, Politics, and the Popular: The Left Behind Series and Christian Fundamentalism's New World Order," *South Atlantic Quarterly*, 102, no. 4 (2003): 773–98.

36. For the ways these concepts, along with other constituent features of religious nationalism, have served U.S. Christian purposes throughout history, see Omer and Springs, *Religious Nationalism*, chap. 3.

37. Carlton Hayes, *Nationalism: A Religion?* (New York: Routledge, 1960).

38. As Weber had it, nationalism shares an elective affinity with (i.e., a tendency to find close association with, symbiotic inter-relation, and mutual reinforcement between) the concepts of ethnicity, culture, and religion. There are important conceptual connections between the basic elements of nationalism, ethnicity, and religion. The Latin root of the word "nationalism," the verb *nascor, nasci, natus*

(and hence the noun *natio*), means "to be born, to be begotten," suggesting that a member belongs to one's people (nation) naturally or by birth. On this view, membership comes innately, perhaps inherited through biological relation—an understanding of nationality that shares many similarities with the concept of ethnicity.

39. Max Weber, *Economy and Society: An Outline of Interpretive Sociology*, 2 vols. (Berkeley: University of California Press), 1:395. For an exhaustive exposition of Weber's use of "elective affinities," see Richard Herbert Howe, "Max Weber's Elective Affinities: Sociology within the Bounds of Pure Reason," *American Journal of Sociology* 84, no. 2 (1978): 366–85. See also Gorski's contribution to this volume.

40. For helpful exposition of these terms, and how they reflect elective affinities when conceptualized through a Weberian lens, see David Little, "Religion, Nationalism, and Intolerance," in *Between Terror and Tolerance: Religious Leaders, Conflict, and Peacemaking*, ed. Timothy D. Sisk (Washington, DC: Georgetown University Press, 2011), 9–28, at 11–12.

41. On such a dichotomous account, to take one example, "nationalism" is intrinsically idolatrous by deifying and worshipping the nation, whereas "civil religion" is a modest, nonidolatrous, virtuously cohesive conceptualization and enactment of people- or nationhood (usually portrayed in civic terms) predicated upon however the group in question may conceive itself in relation to "the transcendent," and often interrelated with its world-historical role (e.g., American exceptionalism). For a nondichotomous account of how the two relate on a conceptual and practical continuum, see Omer and Springs, *Religious Nationalism*.

42. Considering distinctions on a case-by-case basis permits a more fine-grained, context-specific analysis. On this account, even invoking a category of "liberal" or "civic" nationalism (vs. ethnonationalism) is no guarantee that the civic nationalism in question will not behave in ways that reflect ethno- or religious nationalism. Here, political theorist Bernard Yack illustrates such an approach in his skepticism toward an antecedently demarcated, dichotomous civic versus ethnic division between types of nationalism (and also other types of dichotomous opposition—i.e., rational/emotional, voluntary/inherited, western/eastern, good/bad, liberal/illiberal). Yack makes the point as follows: "Designed to protect us from the dangers of ethnocentric politics, the civic/ethnic distinction itself reflects a considerable dose of ethnocentrism, as if the political identities *French* and *American* were not also culturally inherited artifacts, no matter how much they develop and change as they pass from generation to generation. The characterization of political community in the so-called civic nations as a rational and freely chosen allegiance to a set of political principles seems untenable to me, a mixture of self-congratulation and wishful thinking." See Yack, "The Myth of the Civic Nation," in *Theorizing Nationalisms*, ed. Ronald Beiner (Albany: State University of New York Press, 1999), 103–18, at 105.

43. See Omer and Springs, *Religious Nationalism*.

44. I draw the account of Protestant nativism and Anglo-Protestant nativism from José Casanova, "Nativism and the Politics of Gender in Catholicism and Islam," in *Gendering Religion and Politics: Untangling Modernities*, ed. Hanna Herzog and Ann Braude (New York: Palgrave Macmillan, 2009), 21–50. For a succinct example of how such White, Protestant nativism drove anti-Catholic nativism in the nineteenth-century United States (and that compares to certain moments of anti-Muslim nativism in the early twenty-first-century United States), see R. Scott Appleby and John T. McGreevy, "Catholics, Muslims, and the Mosque Controversy," *New York Review of Books*, August 27, 2010, https://www.nybooks.com/daily/2010/08/27/catholics-muslims-mosque-controversy/.

45. See Jenna Johnson and Abigail Hauslohner, "'I Think Islam Hates Us': A Timeline of Trump's Comments about Islam and Muslims," *Washington Post*, May 20, 2017, https://www.washingtonpost.com/news/post-politics/wp/2017/05/20/i-think-islam-hates-us-a-timeline-of-trumps-comments-about-islam-and-muslims/?utm_term=.d010e95d11f0.

46. See Gregory A. Smith, "Most White Evangelicals Approve of Trump Travel Prohibition and Express Concerns about Extremism," Pew Research Center, February 27, 2017, http://www.pewresearch.org/fact-tank/2017/02/27/most-white-evangelicals-approve-of-trump-travel-prohibition-and-express-concerns-about-extremism. See also Gregory A. Smith, "Among White Evangelicals, Regular Churchgoers Are the Most Supportive of Trump," Pew Research Center, April 26, 2017, http://www.pewresearch.org/fact-tank/2017/04/26/among-white-evangelicals-regular-churchgoers-are-the-most-supportive-of-trump; and Myrian Renaud, "Myths Debunked: Why Did White Evangelical Christians Vote for Trump?," The Martin Marty Center for the Advanced Study of Religion, January 19, 2017, https://divinity.uchicago.edu/sightings/myths-debunked-why-did-white-evangelical-christians-vote-trump.

In 2014, negative attitudes and perceptions of Islam actually reached one of their highest points in recent decades, equal to the years immediately following the 9/11 terrorist attacks. Sixty-two percent of Americans stated they were "very concerned about the rise of Islamic extremism around the world," 53 percent "very concerned about the possibility of rising Islamic extremism in the U.S.," and 50 percent affirmed the view that "Islam is more likely [than other religions] to encourage violence among its followers" (while 39 percent say it is not more likely to do so). As of 2016, 57 percent of Americans claimed that the values of Islam stand at odds with American values (while 40 percent disagree). See Robert P. Jones, Daniel Cox, E. J. Dionne Jr., William A. Galston, Betsy Cooper, and Rachel Lienesch, *How Immigration and Concerns about Cultural Changes Are Shaping the 2016 Election: PRRI/Brookings Survey* (Washington, DC: PRRI/Brookings, 2016), 2.

47. Andrew Whitehead and Samuel Perry, *Taking America Back for God: Christian Nationalism in the United States* (New York: Oxford University Press, 2020), 152–53.

48. Ibid., 153–54.

49. For consideration of these themes with reference to science, I point the reader to Yolande Jansen's contribution to this volume (chapter 6).

50. Cultural violence concerns "those aspects of culture, the symbolic sphere of our existence—exemplified by religion and ideology, language and art, empirical science and formal science (logic, mathematics)—that can be used to justify or legitimize direct or structural violence"; see Johan Galtung, "Cultural Violence," *Journal of Peace Research* 27, no. 3 (1990): 291–305, at 291. He goes on, "Cultural violence makes direct and structural violence look, even feel, right— or at least not wrong . . . legitimates violence and the use of violence" (ibid.). Galtung offers an example: "Africans are captured, forced across the Atlantic to work as slaves; millions are killed in the process—in Africa, on board, in the Americas. This massive direct violence over centuries seeps down and sediments as massive structural violence, with whites as master topdogs and blacks as the slave underdogs, producing and reproducing massive cultural violence with racist ideas everywhere. After some time, direct violence is forgotten, slavery is forgotten, and only two labels show up, pale enough for college textbooks: 'discrimination' for massive structural violence and 'prejudice' for massive cultural violence. Sanitation of language: itself cultural violence" (295). For an exposition of the ways that structural and cultural violence are essential to religion, conflict, and peacebuilding, see Jason A. Springs, "'Violence That Works on the Soul': Structural and Cultural Violence in Religion and Peacebuilding," *The Oxford Handbook of Religion, Conflict, and Peacebuilding*, ed. Atalia Omer, R. Scott Appleby, and David Little (Oxford: Oxford University Press, 2015), 146–79.

51. Robert P. Jones, *White Too Long: The Legacy of White Supremacy in American Christianity* (New York: Simon and Schuster, 2020).

52. The Hart–Celler Act reversed explicitly nativist immigration restrictions established in the 1924 Johnson–Reed Act. John Higham describes the distinctively White supremacist orientation to the xenophobia and nativism that underwrote the earlier Johnson–Reed Act: "Nativists during this period argued that the so-called new immigration from southern and eastern Europe was racially inferior to the 'old immigration' from northern and western Europe. It was therefore polluting the nation's bloodstream"; see Higham, "Cultural Responses to Immigration," *Diversity and Its Discontents: Cultural Conflict and Common Ground in Contemporary American Society*, ed. Neil J. Smelser and Jeffrey C. Alexander (Princeton, NJ: Princeton University Press, 1999), 39–62, at 50.

53. John Sides, Michael Tesler, and Lynn Vavreck, *Identity Crisis: The 2016 Presidential Campaign and the Battle for the Meaning of America* (Princeton, NJ: Princeton University Press, 2018); Wong, *Migrants, Evangelicals, and Politics in an Era of Demographic Change*, chap. 2; see also Pippa Norris and Ronald Inglehart, *Cultural Backlash: Trump, Brexit, and Authoritarian Populism* (Cambridge: Cambridge University Press, 2019), esp. 443–71.

54. "Approximately six in ten (57%) white Americans and roughly two-thirds (66%) of white working-class Americans agree that discrimination against whites is as big a problem today as discrimination against blacks and other minorities, an opinion shared by fewer than four in ten (38%) Hispanic Americans and fewer than three in ten (29%) black Americans"; see Robert P. Jones, Daniel Cox, E. J. Dionne Jr., William A. Galston, Betsy Cooper, and Rachel Lienesch, *How Immigration and Concerns about Cultural Changes Are Shaping the 2016 Election: PRRI/Brookings Survey* (Washington, DC: PRRI/Brookings, 2016), 2, June 23, 2016, https://www.prri.org/research/prri-brookings-poll-immigration-economy-trade-terrorism-presidential-race/.

55. Helpful in this regard is Ezra Klein, "White Threat in a Browning America: How Demographic Change Is Threatening Our Politics," *Vox*, July 30, 2018, https://www.vox.com/policy-and-politics/2018/7/30/17505406/trump-obama-race-politics-immigration. Klein points to a number of studies that suggest, for example, that "even gentle, unconscious exposure to reminders that America is diversifying—and particularly to the idea that America is becoming a majority-minority nation—pushes whites toward more conservative policy opinions and more support of the Republican Party." Klein points out that the 2016 PRRI poll (see note 54, above) correlates with a 2017 GenForward poll of White millennials (48 percent of whom agreed with a similar statement), suggesting, Klein argues, that this view is not unique to older whites. He writes, "The experience of losing status—and being told that loss of status is part of society's march to justice—is itself radicalizing. In 2006, Nyla Branscombe, Michael Schmitt, and Kristin Schiffhauer published a fascinating paper: 'Racial Attitudes in Response to Thoughts of White Privilege.' They found that priming White college students to think about the concept of White privilege led them to express more racial resentment in subsequent surveys. The simplest way to activate someone's identity is to threaten it, to tell them they don't truly deserve what they have, to make them consider that it might be taken away."

56. Wong, *Immigrants, Evangelicals, and Politics in an Era of Demographic Change*, 52–53. About 55 percent of White mainline Protestants and White Catholics believe that discrimination against Christians rivals that against other groups (ibid.); see also Michael Lipka, "Evangelicals Increasingly Say It's Becoming Harder for Them in America," Pew Research Center, July 14, 2016, https://www.pewresearch.org/fact-tank/2016/07/14/evangelicals-increasingly-say-its-becoming-harder-for-them-in-america/: "Nearly half of white evangelicals (46%) say things are getting tougher for evangelical Christians in America, similar to the share who took this position in the 2014 survey (42%). In addition, 31% of *nonwhite* evangelicals (mostly blacks and Hispanics) now say it has become more difficult to be an evangelical in the U.S., up from 22% two years ago."

But this is not a recent development. Some trace it to the emergence of evangelicalism in the twentieth century. It did this largely by becoming an identity.

"Over the course of the 20th century, not only were white evangelical leaders by and large intractably blind to their own racism, 'evangelical' also became an *identity* that was intrinsically tied to whiteness (of a particularly American sort) as never before. Evangelicalism has never confronted the fact that its 20th century American iteration was built not so much around a theological identity as it was around a *white cultural* identity. Evangelical became, that is, a political identity for aggrieved white conservatives"; as cited in Gushee, "2018 AAR Presidential Address: In the Ruins of White Evangelicalism: Interpreting a Compromised Christian Tradition through the Witness of African American Literature," *Journal of the American Academy of Religion* 87, no. 1 (2019): 1–17, at 13.

57. Wong, *Immigrants, Evangelicals, and Politics in an Era of Demographic Change*, 53.

58. "77% of white evangelical voters lean toward or identify with the Republican Party, while just 18% have a Democratic orientation. White Catholic voters now are more Republican (54%) than Democratic (40%). While the partisan balance among white Catholic voters is little changed in recent years, this group was more evenly divided in their partisan loyalties about a decade ago"; see "Trends in Party Affiliation among Demographic Groups," Pew Research Center, March 20, 2018, https://www.people-press.org/2018/03/20/1-trends-in-party-affiliation-among-demographic-groups/.

59. Wong, *Immigrants, Evangelicals, and Politics in an Era of Demographic Change*, chaps. 2–3. Among registered voters, 75 percent of White self-identified "born again" Christians voted for Trump in 2016, while Black, Latinx, and Asian "born-again" registered voters voted for Trump at rates of 7 percent, 31 percent, and 37 percent, respectively. In contrast to 69 percent Republican Party identification among White "born-again" self-identifiers, Black, Latinx, and Asian "born-again" self-identifiers reported 8 percent, 26 percent, and 32 percent Republican Party identification, repectively (ibid., 21).

60. Ibid., 22–24.

61. Ibid., 7.

62. Gorski's contribution to this volume (chapter 1) reinforces the point that self-ascribed "victimhood" by White evangelical Christians does not occur ex nihilo. It is, rather, a central feature of the long history of Christian religious nationalism in the United States.

63. Friedrich Nietzsche, *Genealogy of Morals*, ed. Walter Kaufman, trans. Walter Kaufman and R. J. Hollingdale (New York: Vintage), Third Essay, sec. 15. The nature and character of *ressentiment* in Nietzsche's writings is subject to much debate among Nietzsche scholars. My present discussion is aided by the meticulous exposition of *ressentiment* in Nietzsche's writings and the surrounding scholarship by Guy Elgat, *Nietzsche's Psychology of Ressentiment* (New York: Routledge, 2017), esp. chap. 2. On a particular group's self-deception regarding the true source of its experience of suffering, see 50–55.

64. Nietzsche, *Genealogy of Morals*, Third Essay, sec. 28, 162–63.

65. Mark Warren, *Nietzsche and Political Thought* (Cambridge, MA: MIT Press, 1991), 27–30. As Nietzsche has it, it is possible for *ressentiment* to "consummate and exhaust itself in an immediate reaction," and thus not become "poisonous." This is indicative, he says, of a "noble's" response to the experience of *ressentiment* (39).

66. Friedrich Nietzsche, *The Will to Power*, ed. Walter Kaufman, trans. Walter Kaufman and R. J. Hollingdale (New York: Vintage, 1968), 9.

67. For a helpful exposition of Nietzsche's nihilism along these lines, see Tsarina Doyle, *Nietzsche's Metaphysics of the Will to Power* (Cambridge: Cambridge University Press, 2018), 2–4.

68. See Neel Burton, "When Homosexuality Stopped Being a Mental Disorder," *Psychology Today*, September 18, 2015, https://www.psychologytoday.com/us/blog/hide-and-seek/201509/when-homosexuality-stopped-being-mental-disorder.

69. On the nature and character of moral abomination as a form of monstrosity—and homosexuality in the context of certain Christian responses as distinct of example—see Jeffrey Stout, *Ethics after Babel: The Languages of Morals and Their Discontents* (Princeton, NJ: Princeton University Press), 145–62.

70. One finds examples of this in some White Christian responses to the legalization of same-sex marriage in the United States as of 2015. As Daniel Philpott argues, from the perspective of canon law, when two men or two women declare themselves to be married, they "espouse a falsehood and announce their availability for sexual acts that mimic but distort those intrinsic to marriage." From this perspective, legal requirements to provide floral arrangements, catering, or any other services for same-sex weddings—even under the auspices of nondiscrimination laws—is actually compulsion to actively and formally cooperate with sin (that is, to facilitate the wrongful actions of other people). On this account, both the formal cooperation (even the appearance of such) and institutional legitimation of sin (e.g., Christian institutions extending medical benefits to same-sex couples) are intolerable. The only option for Christian persons and institutions that are concerned to witness faithfully to the love of Christ is either to plead for a conscientious exception to the law or to conscientiously refuse to cooperate. This amounts to an explicit refusal to cooperate in any way with the sin of "same-sex 'marriage,'" and to suffer the religious persecution that ensues: "When a Christian organization appears to endorse same-sex unions, even in ways that avoid formal cooperation, the world views it as proclaiming, at least tacitly, that it does not believe that marriage is between man and woman or that sex is reserved for marriage." On this account, the current constellation of laws on the issue of same-sex marriage constitutes conditions of "soft tyranny" and places Christians under conditions of "polite persecution" in the United States. See Daniel Philpott, "Polite Persecution," *First Things*,

April 2017, https://www.firstthings.com/article/2017/04/polite-persecution. See also Gerard Bradley, John Finnis, and Daniel Philpott, "The Implications of Extending Marriage Benefits to Same-Sex Couples," *Public Discourse*, The Witherspoon Institute, February 22, 2015, http://www.thepublicdiscourse.com/2015/02/14522.

71. Allan Chambers, *Leaving Homosexuality: A Practical Guide for Men and Women Looking for a Way Out* (Eugene, OR: Harvest House Publications, 2009); Jonathan Merritt, "The Downfall of the Ex-Gay Movement," *The Atlantic*, October 6, 2015, https://www.theatlantic.com/politics/archive/2015/10/the-man-who-dismantled-the-ex-gay-ministry/408970/.

72. For example, see Jeff Johnston, "The Right to Counseling for Unwanted Same-sex Attractions," Focus on the Family, https://dailycitizen.focusonthefamily.com/therapy-bans-threaten-religious-freedom-free-speech-and-parental-rights/.

73. Jeffrey C. Mays, "New York City Is Ending a Ban on Gay Conversion Therapy. Here's Why." *New York Times*, September 12, 2019, https://www.nytimes.com/2019/09/12/nyregion/conversion-therapy-ban-nyc.html. Conservative U.S. Supreme Court justice Samuel Alito argued publicly in his 2020 keynote address to the Federalist Society that requiring legal recognition and equal treatment for same-sex marriage equality (*Obergefell*) is now the basis for attacks upon religious freedom and freedom of speech. In a textbook example of *ressentiment*, Alito argues that people holding conservative views—despite a Supreme Court newly cemented with a 6–3 conservative supermajority (predominantly Catholic)—are now the victims of cultural and political persecution: "Those who cling to old beliefs will be able to whisper their thoughts in the recesses of their homes. But if they repeat those in public, they will risk being labeled as bigots, and treated as such by governments, employers, and schools. That is just what is coming to pass. One of the great challenges for the Supreme Court going forward will be to protect freedom of speech"; see Josh Blackman, "Video and Transcript of Justice Alito's Keynote Address to the Federalist Society," *Reason*, November 12, 2020, https://reason.com/volokh/2020/11/12/video-and-transcript-of-justice-altos-keynote-address-to-the-federalist-society/.

74. John Fea, *Believe Me: The Evangelical Road to Donald Trump* (Grand Rapids, MI: Eerdmans, 2020) 21.

75. Ibid.

76. Ibid.

77. Ibid.

78. Marie Griffith, *Moral Combat: How Sex Divided American Christians and Divided American Politics* (New York: Basic Books, 2017), 201–2.

79. Griffith affirms the veracity of this general description, but then unpacks the ways that it obscures numerous details about abortion politics and activism among religious citizens over the course of the 1970s. What the broad-brush accuracies of the account obscure is that "religious people were divided on abortion,

and . . . many of the pro-choice feminists were part of Christian communities and still committed to them. Both before and after Roe, prominent Christian voices, from men and from women, made a moral case for abortion rights" (ibid.).

80. Ibid., 84.

81. The Ramsey Colloquium, "The Homosexual Movement," *First Things*, March 1994, https://www.firstthings.com/article/1994/03/the-homosexual-movement. The Ramsey Colloquium was formed by Protestant, Catholic, and Jewish ethicists, under the leadership of Richard John Neuhaus, and including Robert P. George, Gilbert Meilander, David Novak, among others. Though he does not explicitly use the technical terms of "complementarity" and "ontology," Chief Justice John Roberts relies upon these concepts, in effect, in his searing dissent to the *Obergefell* decision. Roberts invokes the "biologically rooted," male/female sexual binary that (he argues) intrinsically serves procreative purposes in the context of a "lasting bond" as essential to the "meaning of marriage that has persisted in every culture throughout human history." This, according to Roberts, is the nature and basis of a fundamental difference between prohibitions of racial intermarriage, on the one hand, and objections to same-sex marriage, on the other. See Roberts, "Dissent," in *Obergerfell et al. v. Hodges*, 576 U.S. 644 (2015), 3–8.

82. Fay Botham, *Almighty God Created the Races: Christianity, Interracial Marriage, and American Law* (Chapel Hill: University of North Carolina Press, 2009).

83. Mark Noll, *The Civil War as a Theological Crisis* (Chapel Hill: University of North Carolina Press), 18.

84. White Christian revulsion at miscegenation was never internally undifferentiated, of course. Distinctions of kinds, and degrees, were interspersed throughout. Antimiscegenation laws aimed their most stringent prohibitions at sex and marriage between White women and Black men. These laws exempted White men from repercussions for violating sexual taboos of "race mixing." Black women suffered the worst of the taboo through the taboo's unnamed, nonregulated status in their case: "Enslaved black women habitually suffered the humiliation of rape by their white masters, so much so that rising numbers of mixed-race babies motivated colonial governments to pass laws declaring the children of enslaved women to hold slave status as well. . . . The legal apparatus developed to prohibit all sexual activity between white women and black men was wholly absent for black women, who were, without penalty, subject to forcible sex, whipping, physical restraints, and public nudity" (Griffith, *Moral Combat*, 86).

85. See Martha Hodes, *White Women, Black Men: Illicit Sex in the Nineteenth-Century South* (New Haven, CT: Yale University Press 1997), 1; and Botham, *Almighty God Created the Races*, 145, 156. See also Griffith, *Moral Combat*, 86–90; Byron C. Martin, *Racism in the United States: A History of the Anti-Miscegenation Legislation and Litigation* (Los Angeles: University of

Southern California Press, 2001), 1026, 1033–34, 1062–63, 1136–37. For similar arguments regarding the nonstatus of same-sex marriage based on natural law and canon law (e.g., that "'same-sex marriages' are in a Catholic understanding not truly marriages at all"), see Bradley, Finnis, and Philpott, "Implications of Extending Marriage."

86. *West Chester and Philadelphia Railroad Co. v. Miles*, Pennsylvania Supreme Court (1867), 211.

87. Again, see the Ramsey Colloquium's treatise, *The Homosexual Movement*, for a variety of arguments in this vein.

88. This point is important to note. Today, many conservative Christians point to the role that Christian progressives played in the suffrage and civil rights movements, and claim that as a historical mantle of their own conservative Christian views. In fact, earlier versions of present-day White Christian conservatism, and White evangelicalism in particular, fought against women's suffrage and civil rights for African Americans. On the role of "militantly masculine" Christianity against women's liberation in early twentieth-century conservative evangelicalism (and its continuities with present-day White evangelical Trumpism), see Kristin Kobes Eu Mez, *Jesus and John Wayne: How White Evangelicals Corrupted a Faith and Fractured a Nation* (New York: Norton, 2020), esp. chaps. 1 and 3.

89. Griffith, *Moral Combat*, 118–19.

90. Nietzsche, *Genealogy of Morals*. To some Christians, the evangelical transvaluation of these values entails the inversion of Christian values. For a profound meditation on precisely this point, see Adam Ericksen, "A God Torn to Pieces: Good Friday, Nietzsche, and Sacrifice," *Sojourners*, April 16, 2014, https://sojo.net/articles/god-torn-pieces-good-friday-nietzsche-and-sacrifice. Ericksen asks of his fellow Christians: "When we incarcerate with a vengeance rather than rehabilitate with mercy, are we following Dionysus or the Crucified? When we deny universal healthcare for the sick, the weak, and the poor, are we following Dionysus or the Crucified? When we deport and demean immigrant laborers, mercilessly separating parents from their children, are we following Dionysus or the Crucified? When we return violence for violence, invading and bombing nations in the name of 'justice,' are we following Dionysus or the Crucified?"

91. Griffith, *Moral Combat*, 118–19.

92. Sam Haselby, *The Origins of American Religious Nationalism* (Oxford: Oxford University Press, 2015), esp. chaps. 3–4.

93. On this account, "secular" does not refer to an all-encompassing process that happens as a result of the onset of a new epoch and hypercontext called "modernity." It is, rather, a contextually multiple, history-specific, multifaceted set of processes, one hallmark of which is the diversification of epistemic justification. For the account of "the secular," and how it accounts for the strengths, and

overcomes the deficiencies, of master narratives that portray "modernity" as a massive, single thing that is, most essentially, a bringer of "the secular," see Jeffrey Stout, *Democracy and Tradition* (Princeton, NJ: Princeton University Press, 2004).

94. For example, Bob Jones University, a White evangelical Christian college, sought for its rejection of racial integration to be tolerated for decades after the respective landmark Supreme Court decisions. It refused to admit African American students until 1971, seventeen years after the Supreme Court ruling that declared laws that segregated schools unconstitutional (*Brown v. Board of Education of Topeka, Kansas*, 1954). Further, Bob Jones University banned interracial dating and refused to admit students who were party to an interracial marriage for decades after the *Loving* decision. In 1983, after a long court battle with the IRS to retain its nonprofit status, the university finally relinquished that status (and the tax exemption it entailed) in order to hold that ban in place. It finally rescinded that rule in 2000 under national scrutiny elicited by a visit from then presidential candidate George W. Bush. The battle against same-sex marriage equality has afforded similar efforts by evangelical colleges to retain their eligibility for federal funding and other considerations while refusing to hire homosexuals or provide benefits for same-sex spouses. See Fea, *Believe Me*, 26–27.

95. Pew Research Center, "Americans Express Increasingly Warm Feelings toward Religious Groups," February 15, 2017, https://www.pewforum.org/2017/02/15/americans-express-increasingly-warm-feelings-toward-religious-groups/.

96. White Christians in the United States reject claims that African Americans suffer from structural forms of racism in far greater proportions than U.S. citizens who do not affiliate with Christianity. See Jones, *White Too Long*.

97. Glen Kessler, Salvador Rizzo, and Meg Kelly, "Trump's False or Misleading Claims Total 30,573 over 4 Years," *Washington Post*, January 24, 2021, https://www.washingtonpost.com/politics/2021/01/24/trumps-false-or-misleading-claims-total-30573-over-four-years/.

98. On this point, I agree with Gorski's chapter in this volume.

99. I am grateful to Josh Lupo for pointing this implication of the argument out to me.

100. Sutton, *American Apocalypse*, 346–54.

101. Stephen Spector, "This Year in Jerusalem: Prophecy, Politics, and the U.S. Embassy in Israel," *Journal of Church and State* 61, no. 4 (2019): 551–71.

102. For helpful exposition and complication of the multiple layers of complexity regarding the different evangelical Christian, commitments, and responses, see *Contending Modernities Blog*, Jerusalem series, https://contendingmodernities.nd.edu/global-currents/jerusalem-unspoken/.

103. Daniel Block, "Is Trump Our Cyrus?," *Christianity Today*, https://www.christianitytoday.com/ct/2018/october-web-only/donald-trump-cyrus-prophecy-old-testament.html.

104. Ibid.

105. "According to Ezra 1:1–4, in fulfillment of Jeremiah's prophecy (Jer. 29:1–14), shortly after Cyrus assumed the rule of Babylon, the Persian king issued a decree authorizing the Judean exiles to return home and to rebuild the Temple of YHWH—with the aid of resources he provided" (ibid.).

106. Adam Gabbatt, "'Unparalleled Privilege': Why White Evangelicals See Trump as Their Savior," *The Guardian*, January 11, 2020, https://www.theguardian.com/us-news/2020/jan/11/donald-trump-evangelical-christians-cyrus-king.

107. Figural interpretation emerged early in the Christian tradition of biblical interpretation in the efforts of the likes of Tertullian and Augustine to reconcile the Old and New Testaments. In an effort to amplify their unity, this interpretative approach reads components of the two testaments as interrelated. Earlier features are understood to be both themselves *and* prophetically prefigure later persons, events, and circumstances in the New Testament. The latter are both themselves, and also the fulfillment of the persons, events, and circumstances that prefigured them. Figural interpretation was perhaps most influentially retrieved in twentieth-century scholarship in Erich Auerbach, *Mimesis: The Representation of Reality in Western Thought* (Princeton, NJ: Princeton University Press, 2003 [1953]); and Auerbach, "Figura," in *Scenes from the Drama of European Literature* (Minneapolis: University of Minnesota Press, 1984 [1959]), 11–76. It was further developed for Christian theological purposes in Hans Frei, *The Eclipse of Biblical Narrative* (New Haven, CT: Yale University Press, 1974), which recounts how this long tradition of Christian scriptural reading was eroded with the onset of the eighteenth century; see also Jason Springs, *Toward a Generous Orthodoxy: Prospects for Hans Frei's Postliberal Theology* (New York: Oxford University Press, 2010).

108. Frei, *The Eclipse of Biblical Narrative*.

109. Eugene F. Rogers, *Sexuality and the Christian Body: Their Way into the Triune God* (Malden, MA: Wiley-Blackwell, 1999). For briefer exposition regarding how Rogers's constructive theology begins from the Triune life of the Christian God and works, by analogy, to the inclusion of same-sex marital unions into the holy sacrament of marriage as a matter of theological necessity, see Jeffrey Stout, "How Charity Transcends the Culture Wars: Rogers and Others on Same-Sex Marriage," *Journal of Religious Ethics* 31, no. 2 (2003): 169–80.

110. Ibid., 172.

CHAPTER 3

Renarrating the Past

The Case of "Modern" "White" "American" Catholics

R. SCOTT APPLEBY

Abstract

Literature on racial-religious nationalism in the United States tends to focus primarily on trends within evangelicalism, a transdenominational movement identified primarily with various Protestant Christian groups. However, this focus can mask the role of American Catholics in relation to these phenomena and obscure the similarities and key differences between historical Catholic and Protestant entanglements with intersecting hierarchies of race, religion, and nationhood. Engaging with the depictions of zombie nationalism and White Christian nationalism outlined by Jason A. Springs (chapter 2) and Philip Gorski (chapter 1) elsewhere in this volume, this chapter examines the unique "both/ and" character of American Catholic engagement with racial-religious constructions of national identity in the United States. As the chapter indicates, the polyglot and racially diverse character of the Catholic Church would seem to resist easy association with ethnonationalist impulses. Indeed, the Church boasts a

> rich (albeit an arguably waning) tradition of radical and liberal antiracist advocacy. On the other hand, some Catholics, despite (or perhaps because of) their own experiences of exclusion in the United States, have historically sought to participate in Whiteness through established forms of othering, including support of anti-Black racism, antisemitism, and xenophobia toward later waves of immigrants, many of whom are Catholic themselves. The generational shift of these Catholics into a "postethnic" status (a status itself associated with the nonmarked category of Whiteness) has thus ironically enabled their embrace of a Christian ethnonationalism that dissolves the "Catholic difference," bringing them into sociopolitical alignment with many White American evangelicals.

The meditations in this volume open up space for the reinterpretation of the past as constructed in narratives of religious, national, ethnic, social, and political histories. Historians can be allergic to theory, especially if it appears to obscure or subordinate the "evidence" painstakingly sifted from archives, culled from correspondences, diaries, demographic data, court records, and the like, and derived from material culture. But in the best-case scenario, second-order theoretical and conceptual reflection illuminates the evidence, provides new lenses by which to see, and forces an encounter with otherwise overlooked subtleties hiding in plain sight.

The studies that make up this volume represent this best-case scenario. This is true not only of the passages that excavate the foundations and elaborate the social psychology of White Christian nationalism, but also of those that expose the layers of deception and self-deception undergirding the practices and policies of self-anointed champions of justice, not least liberal political theologians. Indeed, this volume is an invitation, our editors tell us, to engage in the unmasking of these pretensions, even as the task is undertaken in order to confront Christian categories and histories with an eye to reforming and revising them. The "exposition and demystification of what is really there under multiple liberal facades" masking Euro-Christian White hegemony, write Atalia Omer and Joshua Lupo in the introduction, tell us "what is really there and what subsequently needs to be dismantled." It is not always clear, they continue, "if the dismantling is meant to recover the 'real' that underpins the political projects of modernity or if it is to aid in imagining new, historically located trajectories."

When one considers the case of Catholics and Catholicism, the answer seems to be a favorite Catholic theological-anthropological formula: "both/and." The "dismantling" of Catholic pretensions serves the interrogation of the underlying political and social motivations of Catholic actors, but it also reveals foundations and precedents for renewed historical trajectories less captive to racial and gendered assumptions.

In some important respects the American Catholic experience resonates with the analyses of White American Protestant evangelicalism provided in this volume by Jason A. Springs (chapter 2), who dissects "zombie nationalism," and by Philip Gorski (chapter 1), who sets forth the ingredients of White Christian nationalism and explores its affinities with right-wing populism.

In other important respects, however, the Catholic case is quite different. The differences are rooted in the distinctive character of this global, polyglot, multiracial, multiethnic religious community, which claims to be at once both local *and* "universal," that is, transcending nation, race, and ethnicity (if not gender). In the American context, where waves of Catholic immigrants grappled with the intersection of racial, ethnic, religious, and class bias, a comparison with White evangelicalism is illuminating. For Catholicism in the United States has *both* partaken in and been shaped by White nationalism (and is thereby recognizable in the analyses of Springs and Gorski), *and* it has struggled consistently against confinement in this prison. Tellingly, the struggle to resist White nationalism has been waged by networks of White, Black, and Brown Catholics in the United States, occasionally working in concert across racial and ethnic lines, and waxing and waning in influence over time. Operative in liberal and radical modes, these "resisters" often pit the universal church, headquartered in the Vatican, and its potentially liberating tradition of social doctrine, against the curious xenophobia and intolerance of the local and national church.[1]

In a self-conscious expression of their refusal to assimilate readily to the cultural and national sensibilities of the Protestant mainstream, Catholics strenuously resisted modernity and modernism—a defiant "Catholic medievalism" was the fashion in Catholic intellectual and academic circles, and in local parishes, until the mid-twentieth century[2]—even as modern secular and liberal sensibilities inexorably shaped their ecclesial and social milieux. Their attitudes toward the nation also shifted over time, tracking a social and economic experience of this "chosen nation" that for more than a century was considerably more troubled than that of their White Protestant coreligionists. By the 1970s, however, the majority of White Catholics in the United States had arrived at much the same destination, saluting the Puritan colonist John Winthrop's metaphor of America as a "shining city upon a hill" when it was invoked by Christian nationalist and pseudo-Catholic Ronald Reagan in a much-quoted State of the Union Address in 1988. And they continued proudly to call themselves "American Catholics," thereby blithely ignoring other Americas and other Catholics in the hemisphere.

Given this long-standing resistance to modernity, and the internal diversity and historically shifting self-understandings and behaviors of generations of Catholic immigrants who strived to be counted as White, one wonders: What about the label "modern White American Catholics" is *not* ironic?

In this chapter, I explore the ways Catholics do and do not fit the pattern of White evangelicalism drawn so vividly by Springs and Gorski.

HERE COMES EVERYBODY, AND THEY'RE NOT WHITE

The tens of millions of ethnic Irish, German, Italian, Polish, Lithuanian, and Hispanic (as an array of migrants from Mexico, Central America, and Puerto Rico were then called) immigrants who flooded into urban areas in the northeastern and midwestern United States during the "century of immigration" (1820–1920) strained the popular myth that the United States was a nonviolent, ethnically homogenizing, purifying "melting pot." Rather, assimilation was a messy, often traumatic, incomplete process. For Catholics, it consisted of internal battles over language (would English be mandatory for Germans, Italians, and Poles attending Catholic parochial schools?), ritual (which ethnic saints and local devotions would survive the transatlantic crossing, and at what cost?), and social custom (would the second generation retain the marriage and familial patterns of their parents?). Bitter rivalries among ethnic groups stained both religion and social relations. Hierarchy and status, a staple of these rivalries, were not foreign concepts to the people in the pews, not to mention their clergy and political patrons. Thus, for example, the (English-speaking) Irish quickly asserted themselves, sending their daughters into religious life and their sons to the priesthood and into local and eventually state politics. In mixed parishes, non-Irish were sometimes relegated to the church basement (literally). Polish Catholic women came to resent cleaning the homes of their upwardly mobile Irish American coreligionists. Italians seeking construction jobs despite their "blackness" learned to build their self-preserving patronage networks.

The external enemies were more threatening. Catholics reeled from the economic, political, and physical blows delivered by nativist groups, from the Know-Nothings of the 1850s and the American Protective Association (headquarters: Clinton, Iowa) of the 1880s, to the Ku Klux Klan of the early twentieth century. Portrayed as "subhuman" (as in the *New York Telegraph* cartoon depicting an Irish dockworker as a baboon) or "swarthy" and "unwashed" (by advocates for the forced sterilization of eastern European immigrants), Catholics felt palpably the need to prove themselves "White."[3]

One way of doing so was by differentiating themselves from those nested with them on the lowest rungs of the social hierarchy who had a much harder time passing as White: Black Americans. In 1919, race riots and violent clashes erupted in Chicago between Irish American street gangs and African Americans living in the neighborhoods known as the city's Black Belt. These deadly conflicts mirrored similar events in New York, Philadelphia, and Boston. Middle-class Catholics throughout the twentieth century maintained the tradition of repression by establishing or reinforcing the structural violence through practices such as redlining.[4]

Black Catholics were often caught in a double bind. Attempting to remain faithful to their overwhelmingly White, patriarchal, and racialist church, which did not always understand or accommodate vibrant African American practices, such as lay preaching, gospel blues (as a form of worship), and the blending of urban American and traditional African rites, they were objects of curiosity and criticism from African Americans in Pentecostal, AME Zion, and other Methodist churches.[5] Black Catholic participation in the Harlem Renaissance of the 1920s and 1930s illustrated the dilemma. Harlem, which had become a destination point for African American migration to the urban North, emerged in these years as the center of "a flowering of Negro literature," as NAACP leader James Weldon Johnson termed the proliferation of artistic creativity in theatre, music, fiction, and poetry, as well as in radical social and political criticism and advocacy. Its influence extended to Francophone Black writers from Africa and the Caribbean, who had migrated to Paris. The Marxist and other leftist critics associated with the Harlem Renaissance focused much of their ire on White Christianity, not least Roman Catholicism, whose systemic exclusion of Black Catholics from religious leadership and Catholic education was roundly denounced.[6]

Still, "colored" Catholics participated in the Harlem Renaissance. Claude McKay was perhaps the most prominent. Born in Jamaica to a family enslaved by British colonists and brought from Madagascar and West Africa to the Caribbean, he immigrated to the United States in 1912 and moved to Harlem in 1914, where he published the first book of poetry during the Harlem Renaissance, *Harlem Shadows* (1922), and claimed the first American best-selling novel written by a Black author, *Home to Harlem* (1928). Brenna Moore situates McKay's conversion to Catholicism and theological imagination within the nexus of mysticism, enchantment, and countercultural spirituality, all of which nurtured "his long interest in forms of recalcitrant resistance to modernity."[7]

A Twentieth-Century Tale of Two Catholicisms

Prior to the publication of John McGreevy's landmark study, *Parish Boundaries: The Catholic Encounter with Race in the Twentieth Century Urban North*, the vast literature on race relations among Catholics was biracial: "White" groups were presumed to be "racist" in essentially the same way, distinctions between White populations were elided, and racist patterns of behavior were attributed to working-class and socioeconomic rivalries and resentments. The motivations and biases instilled in the home, and by religion, were given relatively short shrift. And yet, racial attitudes among urban northern Catholics, McGreevy demonstrates, were focused less on the workplace or voting booth and more on the neighborhoods and residential communities. A central claim of his work is that American Catholics prior to the 1970s frequently defined their surroundings in religious terms. Given the fact that in northern cities Catholics in the twentieth century accounted for between 20 percent and 70 percent of the population, McGreevy's thesis cast a new light on American racial dynamics more generally.

In the Catholicism of the enclave, and, eventually, of the intact religious subculture, religion mattered more than money or status or even "race" itself, and more than it would later, when intermarriage (mainly with White Protestants) and other drivers of assimilation accelerated, and Euro-American

Catholics merged into the White American mainstream with all its attendant economic and social rewards—and varieties of racism.

Prior to the 1970s, however, generations of Catholic immigrants struggled to escape the lingering nativist accusation that they were subversive elements undermining a White Anglo-Saxon Protestant nation—mindless disciples of a foreign "potentate" bent on converting the United States to popery, by force of law if possible or, more insidiously, through the machinations of the sinister Society of Jesus (Jesuits). Reactions to these calumnies varied, as did Catholic strategies to escape the stigma and prove their loyalty to the American nation. Offered a haven by Protestant home missionaries, thousands of Catholics simply left the Church. But the vast majority stayed and attempted to live normal lives, raising their families and educating their children, entering the workforce, and participating in civic affairs even as they continued to attend Mass, receive the sacraments, venerate their local saints, and throng by the hundreds of thousands to Eucharistic congresses.[8]

To demonstrate their White American bona fides, a significant minority of Catholics went on the offensive in the twentieth century. In a highly visible demonstration of "belonging," they joined White Protestant nationalists in a wave of campaigns against Blacks and Jews. Operating out of Detroit in the 1930s, the virulently antisemitic and massively popular "radio priest" Rev. Charles Coughlin was a harbinger of a newly aggressive, national racist Catholic public presence. Thousands of Catholics in the urban North, swayed by Father Coughlin's relentless depiction of Jews as "foreign," anti-American traitors who, among other crimes, had bankrolled the Russian Revolution, joined his militant Christian Front organizations, and swelled the numbers of protesters picketing Jewish department stores, blocking Jewish purchases of city buildings, and, in one case, plotting to blow up movie theaters owned by Jews.[9]

Clashes with Black Americans often occurred closer to home in the 1950s and 60s. Neighborhoods in White ethnic parishes across the urban North hardened into enclaves designed to plug the gaps in porous boundaries between the races. Incidents in Boston, Philadelphia, and Chicago, where threats were made to "Negro" families attempting to move into White housing projects, or to attend Mass in White Catholic parishes, were all too typical. Segregation was taken for granted in the South, where aspiring middle-class Catholic minorities "fit in" by helping to keep businesses, schools, civic events, and public spaces White. Structural and cultural violence against African Americans was commonplace. As the civil rights movement gained steam, Catholics were not above participating in murderous violence against even their "colored" coreligionists.

Other Catholics, however, were repulsed by and ashamed of this kind of behavior, even as they remained in many cases blind to subtler expressions of race-based discrimination and oppression.[10]

There was an option available to them, however: Catholic radicalism. A mode of activism dedicated not to the reform of the system but to its dismantling, Catholic radicalism is directly antithetical to White Christian nationalism.[11] An early and influential expression of this campaign, conducted in the name of Christ, to subvert the "rotten, decadent, putrid industrial capitalist system which breeds such suffering" was the Catholic Worker Movement, founded by Dorothy Day and Peter Maurin on May 1, 1933. On that date, Day peddled the first issue of *The Catholic Worker* newspaper (a penny a copy, then and now) in New York City's Union Square.[12] Day, a convert to Catholicism who had been attracted to the Church owing to its mystical and spiritual traditions (including the doctrine of the Church as the mystical body of Christ), found the partner she needed in Maurin, a French peasant, immigrant, and self-taught expert in Catholic social teaching. *The Catholic Worker*, she said, was initially an act of solidarity with the victims of the Depression and an announcement that "the Catholic Church has a social program. . . . There are men of God who are working not only for their spiritual but for their material welfare."[13] She modeled the newspaper on the advocacy journalism she had been practicing in collaboration with socialist and anarchist colleagues in New York.[14] *The Catholic Worker* provided coverage of strikes and unions, denounced the working conditions under which women and African Americans labored, and explained papal teaching on social issues. The movement grew to include agrarian cooperatives, pioneered by Maurin, and houses of hospitality, where Catholic Workers lived with the poor *as* the poor: Day famously rejected the concept of charity, seeing it as a palliative measure, and demanded no less than a nonviolent revolution for social justice.

Day was an original, unique in her way, and yet her example of Catholic radicalism inspired generations of disciples and imitators. Today approximately 180 Catholic Worker communities in the United States remain committed to nonviolence, voluntary poverty, and prayer and hospitality for the homeless, hungry, exiled, and forsaken. Catholic Workers continue to protest injustice, war, racism, and violence of all kinds. And yet the Catholic Worker is but one example of Day's legacy.[15] In her person, Day integrated seemingly irreconcilable positions. On the one hand, she was not blind to the failings of the institutional Church. "I felt that the Church was the Church of the poor," she wrote in her autobiography, "but at the same time, I felt that it did not set its face against a social order which made so much charity in the present sense of the word necessary. I felt that charity was a word to choke over. Who wanted charity? And it was not just human pride but a strong sense of man's dignity and worth, and what was due to him in justice, that made me resent, rather than feel proud of so mighty a sum total of Catholic institutions." Yet she nonetheless made a point of remaining in good standing with her bishop. And although Day was a fierce advocate for women's rights and saw women as natural leaders of the Catholic community—"Women think with their whole bodies and they see things as a whole more than men do," she wrote approvingly—she never wavered in her support of the Church's moral teaching on sexual ethics, which Catholic feminists saw as the expression of a hopelessly unjust bias against women. "When it comes to labor and politics," Day explained, "I am inclined to be sympathetic to the left, but when it comes to the Catholic Church, then I am far to the right."[16]

Despite or perhaps because of these contradictions, not least her patient fidelity to a Church that at times seemed to stand in the way of racial and social justice, Dorothy Day is central, it seems to me, to the task of renarrating the American Catholic past, to interpreting Catholic history as opening the possibility of a renewed "mystical body," liberated from operative (if implicit) and self-defeating assumptions about racial and gender "superiority."

Partly inspired by Day's example, a nucleus of antiracist clergy grew into a national network of Catholic priests, sisters, and laity dedicated to reversing the tide of Catholic bigotry through education, religious formation, and activism. As early as 1949, some enlightened Chicago Catholic clergy and parishes were participating in Saul Alinsky's interreligious community organizing campaigns for fair housing; motivated more by religion than by class, they were "acting upon the Catholic belief that all human beings alike reflect the face of God," as one enthusiast described his motivations, and were seeking to demonstrate "radicalism rooted in religion," according to another.[17] In the 1950s, for example, pastors and Black and White lay Catholics on New York City's West Side objected to the racially discriminatory urban renewal plans drawn up by the city's "master builder," Robert Moses, and endorsed by Cardinal Francis Spellman. Meanwhile, in Maryland, John LaFarge, a Jesuit priest who was serving as pastor of an African American parish, was influenced by the association of Federated Colored Catholics and their leader, Thomas Turner. Subsequently, LaFarge founded the New York Catholic Interracial Council as the first in a series of organizations that would be dedicated to bringing White and Black Catholics together in a coalition to fight racial discrimination and exclusion. His allies proliferated in number and influence.[18]

White American Catholic nationalists found themselves thwarted, if not vanquished, by pushback from the transnational or "universal" Church. They did not see this reversal coming from a church that for centuries had abetted multiple forms of racial oppression and had only condemned the slave trade, and somewhat haltingly, in the previous century.[19] The instinctively cautious LaFarge was encouraged when he sensed an ecclesial sea change on the question of race. Triggered in part by the Church's concern for the plight of German Catholic schools and clergy as Germany came under the control of Nazi officials—an excruciating dilemma brought home to Pope Pius XI when he met with anxious German Catholic bishops in 1937—the revolution was signaled with the publication of *Mit brennender Sorge* (*With Burning Concern*), an encyclical that abruptly rejected theories of racial superiority. "Whoever exalts race," Pius XI proclaimed, "is far from the true faith in God, and from the concept of life which that faith upholds."[20] Influential French theologian Jacques Maritain echoed the pope by arguing that racialism strips thought, science, and art of their "natural 'catholicity.'" LaFarge himself warned that the United States was in no way immune from the pernicious virus of race hatred on display in Nazi Germany; American racism, after all, was a "pale but venomous older cousin" of the ideas sweeping Germany."[21]

The early seeds of interracial Catholic activism sown by LaFarge, Ryan, Monsignor John Egan of Chicago, Rev. Joseph Gremillion of Shreveport, Louisiana, and many others would bear fruit in a myriad of ways, not least through Catholic participation in the southern civil rights movement, which culminated in Selma in March 1965, and in the emergence of "social justice" priests and women religious who led urban ministries in the 1970s and 80s.[22] In Selma, activist priest Daniel Berrigan, SJ (who credited Dorothy Day with introducing him to the pacifist antiwar and racial justice movement) asked: "What is the Church anyway? Is it where we came from, or is it here, being created by Negroes and their White acolytes?"[23]

A compelling answer to Berrigan's question had been provided in 1962 when Pope John XXIII condemned racial discrimination, a move that won applause from U.S. civil rights and religious leaders, including NAACP spokesman Clarence Mitchell, who called it "an unequivocal answer to those bigots and false prophets who like to justify segregation"; and, by Vatican II (1962–65), which conducted a global exercise in *aggiornamento* ("updating") ratified by 2,392 bishops only months after the Selma protests. Hereafter, the Church would be known as "the People of God," drawn from all races of the world and possessed of a special concern for the victims of social and political oppression. In the fall of 1964, Pope Paul VI hosted a visit to the Vatican by Rev. Martin Luther King Jr., who reported that the pope "asked me to tell the American Negroes that he is committed to the cause of civil rights in the United States." King informed the pope, in turn, that "in these counties [of the urban North] the Catholic Church is very strong and a reaffirmation of [the Church's] position on civil rights would mean much."[24]

The new attitude toward the "social question" was summarized memorably in a statement from a subsequent Vatican synod: "Action on behalf of justice and participation in the transformation of the world appears to us as fully constitutive of the preaching of the Gospel, or, in other words, of the Church's mission for the redemption of the human race and its liberation from every oppressive situation."[25]

This surprising, indeed stunning, "updating" on race (perhaps better known as "reversal") by the universal church was welcomed giddily by the likes of LaFarge, Day, and Berrigan, and opened the way for the deepening and popularization of American Catholic resistance to at least the most obvious manifestations of White Christian nationalism. Attitudes toward race and race relations emerged more explicitly than ever as a dangerous and at times bloody dividing line within the community.

At around this point in the historical trajectory, the category "religion" became much more complicated and contested within the Catholic community in the United States. The immigrant church in all its internal diversity, driven largely by ethnoreligious differences, nonetheless hewed to a recognizable shared devotional culture, a core of beliefs and practices common across ethnonational groups, summarized by Jay P. Dolan as a consensus about authority, sin, ritual, and the miraculous.[26] Now, in the aftermath of Vatican II, with its seismic shifts and shocks amplified by the tumult associated with the Vietnam War and the civil rights movement, Catholics fought among themselves about the authority of the Church (a "battle royal" triggered by Pope Paul's 1968 encyclical *Humanae vitae* reinforcing the Church's ban on birth control); about what constituted sin (with *Roe. V. Wade*, the 1973 Supreme Court decision that rendered abortion *the* divisive moral issue between "pro-choice" and "pro-life" Catholics); about which previously hallowed sacraments and rituals were to be preserved and which discarded; and, about whether "the miraculous"—previously, a marker of transcendence separating Catholics from Protestants—could continue to command the Catholic religious imagination. In addition, the postwar assimilation of newly "White" Catholics into the American mainstream set the stage for the harmonization of White Catholic and White Protestant attitudes on a variety of political and social issues, including race, economics, and sexual ethics.[27]

McGreevy's thesis about "religion" shaping Catholic attitudes toward race and ethnicity applied only weakly, if at all, to this new moment. In shaping the political sensibilities and preferences of a majority of Catholics, that is, religion was no longer as decisive as anxieties about threats to the American system of racial and economic inequality that ensures White privilege.

Lessons for Whitey

Two "postethnic" American Catholics, Patrick Buchanan and James Carroll, can stand as representatives of what the contributors to this volume might see not as a "progressive versus conservative" Catholic civil war, but rather as an internecine squabble among plain old liberals.

Patrick J. Buchanan—the journalist, Nixon speechwriter, Reagan advisor, two-time candidate for the Republican presidential nomination, and, later, host of CNN's *Crossfire* and regular commentator on other highly visible media platforms—helped to establish a "respectable" public presence for White supremacist Catholic nationalists. One can trace in the long arc of Buchanan's public career the mix of religious, racial, and socioeconomic grievances leveled against Blacks by Christian/Catholic White nationalists. In the 1960s and 70s, he articulated and exploited the fears of a generation of ethnic Catholics still heady from attaining mainstream status but also threatened by the civil rights movement and the perceived gains of African Americans (historically their bête noire, as we have seen). In 1992, he tried to wrest the Republican presidential nomination from incumbent George H. W. Bush by running on a platform of social conservatism, underscoring his religiously motivated opposition to gay rights and abortion. Tellingly, Buchanan also found a measure of support from "newly arrived" postethnic, upwardly mobile Catholics for his campaign to restrict immigration—a pattern of collective forgetting that would endure and find millions of Catholics joining the rabble echoing Donald Trump's "Build the Wall" mantra.

During the Obama years, Buchanan doubled down on all these themes:

> Governments, businesses and colleges have engaged in discrimination against white folks—with affirmative action, contract set-asides and quotas—to advance black applicants over white applicants.
>
> Churches, foundations, civic groups, schools and individuals all over America have donated time and money to support soup kitchens, adult education, daycare, retirement and nursing homes for blacks.
>
> We hear the grievances; where is the gratitude?
>
> Let [Barack] go to Altoona and Johnstown, and ask the white kids in Catholic schools how many were visited lately by Ivy League recruiters handing out scholarships for "deserving" white kids.[28]

A fervent supporter of Trump, Buchanan, now eighty-three, continues to sing the former president's praises.

For other Catholics, becoming fully American and modern meant becoming "liberal." Yet the liberal Catholicism authorized by Vatican II is not to be conflated with generic political liberalism in the United States—even if a political figure like Joe Biden embodies an unforced compatibility of the two. Rather, liberal Catholics have situated themselves at different points on the "trajectory toward radicalism" established by Dorothy Day and Peter Maurin, and upheld by Thomas Merton, Philip Berrigan, and Daniel Berrigan, S.J.

Others, sympathetic to and admiring of these radical moral and political exemplars, never quite escaped captivity within the reformist assumptions of liberalism. One such liberal Catholic was James Carroll, the journalist, novelist, and National Book Award–winning author of *American Requiem*, a memoir of the generational turmoil in his Irish American Catholic family triggered by the rift between James and his father, Joe, an air force lieutenant general and former FBI agent with ties to J. Edgar Hoover, the sworn enemy of the civil rights movement in general and Martin Luther King Jr., in particular. James had entered the seminary and been ordained a priest in part to please his father, but he soon grew disaffected by the uncritical nationalism and not always subtle racism of both his father's associates and prominent members of the clergy. In *American Requiem*, James recalls that Hoover recruited Cardinal Spellman to intervene with the Vatican in order to cancel King's meeting with Pope Paul VI. "Spellman tried, but it is a measure of the inexorable tilting of the Church's axis that the pope ignored his warning and met with King—a fact I used against my father in our arguments," he writes. "My father was forced to say, as he did one day to me—seismic shifts everywhere—that the pope himself was naïve."[29]

Carroll's "liberal Catholic" moment passed. Increasingly alienated by the bishops' uncritical support for the Vietnam War and the disciplining of Daniel Berrigan for his extralegal acts of civil disobedience, Carroll left the priesthood in 1975. Yet he also admitted to himself that he lacked the nerve to follow Berrigan's path into state- and church-defying Catholic radicalism:

> It was as if, that night in jail [for an act of civil disobedience], I saw into the future, saw the coming collapse of the liberal Catholic impulse, the very thing I was trying to build a life around. . . . In the D.C. lockup, the unclothed despair that I'd been fending off assaulted me like one of the sadistic guards. This was merely a single miserable night in the hoosegow, not the years' worth of prison that Dan [Berrigan] and Phil [Berrigan] and dozens of others were having to survive. Yet I fell into a pit of angst and fear that was also the old pit of my self-loathing.[30]

Carroll became a writer, where he could safely express his rage at the failure of liberal Catholicism and the squandering of Vatican II's promise. For Carroll and thousands of other liberal American Catholics, the council's proclamation of the Church as "People of God" implied a turning away from patriarchy, racism, and war-mongering nationalism. Instead, Paul VI, the opponent of racism and supporter of Martin Luther King Jr., had allowed his pontificate to be compromised by the bitter controversy over sexual ethics unleashed by *Humanae vitae*. Things only got worse, Carroll wrote later, during the long pontificate of John Paul II (r. 1978–2005).[31]

Eventually, both Buchanan and Carroll gravitated to the margins of the American Catholic community, driven there by frustration with their coreligionists for failing to unite behind their respective ideological and political goals for the nation. Instead, the U.S. Catholic community, like the nation itself, became more divided. But, as ever, with a difference.

White Catholics for Trump

The American Catholic resistance to White nationalism soldiered on, but observers of American religion and politics began to ask: "What happened to liberal Catholicism?" The question was by no means new in 2016, when journalists, and millions of Catholics, were astonished to discover that Trump had won 64 percent of the White Catholic vote. Catholics voting in significant numbers along Republican Party lines had been old news since the ascendancy of affluent, college-educated White Catholics into the nation's economic elite had rendered the idea of "the Catholic vote" a myth. The harmonization of White Catholic and White Protestant attitudes on a variety of political and social issues, including race, economics, and sexual ethics, ensued.[32]

Even so, a greater percentage of White Catholics voted for Trump in 2016 than had voted for any of his Republican predecessors. And in the 2020 presidential election, despite the experience of four long years of Trump's divisive, racist, anti-immigrant, antipoor, misogynist, and environmentally insane rhetoric and policies, 57 percent of White Catholic voters still backed non-Catholic (and, arguably, non-Christian) Trump over lifelong practicing Catholic Joe Biden, who has explicitly acknowledged Catholic social teaching as a formative influence on his faith and public service.

The argument that conservative White Catholics, turned off by Hillary Clinton's unapologetically pro-choice position and Biden's own support for reproductive rights and same-sex marriage, turned to Trump as the last hope for an "orthodox" Catholic social agenda goes only so far. It presumes that a significant percentage of Catholic Republican voters are motivated primarily by Church teaching on abortion, same-sex marriage, and LGBTQ rights, as opposed to using that teaching as a convenient "halo" to sacralize raw economic self-interest. And it fails to explain their seeming lack of concern for the imperatives of Church social teaching on solidarity and racial justice, the common good, a preferential option for the poor and the migrant, and care for the Earth, despite concerted campaigns by Roman Catholic dioceses, high schools, and colleges to popularize the "seven principles of Catholic social teaching."

Catholic Democratic voters, one might argue, have become (almost) equally captive to Americanism. Their support of Biden at the polls—less than half of White Catholics voted Democrat—could be interpreted as a repudiation of Trump rather than a ringing endorsement of their fellow Catholic. Beyond voting in a presidential election, in any case, gone are the days when primarily White movements for racial justice were led by liberal Catholics as a buffer against Catholic and American racism. Nor have contemporary Catholics, with too few notable exceptions, worked to bridge racial divisions within the American Catholic community itself. "The election results show that the Catholic Church is as divided as our nation, but the real divide is race and ethnicity, not theology," argues Fordham University's David Gibson. "If the Republican Party continues to try to amplify calls to White grievance and fear of immigrants in order to rally the white Catholic vote, that could create further problems for the Catholic Church itself as it seeks unity."[33]

Black Catholics, understandably, are fed up with their coreligionists of both parties:

> Black people used to be beaten and raped. They used to have their children stolen. I may not be subject to these inhumanities as a Black Catholic today, yet sometimes I feel victim to them. Today, lynching takes a new form in America and is characterized by many Catholics' complacency and implicit participation in an unjust system that upholds white privilege. I have experienced this othering even within the church:

There remain divisions between Black, brown, and white Catholics today. As Thomas Merton stated eloquently in his 1963 "Letter to a White Liberal," "White society has sinned in many ways. It has betrayed Christ by its injustices to races it considered 'inferior' and to countries which are colonized."[34]

The subordination of religious and prophetic dimensions of individual and communal Catholic identity to racial bias and hatred is indisputable. In deference to the tens of thousands of laity (and especially women religious) and clergy who continue to organize and speak out against racial injustice (and against patriarchy and other insidious forms of discrimination), it must be acknowledged that neither liberal nor radical Catholicism in the United States is dead (yet). Still, the question remains: Why so few advocates for justice in a population of 70 million Catholics (including 45 million White Catholics)?

THE CATHOLIC DIFFERENCE(S)

In comparison to the White evangelical version of Christian nationalism, the Catholic variant has more to do today, as it always has, with the Church itself than with the four key elements of White Christian nationalism identified by Gorski, all of which are either absent or muted or minority strains within Catholicism. References in the Bible to blood sacrifice, blood purity, and blood atonement register hardly at all among (largely a-scriptural) conservative Catholics, whose ardent support for the U.S. military has more to do in its twentieth-century origins with the need to prove their "belonging" than with a conflation of their own patriotic self-sacrifice and Christ's martyrdom on the cross. Likewise, most Catholics qua Catholics (that is, apart from their consumption of popular culture) do not embrace *apocalypticism* on anything close to the order of magnitude of influence that Christian premillennialism exercises on the White evangelical imagination.[35] Nor do they harbor *messianic expectations* with anything like the intensity of White evangelicals. Indeed, the only one of Gorski's four elements of White Christian nationalism that resonates strongly with the Catholic experience is the *narrative of persecution and victimization*, which, as we have seen, is buried not far below the surface of Catholic memory, dating back to the era of anti-Catholic nativism and echoed today in the politics of resentment practiced by the likes of Buchanan.

The same can be said of Gorski's characterization of right-wing populism and its four primary actors. With few exceptions, Catholics have not been susceptible to *charismatic leaders* or myths of a *pure people* (how could they be?). Only recently, under the influence of Trumpist populism, have they expressed disdain for *a corrupt elite*. Gorski's mark of populism that rings true of American Catholicism is resentment of *the undeserving other*. American Catholics have always been worried about and resentful of what Gorski calls "line-cutters," those who do not wait patiently for their ticket to the privileges of the mainstream, but instead force their way to the front either through violence and crime (as nineteenth-century immigrants, striving to become White, charged Blacks with doing) or by playing on liberal sympathies (as in the affirmative action policies supposedly advanced by Obama, according to Buchanan). More recently, upwardly mobile Latinx Catholics have become exercised about line-cutting—by "lower-class" Latinos.

The journey of a majority of White Catholics into the company of White nationalists is a function of religious decline, and thus begins with the Church itself. Signs of "decline" include migration from the Catholic Church to other religions or to the growing category of "nones" (no institutional affiliation) and to falling levels of practice (e.g., Mass attendance, reception of the sacraments, parish membership). (The gap between the number of lapsed Catholics and practicing Catholics has been closing rapidly over the last decade.) For the millions who have stayed, the decline is even more profound, in a way: the vaunted claim of mystical-spiritual-sacramental-doctrinal "unity" across ethnic, racial, and political boundaries is sadly suspect. The phenomenon of internal fragmentation is overdetermined.

To mention only a few factors here in the following.

First, for nearly fifty years, since *Roe v. Wade*, the U.S. Catholic bishops, the majority of whom were appointed by John Paul II, have effectively narrowed the scope of Catholic social teaching to one issue: opposition to abortion. More masses, sermons, devotional practices, ecclesial declarations, and political lobbying campaigns have been devoted to pro-life campaigns than to immigrant rights, human rights, racial equality, economic justice, and opposition to nuclear weapons *combined*. Efforts by some bishops and at least one prominent cardinal, Joseph Bernardin of Chicago, to set opposition to abortion within a larger agenda that includes issues such as health care for the indigent and opposition to capital punishment—known as "the seamless garment of life" approach—have been repudiated publicly by the majority of conservative bishops. The casual lay Catholic could be forgiven for assuming that Catholic morality begins and ends with abortion, or, at least with sexual ethics more broadly. This is a woeful reduction of the rich social commitments of the Church.

Second, the clergy sexual abuse scandal has undermined Catholic witness on all social issues, robbing the Church of any prophetic power on issues such as racial justice or immigration; younger Americans, especially, are radically disaffected from the Church as from other institutions. As I write, Pope Francis has made a historic apology to the Indigenous peoples in Canada for abuses, over many decades, at residential schools run by the Catholic Church. His request for forgiveness is the latest in a series of too-little, too-late acknowledgments, apologies, and acts of restitution made by the Church over the last twenty years; in the United States, the crisis of confidence and trust in the clergy—especially in the bishops, who reassigned sexually abusive priests to unsuspecting parishes and schools—peaked in 2002, when a flood of new revelations were reported in the national and international media.

Nevertheless, Francis is by far the most popular (and the most visible) Roman Catholic in the world, and his appeal is particularly strong among religiously unaffiliated and affiliated young adults in the United States, not least among practicing Catholics. They resonate with his pastoral approach to the papacy and to ministry, his vision of the Church as a field hospital attending mercifully to the countless broken bodies and souls, his apparent tolerance of difference and warm embrace of all people regardless of identity markers, and his loving presence. Most of this demographic care less and know even less about doctrine, and find Catholicism's traditional sexual mores hopelessly outmoded.

Can Pope Francis's intentional reconfiguration of the global church, with the goal of lifting up marginalized and "peripheral" local churches and non-European, non-American, non-White populations, liberate the American Church from its captivity to a disgruntled cohort of Republican Party–friendly and Trump-tolerating bishops, whose headquarters in Washington, DC, is known as a "Francis-free Zone"? Can the pope's powerful and influential encyclicals on environmental stewardship (*Laudato si'*) and inclusive social friendship and solidarity to end "global indifference" to the plight of the suffering (*Fratelli tutti*) prove an effective counter to either the nationalist chauvinism of elements of the current American Catholic hierarchy or the trend toward White nationalism I discuss here? Does any of this matter in the long run?

The answer may well turn on the Church's response to the third factor in the fragmentation of U.S. Catholicism's witness to and advocacy of inclusive social justice, namely, the widespread and much-lamented failure of evangelization and catechesis over the last three generations. The papacy of Francis alone will not reverse this trend; the question is whether and how his legacy will endure. One explanation for this failure is the narrowing of evangelization and catechesis, in practice if not in theory, to a select subset of Catholic moral teaching and institutional rules—not merely on abortion, but also to what might be called the etiquette of doctrinal, liturgical, and sacramental practice, a regulatory matter that all but the most indoctrinated younger Catholics find trivial and irrelevant. The alienation of younger White college-educated Catholics—cohorts that tend to be more tolerant of others in general, and particularly opposed to gender-based and racial discrimination—must be reversed if "the meaning of Francis" is to inform the commitments of the coming generation of Catholics who will inherit the institutions that have nurtured generations of Catholic students, nurses, doctors, public officials, and social workers.

How, in short, *could* the McGreevy thesis that religion was the primary determinant of U.S. Catholic identity before the 1970s hold for generations whose independent religious identity has been eclipsed by the preoccupations of mainstream Americans and the failures of the Church itself?

At the opening of this chapter I remarked, ruefully, that although they have taken more than a century to do so, by the 1980s and the presidency of Ronald Reagan, a majority of White Catholics had arrived at the same sociopolitical destination as most White American evangelicals. Notwithstanding "the Catholic difference," one cannot credibly advance an exceptionalist argument exempting American Catholics from vigorous participation in White Christian nationalism. Like other White Americans, White Catholics have become increasingly concerned to retain their (relatively recent) position of socioeconomic privilege, and they have grown accustomed to subordinating creeds and social principles that might inspire resistance to reigning neoliberal capitalism. In recent decades, in fact, White

Catholics have adopted traits and tendencies of populism and nationalism described by Gorski and previously associated almost exclusively with White evangelicals; for example, in a confounding act of collective historical amnesia (or corrupt indifference) regarding the discrimination suffered by their ancestors in this country, a sizable segment of middle- and upper-class Catholics have apparently bought into the myth of Americans as "a pure people" (and placed themselves, a-historically, in this category) and elected and reelected politicians, including Catholic Republicans, who have denigrated brown- and black-skinned immigrants and fellow citizens as "undeserving others."

Sadly, this is not surprising: the ingredients of White American Christian nationalism were present and virulently active in the White Catholic population long before it was granted membership in the ranks of the all-White American religion of "Protestant-Catholic-Jew."[36] They include not only racialist sensibilities and a history of race-based discrimination, exclusion, and violence against non-Whites, but also patriarchal gender norms based on an essentialized conception of nature that is embedded in Catholic ecclesiology and operationalized as a pattern of exclusionary ecclesial politics that has had profound consequences for racial, ethnic, and sexual relations within the Church in the United States.

For decades, American Catholic feminists have offered a sustained critique of this distinctive variant of poisonous intersectionality. They have indicted the theology of the priesthood in particular, which declares the ordained male as alone equipped to stand "in persona Christi" (in the person of Christ) and equates celibacy with "purity."[37] In response to this critique, a network of U.S.-based organizations emerged in the 1980s that was led by Catholic women intent on defending "traditional" American and Christian gender norms and on undermining what they described as the insidious influence of Catholic feminism on American and Catholic values (despite the fact that Catholic feminists had no influence whatsoever on official Catholic teaching). The "Affirmation for Catholic Women" issued by one such group, Women for Faith and Family, articulated the tenets of the movement:

> We believe that through God's grace our female nature affords us distinct physical and spiritual capabilities with which to participate

in the divine plan for creation. Specifically, our natural function of childbearing endows us with the spiritual capacities for nurture, instruction, compassion and selflessness, which qualities are necessary to the establishment of families, the basic and Divinely ordained unit of society, and to the establishment of a Christian social order.[38]

Numerous progressive theologians have noted and lamented the symbiotic relationship between this essentialist philosophy and implicit or explicit sympathy for White supremacy on the part of some American Catholics. This pattern recalls Jason Springs's delineation of the intersection of White Christian nationalism and an American sexual politics informed by an aggressive masculinity.[39]

Black, Brown, and "White" Catholics

Does the modern United States require ethnic and racial minorities to become White and nationalist? Does it choke the faith out of the immigrant and also the "postethnic" Catholic? Brown Catholics may hold the answers to these questions. In 1965, around the time earlier immigrant groups had moved into the mainstream, there were 49 million Catholics in the United States. By 2015, the number had risen to 75 million. Catholics from Latin America and the Spanish-speaking Caribbean account for 78 percent of that growth. Today, a majority of U.S. Catholics under eighteen are Latinx. Yet Latinx cohorts have been leaving the American Catholic Church at a rapid rate. In "exit surveys," so to speak, the departing Latinx Catholics mention the same kind of disillusion with organized religion shared by White youth, adding disdain for Catholic gender discrimination to the mix. But many others complain of the failure of the American Church to escape "Whiteness." Typical of this perspective are the comments of Romero Orozco, the executive director of a day laborer center in Pomona, California, who said that though he appreciates Pope Francis's push for inclusivity, "it has to trickle down to our priests that we go on [sic] Sunday."[40]

The recent failures of the Catholic Church in the United States to effectively welcome and include Latinx Catholics reflects, in part, the waning of the liberal Catholic impulse. Commenting twenty years ago on the pastoral challenge posed by the waves of arriving immigrants from Central America and South America, Timothy Matovina lauded the number of English-speaking Catholics who, in the decades after Vatican II, had been making "considerable efforts to work with their Latino co-religionists and offer them a sense of welcome," particularly, he added, women religious and lay leaders. Owing to their labors, by 2000 approximately 80 percent of all dioceses and 20 percent of all parishes "engage in ministry with Hispanics . . . which encompass efforts to increase Spanish-language Masses, evangelization efforts, renewal movements, and feast day celebrations." Still, he admitted, "an alarming number of Hispanic Catholics feel alienated, rejected and dissatisfied with Catholicism in the United States."[41]

Latinx Catholics retain significant elements of the religious culture of their (or their parents' or grandparents') homeland, but a significant portion of the Latinx population in the United States today clearly seeks to be recognized as postethnic "full-blooded" Americans, not to be singled out from the majority as some kind of hyphenated subculture. This perspective drew national attention in the media coverage of the Latino vote in the 2020 election; in Florida, a battleground state, there was reported backlash against the Democrats for catering to "Latin-Americans" as a distinct minority; some even rejected the labels "Hispanic," "Latino," and, especially, "Latinx."[42]

Yet another lesson for whitey.

How Catholics in the United States Became Negligent

My argument in this chapter, constructed by placing the Catholic story in contrast to the narrative of White evangelical nationalism and populism set forth by Springs and Gorski in this volume, is that the Church (capital C) is the hermeneutical key to comprehending intersectionality, American Catholic style. The Church itself is a doctrine of the Catholic faith; every Sunday, still today, Catholics recite a Creed: "We believe in one, holy, catholic and apostolic Church . . ." For successive generations, Catholic schoolchildren were taught, in so many words, that the Church is *communitas perfecta* ("the perfect community") or *societas perfecta* ("the perfect society"), that is, a self-sufficient, independent community that already has all the necessary resources and conditions to achieve its overall goal (final end) of the universal salvation of mankind. And there was no question, even after Vatican II, that this "eternal" Church is fully present on earth in the Roman Catholic Church. This was precisely the view of the Church held by Dorothy Day, one of Catholicism's great early champions of racial justice.

Indeed, the American Catholic imagination has been captivated by this conception of the Church and also by the way ecclesial leadership has developed the institutional implications (critics would say subjective, arbitrary, and self-serving implications) for religious and moral authority governing the Church (all-male and, until rather recently, all-European, at the highest level). For much of the history of Catholicism in the United States, the polyglot, ethnically and racially diverse body of worshippers, whatever their local religious customs and practices, has had to contend with the teachings, rules, and regulations handed down by this Church, whose range of imperatives comprehends political, economic, social, and religious principles. Translated into secular matters, this complex of ecclesial teachings and practices has served as a framework within which gender, race, ethnicity, class—and the lure of nationalism—has been negotiated by Catholics.

I am also suggesting that this historical dynamic has been altered, perhaps irrevocably, by the passage of successive generations of Catholics into the social and economic mainstream. By the 1970s, millions of postethnic American Catholics had crossed this threshold, and Mexicans, Cubans, and Puerto Ricans were "applying" to the "White" club. At around the same time, crucially, the waning of the influence of the institutional Church over the religious identity and moral agency of Catholics, "White" and otherwise, accelerated. The shift is seismic for Catholics, who (the argument goes) have typically relied on the universal Church (as filtered through and modified by the practices of the local, ethnic worshipping community), in a way it would never be for White evangelical Protestants. For the former, the question is this: What remains of religion as an independent factor in Catholic religious identity when the Church becomes irrelevant? (For the latter, the question might be, Who cares about the Church *beyond* the local community?)

And yet, this is not a story of "simple" religious decline; there is more than a residual attachment to "the Catholic thing," even among so-called lapsed (nonpracticing, or "cultural") Catholics.[43] Might one hope that there is also a reserve of resistance to racist White nationalism despite the spiritual and psychological migration of so many American Catholics away from the once-hallowed and nurturing religious culture enlivened in the home, the parish, the Catholic school, lay Catholic guilds, and networks and associations—a culture that once offered resistance to absorption into the secular American milieu—and into the maw of modern American nationalism?

In their contribution to this volume on "the pull to the right of the right" and Bruno Latour's analysis of the ecological crisis in religio-secular terms, Yolande Jansen and Jasmijn Leeuwenkamp (chapter 6) note that Latour is influenced by Michel Serres's argument that secularity, as such, is not the antithesis of religion. Rather, Serres notes that "scholars interested in religion's etymologies and genealogies 'never say what sublime word our language opposes to the religious, in order to deny it: *negligence*.'" Whoever has no religion should not be called an atheist or unbeliever, Serres continues, but negligent. "'The notion of negligence makes it possible to understand our time'" (see Jansen and Leeuwenkamp herein).

For lapsed and still-practicing Catholics whose internalization of American individualism has authorized them to select specific doctrines and practices that reinforce their sociopolitical (and ethical) affinities, rather than inhabit the whole tradition in its moral complexities and contradictions, gathering together to "reread" the tradition (*religio*) in light of contemporary circumstances, seems to be both necessary and out of the question. Serres's insight calls for a sustained examination of the conditions under which Catholics have become negligent of the encompassing tradition, including its bracing social doctrines that serve as a foundation for a radical reimagining of Catholic public presences. Can negligence be reversed? How might that goal be envisioned and pursued? Developing an antidote to virulent White Catholic nationalism might hang in the balance.

NOTES

1. On other issues—e.g., the benefits of religious pluralism, the separation of church and state, the resilience and witness of the local churches—liberal/progressive Catholics of the United States are quick to assert that the universal church has learned from the American experience. On the range of Catholic efforts to resist White nationalism, see, inter alia, Cyprian Davis, *The History of Black Catholics in the United States* (New York: Crossroad, 1990); Stephen J. Ochs,

Desegregating the Altar: The Josephites and the Struggle for Black Priests, 1871–1960 (Baton Rouge: Louisiana State University Press, 1990); Timothy Matovina and Gerald E. Poyo, eds., *¡Presente! U.S. Latino Catholics from Colonial Origins to the Present* (Maryknoll, NY: Orbis, 2000).

When I capitalize "Church," I mean the Roman Catholic Church, unless otherwise noted.

2. William Halsey, *The Survival of American Innocence: Catholicism in an Era of Disillusionment, 1920–1940* (Notre Dame, IN: University of Notre Dame Press, 1980); Philip Gleason, *Contending with Modernity: Catholic Higher Education in the Twentieth Century* (New York: Oxford University Press, 1995).

3. Noel Ignatiev, *How the Irish Became White* (London: Routledge, 2008); M. F. Jacobson, *Whiteness of a Different Color* (Cambridge, MA: Harvard University Press, 1999); Jay P. Dolan, *The American Catholic Experience: A History from Colonial Times to the Present* (Notre Dame, IN: University of Notre Dame Press, 1992), 195–220.

4. John T. McGreevy, *Parish Boundaries: The Catholic Encounter with Race in the Twentieth-Century Urban North* (Chicago: University of Chicago Press, 1996).

5. On Black Protestant religious culture, see Michael W. Harris, *The Rise of Gospel Blues: The Music of Thomas Andrew Dorsey in the Urban Church* (New York: Oxford University Press, 1992).

6. The Catholic Church in the United States routinely excluded Black men from the priesthood and Black women from religious life. One widely circulated critique was provided by George Joseph MacWilliam, "The Catholic Church and the Negro Priest," *The Crisis* 19, no. 3 (1920): 122–23. After repeatedly being denied entry into Catholic seminaries on account of his being "colored," MacWilliam concluded, "Since we are not allowed in any capacity to pursue a religious vocation, colored young men and women are not admitted to Catholic high schools and colleges, notwithstanding the fact that they are dissuaded from attending those under Protestant influence. This accounts for the great percentage of ignorance among colored Catholics . . . making us the most backward, the most depraved sect of American Negroes. We are governed by the most prejudiced men on this continent, who impose their conditions upon us and tell us it is God's will" (123).

7. Brenna Moore, "'To Confound White Christians': Thinking with Claude McKay about Race, Catholic Enchantment, and Secularism," in *Religion and Broken Solidarities: Feminism, Race, and Transnationalism* (Notre Dame, IN: University of Notre Dame Press, 2022), 133–57.

8. On the culture of Catholic devotionalism, see Dolan, *The American Catholic Experience*, 223–35. See also, Robert Orsi, *The Madonna of 115th Street: Faith and Community in Italian Harlem* (New Haven, CT: Yale University Press, 1985).

9. In 1938, Coughlin published *Social Justice*, a newspaper that filled its pages with diatribes against Jews. Coughlin endorsed Hitler and Mussolini, and he delivered a speech in the Bronx, during which he gave a Nazi salute. See Alan Brinkley, *Voices of Protest: Huey Long, Father Coughlin, and the Great Depression* (New York: Vintage, 1982).

10. McGreevy, *Parish Boundaries*.

11. Mel Piehl, *Breaking Bread: The Catholic Worker and the Origin of Catholic Radicalism in America*, 2nd ed. (Tuscaloosa: University of Alabama Press, 2006).

12. The phrase in quotation marks is Day's.

13. Day was referring to the program of social reconstruction issued by the U.S. Catholic Bishops Conference in 1919. See Joseph M. McShane, SJ, *Sufficiently Radical: Catholicism, Progressivism, and the Bishops' Program of Social Reconstruction* (Washington, DC: Catholic University of America Press, 1986).

14. Born in Brooklyn in 1897, Day returned to New York at age eighteen after attending the University of Illinois briefly and was drawn to leftist circles. "When I read Tolstoy, I was an Anarchist," she later recalled. "My allegiance to *The Call* kept me a Socialist though a left-wing one, and my Americanism inclined me to the I.W.W. (the Industrial Workers of the World)"; see Dorothy Day, *The Long Loneliness* (San Francisco: Harper, 1997), 62. At twenty she was arrested in Washington, DC, for picketing at the White House for women's suffrage, the first of many nights in jail, which continued into her mid-seventies. Day died in 1980.

15. See https://www.catholicworker.org.

16. "To feed the hungry, clothe the naked and shelter the harborless without also trying to change the social order so that people can feed, clothe and shelter themselves is just to apply palliatives. It is to show a lack of faith in one's fellows, their responsibilities as children of God, heirs of heaven." "As we come to know the seriousness of the situation, the war, the racism, the poverty in our world, we come to realize that things will not be changed simply by words or demonstrations. Rather, it's a question of living one's life in a drastically different way" (Day, *The Long Loneliness*, 2).

17. McGreevy, *Parish Boundaries*, 111.

18. LaFarge's network included nationally prominent Catholics such as Monsignor John A. Ryan, "the Right Reverend New Dealer," who earlier had turned on Coughlin for his antisemitic tirades and helped build a coalition of bishops, cardinals, and influential laymen, such as Joseph P. Kennedy, to have Coughlin silenced by the Vatican. See Marilyn Wenzke Nickels, *Black Catholic Protest and the Federated Colored Catholics, 1917–1933: Three Perspectives on Racial Justice* (New York: Garland, 1988); John LaFarge, *Interracial Justice: A Study of the Catholic Doctrine of Race Relations* (New York: America Press, 1937).

19. In 1839, Pope Gregory XVI issued a bull, *In supremo apostolatus*, in which he condemned slavery, with particular reference to New World colonial slavery and the slave trade, calling it "inhumanum illud commercium." The exact meaning and scope of the bull was disputed at the time and remains disputed among historians. That new enslavements and slave-trading are condemned and forbidden is clear, but the language in the passage was not sufficiently specific to make clear what, if anything, the bull had to say about the ongoing ownership of those already slaves, but their sale seemed to be prohibited. In any case, it was certainly no clear call for the emancipation of all existing slaves, as had already happened in the British and French Empires.

20. Pope Pius XI, "On the Church and the German Reich," http://www.vatican.va/content/pius-xi/en/encyclicals/documents/hf_p-xi_enc_14031937_mit-brennender-sorge.html.

21. Quoted in McGreevy, *Parish Boundaries*, 50.

22. R. Scott Appleby, "Present to the People of God: The Transformation of the Roman Catholic Parish Priesthood," in *Transforming Parish Ministry: The Changing Roles of Catholic Clergy, Laity, and Women Religious*, ed. Jay P. Dolan, R. Scott Appleby, Patricia Byrne, and Debra Campbell (New York: Crossroad, 1989), 54–89.

23. Quoted in McGreevy, *Parish Boundaries*, 58.

24. Pope John XXIII, *Pacem in terris*, http://www.vatican.va/content/john-xxiii/en/encyclicals/documents/hf_j-xxiii_enc_11041963_pacem.html; see also McGreevy, *Parish Boundaries*, 152, 173.

25. World Synod of Bishops, "Justice in the World" (1971), para. 6, http://www.stjosephsbrackenridge.com/uploads/3/7/8/4/37843139/justice_in_the_world.pdf.

26. Dolan, *The American Catholic Experience*, 221–46.

27. Leslie Woodcock Tentler, *Catholics and Contraception: An American History* (Ithaca, NY: Cornell University Press, 2004).

28. Patrick J. Buchanan, "A Brief for Whitey," Patrick J. Buchanan Official Website, March 21, 2008, https://buchanan.org/blog/pjb-a-brief-for-whitey-969.

29. James Carroll, *An American Requiem: God, My Father, and the War That Came between Us* (New York: Mariner Books, 1996), 146.

30. Ibid., 239.

31. James Carroll, *Practicing Catholic* (Boston: Houghton Mifflin Harcourt, 2009), 242–44, 251, 259–60.

32. By the 1970s, following Pope Paul VI's encyclical *Humanae vitae* (1968)—the use of "artificial contraception" by American Catholics actually increased after the pope banned it—social surveys consistently found negligible differences between Catholic and Protestant attitudes toward and practice of

religiously banned behaviors, such as birth control and abortion, much less "mixed marriage."

33. "Survey: Biden and Trump Split the 2020 Catholic Vote Almost Evenly," *America*, November 6, 2020, https://www.americamagazine.org/politics-society/2020/11/06/catholic-vote-donald-trump-joe-biden-election-split.

34. Patrick Saint-Jean, SJ, "There Remain Divisions between Black, Brown, and White Catholics Today," *US Catholic*, https://uscatholic.org/articles/202009/we-need-to-talk-about-racism-in-the-catholic-church/.

35. The exception is Marian apocalypticism, prominent during the early stages of the Cold War. Typically, the focus was on the threat "atheistic" communism posed to the Church, symbolized by the figure of the Virgin, not to the American nation. Nonetheless, the Legion of Mary, the Blue Army, and the Catholic crusades for the Rosary were an important way by which American Catholics did their part in the national fight against Soviet Russia and thus reinforced their patriotism. On contemporary Christian premillennialism, see the riveting documentary film *'Til Kingdom Come* (and note the absence of Catholics among the [anti-Jewish] Christian Zionists!), directed by Maya Zinshtein, metfilm (London: Ealing Studios, 2020).

36. Will Herberg, *Protestant, Catholic, Jew: An Essay in American Religious Sociology* (Garden City, NY: Doubleday, 1955).

37. Mary J. Henolds, *Catholic and Feminist: The Surprising History of the American Catholic Feminist Movement* (Chapel Hill: University of North Carolina Press, 2008).

38. Reprinted in Helen Hull Hitchcock, "Women for Faith and Family: Catho-lic Women Affirming Catholic Teaching," in *Being Right: Conservative Catholics in America*, ed. Mary Jo Weaver and R. Scott Appleby (Bloomington: Indiana University Press, 1995), 163–85, at 177.

39. See also Jeannine Hill Fletcher, *The Sin of White Supremacy* (Maryknoll, NY: Orbis, 2017). Also see M. Shawn Copeland's denunciation of "the spread of a race-based hierarchical/patriarchal system that supported the enslavement not just of other human beings but of other Christians, the dehumanization of women and persons of color"; see Copeland, ed., *Uncommon Faithfulness: The Black Catholic Experience* (Maryknoll, NY: Orbis, 2009).

40. Alejandra Molina, "US Latinos Are No Longer Majority-Catholic, Here's Why," Religion News Service, November 8, 2019, https://abcnews.go.com/US/wireStory/us-latinos-longer-majority-catholic-66856012. In 2018–19, 47 percent of Latinos identified as Catholic, down from 57 percent a decade ago. The Pew Research Center study reported by Molina found the share of Latinos who say they are religiously unaffiliated is now 23 percent, up from 15 percent in 2009.

A majority of U.S. Catholics under eighteen are Hispanic. The median age of Hispanics is twenty-eight, significantly younger than White (43), Asian (36), and Black (33) populations. About 60 percent of all U.S. Catholics younger than eighteen are Hispanic. Of that population, 93 percent were born in the United States. Most young Hispanics remain significantly influenced by their immigrant families, retaining their faith, culture, and language. More than half of all U.S.-born Hispanics older than five—about 20 million—speak Spanish at home.

    41. Timothy Matovina, "Hispanic Catholics: 'El Futuro' Is Here," *Commonweal*, September 14, 2001, https://www.commonwealmagazine.org/hispanic-catholics.

    42. Raymond Arroyo, "LatinX: A Label without a Cause," *Latino Leaders*, https://www.latinoleadersmagazine.com/winter-2019/2020/1/31/latinx-a-label-without-a-cause.

    43. Rosemary Haughton, *The Catholic Thing* (Springfield, IL: Templegate, 1979).

CHAPTER 4

Constructing "Religion," Performing "The People"

Political Theology and the Paradox of Popular Sovereignty

RICHARD AMESBURY

Abstract

Scholars of religion and populism have long noted the instrumental role that religious categories can play in drawing in-group/out-group distinctions that define a "people." This chapter explores the overlooked role of theological language not simply in drawing such distinctions, but in legitimating them. Democratic nation-states uniformly face a paradox of popular sovereignty, the chicken-or-egg problem of rooting authority in a particular conception of the demos whose precise bounds cannot be established through democratic procedures. By reconsidering the discursive entanglements between concepts such as religion, race, and nation, this chapter argues that theological language posits a constitutive prior authority for grounding these distinctions that purports to break free from this paradox. Drawing on examples of so-called right-wing populisms in the United States and Germany, and on the idealized liberal order with which populism is typically contrasted, it shows how movements invoke divine sovereignty to perform popular sovereignty.

It had a mythical beginning, still visible, if ambiguous, to itself and to its audience: before there was Russia, there was Russia; before there was France and England, there was France and England; but before there was America there was no America. America was *discovered*, and what was discovered was not a place, one among others, but a setting, the backdrop of a destiny. It began as theater.

—*Stanley Cavell, "The Avoidance of Love:*
A Reading of King Lear"

In December 2015, Jerry Falwell Jr., son of the late preacher Jerry Falwell Sr. and then president of Liberty University in Lynchburg, Virginia, urged students at the private Christian university to carry guns on campus following a mass shooting in San Bernardino, California. The *Washington Post* reports that Falwell touted a free course for students wishing to acquire permits to carry concealed weapons:

> "It just blows my mind that the president of the United States [Barack Obama] [says] that the answer to circumstances like that is more gun control," he said to applause.
>
> "If some of those people in that community center had what I have in my back pocket right now . . ." he said while being interrupted by louder cheers and clapping. "Is it illegal to pull it out? I don't know," he said, chuckling.
>
> "I've always thought that if more good people had concealed-carry permits, then we could end those Muslims before they walked in," he says, the rest of his sentence drowned out by loud applause while he said, "and killed them."[1]

Falwell's remarks were denounced by numerous commentators, and Falwell later said that he had been referring to Islamist terrorists, not to Muslims generally. Be that as it may, his remarks point to a troubling dimension of the nexus of American evangelicalism and right-wing politics that came to particular prominence with the political ascendancy of Donald J. Trump, who—seemingly improbably, given his reputation as an irreligious libertine—garnered approximately 81 percent of the White evangelical vote in 2016 and 76 percent in 2020.[2] In addition to their explicit endorsement of violence, Falwell's remarks are notable for the way they frame the conflict as between "good people" and two mortal enemies—first, "those Muslims," and second, a president who fails to appreciate the significance of this purported threat and cannot be trusted to protect the good people from it.

Falwell's enthusiasm for the Second Amendment and gun culture is of course a distinctively American phenomenon, but his anti-Islamic rhetoric and suspicion of elites are not. Anti-Muslim rhetoric is also on the rise in much of Europe, and there too the "good people" are often conceived as threatened from both above/within (by feckless "elites") and below/outside (by Muslims and non-White immigrants).[3] Though myriad examples might be noted—including Fidesz in Hungary, Lega and the 5-Star Movement in Italy, Independent Greeks and Golden Dawn in Greece, Law and Justice in Poland, the Swiss People's Party, the UK Independence Party, and the Austrian Freedom Party, to name just a few—I turn for comparative purposes to Germany, and, in particular, the Alternative for Germany (AfD) party, because the German examples are interestingly similar and dissimilar to some of the U.S. ones and are useful in distinguishing different threads within the assemblage of contemporary political movements commonly dubbed "right-wing populisms." Though much could be said about these movements—their origins, aims, methods, family resemblances, global ecology, and the grievances they cultivate and draw upon—my interest in comparing them here is limited: I would like to consider some of the various ways in which *discourse about religion*, particularly about Islam and Christianity, functions and circulates in them, how it is used to demarcate and legitimate the boundaries of "the people," and what this says about the anxieties of popular sovereignty and the larger Euro-American political-theological imagination.

Within these movements, discourse about religion often functions to delimit "the people," separating an in-group (often "Christians") from an out-group (often "Muslims"). In the introductory chapter of *Saving the People*, a volume they coedited with Olivier Roy, Nadia Marzouki and Duncan McDonnell contend that "the populist use of religion is much more about 'belonging' than 'belief.'"[4] On this reading, "Christianity" names a collective identity, not a set of doctrinal commitments. Similarly, Rogers Brubaker argues that "the Christianity invoked by the national populists . . . is not a substantive Christianity; it is a 'secularized Christianity-as-culture,' a civilizational and identitarian 'Christianism.' It is a matter of belonging rather than believing, a way of defining 'us' in relation to 'them.'"[5] But "religion"—as deployed in these endeavors—is not simply a sociological category: if not about "belief" per se, it is implicated nevertheless in political-theological debates about authority. Indeed, I suspect that questions of the latter type have been neglected in the academic literature partly because its secular frame tends to reinforce a normative distinction between *genuine or authentic religion*, on the one hand, and *politics*, on the other. The subtitle of *Saving the People*, *How Populists Hijack Religion*, implies that *real* religion is *not* political, and that its political "uses" are merely strategic.[6] By contrast, I regard such a distinction as itself ideological: a normative move within a political-theological game from which it is difficult to achieve exteriority. Rather than assuming an evaluative conception of religion and its proper limits, I treat "Christianity" as a contested category, a signifier the grammar of which is perpetually in dispute.

It is important to point out that *religion* is not the only category in terms of which so-called populist movements articulate belonging, and that claims framed in terms of religion intersect with claims framed in terms, for example, of race, gender, and sexuality. The category of religion has historically been co-constituted with these latter categories and continues to work together with them in complex ways. Any general account of political belonging would need to trace the genealogies in terms of which these categories came to be differentiated in theory, if not always in practice. This chapter, however, is not primarily intended to make that case, which has been made at length elsewhere.

Rather, I am interested in a dimension of theological language that the scholarship on populism and religion tends to elide, namely, *sovereignty*. Indeed, I argue that the significance of theological language in these debates is only secondarily a function of its utility, much discussed in the sociological literature, in drawing in-group/out-group distinctions.[7] What is of primary significance is its function in conferring *legitimacy* on these exclusions. By comparing the AfD with right-wing evangelical movements in the United States, I argue that the category of *religion*, which historically has been constructed monotheistically, provides the discursive framework within which sovereignty is conferred on specific "peoples."

The argument I outline here shares in the concerns of the other contributors, but it can be read especially in critical conversation with the contributions herein of Zubrzycki (chapter 5) and Gorski (chapter 1). Zubrzycki argues that the sovereignty of the majority Catholic population in Poland is affirmed by identifying Jews as outside the boundaries of Polishness. Further, the attempt to challenge Catholic Polish identity by appropriating Jewish practices serves, ironically, to reinscribe its logic. Gorski focuses on Trump's claim to be the "voice" of the people and argues that Trumpism is a form of White Christian nationalism.

CATEGORIES AND METHODS

Here, however, I would like to put forward a methodological proposal: instead of approaching *religion*, *politics*, *race*, and such as analytically distinct phenomena that happen to have become entangled, and that it is the task of the scholar to distinguish, we conceive the object of our inquiry as an undifferentiated whole. That is, I propose to follow Michel Foucault in treating universal categories not as an a priori grid of intelligibility, but as historical artifacts. Commenting on his approach to how the history of governmental practice has come to be organized and understood, Foucault writes, "I start from the theoretical and methodological decision that consists in saying: Let's suppose that universals do not exist. And then I put the question to history and historians: How can you write history if you do not accept a priori the existence of things like the state, society, the sovereign, and subjects?"[8] Rather than taking these "universals" as given, as constituting "an obligatory grid of intelligibility for certain concrete practices," Foucault's strategy—which might be called *methodological nominalism*—invites us to appreciate their historical contingency.[9] By performing a sort of *epoché*—a suspension of essentializing assumptions about social ontology—we can come to view otherwise familiar categories of analysis as themselves being appropriate objects of historical inquiry and critique. Analogously, I strive to suspend the assumptions, for example, that *religion* has an essence distinct from that of *politics*, and that what is called "race" is only externally and contingently entangled with what is called "Christianity." The question is not, *How did religion, politics, race, and so on become entangled?* but *Why do certain parties wish to distinguish them?* What is at stake, for example, in the claim that right-wing populists in Germany or the United States are "perverting" Christianity? Unlike Gorski's Weberian account of "elective affinities" in this volume, I argue that religion and the nation-state are not two categories that are sometimes combined, but rather one category that is sometimes differentiated. To the extent that speaking of "religion" is a way of *not speaking* about "race," "politics," "gender," and such, it is, I want to insist, important to recognize that the discursive logics these various categories attempt to foreground are implicated from the outset.

Elsewhere I have argued that "religion" comes into view as a discrete phenomenon only in the context of a bundle of historically contingent but institutionally normalized assumptions, dispositions, and affects I call "the secular."[10] I will say more about that later in the chapter. Here, however, we can already note an important similarity between the discourse of religion and the discourse of race: the secular and Whiteness are alike in being "unmarked" categories, the invisibilized background against which difference is configured and managed. If one recognizes that Whiteness is not primarily a phenotypical difference but rather a hegemonic *position*—to quote W. E. B. Du Bois, "whiteness is the ownership of the earth forever and ever, Amen"[11]—then this formal similarity can be seen to be more than a mere analogy. As Vincent W. Lloyd has put the point, "whiteness is secular, and the secular is white. The unmarked racial category and the unmarked religious category jointly mark their others. Or, put another way, the desire to stand outside religion and the desire to stand outside race are complementary delusions, for the seemingly outside is in fact the hegemonic."[12]

Standing *outside* is prized by academics, and it is central not simply to the academic study of religion, but also in scholarship on populism. In contemporary political commentary, the term "populism" is often used pejoratively to denote a narrow, homogeneous conception of "the people," one constructed over against both outsiders and "elites." *Populism* is, according to this usage, primarily an outsider term, what we call it when we don't like what we see in the mirror that elections and referenda hold up to democracy. Yet historically the term has been self-applied by diverse figures and movements on the right, left, and center of the political spectrum, including, just a few years ago, by Barack Obama.[13] Most basically, a populist is someone who speaks on behalf of *the people*. Conceived broadly, I want to suggest, *we are all populists*; that is, we are engaged, whether or not we acknowledge it, in the construction of "the people." To reject any particular conception of the people is necessarily to endorse, at least tacitly, another. Neither "religion" nor "the people" is a politically neutral, descriptive term, and attempts to isolate the genuine article in its purity—whether by "populists" or by the scholars who study them—are always already political.

To say that we are all populists is also to imply that "populism" is of limited value as a political classification, and that we need more substantive descriptors. Accounts of populism that frame it in purely structural terms— as antielitist, as concerned with the interests of the people, or as a politics of fear—are too formal and ahistorical to be of use in capturing the salient features of, say, the Trump phenomenon or the appeal of Podemos. Moreover, they invite dubious groupings and a false sense of equivalence. Finally, as I shall argue here, even among movements that share substantive features, there are often important differences, and movements are themselves rarely internally consistent. Attending to the nuances of these movements is arguably of greater value than categorizing them in terms of purely formal similarities.

But if the differences among "populist" movements are generally more interesting than the similarities, the similarities between the movements categorized as "populist" and their assumed contrast case—the "normal" democracy of which populism is imagined to be the shadow—are worth emphasizing. That the term "populism" ranges indifferently over such a wide and ideologically disparate variety of movements suggests that it tells us less about these movements than about the perspective of those who use the term pejoratively. What, it might more helpfully be asked, is *not* populism? The conventional answer is *liberal democracy*. What critics of "populism" seem concerned to defend is, in other words, some version (typically idealized) of the postwar international liberal economic and political order. Though nominally democratic, this order operates, as I attempt to show below, according to a similar sovereign logic of identity and exclusion. By treating threats to this order as pathologies of democracy, rather than as (quasi-)democratic challenges to a historically particular international regime (the democratic *bona fides* of which are not beyond question), the scholarship on populism works to naturalize a particular idea of democratic sovereignty (and, in the case of at least some scholarship on "left populism," a capitalist economic order). In this respect, *discourse about populism* is formally similar to *populist discourse*, demarcating boundaries of peoplehood and seeking to institutionalize certain claims to political authority.

When it comes to religion, what is commonly called "populism" takes various forms. In the United States, the "elites" against whom "the people" are positioned are of multiple stripes—Washington insiders, Hollywood types, "liberal" academics—but they tend to be portrayed as *secular* in the sense of *lacking in religious commitment*, and as hostile to those forms of religion that make truth claims, particularly evangelical Christianity.[14] "Islam" is opposed to "the people" not because it is not secular, but because it is not Christian, that is, because it makes a rival claim to truth. In other cases, however, "secularity" is regarded not as a problem to be overcome but as a legacy to be defended, and Muslims are deemed unassimilable precisely because they are said to reject secular law and liberal values. Movements of the former kind might be thought more *religious* than movements of the latter type, but I shall argue that it is not so simple: the more avowedly theological movements—according to which Christianity is a "relationship" or faith claim—quickly become entangled in the secular, whereas apparently more secular approaches to religion, often couched in terms of cultural heritage and tradition, are often crypto-theological. Claims to truth are flattened into claims to identity, but claims to identity sometimes mask claims to truth. Movements of both types are present in various contexts, but the former seem to be more prominent in the United States and in the UK, whereas the latter appear to be more common in other parts of Europe, including Germany.[15] It is tempting to view this distinction as tracking a Protestant/Catholic divide, but the reality is more complicated, a result partly of different secular settlements, and both projects are best viewed as idealized types, with considerable circulation of ideas complicating any hard-and-fast distinction.

Although this chapter discusses the United States and, to a lesser extent and for comparative purposes, the AfD, it does not aspire to provide a comprehensive account of either.[16] Rather, my aim is to advance four theoretical and/or interpretive theses:

1. Democratic states rest their claim to legitimacy on the will of the people, but there is no democratic way of answering the question of who "the people" are. I call this the *paradox of popular sovereignty*.
2. "The people" and "religion" are both normative, performative categories.
3. There are at least two different ways in which contemporary so-called populist movements in the United States and Germany understand the relationship between religion and secularity, but they are both implicated in a broader imaginary I term *the secular*, a characteristic feature of which is that "religion" is thematized as a discrete category.
4. Appeals to "Christianity" are not simply strategic and should be understood as theological gestures aimed at resolving the paradox of popular sovereignty by conferring sovereignty from "above."

The Paradox of Popular Sovereignty

To understand the political-theological significance of invoking God within an ostensibly secular, democratic political order, it is necessary to appreciate that popular sovereignty—the doctrine that political authority derives from the consent of the governed, which is conventionally understood as having inverted the notion of the divine right of kings—involves a paradoxical element of recursivity that threatens to destabilize the boundary between citizens and noncitizens. This is a problem not simply for the various right-wing movements commonly called "populisms," but, importantly, for any politics that purports to draw authority from a bounded conception of *the people*. Indeed, the premise here is that there is little novel or surprising about the present moment in terms either of substance or form: instead, we are observing the iteration of well-established patterns that coil through history and circulate much more widely than is commonly acknowledged by populism's critics.

Consider, if you will, a familiar, if paradoxical, image: *Drawing Hands*, a well-known 1948 lithograph by M. C. Escher, depicts two hands emerging, in *trompe-l'oeil* fashion, from a sheet of paper, each drawing the other into existence. Douglas Hofstadter describes the image as a (representation of a) *strange loop*, that is, "not a physical circuit but an abstract loop in which . . . there is a shift from one level of abstraction (or structure) to another, which feels like an upwards movement in a hierarchy, and yet somehow the successive 'upward' shifts turn out to give rise to a closed cycle."[17] It is just such a strange loop that we find at work in the founding documents of the United States with their references to "the people."

As Jacques Derrida once noted with reference to the Declaration of Independence, "This people does not exist. They do not exist as an entity, it does not exist, before this declaration, not as such. If it gives birth to itself, as free and independent subject, as possible signer, this can hold only in the act of the signature. The signature invents the signer. The signer can only authorize him- or herself to sign once he or she has come to the end . . . , if one can say this, of his or her own signature, in a sort of fabulous retroactivity."[18] By speaking in the name of a community yet to be imagined as such, the Declaration *invents* the very "people" its signatories claim to represent. Like Escher's hands, the American people is imagined to have inscribed itself into existence by a sovereign act of will. The Declaration enacts, illocutionarily, the investiture of a popular sovereign.

This idea of a self-authorizing people is in one sense little more than a comforting myth—on par with the Athenian idea that an autochthonous *polis* had sprung, cicada-like, from the Attican soil. It imagines "America" as a self-contained whole, created *ex nihilo* on an otherwise empty continent, without taking into account the histories of genocide and slavery. The Declaration's claim to sovereignty is asserted not simply against Britain but also against the Indigenous nations that already occupied the North American continent, into whose homelands the United States would expand. As Juliana Barr notes, "At the time of European invasion, there was no part of North America that was not claimed and ruled by sovereign Indian regimes. The Europeans whose descendants would create the United States did not come to an unsettled wilderness; they grafted their colonies and settlements onto long-existent Indian homelands that constituted the entire continent."[19] To the (limited) extent that it situates this project within an historical narrative, the Declaration itself foregrounds the experience of the colonists, not that of the colonized. From the beginning, "the people" are framed in opposition to both elites and barbarians.

Oppressed from above by the British Crown, the "good People of these Colonies" are portrayed in the Declaration as simultaneously harried from below (with encouragement on the king's part) by "merciless Indian Savages, whose known rule of warfare, is an undistinguished destruction of all ages, sexes and conditions." Like all sovereign bodies, "the people" on which the founding documents rest their claim to authority—and to which they give birth—was characterized principally by whom it excluded. At the time of the founding, 20 percent of the population lived in bondage, and Thomas Jefferson, who penned the Declaration's famous line "all men are created equal," enslaved more than 600 people over the course of his life. The American body politic has never been an abstract, purely formal category, but a *body* of a particular kind, masculine, Christened, and distinguished, above all, by its ontological *Whiteness* (particularly, its anti-Blackness).[20] "America never was America to me," Langston Hughes wrote in 1935.[21] Appreciating the interrelation between abstract structures of exclusion and concrete exclusions is a central challenge for any historical—as opposed to purely philosophical—account of popular sovereignty. Indeed, part of the rhetorical function of the discourse of popular sovereignty is, as we shall see, to render this historical violence invisible, ensuring that its victims, too, are "disappeared." Insofar as it pretends to locate authority in a sovereign unit that cannot account for itself democratically or historically, the myth of popular sovereignty builds its conclusion into its premises.

Precisely *in* its mythological character, however, the Declaration's performance of sovereignty points to an interesting set of anxieties about legitimacy—anxieties submerged, as it were, in the national psyche, which must constantly be repressed. Derrida writes: "There was no signer, by right, before the text of the Declaration which itself remains the producer and guarantor of its own signature. . . . It opens for itself a line of credit, its own credit, for itself to itself."[22] In this way, the founders' "we" can be read as performative, rather than constative: its referent is not an already existing entity, but an entity in the act of constructing and legitimating itself, a not yet fully present referent.[23]

The result is a paradox at the heart of the democratic enterprise. On the one hand, democracy is possible only when there is a *demos*, and constituting a *demos* in a context of multiple sovereign states inevitably produces exclusions.[24] In other words, citizenship requires that we distinguish insiders from outsiders, and the democratic struggle among citizens to be treated equally to one another is almost always, in effect, a quest to be treated differently from those outside the polity. As Talal Asad has noted,

> The democratized ethical subject is first and foremost a loyal citizen, and thus a member of liberal democracy's privileged circle of "we." The benefits provided by the welfare state to the citizen—security against destitution, minimum wages, education and health care benefits, retirement pensions and so on—are confined to this circle of "we." Ideologically, at least, the citizen is expected to die for his or her homeland. In return, the subject expects equal treatment from the liberal democratic state of which he or she is a citizen. These reciprocal bonds inevitably construct an "outside" to the circle: a world of aliens not entitled to benefits and enemy aliens not entitled to sympathy.[25]

The political equality of citizens is not the moral equality posited by human rights; indeed, the two are often in conflict. On the other hand, there is no *democratic* way of distinguishing between insiders and outsiders, of determining, from *within* the procedures that democracy authorizes, who belongs and who does not. The question of who is eligible to vote, for example, cannot be decided, but only begged, by a vote. In short, democracy, as practiced within the borders of sovereign states, seems both to demand and to resist closure: the logic of state sovereignty requires exclusions, but no particular exclusion can be justified democratically. The sovereign people on which the legitimacy of everything else depends is not itself democratically legitimate. As a consequence, the moral borders of a democratic state are inherently fuzzy and contestable, always provisional and subject to being redrawn.

The logic of popular sovereignty—the idea that democratic government depends for its legitimacy on the will of the people—is circular: the *people* said to authorize the state is constructed and maintained *by* the state. What matters, in other words, are not *people* in the plural, but *the people*: the sovereign people make up a singular, enduring entity, and the question is, *Who belongs* to this entity? Individuals matter distributively only insofar as they are *citizens*, members of the collective. The quotation by Stanley Cavell at the beginning of this chapter points to the performativity (the "theater") through which the United States came to be constituted. There was no "America"—no sovereign unit on which the United States could rest its claim to legitimacy—prior to this performance. In this respect, Cavell seems to suggest, the United States is different from "France" or "England." But in fact, *all* democratic nation-states are implicated in a similar circularity. Part of the explanation for why the paradox of popular sovereignty—the inability of giving a fully democratic account of the *demos*—tends to escape notice is that most modern constitutional states emerged not through revolutionary acts of self-assertion but through the democratizing of nondemocratic regimes. In the process, subjects became citizens, but preexisting boundaries of belonging were simply taken as given, importing the vagaries of historical memory and forgetfulness into the very definitions of *peoples*. These boundaries cannot themselves be authorized democratically—by appeal to the sovereign people—without begging the question of which people are here relevant.

Iterated through repeated performance over time, a *people*, however fictive in its inception, takes on a life of its own. As historically contingent exclusions are *grandfathered* into the definition of a "people," they come to seem necessary. Artifice comes to resemble nature, and time is conceived as looping. What matters is an imagined past and a hoped-for future, which is also a return to the imagined past: *Make America Great Again*.[26] By backdating a preferred future, the present, the space of political agency, is minimized, and with it the opportunity to imagine differently. Once written out of this definition of the people, the excluded are refused the access needed to contest their exclusion. They are denied what Hannah Arendt called "the right to have rights."[27] It is worth noting here that the term "grandfather clause" first referred to a provision in certain southern U.S. state constitutions and Jim Crow laws that waived voting requirements—literacy tests, poll taxes, and such—for descendants of people who voted prior to the Civil War, thus exempting Whites from a supposedly universal requirement that functioned in practice to disenfranchise Black Americans.

Perhaps not surprisingly, the doctrine of popular sovereignty has long been invoked to exclude. Honoring the will of the people has often in practice meant permitting discrimination against those in opposition to whom "the people" is defined. During the Antebellum period, for example, "popular sovereignty" referred to the idea, championed by Stephen Douglas, that states ought to be able to decide for themselves whether or not to permit slavery. Perversely, slavery was justified by appeal to the consent of the governed. The peculiar logic of popular sovereignty lay at the heart of the Supreme Court's infamous 1857 *Dred Scott* decision, which denied Scott the legal standing to contest his own enslavement, and explains why, in 1919, only men could vote on whether to enfranchise women. The very exclusions at issue rendered the excluded officially inaudible, incapable of contesting their exclusion within the procedures said to be underwritten democratically.[28] The phrase "We the people" is today popular among the Far Right in the United States, for whom it signifies *us* versus *them*, and popular sovereignty is routinely invoked by conservatives opposed to immigration.[29]

Still, justification can never quite catch up with itself, and bordered democracy invariably is left begging the question. One implication of this paradox endemic to popular sovereignty is that the popular sovereign presents a standing question to itself: Who are "We the people"? To this question, various answers can be given, including those characteristic of "populism," as this is commonly understood today. Indeed, populism is, at its most basic, simply the claim to speak on behalf of *the people*. Because democracy requires a "we," there is a sense in which populism is unavoidable: every democratic system presupposes, and must occasionally attempt to articulate and reaffirm, certain boundaries. For the reasons just noted, however, no answer to this question can itself be authorized democratically. Consequently, the most basic political question in a democracy—the question on which all other political questions turn—is a question democracy cannot easily answer: the question of who belongs to the popular sovereign.

A Political Theology of "The People"

In times of perceived crisis, when sovereignty is taken to be under threat, there may be significant pressure to shore up "the people"—to harden its boundaries and anchor it in something immutable—and this demand is met, if never actually satisfied, by answers that attempt to break the strange loop of self-authorization. Indeed, such a move can be detected in the Declaration of Independence, which begins by averring self-evident truths and concludes its performance of self-authorship by "appealing to the Supreme Judge of the world for the rectitude of our intentions." In this way, Derrida argues, the signers present themselves as cosigners:

> It is still "in the name of" that the "good people" of America call themselves and declare themselves independent, at the instant in which they invent (for) themselves a signing identity. They sign in the name of the laws of nature and in the name of God. They pose or posit their institutional laws on the foundation of natural laws and by the same coup (the interpretive coup of force) in the name of God, creator of nature. He comes, in effect, to guarantee the rectitude of popular intentions, the unity and goodness of the people.[30]

On Derrida's reading, these invocations of self-evidence, of "the Laws of Nature and of Nature's God," represent the founders' attempts, however oblique, to escape the vicious circle of self-authorization by anchoring the legitimacy of the new polity in something constative rather than performative, something stable, "given," and enduring. As Derrida puts it, "for this Declaration to have a meaning and an effect, there must be a last instance. God is the name, the best one, for this last instance and this ultimate signature."[31]

"God" is here Derrida's term of art for whatever is said to arrest the performative regress inherent in constituting a *demos*—to fund the promises on which, according to Locke, social contracting depends—be it Providence, Nature, History, Race, *Volk*, *Heimat*, or any of the other putative constatives that have lent an aura of necessity and immutability to contingent political arrangements. It is in this context that I propose to understand talk of "Christianity" and "Islam," but it is important to stress that theological language need not be couched in terms of "religion." *Race*, for instance, functions theologically when it acts as a "god" in Derrida's sense, providentially securing the borders of the community. So understood, theological language is not simply an ad hoc criterion for distinguishing an in-group from an out-group (even if it performs that function indirectly). Rather, its significance lies in its promise to break free of the vicious cycle of self-authorization by positing a prior authority, constative rather than performative, on which a community of "good people"—one nation *under God*—is imagined to depend.

Because "the people" cannot, without circularity, answer the question of its own definition, it seeks a source beyond itself, which it can find only in a will imagined as independent of, but willing, *this precise people*. When asked to account for itself, popular sovereignty is forced back onto divine sovereignty. The people elect their leaders, but God elects *the people*. The God of "civil religion" is not, as sometimes thought, a metaphorical deity, only tenuously connected to historical piety. Rather, it is at the heart of what we have learned to call "religion." Indeed, by calling it "religion," and imagining it as something self-contained, we manage conveniently to forget that secular democracy is itself indebted to the work of gods. These various (seemingly) extrasystemic "guarantees" serve to conceal and/or justify the violence required to institute and maintain the polity and to reify the distinction between insiders and outsiders.

Arendt found it ironic that the ostensibly secular founders of the United States appealed to God in moments of exception: "What saved the American Revolution was neither 'nature's God' nor self-evident truth, but the act of foundation itself."[32] But it is significant that such appeals have never disappeared from the national conversation. What Robert Bellah famously called "American civil religion" is an archive of repeated efforts aimed at tying off the question of popular sovereignty, but the very ubiquity of these expressions—indeed, their ritualized, liturgical structure—suggests that the question has never finally been laid to rest and in fact constitutes a kind of ever-receding horizon of American political life.[33]

The German Alternative

All ostensibly democratic nation-states depend on extrademocratic accounts of the *demos*, but the situation in the United States is, of course, different in a number of important ways from that in Europe. Indeed, it is not entirely clear what the appropriate units of comparison should be: Ought the United States be compared to one or another European country, such as Germany or the Netherlands? Or ought it be compared with "Europe" or the EU? This question is further complicated by the fact that "Europe" is itself an ambivalent concept in some of these same discourses—naming, on the one hand, a civilizational identity imagined to be shared by people from various nations, and, on the other hand, an administrative apparatus, run by "Eurocrats" in Brussels, viewed as posing a threat to national sovereignty and permitting the migratory flows said to dilute and pollute

Europe's civilizational identity.[34] For example, the 2017 manifesto of the AfD, at the time of my writing Germany's largest opposition party, decries "the relinquishing of national sovereignty to the EU."[35]

This ambivalence is related to the double threat noted earlier: identity and sovereignty are imagined to be under attack from both above/within and below/without. The AfD manifesto presents the party as engaged in a struggle for German sovereignty, which draws inspiration from revolutionary sources: "The recollection of the two revolutions of 1848 and 1989 drive our civil protest and the determination to complete our national unity in freedom, and create a Europe of sovereign and democratic nation states, united in peace, self-determination and good-neighbourliness."[36] This vision of Europe—a Europe of "sovereign, but loosely connected nation states"—is threatened, from above, by transnational institutions: "At the latest since the Schengen (1985), Maastricht (1992) and Lisbon (2007) Treaties, the inviolability of national sovereignty as the foundation of our state has been exposed as a fiction."[37] Having been deprived of the ability to control their borders and limit free movement, these nation-states are, moreover, threatened by migration, particularly by Muslims. Reclaiming political sovereignty is thus a project with an explicitly religious, and racialized, dimension.

"Europe" is popularly imagined to be more "secular" than the United States, but it is notable that discourses about religion remain prominent in both contexts, even if they differ in interesting ways. Earlier I distinguished between movements in which the "good people" are seen as having true faith, and as in conflict with those who lack it, and conceptions of the people that treat Christianity more as an historical source or reservoir of civic identity. Movements of the first type can themselves take more than one form, ranging from "moral majority"-style campaigns to Christianize the state, such as that pioneered by Jerry Falwell Sr., on the one hand, to minority-rights approaches that represent Christianity as a beleaguered identity in need of special protections, on the other. Often these two strategies coexist uneasily and alternate depending on the context. In the United States, for example, conservative Christian groups have been influential both in securing religious exemptions in the courts and in influencing the nomination and appointment of judges. What both strategies have in common is a conception of the state as at least potentially *in competition with* Christianity. Such efforts are commonly represented as attempting to push back against secularity—whether by evangelizing the public sphere or by carving out protected spaces within it—but they are also entangled in its technologies. In the process of attempting to shore up Christian identity, influence, and privilege, Christianity comes to be treated as a "religion"—in competition with other religions, such as "Islam," and with the nonreligious, secular world. It names, on this construal, an identity in a multicultural market and, like the identities with which it finds itself in competition, is viewed as deserving of rights-based protections.[38] In this way, the rhetoric of minority rights is appropriated in defense of comparatively privileged identities.

The use of rights claims to defend the very identities whose hegemony such claims are often conceived of as guarding against is of course not unique to religion. Another obvious example is provided by the White identity politics with which Christian identity politics is in many cases intertwined (and from which it is sometimes indistinguishable). Indeed, it might be argued that rights claims—in their formality and indifference to normative questions about the good—lend themselves to precisely this sort of reciprocal, lateral deployment. The appropriation of the rhetoric of religious rights, however, presents an especially interesting set of quandaries, because "religion" is a secular category. I lack the space to explore this here, but I have argued elsewhere that secularity is best conceived not as the inverse of religion but as an *episteme*, an ensemble of dispositions, affects, and ethical intuitions that structure knowledge.[39] Within the secular episteme, religion comes into view as a limited and discrete domain, an object variously of interest, anxiety, regulation, and academic study. The ambivalence of appropriating religious freedom has recently been explored in relation to minority, Indigenous, and nonwestern groups, which often find themselves obliged to submit (or adapt) to the Procrustean contours of Protestant Christianity.[40] But "religion" can sometimes be an awkward fit for Protestant majorities. Historically, American evangelicals have often rejected the claim that Christianity is a religion—both because twentieth-century dialectical theologians had tended to view "religion" as an anthropological phenomenon and because of an unwillingness to accept for Christianity the relativized status of one "option" among others in a secular, pluralist framework. Insofar as they appropriate the concept of religion and the discourse of religious freedom, contemporary evangelicals in the United States find themselves on a secular playing field, struggling to repackage emic understandings in deflationary secular categories. Moreover, by petitioning the state for legal relief, they defer to its authority: sovereign is that which grants the exemptions.

The second type of movement alluded to a moment ago starts from a conception of Christianity as identity, but here the identity is not individual or characteristic of an internal minority but national or civilizational: Christianity is conceived as a cultural marker, and the competition is not so much with other identities in a pluralist society but with other societies or civilizations.[41] Instead of presupposing a multicultural milieu, within which Christianity is seen as a besieged minority, movements of this latter type reject multiculturalism altogether. A distinctive feature of this constellation of movements is that secularity tends to be embraced as consistent with Christianity, rather than being viewed as in competition with it. According to its manifesto: "The AfD is committed to German as the predominant culture (*Leitkultur*). This culture is derived from three sources: firstly, the religious traditions of Christianity; secondly, the scientific and humanistic heritage, whose ancient roots were renewed during the period of Renaissance and the Age of Enlightenment; and thirdly, Roman law, upon which our constitutional state is founded."[42] Whereas right-wing American evangelicals such as Falwell Sr. tend to view Christianity as under threat from the "scientific and humanistic heritage" of the Enlightenment, the AfD sees these "sources" as compatible and mutually reinforcing.

Are the latter appeals to Christianity sincerely *religious* or merely strategic? As Marzouki and McDonnell note, so-called right-wing populists in Europe often come into conflict with established churches, whose leaders they tend to perceive as "elites" in a pejorative sense.[43] For example, the AfD has been sharply criticized by representatives of both the Protestant and Catholic state churches in Germany, who have accused it of perverting Christianity. It is consequently tempting to view populist appeals to Christianity as entirely negative. As Olivier Roy puts it, "The European right advocates a Christian identity for Europe not because it wants to promote Christianity, but because it wants to fight Islam and the increased presence within European societies of Muslims."[44] However, these tensions are, I argue, better interpreted as a theological contest for control of the meaning of Christianity itself. To be sure, the Christianity the AfD seeks to promote is not identical to that of Catholic and Lutheran clergy, but since the views of "elites" are part of what is in dispute, the latter cannot be treated as authoritative without begging the question.

Although viewed from a largely secular standpoint, Christianity continues to be treated by right-wing critics of the German church leadership as a source of authority with a normative status altogether different from that assigned to Islam. Concealed within the appeal to identity is a claim to truth, which is revealed when it is perceived to come into conflict with rival claims to political authority or "true religion," on the part both of church elites and of Muslims. For the AfD, assertions of Germany's so-called Christian heritage are simultaneously assertions of national sovereignty: a "sovereign Germany" requires the subordination of claims to religious authority outside the scope of Christianity.[45] Thus, though it makes no corresponding claim about *Christian* theologians in German universities, the AfD manifesto insists that "theological chairs for Islam studies at German universities are to be abolished and the positions transferred to the faculty of non-denominational religious studies."[46] That is to say, Christian theology may continue to be taught in public universities, but Islam can only be taught *about*.

Islam, on this account, is incompatible with German nationhood not simply because it represents a cultural "other," but because it is perceived as making a claim to sovereignty at the same level as—and potentially rivaling—the claim made by the German state. According to the manifesto, "An Islam which neither respects nor refrains from being in conflict with our legal system, or that even lays claims to power as the only true religion, is incompatible with our legal system and our culture."[47] Thus, Islam is sometimes portrayed not as a "religion" at all, but as a political movement. For example, in 2016, Alexander Gauland, then floor leader for the AfD in the Brandenburg state parliament and deputy party leader (and currently the AfD leader in the Bundestag), was quoted in the *Frankfurter Allgemeine* as saying, "Islam is not a religion like Catholic or Protestant Christianity but is rather always associated intellectually with the take-over of the state. For this reason, the Islamicization of Germany is a threat."[48] Naomi Goldenberg has argued that *religions* can best be understood as vestigial *states*, sovereignties defeated and limited—at least for now—by the dominant governing order: "They are 'once and future' governments, alternative ruling orders, governments in waiting."[49] Allowed their own modest sphere of influence, religions are simultaneously circumscribed and contained. One might accordingly detect in the claim that Islam is "not a religion" political-theological anxieties about a sovereignty that is perceived as not yet having capitulated to the authority of a nation-state that has long since co-opted its established churches as a constituent feature of its self-understanding as secular. Germany is secular *because* it is Christian, and for this reason "Islam does not belong to Germany."[50] Because secular Christian Europe is tolerant, it cannot tolerate Islam. According to this understanding, "Islam" is seen to posit an as-of-yet-unconquered god and thus to mobilize a different configuration of the people. It is not yet a "religion," in the sense of a having been brought within the sovereign power of the state. Its god is as yet sovereign, and thus threatening.

By contrast, Christianity is permissible not because it is nonpolitical per se (a defeated opponent that can now be graciously tolerated), but, on the contrary, because it is regarded as a submerged source of the state's political authority. It appears nonpolitical only because its politics are imagined to align with the political structure of the state, as both are idealized by the AfD. Unlike in the case of "moral majority" evangelicals in the United States, there is no need to wrest control of the state from secularists, because Christianity and secularity are not viewed as rivals.[51]

"Religion" as a Secular Category

Elizabeth Shakman Hurd has distinguished two forms of secularity—laicism and what she calls "Judeo-Christian secularism." Where the former advocates for strict separation between religion and politics, the latter "emphasizes the role of Christianity, and more recently Judeo-Christianity, as the foundation for secular public order and democratic political institutions."[52] The AfD manifesto situates itself within the tradition of Judeo-Christian secularism, even using the construct "Judeo-Christian," without apparent irony, to describe Germany's cultural heritage.[53] The erosion of Christian identity is troubling, on this view, because it signals the erosion of state sovereignty.

The question of how to characterize American movements like that of the since-disgraced Jerry Falwell Jr. is more complicated. Although U.S. courts take a broadly accommodationist approach to religion, in contrast with French-style *laïcité*, Falwell and figures on the evangelical right would appear to regard the state with considerable ambivalence and suspicion. Even in touting the ostensibly Christian foundations of the United States, they tend to view the state as having fallen from grace (needing to be redeemed or "made great *again*") and thus as at least potentially hostile to Christianity: the state belongs to *the world*. Unlike in the case of the AfD, Christianity is not viewed as coterminous with secularity. Indeed, the two are seen as in zero-sum competition. Whether hoping eventually to (re-)Christianize the state via a moral majority or (in the meantime) to claim religious exemptions from its sovereign authority, they take for granted a *conceptual* separation of church and state.

But by adopting a secular, broadly liberal *descriptive* account of their relation to the state, these movements find themselves entangled, paradoxically, in the secular episteme they claim to reject. Indeed, the very idea that the United States has abandoned its "Christian heritage"—if such a thing ever existed—seems to read history through the lens of a secular, liberal set of categories, treating whatever changes have occurred primarily as demographic and not conceptual, that is, as though the interesting differences between a supposedly Christian past and an ostensibly secular present were the extent and political influence of the group of people for whom Christianity is a *religious identity*, when in fact this whole idea of a Christian identity as one among others internal to American life only makes sense from a contemporary pluralist vantage point. It is precisely this conception of "religion" (and of Christianity *as religion*)—and not religion's supposedly having lost ground—that is, I would argue, the defining element of the secular.

This latter idea of Christianity as identity is also central to the discourse of right-wing European "populist" movements, including the AfD, but here it tends to be deployed differently, not as in competition with the state but as its basis. Thus, where right-wing evangelicals in the United States imagine themselves to be fighting a two-front battle against secularity and Islam, groups such as the AfD seem to see Christianity and secularity not as antagonists but as coterminous, or as parent and child. Indeed, the problem with Islam, on this view, is not that it is a religion but that it is a *politics*. The quarrel for European populists is not with secularists, but with church elites over the meaning of Christianity.[54] The latter might naturally view this as a matter of Christianity having been perverted or "hijacked," but I have suggested that that characterization is, from a descriptive standpoint, tendentious.

The deployments of religion I have attempted to briefly describe here are characteristically secular, but they cannot for that reason be dismissed as instances of religion being manipulated for independent political purposes. On the contrary, "religion" is a secular category, inextricably implicated in the theo-politics of modernity. In response to anxieties about sovereignty, claims to truth are repackaged as claims to identity, while claims to religious identity can give expression to claims to political truth. How one thinks about religion will depend on how one conceives of the people, and vice versa.

Conclusion: Performing Differently

I noted earlier that the paradox of popular sovereignty—the performativity involved in appeals to "the people"—generates a demand for constatives, for extrademocratic "guarantees." These givens, which Derrida calls "gods," are imagined to ground the performance from somewhere outside it. Appeals to God, however, are themselves *part of* the performance, and so cannot finally break the strange loop of self-authorization. Consider, for instance, the opening words of the Declaration of Independence: "We hold these truths to be self-evident." As Arendt famously observed, self-evident truths do not *need* to be stated. That Jefferson begins the sentence with "We hold" suggests that it is the *holding*, rather than the purported self-evidence, that is doing the work. We the people depend upon gods, but the gods are of our own imagining. We make the gods that make "the people." Sylvia Wynter captures this dialectic:

> As humans, *we cannot/do not preexist our cosmogonies*, our representations of our origins—even though it is we ourselves who invent those cosmogonies and then retroactively project them onto a past. We invent them in formulaic storytelling terms, as "donor figures" or "entities," who have *extrahumanly* (supernaturally, but now also *naturally* and/or bioevolutionarily, therefore secularly) *mandated* what the structuring societal order of our genre-specific, eusocial or cultural *present* would have to be.[55] (emphasis original)

The gods of civil religion are reverse engineered to ordain and underwrite the prevailing social order, and they are, by design, jealous, territorial deities: under God, one nation. Hence the violence with which Jerry Falwell Jr. pits "good people" against "those Muslims." But because these gods are of our own making—because their authority is identical to that of the ostensible community they are invoked to justify—they cannot finally satisfy the demand for justification without begging the question.

Sovereignty is a theological category, and as long as there are states, there will be gods. But the gods can be imagined in new ways, and "the people" performed differently. The same performativity that creates the demand for constatives holds open the possibility of alternative, more expansive conceptions of peoplehood, other "populisms," some of which exist already and others that await imagining, as counterperformances of theopopular sovereignty.

NOTES

1. Sarah Pulliam Bailey, "Jerry Falwell Jr.: 'If More Good People Had Concealed-Carry Permits, Then We Could End Those' Islamist Terrorists," *Washington Post*, December 5, 2015, https://www.washingtonpost.com/news/acts-of-faith/wp/2015/12/05/liberty-university-president-if-more-good-people-had-concealed-guns-we-could-end-those-muslims/?noredirect=on.

2. I say "seemingly," because—for reasons I hope to explain—I see no obvious contradiction here. Falwell Jr. was a staunch supporter of Trump's presidency. See Jessica Martínez and Gregory A. Smith, "How the Faithful Voted: A Preliminary 2016 Analysis," *Pew Research Center*, November 9, 2016, https://www.pewresearch.org/fact-tank/2016/11/09/how-the-faithful-voted-a-preliminary-2016-analysis/; "Analysis Exit Polls 2020," *NBC News*, https://www.nbcnews.com/politics/2020-elections/exit-polls.

3. A recent study from the UK found that whereas around three-quarters of participants said they were comfortable with a close relative marrying an Asian or Black partner, fewer than half said they were comfortable with a close relative marrying a Muslim. See Julian Hargreaves et al., "How We Get Along: The Diversity Study of England and Wales 2020: Executive Summary," Woolf Institute, 10, https://www.woolf.cam.ac.uk/research/projects/diversity.

4. Nadia Marzouki and Duncan McDonnell, "Populism and Religion," in *Saving the People: How Populists Hijack Religion*, ed. Nadia Marzouki, Duncan McDonnell, and Oliver Roy (New York: Oxford University Press, 2016), 1–11, at 2.

5. Rogers Brubaker, "Between Nationalism and Civilizationism: The European Populist Moment in Comparative Perspective," *Ethnic and Racial Studies* 40, no. 8 (2017): 1191–1226, at 1199.

6. A similar claim is made by Wolfgang Palaver, who claims that "populists hijack religion but are often more interested in belonging than believing"; see Palaver, "Fraternity versus Parochialism: On Religion and Populism," *Religions* 11, no. 7 (2020): 1–13.

7. Gorski and Springs both explore this in detail in their respective chapters. The current heightening of otherizing discourses continues despite—or rather because of—demographic changes and shifts in mores that threaten various forms of entrenched privilege.

8. Michel Foucault, *The Birth of Biopolitics: Lectures at the Collège de France 1978–1979*, ed. M. Senellart, trans. G. Burchell (New York: Palgrave Macmillan, 2008), 3.

9. Ibid., 2–3.

10. Richard Amesbury, "Secularity, Religion, and the Spatialization of Time," *Journal of the American Academy of Religion* 86, no. 3 (2018): 591–615; and Amesbury, "Expanding 'Religion' or Decentering the Secular? Framing the Frames in Philosophy of Religion," *Religious Studies* 56, no. 1 (2020): 4–19.

11. W. E. B. Du Bois, *Darkwater: Voices from within the Veil* (Mineola, NY: Dover, 1999), 18.

12. Vincent W. Lloyd, "Introduction: Managing Race, Managing Religion," in *Race and Secularism in America*, ed. Jonathon S. Kahn and Vincent W. Lloyd (New York: Columbia University Press, 2016), 1–19, at 5.

13. For a historical overview and critique of the term "populism," see Anton Jäger, "The Myth of Populism," *Jacobin*, January 3, 2018, https://www.jacobinmag.com/2018/01/populism-douglas-hofstadter-donald-trump-democracy.

14. Claims to identity, on the other hand, can more easily be accommodated by elite pluralist frameworks.

15. Referring to English evangelicals, Méadhbh McIvor writes, "Evangelicals frequently reject the language of 'religion' as regards their own beliefs and practices, preferring to view Christianity as a *relationship with God*, something fundamentally different (in their eyes) from the kinds of creeds and ritual systems typically labelled 'religious.' In this sense, to rely on the right to freedom of religion as a Christian is to relativize one's faith, accepting that it is merely one religious option among others. But in England—with its 'Christian heritage' and established church—it is also to sift Christian values out from the national fabric, portraying the moral norms that evangelicals believe to have *universal* application as the *particular* interests of a minority group. In other words, challenges to the liberal consensus on religion—the idea that it ought to be accommodated so long

as it is spatially interior, a phenomenon largely reducible to claims of conscience—can shore up its power even as they reveal its potentially oppressive force"; see Méadhbh McIvor, *Representing God: Christian Legal Activism in Contemporary England* (Princeton, NJ: Princeton University Press, 2020), 14–15 (emphasis original).

16. For sustained examination of American evangelical movements, see the contributions to this volume by Gorski (chapter 1) and Springs (chapter 2).

17. Douglas R. Hofstadter, *I Am a Strange Loop* (New York: Basic Books, 2007), 101–2.

18. Jacques Derrida, "Declarations of Independence," in *Deconstruction: Critical Concepts in Literary and Cultural Studies*, ed. Jonathan Culler (New York: Routledge, 2003), 4:24–31, at 27.

19. Juliana Barr, "Borders and Borderlands," in *Why You Can't Teach United States History without American Indians*, ed. Susan Sleeper-Smith, Juliana Barr, Jean M. O'Brien, Nancy Shoemaker, and Scott Manning Stevens (Chapel Hill: University of North Carolina Press, 2015), 9–25, at 9.

20. It is significant that the pro-gun, anti-Muslim rhetoric of Jerry Falwell Jr. with which I began was also directed against Barack Obama, whose credentials as a "Christian" were routinely impugned by White evangelicals on the right. "Black" and "Muslim" functioned synonymously to suggest that *Barack Hussein Obama* was not, and indeed *could not be*, part of the American people. What lay behind the rhetoric of the "birther" movement on which Donald Trump rose to political prominence was the conviction that Obama was *ontologically* incapable of representing the popular sovereign. I am indebted on this point to insightful feedback from J. Kameron Carter and Gil Anidjar.

21. Langston Hughes, "Let America Be America Again," in *The Collected Poems of Langston Hughes*, ed. Arnold Rampersad (New York: Vintage, 1994), 189.

22. Derrida, "Declarations of Independence," 27.

23. See ibid., 25.

24. Anything resembling an actual "global democracy" or "world governance" would arguably produce exclusions of its own, e.g., of those deemed incompetent, underage, nonhuman, etc.

25. Talal Asad, "Reflections on the Origins of Human Rights," lecture at Berkley Center, Georgetown University, September 28, 2009.

26. Most recently associated with Trump, this phrase has a much longer history, with variants being used by Barry Goldwater, Ronald Reagan, and Bill Clinton, among others. A more ambivalent variation on the theme is found in Hughes's "Let America Be America Again."

27. Hannah Arendt, *The Origins of Totalitarianism* (New York: Harcourt, 1966), 296.

28. This is one reason voting is an inadequate tool for effecting structural change.

29. Writing in the conservative journal *American Affairs*, R. R. Reno asks, "Who is a member of the polis, and thus entitled to have a say in its future? This would seem to be a fundamental political question, if not the fundamental question. It was a crucial issue in the democratic era, defining nineteenth- and twentieth-century struggles against imperial domination and for the popular franchise. Now, however, we are increasingly told that we cannot decide, as a nation, who can migrate and immigrate"; see Reno, "Negative Piety," *American Affairs* 1, no. 3 (2017), https://americanaffairsjournal.org/2017/08/negative-piety/.

30. Derrida, "Declarations of Independence," 28.

31. Ibid., 28–29. In *On Revolution*, Arendt raises this same issue in terms borrowed from Rousseau: "'The great problem in politics, which I compare to the problem of squaring the circle in geometry . . . [is]: How to find a form of government which puts the law above man.' Theoretically, Rousseau's problem closely resembles Sieyes's vicious circle: those who get together to constitute a new government are themselves unconstitutional, that is, they have no authority to do what they have set out to achieve. The vicious circle in legislating is present not in ordinary lawmaking, but in laying down the fundamental law, the law of the land or the constitution which, from then on, is supposed to incarnate the "higher law" from which all laws ultimately derive their authority. And with this problem, which appeared as the urgent need for some absolute, the men of the American Revolution found themselves no less confronted than their colleagues in France. The trouble was—to quote Rousseau once more—that to put the law above man and thus to establish the validity of man-made laws, il faudrait des dieux, 'one actually would need gods'"; see Hannah Arendt, *On Revolution* (New York: Penguin, 1963), 183–84. For an insightful comparison and analysis of Arendt and Derrida on the Declaration of Independence, see Bonnie Honig, "Declarations of Independence: Arendt and Derrida on the Problem of Founding a Republic," *American Political Science Review* 85, no. 1 (1991): 97–113.

32. Arendt, *On Revolution*, 188.

33. Robert N. Bellah, "Civil Religion in America," *Daedalus*, 96, no. 1 (1967): 1–21.

34. See, e.g., the 2017 document, drafted by European conservative thinkers, titled "A Europe We Can Believe In." Dubbed "The Paris Statement," it distinguishes a "true Europe" from a "false Europe," which is said to be "utopian and tyrannical." According to the document, "The true Europe is a community of nations. We have our own languages, traditions and borders. Yet we have always recognized a kinship with one another, even when we have been at odds—or at war"; see A Europe We Can Believe In, "The Paris Statement: A Europe We Can Believe In," https://thetrueeurope.eu/a-europe-we-can-believe-in/. That Europe is conceived as something to be "believed in"—an article of faith—is telling.

35. Alternative für Deutschland [AfD], *Manifesto for Germany: The Political Programme of the Alternative for Germany* (2017), 8, https://www.afd.de/wp-content/uploads/sites/111/2017/04/2017-04-12_afd-grundsatzprogramm-englisch_web.pdf. It adds: "We oppose the idea to transform the European Union into a centralized federal state. We are in favour of returning the European Union to an economic union based on shared interests, and consisting of sovereign, but loosely connected nation states" (15). That the manifesto, which stresses "the German language as focal point of our identity," is available on the party's website in six languages attests to the international circulation of nationalist discourses—a phenomenon abetted by what, paraphrasing Benedict Anderson, might be termed *digital capitalism*. See Benedict Anderson, *Imagined Communities: Reflections on the Origin and Spread of Nationalism* (London: Verso, 1983).

36. AfD, *Manifesto for Germany*, 5.

37. Ibid., 7.

38. For an illuminating discussion of these tensions in the UK, see McIvor, *Representing God*.

39. See, e.g., Amesbury, "Secularity, Religion, and the Spatialization of Time."

40. See, inter alia, Tisa Wenger, *We Have a Religion: The 1920s Pueblo Indian Dance Controversy and American Religious Freedom* (Chapel Hill: University of North Carolina Press, 2009); Tisa Wenger, *Religious Freedom: The Contested History of an American Ideal* (Chapel Hill: University of North Carolina Press, 2017); Anna Su, *Exporting Freedom: Religious Liberty and American Power* (Cambridge, MA: Harvard University Press, 2016); and Winnifred Fallers Sullivan, *The Impossibility of Religious Freedom*, new ed. (Princeton, NJ: Princeton University Press, 2018).

41. Brubaker calls this "civilizationist" populism. The cluster of civilizationist movements he discusses does not include the AfD, which, writing in 2017, he viewed as too internally divided to confidently label. See Brubaker, "Between Nationalism and Civilizationism," 1193.

42. AfD, *Manifesto for Germany*, 46.

43. Marzouki and McDonnell, "Populism and Religion," 8.

44. Olivier Roy, "Beyond Populism: The Conservative Right, the Courts, the Churches and the Concept of a Christian Europe," in Marzouki, McDonnell, and Roy, eds., *Saving the People*, 197. In a similar vein, Brubaker writes, "Crudely put, if 'they' are Muslim, then 'we' must, in some sense, be Christian. But that does not mean that 'we' must be religious" (Brubaker, "Between Nationalism and Civilizationism," 1199).

45. See AfD, *Manifesto for Germany*, 5. Zubrzycki in her chapter herein shows how a similar rhetoric of heritage is used by conservative Catholics in Poland to demarcate national boundaries.

46. Ibid., 49.

47. Ibid., 48.

48. Von Storch, "Islam nicht mit Grundgesetz vereinbar," *Frankfurter Allgemeine*, April 17, 2016, http://www.faz.net/aktuell/politik/inland/von-storch-islam-nicht-mit-grundgesetz-vereinbar-14182472.html (translation mine).

49. Naomi Goldenberg, "Religion and Its Limits," *Journal of the British Association for the Study of Religion* 21 (December 2019): 1–15, at 4.

50. AfD, *Manifesto for Germany*, 48.

51. It is worth noting, however, that in response to criticism from church leaders, the AfD has emphasized the separation of church and state and the freedom of Christian conscience. See AfD-Fraktion im Landtag Rheinland-Pfalz, *Kirchenpolitisches Manifest*, September 7, 2017, http://www.afd-rlp-fraktion.de/kommentare/kirchenpolitisches-manifest.

52. Elizabeth Shakman Hurd, *The Politics of Secularism in International Relations* (Princeton, NJ: Princeton University Press, 2008), 5.

53. AfD, *Manifesto for Germany*, 47. It is significant that discourse about Jews also circulates within right-wing movements in both the United States and Germany (among other countries) and intersects with language about Muslims and Christians in complex ways. A full treatment of this topic exceeds the scope of this chapter, but two features of this discourse can be noted briefly. First, whereas Muslims tend to be presented as a threat from outside or below, when Jews are represented as a threat, they tend to be framed as a threat from above, i.e., as an "elite" threat to "the people." And second, it is important to note that antisemitism coexists alongside philosemitism, and that the latter provides cover for anti-Islamicism. Antipathy to Muslims is thus justified on the basis of the claim that Islam is anti-Jewish, or that Muslims are hostile to Israel. Through the invention of a "Judeo-Christian tradition" to which Islam is said to be antagonistic, Muslims are made the scapegoat for a long history of Christian and European antisemitism. This second feature of discourse about Jews and Muslims is not unique to the right-wing movements discussed in this chapter. For further discussion of the ideological uses of alleged Jewish–Muslim enmity, see, e.g., Gil Anidjar, *Blood: A Critique of Christianity* (New York: Columbia University Press, 2014); and Santiago Slabodsky, *Decolonial Judaism: Triumphal Failures of Barbaric Thinking* (New York: Palgrave Macmillan, 2014). For a detailed exploration of philosemitism in Poland, see Zubrzycki's contribution to this volume (chapter 5).

54. Zubrzycki notes a similar hostility among some conservative Catholic Poles toward liberal Polish bishops and even John Paul II, who are pejoratively framed as "Jewish," in a logic, which, following Adam Michnik, she terms "magical antisemitism."

55. Sylvia Wynter and Katherine McKittrick, "Unparalleled Catastrophe for Our Species? Or, to Give Humanness a Different Future: Conversations," in *On Being Human as Praxis*, ed. Katherine McKittrick (Durham, NC: Duke University Press, 2015), 9–89, at 36.

CHAPTER 5

Anti/Philosemitism, Religion, and the Logic of Ethnic Nationalism in Poland

GENEVIÈVE ZUBRZYCKI

ABSTRACT

National identity in Poland is understood primarily in ethnic terms and is tightly associated with Catholicism. Poles proposing a secu-lar definition of national identity, and associated with socialism and cosmopolitanism, are discursively othered as "Jews" by figures on the political right. If that ethnicization of ideological otherness functions as a form of "antisemitism without Jews," it also facilitates philosemitisms, that is, the promotion of Jewishness as an alternative secular, civic, multicultural vision of the national polity. These contrasting invocations of Jewishness illustrate how symbolic categories can function in the construction of both exclusive ethnoreligious nationhood and inclusive secular alternatives. However, as this chapter demonstrates, philosemitism preserves many of the same inner logics as antisemitism. By formulating ostensibly progressive alternatives as inversions of the antisemitism of ethno-Catholic Polish nationalism, philosemitism still tacitly accepts the former's discursive positioning of Jews as the traditional Other of Polish society, perpetuating forms of symbolic

> violence even while seeking to expand the symbolic boundaries of
> Polish nationalism.

What Poland "should be" has been at the center of political debates since the fall of communism. That battle is fiercer now than ever, as Polish society has become even more polarized with the rise of populism in recent years. One section of Polish society favors the nationalist vision represented by the Law and Justice Party and the hierarchy of the Catholic Church. In their vision, the identity of Poles should be crystallized around Catholicism, conservative values, and a national narrative articulated around Polish martyrdom and heroism.[1] The other supports Poland's membership in the European Union (EU), espouses progressive civic values and secularism, and is engaged in significant soul-searching about the participation of Poles in violent crimes against Jews during and after World War II. In both camps, the figure of the Jew plays a prominent role, portrayed as a threat to the nation for some, and as a quasi-savior for the other. How can we make sense of these seemingly contradictory phenomena: right-wing populism and antisemitism, on the one hand, and Polish liberalism and philosemitism, on the other?[2] And what is the meaning of antisemitism and philosemitism in a society with very few Jews?[3] One might be tempted to see Polish liberalism as a reaction, or opposition, to right-wing populism. In this chapter, however, I show that both are related to the logic of Polish ethnic nationalism whereby Catholicism is folded into ethnonationality and into the specific demographic features of late-modern Poland.[4]

As we know from a rich literature on nationalism,[5] ideological forms of exclusion are typical of places where the nation is understood in civic terms, and where therefore one's national identity, at least ideally, is determined by adherence to the principles of the social contract, whatever its terms may be. Consider the case of the United States, where "being" American implies the support of a specific set of values and practices, and therefore where it is possible to be considered "un-American" because of political beliefs. This was the case during the "red scare" and McCarthyism in the 1950s, when those suspected of supporting communism were accused of being un-American and as a result suffered discrimination of varying degrees. The trope of un-Americanness resurfaced after September 11, 2001, to characterize critics of the Bush administration, or more recently to delegitimize "Obamacare" or those embracing "democratic socialism."[6]

Nations imagined in the ethnic mode emphasize instead common descent, language, and cultural traits, such as religion, passed on to individuals through birth. Since national identity "flows through one's veins," inclusion in the national community is primarily determined by one's ethnic or racial origins. The national community is essentialized to the extent that identity cannot be chosen, acquired, or escaped. Exclusion on the basis of one's politics or ideological leanings therefore ill befits places where the nation is primarily understood in ethnic terms. And yet, the Catholic Right in Poland routinely excludes ethnic Poles from the imagined boundaries of the nation because of their ideological leaning, political identities, religious affiliation, or sexual orientation.[7]

How is the tension between these two modes of boundary-keeping, one based on blood and culture, the other based on ideological orientations and political bonds, reconciled? How is that paradox resolved?

MAGICAL ANTISEMITISM AND THE ETHNICIZATION OF IDEOLOGICAL OTHERNESS

In Poland, that tension is primarily solved through the ethnicization of ideological divergence: deviance from normative ethno-Catholic Polishness is ethnicized in such a way that individuals and groups that are not defending the prominent place of Catholicism and its symbols in the public sphere, and are advocating instead for a civic and secular Poland, are discursively turned into "Jews" by the Far Right. That process makes ideologically based exclusion conform with the logic of ethnic nationalism. But why Jews? One key reason is that Jewishness is perceived as the opposite ethnoreligious category of the *Polak-katolik*. According to Sergiusz Kowalski and Magdalena Tulli, the invention of Jews in right-wing milieus is a response to their ideological creation of "imaginary Poles."[8] Imaginary Poles embody the "true" qualities and values of Polishness, namely, Catholicism, patriotism, traditionalism, and economic conservatism. As this ideal Pole is rarely matched by actual persons, right-leaning social actors suffer from a cognitive dissonance that they solve by spinning conspiracy theories of Jews infiltrating the nation. (I return to the racist trope of "passing" later in the chapter.) Another reason is that Jews are traditionally associated, in Polish society, with both capitalism and socialism, and with cosmopolitanism.[9]

The ethnicization of deviation from an idealized national self is thus at the source of Poland's "antisemitism without Jews." Jean-Paul Sartre famously claimed that "if the Jew did not exist, the anti-Semite would invent him."[10] For Enzo Traverso,[11] one can be Jewish merely by virtue of the Antisemite's gaze. Former political dissident and Solidarity activist Adam Michnik, now editor in chief of Poland's most important daily, *Gazeta Wyborcza*, calls this specific form of antisemitism "magical antisemitism." He explains its workings: "The logic of normal . . . antisemitism is the following: 'Adam Michnik is a Jew, therefore he is a hooligan, a thief, a traitor, a bandit etc.' Magical antisemitism however works this way: 'Adam Michnik is a thief, therefore he is most probably a Jew.'"

The collage of figure 1 is a powerful example of such magical antisemitism. Formerly posted on a Far Right webpage, it is entitled "A Very Virtual Poland," implying that the Poland represented here by President Aleksander Kwaśniewski (1995–2005) is not the "real thing," nor what it should be. It depicts Kwaśniewski with his mouth covered with a photograph of Joseph Stalin. The president, the author of the collage thus implies, is a communist mouthpiece. Prominently displayed on the top-right corner of the image is the insignia of the Soviet NKVD, the organization that preceded the KGB and that was responsible for murdering 20,000 Polish officers during World War II. The cloth Star of David that Jews were forced to wear in Nazi-occupied Europe, on the top-left corner, suggests that Kwaśniewski is not only associated with violent communism but is also a Jew, replicating the long-standing trope of Judeo-communism.[12] The juxtaposition of the Star of David with the yellow stars of the EU flag, which Poland joined in 2004 under Kwaśniewski's leadership, visually alludes to a conspiracy theory commonly articulated in right-wing media, according to which the EU is part of a communist/Zionist plot to take over Poland.[13]

Another example of magical antisemitism found on the same website did not associate symbols of cosmopolitanism, communism, and Judaism with a single political figure and (leftist) political formation, but instead visually transformed various elites representing a wide range of political positions on both the left and right, into Orthodox Jews. The meme's author added kippas to some figures, and sidelocks, beards, and fur hats to others. The visual claim of the meme is that Poland is ruled by Jews, a claim clearly articulated also with the caption "List of Jews in Enslaved Poland." Some of the political figures depicted did have Jewish roots, but most did

Figure 1. Antisemitic photo collage presenting former president of Poland Aleksander Kwaśniewski as a Jew and communist agent, replicating the trope of *żydokomuna*. Source: http://bardzo-wirtualna-polska.abceblog.com/wp-content/uploads/sites/10/2013/08/zydzi-w-polsce.jpg.

not. And that is the point: it does not matter who actually is Jewish, but what Jewishness represents to the author of the cartoon.

These two shocking examples are representative of visual discourses commonly displayed on far-right social media, but that are too extreme to be found on mainstream right-wing forums.[14] Magical antisemitism and discourses articulated around *żydokomuna* are very much present in the public sphere, however, and commonplace in right-wing publications.[15] It is also commonplace on the airwaves of Radio Maryja, a popular radio station established in Toruń in 1991, which quickly expanded into a nationwide network that now includes a television station and local chapters of listeners forming "families" of supporters.[16] In those circles, for example, Poland's most popular daily, the progressive *Gazeta Wyborcza*, is nicknamed "Gazeta Koszerna," "the kosher newspaper." In the same vein, the personalist Catholic weekly *Tygodnik Powszechny*, with which John Paul II was associated before his papacy and which has long worked toward building Polish– and Christian–Jewish dialogue, is nicknamed "Żydownik powszechny" ("Universal Jewishy Weekly") by people on the Far Right.[17]

That process of turning opponents into "Jews" is so prevalent that some liberal Catholic bishops are accused by far-right supporters of being

Jewish. Even John Paul II, canonized in 2014, is not immune to this magical antisemitism. Graffiti defacing a mural dedicated to the memory of the late "Polish Pope" accused him of being an "actor and an impostor"—and a Jew! (most likely because of his ecumenical preaching and rapprochement with Judaism and Jews, whom he commonly referred to as "our older brothers in faith"). A Star of David was spray-painted over the pope's face, and he was cursed with a play on the vulgar "son of a bitch" insult, replacing the word "son" with "Jew" ("Jew of a bitch"—*z kurwy żyd*). The word "Jew" was sprayed over a few times to achieve a bold effect. The graffiti was not signed, but its author included the symbol of "Poland Fighting" (*Polska walcząca*) in the bottom-left corner, a symbol used in the resistance against the Nazis during World War II, against communism in the postwar era, and now used by the Right and Far Right in their fight against a multitude of liberal issues.

Similar discourse finds more "banal" expressions in everyday life. During my fieldwork at the Auschwitz-Birkenau Museum and in the town of Oświęcim for my book *The Crosses of Auschwitz*,[18] it was explained to me on several occasions that the more liberal wings of the Catholic Church were led by Jews who had infiltrated the organization by "passing." A common story circulating is that many Jewish children who were hidden and saved by the Catholic Church during World War II later entered the priesthood for convenience and eventually rose in the Church hierarchy. They are now ideally situated to destroy the institution from within, the argument goes. The fact that many Jewish children were in fact hidden in Catholic institutions, and that some of them did later become priests and nuns, renders that conspiracy theory all the more powerful.[19]

In the examples cited here, Jewishness is understood as an ethnic or even racial category rather than a religious one. The trope of "passing"—by converting and/or changing one's name to hide Jewish origins—is therefore ever present in the discourse of the Far Right because conversion cannot alter one's ethnicity or race. Revelations about public figures' "real names" in traditional and social media platforms, or the use of adjectives such as "Polish-speaking" or "Polish-language" (instead of "Polish") are therefore common discursive strategies meant to unveil that passing and unmask "impostors." Long before I started conducting research on antisemitism and philosemitism, someone's "real" identity would be "revealed" to me

Anti/Philosemitism, Religion, and Ethnic Nationalism in Poland   165

by others in confidence or casual conversations, about public figures, acquaintances, or colleagues.

It is that specific form of magical antisemitism that street artist Peter Fuss highlighted in his billboard "Jesus Christ King of Poland," in the northwest city of Koszalin in January 2007. It depicted fifty-six stylized photographs of Polish public figures, with the caption "Jews Get Out of This Catholic Country!" By including several prominent figures from the Catholic Right—such as then president of Poland, Lech Kaczyński—Fuss underlines the logic (and hysteria) of magical antisemitism.[20] Part of the project was for the artist to observe and photograph the reactions of passersby examining the billboard and that of police investigating the issue. These became part of a multimedia exhibit in which Fuss blew up and framed antisemitic threads posted on popular web platforms, while playing recorded fragments from Radio Maryja.[21] The billboard was deemed racist and antisemitic by the Koszalin police, and the exhibit was shut down for propagating hate speech, which Fuss documented as part of the project and posted on his website.

These examples (and Fuss's artistic critique) highlight the ways in which Jewishness is constructed as a symbol standing for a liberal, civic, and secular Poland, and how the conservative Catholic Right can claim Poland to be ruled by "Jews," calling upon "real Poles" to neutralize them. This is how Poland can be host to the seemingly curious phenomenon of antisemitism in a country with very few Jews.[22]

Magical Philosemitism

If the discursive ethnicization of deviation from the ethno-Catholic model of Polishness is at the source of magical antisemitism, it is also at the source of magical *philosemitism*. Ethnoreligious nationalists contend that "Jews" are contaminating the nation with their civic ideals, building a pernicious cosmopolitan world, and must therefore be politically marginalized, but "Jews" must for the same reason be resurrected and Jewishness promoted, according to proponents of a civic and secular vision of the polity. This thesis is strongly supported by a multitude of data I collected over the course of ten years in multiple Polish cities and smaller towns. To uncover the various meanings of Jewishness for Poles participating in Poland's so-called Jewish revival, and to identify the different "registers" of engagement in the revival,[23] I was a frequent participant observer at the Kraków Festival of Jewish Culture, which in addition to the usual concerts organizes a series of workshops, courses, and tours aimed at educating Jewish and non-Jewish Polish participants about Poland's Jewish past and present. I analyzed the core exhibit of the newly opened POLIN Museum of the History of Polish Jews and observed visitors during seventy visits. My participation in mundane, everyday work at Kraków's Jewish Community Center (JCC), was also a significant source for analyzing the meaning Jewishness carries for Poles rediscovering theirs as well as for the staff and volunteers who work there. In addition to this participant observation, I conducted more than 100 open-ended interviews with key actors and representatives of institutions involved in major Jewish-related initiatives and activities. Interviewees included rabbis, cultural entrepreneurs, communal leaders, museologists, artists, and public intellectuals as well as participants in communal and cultural events. About half of my interviewees were non-Jewish volunteers at Jewish institutions, non-Jewish members of a Jewish dance group, Christian evangelicals observing Jewish holidays, and non-Jewish Poles who are in the process of converting to Judaism or who recently discovered they have some Jewish ancestry and are recovering a Jewish identity through an active schedule of classes and practices.

My analysis of these rich qualitative data clearly shows that philosemitism in contemporary Poland is not anti-antisemitism, but related more broadly to the inner logic of ethnic nationalism in that country. Precisely because Jewishness carries specific significations and symbolic capital that other minorities in Poland (such as Ukrainians, Silesians, or the Vietnamese) do not possess, it is primarily through Jews and Jewishness that a modern multicultural and secular Poland is articulated and civic nationalism promoted.[24] Hence you see liberal, leftist youth wearing T-shirts and brandishing posters in protests against self-declared "Poles Catholics," subversively claiming that they are "Jews." With this display they mock antisemitic conspiracy theories of the Right claiming that Jews rule Poland, but they also call for a different kind of Poland, one in which the Right's distinctions between "real Poles," "Jews," and "bad Poles" would have no political traction.

Figure 2. Rehearsal of amateur Jewish dance troupe at Kraków's Popper synagogue, March 2012. Photo by author.

"I'm a Jew" T-shirts were part of a campaign by the Foundation for Freedom that consisted in "spreading . . . slogans signaling the existence of some taboo topics . . . and discriminated against social groups in Poland," including atheists and homosexuals,[25] while a hip clothing label in Warsaw launched a new "Jewish" line called "Oy." Initially targeted at young Jews, the brand Risk Oy for a while produced pricey T-shirts and hoodies with slogans such as "Thanks to My Mom" or "You Had Me at Shalom" adorned with a variety of Star of David designs and Hebrew inscriptions. The (Polish-Jewish) owner of the brand told the *Times of Israel*, "What we really want . . . is to rebrand Jewish identity. We want to show the modern, positive aspects of it. What we are doing is showing that being Jewish is cool and sexy."[26] According to Kraków's JCC director, Jonathan Ornstein, there might be no need to "rebrand" Jewish identity, since he has been insisting for years now that "it's hip to be Jewish in today's Poland."[27] Several non-Jewish volunteers at the JCC and non-Jewish members of a Kraków-based Israeli dance troupe (see fig. 2) I interviewed made similar observations, commenting on the fact that "Jewishness is fashionable," one even adding that "just like in Warsaw it's fashionable to have a gay friend."[28]

The important question here is why Jewishness (and gayness) is "fashionable" for some non-Jewish Poles. What does it signify for them? The president of the Joint Distribution Committee (JDC) in Warsaw, Karina Sokołowska, addressed this issue in the *Times of Israel* article on the Risk Oy clothing line: "In general, Jews in Poland are looking for ways to express being Jewish, [but the clothing line] *is an attractive item for Poland's many philo-Semites*" (my emphasis). One such non-Jew quoted in the story, a forty-year-old lawyer living in Warsaw, explained, "Wearing [Risk Oy] is like taking part in a public discussion about Jews in Poland—that Jews live here and that Jews can live here." This is an important comment: public discussion about Jews in Poland is actually one about the very identity of Poland and a critique of the still dominant vision of the nation as ethnically Polish and (nominally) Catholic, a clear finding of my research.[29]

Consuming Jewish food, whether in its Ashkenazi form or in its contemporary Israeli versions, is also a way to acquaint oneself with either the "known" and recognizable Ashkenazi cuisine, very similar to, because in part constitutive of, Polish cuisine, or the mysterious and exotic Israeli cuisine. It is that mix of "ours" and "other," of the familiar and the exotic, likewise that attracts many (non-Jewish) young women to take part in an Israeli dance group. One of the dancers, a young Protestant woman who majored in Judaic studies and art history and is now a museum educator in a Catholic institution, explained to me: "On one hand, [Jewish culture] is, let's say, 'oriental.' But on the other hand, because it developed in Poland, in spite of everything it's somehow very much tied with Poland, yes? It's kind of an exotic element in our environment. It's not something like . . . Swahili somewhere far off in Africa, but [rather] something that is different from Polish culture yet at the same time related to it, inseparable even." Performing various forms of Jewish dances—Ashkenazi, Sephardic, or contemporary Israeli hip-hop—brings those young women (and, one presumes, their audiences) closer to a different side of Polish history than the one exalted in Polish national mythology and its sensorium. At the same time, as this woman's explanation suggests, the dances transport them to faraway, exotic, "oriental" places, such as Israel.

Wearing a "Jewish" sweatshirt, dancing to Jewish music, eating Jewish foods, and drinking kosher vodka become embodied practices meant to challenge a restrictive definition of Polishness. These practices serve to *de-* and *re-*construct identity along new lines. Polishness is being challenged and redefined by activists and artists and also by ordinary people in their mundane activities. Ordinary Poles come to assimilate Jewishness through embodied and repeated actions. They remake Polishness by learning how to "cook Jewish" or how to serve and consume Jewish foods during a festival, at a café all year round, or at a Sabbath dinner at the JCC; by singing and dancing, by learning Jewish paper-cutting techniques, or by donating their time and energy to Jewish individuals and organizations. This implies a certain objectification of Jewishness and "Jewish culture" and its appropriation by non-Jews. But that "cultural appropriation" is motivated by a political project, a national vision defined by openness. It serves to undermine the political claim and the dominant view that Poland is essentially, primordially ethno-Catholic.

Indeed, since the 1990s, the Catholic Right and the official hierarchy of the Catholic Church have routinely emphasize the "objective" homogeneity of Poland's population, wielding Poland's demographic statistics ("96 percent ethnically Polish, 95 percent Catholic, and 95 percent believers") to bolster claims of monolithic unity and to legally enforce a narrow vision of Poland. Such statistics were used to support and justify the inclusion of an *invocatio Dei* in the 1997 Constitution, and are often invoked to defend the state's policing of social movements that deviate from an imagined national norm. They were thrown around, for example, when gay pride parades were banned in Warsaw in the name of "public morality." Religious discourse since 1989, then, has been used primarily to constrain individual rights and to *shrink* the boundaries of Polishness by symbolically excluding those considered "morally unworthy" for full membership—"Jews," secularists, "bad Catholics," Masons (all code names for Jews), and, increasingly, "feminists-terrorists" and the "gay lobby." It is against that right-wing vision and its social, political, and cultural implications that many non-Jews participate in the revival of Jewish culture.

Multiculturalism and Secularism

Building and promoting a plural society in a nation-state with an ethnically and denominationally homogenous population is no easy task. Many activists and NGOs therefore create visible, countable, "objective" counterweights by reviving Jewish culture, supporting the institutional growth of

Jewish communities, promoting knowledge about Poland's Jewish past and present, and even introducing Jewish symbols in the public sphere. There thus exist more than forty festivals of Jewish culture in Poland today, many new (and impressive) museums on the history of Polish Jews and the Holocaust, and Jewish cuisine restaurants, Jewish bookstores, Klezmer music clubs, and so on.[30]

The promotion of Jewishness in festivals, memory projects, and many other institutional projects is perceived by their organizers to be instrumental in bringing Poland back to its "true essence," as Janusz Makuch, cofounder and director of Kraków's Festival of Jewish Culture, expresses here: "Kraków was always a multicultural place, where cultural pluralism was often very obvious. However this national monotheism, religious monotheism, that was created after the second world war is scorching me, hurting me. I really don't like this—so let's go back here to what is the basis of our spirituality, actually, since Jews were Polish citizens."[31]

For Makuch, it is important that Poles reconnect with that culture:

> Whether people know it or not, it is a *fact* that Jews, for many many centuries . . . , made tremendous contributions to Polish culture. So when we're talking about Polish culture, we're equally talking about Jewish culture. Without the contribution of Jews, true Polish culture couldn't exist. Forget it! Literature, architecture, sculptures, historians, intellectuals, music, economics, politics, food. So everything was intertwined and still is, thank God. What I'm trying to do . . . is to help Poles realize what is theirs.[32]

In a context where national identity is primarily understood in ethnic terms, and where civic discourse is either perceived as a remnant of Communist Party/state speak or as an import from the EU, civic nationalists must work doubly hard at rendering that vision of the nation legitimate and "truly Polish." Public intellectuals have therefore tried to sell this vision to the population by reconstructing a distinctively Polish narrative that emphasizes the civic heritage of the nation in Poland, by, for example, going back to sixteenth-century religious tolerance, to the First Republic's multiethnic and multiconfessional state, to the Democracy of Nobles' elective monarchy, to the Constitution of May Third, to the Polish legions (fighting "for your freedom and ours"), to interwar liberal traditions, and to a certain extent to Komitet Obrony Robotników's and Solidarity's peaceful resistance and civic activism. Since the Right also uses some of these historical themes, the Jewish trope becomes especially salient. The large number of Jews who settled in Poland is key for that narrative. As I heard many times in various venues, "When Jews were being kicked out from Southern and Western Europe, King Kazimierz the Great was welcoming them in Poland." Embracing elements of Jewish culture becomes a way to plausibly demonstrate that to be Polish is not merely to participate in Catholic practices and folklore, but that it is also to welcome Jewish refugees, making Poles European avant la lettre.

Engaging in that process of resurrecting Jewish culture and supporting an ongoing Jewish renewal therefore allows both the creation of a symbolic multiculturalism and the promotion of secularism. Ethnographic data is helpful here: Aga, a non-Jewish student in Kraków who volunteers in Jewish organizations, is expressly anticlerical, and declares herself an atheist, explained to me during a Shabbat dinner at the JCC in Kraków: "I think it's great to see all of that [Jewish religious activity]. I'm not religious but I think it's good to see that there's something else than what we already know—and frankly speaking—that we're sick of: processions, pilgrimages here and there, crosses everywhere." This suggests that the presence of non-Christian symbols and of visibly different religious groups in the public sphere are embraced because their presence weakens the hegemony of Catholicism. Another young woman, a self-declared feminist in her early twenties, explained to me in an interview that she's happy to see ultra-Orthodox Jews in the streets of Kraków, "because it breaks the Catholic 'black cassocks' monopoly."

Unlike the cross, which has come to be associated with the Right in the past quarter century, the menorah (or Hasidic garb) has no such acquired "baggage" for left-leaning Poles who support a civic and secular vision of the nation. On the contrary, Jewish markers, be they religious or secular, serve to visibly create diversity, thereby somewhat diluting the weight of Catholicism and potentially *neutralizing* it. By dissociating Polishness from Catholicism and expanding what is considered "national" culture, the embrace of Judaism and Jewishness secularizes Polishness. Secularism, in the Polish context, is therefore not being fought for by attempting to erase all religious elements from the public sphere, but rather through an effort to build a neutral space where Catholicism is only one among many other value systems (religious and nonreligious) in which none is hegemonic. Many evangelical Christian groups also support the Jewish revival in Poland. They do so for theological reasons, but also to build a counterweight to the all too heavy presence of Catholicism. And Catholic groups invested in the Jewish revival often do so in explicit support of so-called open Catholicism and John Paul II's call for ecumenical exchanges and respect for "our older brothers in faith," in explicit opposition to the reactionary and antisemitic Catholicism of Radio Maryja. This is most likely why John Paul II—his message and image—is often used to counter antisemitism, and also likely one of the reasons why a mural dedicated to his memory in Kraków was vandalized with antisemitic graffiti, in a powerful example of magical antisemitism.

This is not to say that the hegemonic place of Catholicism in Poland is only or even primarily contested and countered via the support of Judaism and Jewish culture; it is also contested via critiques of the Church and of traditional forms of Polish Catholicism, formal demands for a stricter separation of church and state and apostasy movements, and in the support of the rights of various alternative groups, primarily sexual minorities and feminists, who, significantly enough, also support the revival of Jewish communal life as they understand their minority status and their struggle as ones shared by Jews.[33]

This is also not to say, either, that the revival is not about other properly Jewish processes. For it obviously is.[34] What I argue here is that one must nonetheless see a relation between non-Jewish Poles' support of, and participation in, the Jewish revival and the desire to build a Poland that is different from the one forcefully promoted by the Catholic Church and the Right.

What are some of the contributions of the Polish case to our understanding of religion, ethnicity, and nationalism in late modernity?

First, it shows us how a symbolic category—here Jewishness—can serve as a foil to construct not only an exclusive ethnic nation, but also to build an inclusive, civic, and secular nation. I have shown that in Poland the national self is being built not only *against* the Other (the Jew), but also *through* that Other in opposition to an alleged primordial "self"—the ethno-Catholic Pole. This is more than the simplistic story of philosemitism opposing antisemitism—or "anti-antisemitism." Rather, Polish philosemitism is part of a larger process of redefining national identity. Polish philosemitism articulates and legitimates a new national identity, but are notions of sovereignty being expanded in the process, as Richard Amesbury suggests (chapter 4) in this volume? Alas, not. The inclusion of "Jews" within the symbolic perimeter of the nation in order to redefine and expand Polishness is problematic, for the Jew must irremediably remain Other to achieve the goal of civic nationalism and multiculturalism. And whether real or symbolic, the Jew remains malleable at the hands of those who control the category. Jews—past, present, symbolic, or real—may become legitimate members of an imagined Polish civic nation, but they are still deprived of sovereignty in that process. The symbolic power exerted to "articulate the principles of vision and division" for a particular group, to quote Bourdieu, is thus still "violent" even when it is used in progressive projects meant to expand the symbolic boundaries of the group.[35]

The case also highlights how challenging it is for proponents of a civic vision of the nation to promote a national vision that is based on abstract principles, especially when those are perceived to be "foreign." Without political stories and symbols that they can mobilize, civic nationalists must resort to recreating Jewish culture as "real," as a visible counterweight to the ethnoreligious national community. Paradoxically, then, ethnicity remains the prism through which social actors attempt to transcend ethnonationalism. That conundrum is at the basis of what I call the "tragedy of Polish civic nationalism": to escape ethnic nationalism, civic nationalists must resort to the very categories they are seeking to transcend. This, I have shown, is because of the very logic of ethnic nationalism, but it is also because of the previous association of civic discourse with Soviet-imposed communism and a relative deficit in stories, symbols, and material culture that could be mobilized in the service of civic nationalism.

The case also shows how what Brubaker has called "idioms of nationhood"—cultural schemes or ways of conceiving one's nation—shape not only formal rules of membership (i.e., citizenship), but also the logic of symbolic membership.[36] That the nation is generally imagined in ethnic terms in Poland (and in the region more broadly) explains how certain members are symbolically excluded from the national community for their political ideas or values by being "ethnicized," by being turned into ethnonational Others. That observation also helps us to understand other cases. Consider France, the archetype of civic nationhood, where inclusion into the national community is, ideally speaking, premised not on blood but upon one's adherence to the social contract. How can the French Right legitimately exclude ethnic and racial others? It does so by ideologizing them, by turning Arabs and Africans into dangerous, observant Muslims, who threaten the Republic by infringing upon *laïcité*, a sacred tenet of the social contract. This discursive "trick" has been used by French political elites for decades, but was given new life recently, with the Macron government's proposed bill against "political Islam," "communautarisme," and "séparatisme."[37]

As Gorski (chapter 1) and Springs (chapter 2) demonstrate in this volume, White evangelical Christians, in attempts to shore up their legitimacy, have identified various others that threaten their hegemony.

Finally, and most importantly for this volume, the analysis shows how religion in this case acts not merely as an ethnic marker, but perhaps even as a racial category, or at the very least a racialized one. By working toward the "resurrection" of Jewish culture in Poland, then, Poles attempt to build a symbolically multicultural, "multiracial" society, but without actual ethnic and racial minorities. Supporting the revival of Judaism, in turn, becomes a tool to build secularism. Ethnicity, race, and religion remain intertwined in political projects attempting to transcend those very categories.

NOTES

1. The Roman Catholic Church in Poland is a diverse and vibrant institution. The hierarchy is primarily constituted by what I call "traditional-conservatives." This is the so-called Catholicism of continuity, supported by the late Cardinal Glemp, Abp Michalik, and the current primate of Poland, Cardinal Wojciech Polak. It is also the type of Catholicism embraced by the majority of clergy and by many political figures on the right. Traditional-conservative Catholicism, in the Polish context, is characterized by the explicit engagement of Catholics qua Catholics in public life, since the nation is cast as a divine community and the Church portrayed as its holy guardian. See Jarosław Gowin, *Kościół po komunizmie* (Kraków: Znak, 1995); and Jarosław Gowin, *Kościół w czasach wolności 1989–1999* (Kraków: Znak, 2000). According to those traditional-conservative Catholics, the specificity of the Polish way of life resides primarily in the tight relationship between religion and national identity. Another wing within the Church is that of Radio Maryja. The voice of anticommunism, anti-EU sentiment, and antisemitism, in recent years it added to its arsenal a vociferous propaganda against refugees, and

against women's and LGBTQ equality movements. Radio Maryja is not the dominant face of Catholicism in Poland, but it is the most vocal and occupies public space with immense semiotic force: through related publications such as *Nasz Dziennik* (*Our Daily*) and *Nasza Polska* (*Our Poland*) it exerts a significant influence on the public face of Catholicism in Poland by affixing the terms and relative positions that bind public debate. With the coming to power of Law and Justice in 2015 and Poland's sharp right turn, the radical positions of Radio Maryja are now offering solid competition to the "mainstream" of the Catholic Church. Finally, self-proclaimed "open Catholics" are a small elite group of intellectuals who were initially associated with personalist Catholic publications, such as *Tygodnik Powszechny*, *Znak*, and *Więź*, but in the last two decades have expanded their reach to liberal secular outlets, such as the daily *Gazeta wyborcza*. For that group, traditional Catholicism in Poland is associated with politics to such an extent that it has become a political religion. See Gowin, *Kościół w czasach wolności 1989–1999*; Geneviève Zubrzycki, *The Crosses of Auschwitz: Nationalism and Religion in Post-Communist Poland* (Chicago: University of Chicago Press, 2001); Stanisław Obirek, "The Many Faces of John Paul II," in *Religion, Politics, and Values in Poland: Continuity and Change since 1989*, ed. Sabrina Ramet and Irena Borowik (New York: Palgrave Macmillan, 2017), 41–59. Open Catholics therefore warn against the conflation of nation and religion and stress instead the universality of Catholicism. Open Catholics also consistently promote the principles of Vatican II and engage in ecumenical dialogue. Following the personalist tradition, they emphasize the need for a deepening and active internalization of faith. For a typology of Catholicisms within the Polish Catholic landscape, and different orientations' specific rapport with Jews and antisemitism, see Geneviève Zubrzycki, "'Poles-Catholics' and 'Symbolic Jews': Jewishness as Social Closure in Poland," *Studies in Contemporary Jewry* 21 (2005): 65–87; and Geneviève Zubrzycki, "Quo Vadis, Polonia? On Religious Loyalty, Voice, and Exit," *Social Compass* 67, no. 2 (2020): 267–81.

2. The term "philosemitism" was coined by self-avowed antisemites in Germany in the 1880s to denigrate their opponents, but I adopt it here to denote a wide spectrum of practices motivated by a curiosity and desire to learn about Jewishness. See Jonathan Karp and Adam Sutcliff, eds., *Philosemitism in History* (New York: Cambridge University Press, 2011). These attempts aim to uncover and preserve the remnants of Jewish life and to honor the lives of the millions of Jews (Polish and non-Polish) who were murdered on Polish soil. For a discussion of the history and theoretical underpinnings of the terms "antisemitism," "anti-antisemitism," "philosemitism," and "allosemitism," see Zygmunt Bauman, "Allosemitism: Premodern, Modern, Postmodern," in *Modernity, Culture, and "the Jew*," ed. B. Cheyette and L. Marcus (Cambridge: Polity Press, 1998), 143–56; Thomas Alteflix, "The 'Post-Holocaust Jew' and the Instrumentalization of Philosemitism," *Patterns of Prejudice* 34, no. 2 (2000): 41–56; and

Jonathan Judaken, "Between Philosemitism and Antisemitism: The Frankfurt School's Anti-Antisemitism," in *Antisemitism and Philosemitism in the Twentieth and Twenty-First Centuries: Representing Jews, Jewishness and Modern Culture*, ed. Phyllis Lassner and Lara Trubowitz (Newark: University of Delaware Press, 2000), 23–46. For empirical studies, see Frank Stern, *The Whitewashing of the Yellow Badge: Antisemitism and Philosemitism in Postwar Germany* (New York: Pergamon, 1991); Marion Mushkat, *Philo-Semitic and Anti-Jewish Attitudes in Post-Holocaust Poland* (Lewiston, NY: Edwin Mellen Press, 1992); Jonathan Karp and Adam Sutcliff, eds., *Philosemitism in History* (New York: Cambridge University Press, 2011). On philosemitism in Poland, see Geneviève Zubrzycki, "Nationalism, 'Philosemitism,' and Symbolic Boundary-Making in Contemporary Poland," *Comparative Studies in Society and History* 58, no. 1 (2016): 66–98; and Elżbieta Janicka and Tomasz Żukowski, *Przemoc filosemicka? Nowe polskie narracje o Żydach po roku* (Warsaw: Instytut Badań Literackich PAN, 2016).

3. Before World War II, Poland had the largest Jewish population in Europe (about 3.5 million), representing approximately 10 percent of its population. Ninety percent of Polish Jews were exterminated in the Holocaust. Of those who survived, many left to start their lives over elsewhere. Following the war, violence against those who remained was common. See Jan. T Gross, *Fear: Anti-Semitism in Poland after Auschwitz* (New York: Random House, 2006); and Anna Cichopek-Gajraj, *Beyond Violence: Jewish Survivors in Poland and Slovakia, 1944–48* (Cambridge: Cambridge University Press, 2014). In 1968, about 20,000 Polish Jews were expelled from Poland in an anti-Zionist and antisemitic purge; see Dariusz Stola, *Kampania antysyjonistyczna w Polsce 1967–1968* (Warsaw: Instytut Studiów Politycznych Polskiej Akademii Nauk, 2000); and Dariusz Stola, *Kraj bez wyjścia? Migracje z Polski 1949–1989* (Warsaw: Institute of National Remembrance, 2010). As a result, there are only between 7,000 and 40,000 Jews living in that country now, the numbers varying depending on sources, the criteria used to determine Jewishness, and the year the data was collected; see Sergio Della Pergola, "World Jewish Population, 2019," in *American Jewish Year Book 2020: An Annual Record of the North American Jewish Communities since 1899*, ed. Arnold Dashefsky and Ira M. Sheskin (New York: The American Jewish Committee, 2020), 119:263–353; author interview with chief rabbi of Poland Michael Schudrich on September 28, 2012.

4. I specifically discuss the effects of the fall of communism, ongoing debates about Polish violence against Jews during World War II and its immediate aftermath, Poland's accession to the EU, and the promotion of Holocaust and heritage tourism in other publications. See Geneviève Zubrzycki, "Narrative Shock and Polish Memory Remaking in the Twenty-first Century," in *Memory and Postwar Memorials: Confronting the Violence of the Past*, ed. Marc Silberman and

Florence Vatan (New York: Palgrave Macmillan, 2013), 95–115; Zubrzycki, "Nationalism, 'Philosemitism,' and Symbolic Boundary-Making in Contemporary Poland"; and Zubrzycki, "Traces and Steps: Expanding Polishness through a Jewish Sensorium?," in *National Matters: Materiality, Culture and Nationalism*, ed. Geneviève Zubrzycki (Stanford, CA: Stanford University Press, 2017), 193–215.

5. See Rogers Brubaker, *Citizenship and Nationhood in France and Germany* (Cambridge, MA: Harvard University Press, 1992); Dominique Schnapper, *La communauté des citoyens: Sur l'idée moderne de la nation* (Paris: Gallimard, 1994); Bernard Yack, "The Myth of the Civic Nation," *Critical Review* 10, no. 2 (1996): 193–211; Kai Nielsen, "Cultural Nationalism, Neither Ethnic nor Civic," *The Philosophical Forum: A Quarterly* 28, no. 1–2 (1999): 42–52; Geneviève Zubrzycki, "'We, the Polish Nation': Ethnic and Civic Visions of Nationhood in Post-Communist Constitutional Debates," *Theory and Society* 30, no. 5 (2001): 629–69.

6. The prefix *un*, unlike the more neutral *non*, underlines that it is contrary to what is normatively considered "American."

7. On sexual minorities, see Agnieszka Graff, *Rykoszetem: Rzecz o płci, seksualności i narodzie* (Warsaw: W.A.B., 2008). She argues that gays are the "new Jews," and notes the ideological alliance between minority groups toward which the Catholic Right and the Catholic Church are not especially benevolent. This argument has also been made by feminist scholar and public intellectual Magdalena Środa in an editorial called "The New Jews," in which she analyzes the witch hunt against feminists and the Catholic Church's blaming "gender ideology" for all sorts of social ills, from broken families to pedophile priests. See Agnieszka Graff, "Nowi Żydzi," *Wprost*, January 19, 2014, http://www.wprost.pl/ar/432887/Nowi-Zydzi/. On the use of Jewishness and homosexuality as tropes for symbolic exclusion from the national community, see also George Mosse, *Nationalism and Sexuality: Respectability and Abnormal Sexuality in Modern Europe* (New York: Fertig, 1985); and Matti Bunzl, *Symptoms of Modernity: Jews and Queers in Late-Twentieth-Century Vienna* (Berkeley: University of California Press, 2004). For an analysis of LGBTQI as ideological others in Poland, see Ian Bratcher, "Ideological Others and National Identifications in Contemporary Poland," *Nations and Nationalism* 26, no. 3 (2020): 677–91.

8. Sergiusz Kowalski and Magdalena Tulli, *Zamiast procesu: Raport o mowie nienawiści* (Warsaw: Instytut Studiów Politycznych PAN, 2003), 486–89.

9. On antisemitism in contemporary Poland, see Ireneusz Krzemiński, ed., *Czy Polacy są antysemitami? Wyniki badania sondażowgo* (Warszawa: Oficyna Naukowa, 1997); Ireneusz Krzemiński, "Polacy i Żydzi: wizja wzajemnych stosunków, tożsamość narodowa i antysemityzm," in *Trudne sąsiedztwa: Z socjologii konfliktów narodowościowych*, ed. Aleksandra Kania (Warsaw: Wydawnictwo narodowe Scholar, 2005), 171–200; and Michał Bilewicz, Mikołaj Winiewski, and Zuzanna Radzik, "Antisemitism in Poland: Economic, Religious, and Historical

Aspects," *Journal for the Study of Antisemitism* 4 (January 2012): 2801–20; on antisemitism and opposition to it, see Robert Blobaum, ed., *Antisemitism and Its Opponents in Modern Poland* (Ithaca, NY: Cornell University Press, 2005); and Adam Michnik, "Wstęp," in *Przeciw Antysemityzmowi 1936–2009*, ed. Adam Michnik (Kraków: Universitas, 2010), 1:iii–xiii. On representations of Jews in Poland, see the now-classic studies by Alina Cała, *The Image of the Jew in Polish Folk Culture* (Jerusalem: Magnes Press, 1995); Joanna B. Michlic, *Poland's Threatening Other: The Image of the Jew from 1880 to the Present* (Lincoln: University of Nebraska Press, 2006); Joanna Tokarska-Bakir, "Żyd z pieniążkiem podbija Polskę," in *PL: tożsamość wyobrażona*, ed. J. Tokarska-Bakir (Warsaw: Czarna Owca, 2013), 6–31; and Erica Lehrer, *Jewish Poland Revisited: Heritage Tourism in Unquiet Places* (Bloomington: Indiana University Press, 2013). For studies on "lucky Jews," wooden statues, paintings, and other kitsch lucky charms, see Tokarska-Bakir, "Żyd z pieniążkiem"; Erica Lehrer, ed., *Lucky Jews: Poland's Jewish Figurines* (Kraków: Korporacja Ha!art, 2014); and Paweł Dobrosielski, "'Żyd z pieniążkiem' jako praktyka polskiej wernakularnej: Wstępny raport z badań," *Kultura współczesna* 3 (2015): 61–75.

10. Jean-Paul Sartre, *Anti-Semite and Jew* (New York: Schocken, 1986 [1946]), 12.

11. Enzo Traverso, *L'Histoire déchirée: Essai sur Auschwitz et les intellectuels* (Paris: Ed. Cerf., 1997).

12. "Żydokomuna" is a pervasive antisemitic narrative claiming that Jews collaborated with the Soviet Union to import and then impose communism in Poland. The creation of a single term joining "Jews/Jewishness" and "communism" underlines the fusion of both categories. On Judeo-Bolshevism in Eastern Europe, see Andre Gerrits, "Antisemitism and Anti-Communism: The Myth of 'Judeo-Communism' in Eastern Europe," *East European Jewish Affairs* 25, no. 1 (1995): 49–72; and Paul Hanenbrink, *A Specter Haunting Europe: The Myth of Judeo-Bolshevism* (Cambridge, MA: Harvard University Press, 2018). For analyses on its Polish variant, see Michlic, *Poland's Threatening Other*; and Paweł Śpiewak, *Żydokomuna* (Warsaw: Czerwone i Czarne, 2012).

13. It was expressed numerous times in my interviews in the early 2000s. One elderly interviewee, for example, explained to me that the Jews knew that their situation in Israel was untenable in the long term and were therefore trying to come back to Poland, the "real Promised Land." The EU was the structure through which they could accomplish that goal, according to that interviewee.

14. These images could be found on a popular far-right website and are circulated on the web, but it is impossible to find the site's author or even get in touch with the webmaster. As such, they are "anonymous."

15. For example, *Nasz Dziennik* (*Our Daily*), or the weeklies *Gazeta Polska* (*The Polish Gazette*) and *Niedziela* (*Sunday*).

16. Often accused by the Left and by progressive Catholics of having created a sect that borders on heresy, its charismatic leader, Fr. Tadeusz Rydzyk, has managed to create a social movement around Radio Maryja's right-wing politics, consistently mobilizing followers devoted to restoring a "true Poland." See Ireneusz Krzemiński, ed., *Czego nas uczy Radio Maryja?* (Warszawa: WAiP, 2009); Ireneusz Krzemiński, "Radio Maryja and Fr. Rydzyk as a Creator of the National-Catholic Ideology," in *Religion, Politics, and Values in Poland: Continuity and Change since 1989*, ed. Sabrina Ramet and Irena Borowik (New York: Palgrave Macmillan, 2017), 85–112; and Kinga Sekerdej and Agnieszka Pasieka, "Researching the Dominant Religion: Anthropology at Home and Methodological Catholicism," *Method and Theory in the Study of Religion* 25 (2013): 53–77, at 61–65. In 2011, the Family of Radio Maryja was estimated to number 1 million members. The group organizes an annual pilgrimage to Częstochowa, which averages more than 100,000 participants. See Editors, "Rodzina Radia Maryja się powiększa. Rozgłośnia Rydzyka ma milion słuchaczy," *Polska Times*, July 12, 2011, https://polskatimes.pl/rodzina-radia-maryja-sie-powieksza-rozglosnia-rydzyka-ma-milion-sluchaczy/ar/425998.

17. The word "weekly" (*tygodnik*) is transformed into "Jewishy" (*żydownik*). In a bold reversal, the weekly adopted *Żydownik Powszechny* on its first page for its sixty-fifth anniversary issue in 2010, commemorating its long-standing engagement with Polish–Jewish and Christian–Jewish relations.

18. Zubrzycki, *The Crosses of Auschwitz*.

19. See Paweł Pawlikowski's Oscar-winning film *Ida* about a novice nun about to take her vows who is told by a family member that she is Jewish. See also the documentary *Torn*, by Ronit Kertsner, about Fr. Romuald-Jakub Weksler-Waszkiniel, a Roman Catholic priest who found out at age thirty-five that he had been given by his Jewish birth mother to a Polish Catholic family in Święcany (near Vilnius) before the liquidation of the town's ghetto in 1943. Weksler-Waszkiniel made *Aliyah* in 2008. See SFJewish Film, "Torn Trailer," YouTube Video, https://www.youtube.com/watch?v=DM4N2ecEaCo; and Museum of the History of Polish Jews, "Weksler-Waszkinel Romuald Jakub," https://sztetl.org.pl/en/biographies/4136-weksler-waszkinel-romuald-jakub.

20. Other usual suspects on the billboard included former prime minister Tadeusz Mazowiecki and Nobel laureate Wisława Szymborska, both associated with *Tygodnik Powszechny*; Adam Michnik; former minister of finance Leszek Balcerowicz (center-right); and Leszek Miller (postcommunist Left).

21. For photographs of the exhibition, screenshots, and radio segments used in the project, see Peter Fuss, "Jesus Christ King of Poland," http://peterfuss.com/jesus-christ-king-of-poland/. The conservative weekly *Wprost* published a story on the project, with the title "Police Searching for Author of Racist Billboard," January 26, 2007, https://www.wprost.pl/kraj/100441/jutro-spotkanie-kaczynski-tusk.html.

22. In 1989, approximately 2,000 individuals were registered with Jewish communities (*American Jewish Year Book 1989*). By the beginning of the new millennium, the number of Polish Jews registered with communities, belonging to Jewish organizations, or receiving aid from the American Jewish Joint Distribution Committee had nearly quadrupled. See Della Pergola, "World Jewish Population, 2019," Berman Jewish DataBank, https://www.jewishdatabank.org/content/upload/bjdb/2019_World_Jewish_Population_(AJYB,_DellaPergola)_DataBank_Final.pdf. As many as 40,000 Polish citizens are now thought to have some Jewish ancestry. When asked how many Jews currently live in Poland, the chief rabbi of Poland, Michael Schudrich, often responds: "How many do you think there are? Take that number and double it. And now add 1. There's always one more coming out of the closet" (informal conversation, Warsaw, March 22, 2013).

23. I have also conducted extensive research on the renewal of Jewish communal life itself. I was invited to numerous communal events in the Kraków and Warsaw Jewish communities, such as Sabbath dinners, anniversaries, and other life event celebrations (weddings, bat mitzvahs), and religious holidays (Purim, Yom Kippur, Passover), and attended the 2016 Polish edition of LIMUD, a four-day gathering of members of the Jewish community, during which they learn from each other in workshops, panels, and book readings. Last, I was included in a Polish Birthright trip to Israel, spending twelve days with Polish Jewish youth as they discovered that country and explored their Jewishness. Analysis of these materials constitutes a separate chapter in Geneviève Zubrzycki, *Resurrecting the Jew: Philosemitism, Nationalism, and Poland's Jewish Revival* (Princeton, NJ: Princeton University Press, 2022).

24. Zubrzycki, "Nationalism, 'Philosemitism,' and Symbolic Boundary-Making in Contemporary Poland."

25. Other T-shirts that were part of the 2004 campaign included "I Don't Go to Church," "I Don't Want to Have Kids," or "I'm Gay." See http://www.tiszertdlawolnosci.tiszert.com/.

26. Renne Ghert-Zand, "Polish Fashion Entrepreneur Makes Being Jewish Sexy," *Times of Israel*, January 31, 2014, http://www.timesofisrael.com/polish-fashion-entrepreneur-makes-being-jewish-sexy/?utm_source=Newsletter+subscribers&utm_campaign=0c5a586595-JTA_Daily_Briefing_1_31_2014&utm_medium=email&utm_term=0_2dce5bc6f8-0c5a586595-25416689.

27. Personal communications, March 2011, March 2012, and March 2013.

28. Interviews, March 2012.

29. Zubrzycki, "Nationalism, 'Philosemitism,' and Symbolic Boundary-Making in Contemporary Poland."

30. See Ruth Ellen Gruber, *Virtually Jewish: Reinventing Jewish Culture in Europe* (Los Angeles: University of California Press, 2002); Magdalena Waligórska, *Klezmer's Afterlife: An Ethnography of the Jewish Music Revival in Poland and Germany* (New York: Oxford University Press, 2013); Lehrer, *Jewish Poland*

Revisited; Zubrzycki, "Nationalism, 'Philosemitism,' and Symbolic Boundary-Making in Contemporary Poland." Kraków's Galicja Jewish Museum was founded in 2003; Schindler's Factory Museum on occupation in World War II Kraków opened in 2010; the Museum of Kraków's ghetto, The Eagle Pharmacy, opened in 2013; and the Museum of the History of Polish Jews in Warsaw opened its building in April 2013 and its main exhibit in October 2014. There are many other smaller museums and educational centers throughout Poland, such as the Świętokrzyski shtetl in Chmielnik, which opened in 2014.

31. Interview, March 19, 2011.

32. Interview, March 1, 2012. Original conversation in English.

33. Geneviève Zubrzycki, "Quo Vadis, Polonia? On Religious Loyalty, Voice, and Exit," *Social Compass* 67, no. 2 (2020): 267–81.

34. Jewish life proper has also gone through an important renewal since the fall of communism. That renewal is aided by the lifting of taboos around Jewishness, which makes it possible for people who have Jewish roots to accept and embrace them, and has inspired many to dig into their family histories to potentially recover Jewish identities. It is also boosted by the financial support of Jewish communal life by international organizations and philanthropies, and the return of communal property to Jewish communities. I discuss the revival of Jewish communal and religious life elsewhere; see Geneviève Zubrzycki, *Resurrecting the Jew*.

35. Pierre Bourdieu, *Language and Symbolic Power*, ed. John B. Thompson, trans. Gino Raymond and Matthew Adamson (Cambridge, MA: Harvard University Press, 1991). On philosemitism as symbolic violence, see Janicka, *Przemoc filosemicka?*

36. Brubaker, *Citizenship and Nationhood in France and Germany*.

37. For a description of the bill, with amendments and transcripts of parliamentary debates and public speeches, see "Projet de loi confortant le respect des principes de la République," https://www.vie-publique.fr/loi/277621-loi-separatisme-respect-des-principes-de-la-republique-24-aout-2021.

CHAPTER 6

The Pull to the Right of the Right, Religion, and the Ecological Crisis

Evaluating a Religio-Secular Perspective through a Reading of Bruno Latour's Late Work

YOLANDE JANSEN AND JASMIJN LEEUWENKAMP

ABSTRACT

What is the relationship between the ecological crisis and the rising global tide of right-wing politics, populism, and the particular phenomenon of Trumpism? Drawing on the late work of philosopher of science, sociologist, and anthropologist Bruno Latour, this chapter brings an ecological perspective to bear on the "pull to the right of the right." The use of concepts such as the "Right," "Far Right," and "right-wing populism" implies a certain boundedness and distinction between the political attitudes and actions that each one denotes. The pull to the right of the right, by contrast, conveys a global rightward lurch of political discourse in general, driven by the worldwide proliferation of far-right anti-egalitarian discourse that oversaturates the political imaginaries available to more moderate politics on the political Right, and even those on the political Left, with particular ramifications for efforts to understand and respond to the climate catastrophe.

Latour locates climate change denial at the heart of the right-wing drive, as the prospect of global migration increases, and attendant questions around social and economic inequality pose threats to right-wing constructions of the nation as access to a territorially situated (and racialized) "way of life." Latour sees the religious and philosophical dimensions of the ecological crisis as traceable to the coincidence of modern developments in (Cartesian) philosophical and scientific rationalism and (Gnostic) Christian reconfigurations of the relationship between immanence and transcendence. Together these transformations produced an essentially modern Manichaean distinction between progress through "Science,"[1] "discovering" the laws of nature (mind), and a corresponding contempt or negligence toward the actual natural world (matter). To combat this modern tendency of attempting to "escape" attachments to the natural world, Latour advocates the cultivation of "Earthboundedness," a novel reconception of the sciences oriented toward care for the "secular figure of Gaia" in contradistinction to the negligence of the material world that Latour locates in both modern Science and postmedieval Christianity.

However, this chapter also challenges Latour's diagnosis and proposed remedy to the coimbrication of the ecological crisis and the rising global tide of right-wing populism. First, it raises key critiques of the "religio-secularism" of Latour's account, demonstrating how its central secularization narrative remains beholden to Eurocentric imaginaries for diagnosing the pull to the right of the right in relation to the ecological crisis. The authors stress the coemergence of modern Science alongside the material and political dimensions of Europe's modern colonial and imperial projects. These produced a racialized, "imperial mode of living" in Ulrich Brand and Markus Wissen's terms, dependent on exploitation and extractivism. The analysis of this dimension of the ecological crisis remains out of focus from within a religio-secular approach. The authors also show how the Eurocentrism of Latour's proposed solution of Earthboundedness and his preferred cultural archive (Gaia) similarly neglects many of the material and planetary dimensions of these interlinked crises, including the globalization of capitalism's interlocking racial and gendered hierarchies. The chapter closes by advocating instead for a more open and decolonial approach to combating the combined threats of the ecological crisis and the pull to the right of the right.

INTRODUCTION

In attempts to understand the worldwide tide of right-wing and far-right politics, and to formulate alternatives to it, the focus is often placed on the dynamics between the political economy of globalization and counterreactions to it in terms of race, nationalism, and civilizationism, with religion and secularization playing complex roles both in the push toward globalization and in the counterreactions. In this chapter, we contribute an ecological perspective by critically discussing the late work of the philosopher of science, sociologist, and anthropologist Bruno Latour. We argue that his account of the modern Gnostic origins of the ecological crisis is pivotal for adequately understanding the right-wing moment, but we also propose a critical engagement with his religio-secular and Eurocentric framework.

In a short essayistic publication, *Down to Earth* (2018),[2] Latour argues that the ecological crisis is a key explanatory factor for the rise of right-wing populism, and of Trumpism, in particular. Although he does not explicitly link populism to the political-religious origins of the ecological crisis in this essay, he traced these origins in his earlier *Facing Gaia* (2017).[3] In this chapter, we reconstruct how the tide of right-wing populism can be related to the religious and philosophical dimensions of the ecological crisis from within Latour's perspective, and we also propose a critical reading of that perspective.

Latour sees a failed secularization after a transformation in Christianity during the Renaissance as the main driver of the dramatically flawed European and Euro-colonial relations to living nature, the planet, and other peoples, manifesting itself in the idea of modern Science, and culminating in the ecological crisis and the right-wing promise that we will not have to share the burden equally.

We read Latour's contribution as a compelling narrative of secularization that helps to understand some of the deeper layers in the rise of right-wing populism, and its roots in the modernist relation to nature. However, we problematize Latour's reliance on what we call "religio-secularism." By religio-secularism, we mean the understanding of complicated societal problems and their histories in terms of a conceptual framework in which religion and secularization (process), secularity (condition), or secularism (ideology) play key explanatory roles.[4] We evaluate the limitations of religio-secularism, and the broad philosophical-theological approach accompanying it, for the diagnosis of what we call the pull to the right of the right in relation to the ecological crisis, and for thinking about alternatives.

We argue that Latour's religio-secularism leads him to a diagnosis of the ecological crisis that remains overly concentrated on Europe and European legacies, while his proposal for "Earthboundedness" as a response to the ecological crisis needs revision too, because of the almost exclusive references to, first, the sciences in connection to what he calls the "*secular figure of Gaia*,"[5] and second, to recent ecological steps in Catholicism developed by Pope Francis in his encyclical *Laudato si'*.[6] In our view, these references are surely important, but they follow the typical European Greek/secular–Christian/religious dyad, and, not coincidentally, they are also close to the preferred cultural references of the Right and remain attached to the same cultural-political archive.

To underline the importance of reflexivity toward this archive, we introduce our notion of a "pull to the right of the right." By this concept we mean the process of how specific European themes, perspectives, and archives cherished by the intellectual Far Right have captured the Euro-Atlantic political imagination in a variety of ways that are not reserved for the Far Right itself, but that "pull" the Right further to the right, generally, and in many places draw the Left with it. Surely, the Far Right didn't invent these themes and archives, but it is rather a matter of a "recapturing" of the political imagination with colonially and racially loaded themes and archives (we explain this more elaborately in our first section).

Finally, and in connection to our critique of the religio-secularism and the related Eurocentrism of Latour's approach, we propose to focus on the way that the ecological crisis is connected to capitalism as a practice or an "imperial mode of living," in sociologists' Ulrich Brand's and Markus Wissen's terms, and is dependent upon "cheap nature," in philosopher Jason Moore's terms.[7] Taking matter into account literally and practically enables us to understand the relations between ecology and the pull to the right of the right during the early decades of the twenty-first century more fruitfully than Latour is able to from within religio-secularism. We also argue that addressing this is important not only for political reasons, but also because sources and practices from beyond the Euro-colonial boundaries are at least as important for conceptualizing Earthboundedness, and for ecological responsibility and solidarity.[8] By thus reflecting on the premises of the religio-secular framework that Latour proposes, we hope to contribute to a philosophical and political *contrepoids* to the right of the right by showing how we can move away from it more radically than Latour can do from within religio-secularism.

The Pull to the Right of the Right and Its Irreligious Tendencies

The worldwide "pull to the right of the right" has become visible through the political successes of the last decade of Trump, Bolsonaro, Erdogan, Putin, Baudet, Wilders, Orbán, Duterte, Modi, Netanyahu, and others. These successes have been prepared, however, by a few decades of discursive transformation during which neoliberal, pro-capitalist, and conservative right-wing discourses have become increasingly entangled with racism, Islamophobia, masculinism, and colonial and imperial nostalgia. Many of these themes were legacies from European imperialism and only had to be recovered after a relative "dip" in the 1960s through the 1990s.

The success of this transformation is what we denote with the notion of a "pull to the right of the right," instead of the more common "right-wing populism" or "Far Right." The latter terms denote an actual political shift from one political genre to another, from the "Right" to the "populist Right" or the "Far Right," and suggest a quite strict divide between them. Our notion of a "pull to the right of the right" refers to a discursive process ("the pull to") whereby anti-egalitarian ideas, themes, and images about race, migration, the nation, Christianity, Whiteness, and gender and sexuality, initially spread within the budding far-right movements from around the 1970s but were infused, sometimes in diluted ways and sometimes explicitly, into more mainstream right-wing discourses and public imaginaries in the course of the twenty-first century, and are still being further spread across the political spectrum and at a global scale.

The pull to the right of the right has been prepared in European, and in particular in French intellectual discourses, making up the so-called *nouvelle droite*, an intellectual movement with legacies of fascism that took shape during the course of the 1970s. Authors such as Dominique Venner, Renaud Camus, Alain de Benoist, and Jean Raspail introduced now widespread notions and themes, such as, first, the emphasis on a so-called *ethno-differentialisme* or *ethno-pluralisme*, where ethnic diversity has been presented as laudable and to be protected, but for each ethnicity (often used as a euphemism for race) in its "country of origin"; second, the interpretation of migration as a reverse colonization; and, third, and more recently, the idea of a *grand remplacement*.[9] The translated term ("great replacement") has been picked up by the American Alt-Right movement through the website Breitbart, and has since become widespread across the Euro-Atlantic. When Renaud Camus restated his replacement theory for an English audience by publishing *You Will Not Replace Us* in 2018, this title became a slogan of the Alt-Right in the United States.[10]

The ambition of these authors has mostly not been directly political, but rather to spread a discourse that would become culturally dominant first, and that could counter what was called "cultural Marxism" after May 1968. Therefore, some scholars talk about a "Gramscism of the Right," because it aims at cultural hegemony instead of political power and seeks to prevent identification with fascism.[11] The ideas of the *nouvelle droite* have not only inspired the North American Alt-Right (as it is euphemistically called), but also European movements to the right of the right, and political parties such as, of course, the National Front (renamed Rassemblement National since 2018), but also the Dutch Forum voor Democratie and the Swedish Far Right.[12] This is why some use the notion of a "European New Right," denoting a movement with intellectual and political representatives increasingly interconnected across Europe.[13]

The identitarian dimensions of the right of the right often exceed strictly national identities by implicitly or explicitly using racial and racial-religious markers inherent to the national ones. As early as the 1960s, the far-right historian Dominique Venner attempted to "refound nationalism by dragging it out of the idea of the nation" and use it for the "defense of the white world."[14] Today, the right of the right constructs a Whiteness that is a complex mix of race, nation, and religion (Christian and/or secularist), but not everywhere in the same manner. In the U.S. context, Whiteness has been thoroughly Americanized, and often figures as White nationalism but is also often recast in terms of (White) Christianity as explored by Philip Gorski (chapter 1), Jason A. Springs (chapter 2), and R. Scott Appleby (chapter 3) in this volume. In the European context, majorities pulled to the right of the right often identify themselves in civilizational terms concerning Europe, rather than in national ones.[15] Often, a secular-religious dyad is used as a criterion, for example, when Europe is identified as a secular, pagan, or Judeo-Christian region, and Islam and "illegal migration" serve as central oppositional categories. Over the last decade, however, the civilizational markers have increasingly been complemented by explicitly racial references, for example, to a so-called European "boreal," or an "Indo-European" civilization, instead of a Judeo-Christian, Christian, or secular one,[16] and by the discursive turn of the European New Right toward the vision of a "great replacement" of White majorities by non-Whites, and the breeding of a "fear of white extinction."[17]

The dire fears of the future conjured up in these discourses ask for out-of-the-ordinary politics. Journalist Thomas Chatterton Williams puts it this way when tracing the French influences on the U.S. right of the right: "The belief that a multicultural society is tantamount to an anti-white society has crept out of French salons and all the way into the Oval Office. The apotheosis of right-wing Gramscism is Donald Trump."[18] The politicians leading the movements to the right of the right regularly acquire religious features when being figured as the "Saviors" of the people, against the presumed lies of all other political actors and media, of which perhaps the most ironic, or rather, absurd, example has been Donald Trump featuring as Esther or Cyrus the Great, leading the Jewish people out of Babylonian exile.[19]

However, the general outlook of these movements seems singularly "irreligious" if we take seriously French philosopher Michel Serres's understanding of religion. Serres puts forward that religion should not be understood as a belief in a specific doctrine or even as a set of practices related to particular groups and beliefs. Drawing on the etymology of *religio*, he understands religion in terms of "to assemble, gather, lift up, traverse, or reread."[20] Serres notes that scholars interested in religion's etymologies and genealogies "never say what sublime word our language opposes to the religious to deny it: *negligence*. Whoever has no religion should not be called an atheist or unbeliever, but negligent. The notion of negligence makes it possible to understand our time."[21]

As we think with Serres for a moment, what characterizes the right of the right seems to be a general carelessness toward the world and everything vulnerable that is "not-us." At the same time, "us" is being imagined as stronger than, but still endangered by, "not-us." The way "not-us" is reconfigured and reimagined is characterized by a fear of *ensauvagement* and *remplacement*,[22] insecurity, barbarism, streaming, and flooding—all phenomena considered more "natural" and less "cultural/modern/civilized/White/masculine" than "us," and therefore dangerous. These other "dangerous" phenomena can be humans, but then especially those without homes, citizenship rights, and properties, flooding "our" well-ordered ("White-ordered") societies (and land registers).[23] Like natural phenomena, they can happen to "us," but they are not "us."

For Latour, who mentions Serres's work as one of his major sources of inspiration, it is particularly the attitude of neglect and even contempt for nature, and everything and everyone relegated to it, that lies at the root of the general inability to respond adequately to the climate crisis. According to Latour, the underlying motive in Trumpism and what he calls "populism" is a specifically modern irreligious attitude in Serres's sense: a general carelessness toward the Earth and its inhabitants. Latour sees Trumpism as a form of hypermodernism, aggressively defending the American way of life, which can be seen as the culmination of a tendency that had been expressed before him in George W. Bush's slogan that "the American way of life is not negotiable."[24]

An ultimate resource, according to Latour, for the attachment to the "American way of life," or what we call, with Brand and Wissen, the "imperial mode of living," is a "contempt for matter." In the footsteps of the German American philosopher Eric Voegelin (1901–85), Latour sees such contempt as a religious motive that developed specifically in European Christianity during the Renaissance and eventually became a determining feature of modernity. This contempt is not "religious" in Serres's sense—rather the opposite. However, it does refer to a specific turn within Christianity, moving it toward the contempt for material, living nature. This attitude eventually permeated modernity in its entirety through the modern idea of Science, philosophy (Descartes), and capitalism.[25] This transformation and its devastating consequences for nature and, increasingly, for the entire planet, are intimately linked to the pull to the right of the right, for this is the latest articulation and culmination of the kind of negligence and contempt that Latour and Serres put forward as the defining features of modernity. Latour sees this development as a failed secularization because it is dependent on a Manichaean, Gnostic turn in Christianity, opposite to secularity in the sense of being worldly, earthly, materially. Therefore, it is also insensitive to ecological matters. Let us further explain.

The Philosophical and Religious Origins of the Ecological Crisis in Latour's Work

In recent years, politicians to the right of the right in different political contexts have been raising doubts about the truth of scientific reports on climate change.[26] They argue that these reports are based on a misguided belief in abstract uncertainties rather than common sense and claim that "believing" in the doom scenario portrayed by scientists will necessarily result in rapid economic decline and overall chaos. Condemning such "hysteria," these politicians have rendered modern science as suspicious, hence the emphasis on "alternative truths" and the skepticism toward the "scientist elites." A painful example from the United States were the attacks against public health officials during the COVID-19 pandemic.

The resistance to climate science is a crucial part of the right-wing populist narrative, argues Latour. He explains in *Down to Earth* that the climate skeptic response is at the center of the discourse of "so-called 'populist' parties," as it stems from the idea that the nation (often perceived as White and Christian) must be recast as an exclusive access to a certain "way of life" that is "not negotiable." The climate crisis is therefore necessarily also a crisis of migration and socioeconomic inequality, because these phenomena together cause a fear of losing one's habitat, an exclusive territory, and the wealth and ways of life connected to it. Unfortunately, the response to this fear of those drawn to the right of the right has been to turn to "the false protection of identities and rigid borders," recast in civilizationist, nationalist, and/or racial terms.[27] As such, right-wing "populism" must be seen as a symptom of a longer and broader phenomenon that has resulted in these multiple crises. Latour writes: "We understand nothing about the terrifying growth in inequalities, the 'wave of populism' or the 'migration crisis' if we do not understand that these are three different responses . . . to the powerful reaction of the Earth to what globalization has done to it."[28] What strengthens those on the right of the right is their responsiveness to the widespread fear of losing a safe haven in an increasingly complex world, a fear that they racialize and culturalize in accordance with the classical right-wing strategy.[29]

Latour adds that it is against the backdrop of the increasingly experienced lack of a shared "common ground" (the "Local"[30] in a very literal sense, in the sense of a "feeling at home") that we must understand the fear of losing one's land and habitat. He relates this to the realization that because "what had to be abandoned in order to modernize" was "the Local," the territory reinvented by modernism as "backward," serving as the opposite of "progress,"[31] modernization was no longer a desirable option, but rather one to fear. This fear is first and foremost an effect of the "disorientation" that "derives entirely from the emergence of an actor that reacts and will continue to react to human actions [Gaia] and that bars modernizers from knowing *where they are, in what epoch*, and especially *what role* they need to play from now on."[32] In other words, if we want to understand why the right of the right has become an attractive alternative, and assess how we must respond to the fears it appeals to, we need to face the emerging reality of an Earth that seems no longer accessible and habitable for everyone and as such urges us to find an alternative promise to secure a place on Earth.

Contempt for Matter, Gnosticism, and "Immanentization"

In *Facing Gaia*, Latour traces the ecological crisis back to the (counter) religious and philosophical origins of modernity by looking at the juncture of the idea of Science, developments within Christianity, and global politics. This reconstruction shows how a Gnostic "contempt for matter" shaped the modernist stance to "nature," which in Latour's view is the main explanation for the general insensitivity to the ecological crisis and our inability to respond to it adequately.

In exploring the religious origins of this attitude, Latour, drawing on the work of Voegelin, links the modernist contempt for matter to a particular shift in the apocalyptic message of Christianity.[33] Voegelin locates this shift to medieval monk Joachim de Flore. He added to the Christian faith the idea that the Kingdom of the Spirit, imagined as the incarnation of eternal heaven, is not reached in a wholly distant and obscure eternal world, as was believed, but rather is an "end" that can be realized on Earth and within the passage of time. This shift created a tension between the contingency of the sublunary world[34] and the universality and eternity of the transcendent world (as they were now both localized within this world), which was then resolved by the transformation of immanent earthly things, "into what is able to bear eternity for good."[35] This meant that realizing the Kingdom of the Spirit here below could only be done "by radically transforming the earthly one" into the reality of "Paradise itself."[36] In other words, since the theological reform instigated by Joachim de Flore, "paradise" (the "end" of life itself), was localized *on Earth* and *within this time*, rather than elsewhere and beyond. This ultimately resulted in the conviction of the Moderns that one could reach "the completion, the achievement, of the world here below by the intrusion of the Spirit."[37]

Latour adds to this reconstruction the concept of counterreligion, which he borrows from Egyptologist Jan Assmann. Assmann coined the concept to distinguish the major monotheistic religions from earlier religious traditions, regarding these religions as essentially countering other existing religions by means of elevating their own religion as the only true one, and thereby establishing their Truth as absolute, universal, and eternal.[38] It means seeing Truth (and the promise connected to it) as the only conceivable one. Latour emphasizes that as eternity, because the end of time and the promise of salvation, was now being located within history, it became reachable, and gave rise to the belief that *all uncertainty*, once the most essential aspect of Christianity,[39] must and can eventually be overcome.

In the footsteps of Voegelin, Latour suggests that it was particularly through the influence of Gnosticism that this immanentization of the Truth resulted in the Moderns metaphysically disconnecting themselves from the Earth. Gnosticism, a heretic tradition within Christianity that conceived of matter (and the body) as evil and as separate from the Good, emerged from the fear that arose from the uncertain relation that Christians had with their world-transcendent God. In a counterreligious move, Gnosticism modified the obscure and uncertain character of the Christian message by localizing the Absolute Truth in "assured knowledge."

This influenced the belief of presumably secular science in a system of perfectible knowledge of general laws,[40] which superimposes on materiality a "contempt for matter" that is "insensitive to the specific agency of Earthly things and living entities from bacteria to worms to human individuals."[41] As the Earth itself became the locus of eternity in the form of universal laws, final ends, causality, and *Dinge an Sich*, its former agents became petrified, dead objects waiting for man to analyze, quantify, and control them, making "any contact with the down-to-earth, with materiality" impossible.[42] Imagining the realm here below as an immanentized paradise was thus inextricably linked to the Moderns' Gnostic contempt of matter. This contempt thus resulted in a Science that transformed materiality into passive, dead, controllable, objective matter ("matters of fact"), stripped from all agency or freedom,[43] that had to be grasped, categorized, and brought into formal and causal relations by the universal power of reason, without which these phenomena remained meaningless objects—hence the "death of nature."[44] Modernization in this regard is the endeavor to move toward the promise (salvation) of progress through Science for the higher (final and absolute) promise (end) of "civilization."

Latour connects this counterreligious move of immanentizing the earthly world to the Moderns' insensitiveness to the ecological crisis, by suggesting that the belief that it is possible to create "paradise on Earth," that heaven could become "immanentized," had as its countereffect that there no longer was an accessible Earth.[45] Hence the apocalypse in the form of the ecological crisis could not be perceived as a real threat because the Moderns are convinced with blind (counterreligious) certainty that they have already created paradise here on Earth (salvation through capitalist growth and scientific progress) and that the end-time has already been reached.[46] Latour writes: "Telling Westerners . . . that the time has come, that their world has ended, that they have to change their way of life, can only produce a feeling of total incomprehension, because, for them, the Apocalypse *has already taken place*. They have already gone over to the other side."[47] Because the Moderns *believe* that they have already reached the promised land of eternally appropriating dead nature-as-matter, they are not able to see the response of this "matter" that was supposed to be inert, because the Moderns superimposed on materiality the "*contempt for matter* that is one of the ancient features of Gnosticism."[48]

In sum, a person's modern scientific relation to nature is thoroughly Gnostic in the sense that nature is conceived as being in one sense the realm of eternal laws (immanentized), without historicity and agency, and in another sense simultaneously proving time and again beyond our control (hence the contempt). The "Manichaean feature" of Gnostic modernity thus resulted in the "mistrust, disgust, hatred even, toward matter" for its unfitness "to be transformed by Ideas," and for its resistance through the differentiated agency of small things as uncovered by the sciences in practice, and through the imminent response by the Earth to its ecological maltreatment.[49] The Moderns did not realize that modernity has not been a rejection of religion, or an emancipation from it—a "secularization"—but rather a "counterreligion" itself, where science is treated as an absolute truth that does not need to attend to the specific agency of things. The latter is, however, what the sciences in practice do when they function well, which is why in the eyes of Latour they do the opposite of what the modern idea of science assumes.[50]

Connected to the promise of civilization and the contempt for matter is the need to transcend the crude "state of nature" and the brutish condition of its inhabitants, to "enlighten" oneself with the universal laws and principles of Science and Civilization. There are thus immediate material, political, and imperial dimensions to the "Gnostic temptation" that became stronger in early modernity. As the sciences developed and new forms of land and wealth emerged on the horizon of the colonial enterprise after 1492, modernity moved to a "situation in which we believe we can grasp, realized here on earth, the promised presence of the world beyond" (the "New World").[51] The modernizing impulse thus has an inherently imperial and violent side: "By believing oneself to be a bearer of salvation," the West became "the apocalypse for others."[52]

In his *Race: A Theological Account*, J. Kameron Carter traces how Gnosticism already in antiquity and the early Middle Ages was connected not only to a contempt of matter in a general sense, but also to a division between specific groups associated with nature, matter, or the body. Jews in particular were cast in contrast to a superior "race" of pneumatic (spiritual) men.[53] These early practices of racial othering through the mind/body dichotomy returned with modernity in the fraught and complicated but always hierarchical presentation of the relation between "Man" and nature/animal/woman, *humanitas* and *anthropos*, White and Black. In short, the binaries that the recent humanities have been opposing and deconstructing are the same as those pulling the right to the right are celebrating and exacerbating again, especially in their constructions of a patriarchal Whiteness.[54]

Sylvia Wynter sees these hierarchical relations as part of what she calls "the overrepresentation of Man." By "Man" Wynter means the European bourgeois, White male "ethnoclass" that in colonial modernity has represented itself, and still does, as the essence of Being, Power, Truth, and Freedom, repressing other forms of being (human).[55] She explicitly links the "struggles with respect to race, class, gender, sexual orientation, ethnicity" to environmental struggles and the unequal distribution of resources, by explaining them as an expression of the struggle between the overrepresented "Man" and the underrepresented "human." Wynter's "Man" could be read as analogous to the all-knowing rational subject of modern Gnosticism and Science, and "human" as her terminology for the disregarded material being. More strongly than Latour, however, she explains the emergence of "Man" in the context of the Renaissance humanists' confrontation with the "New World" and the racial hierarchies that were constructed in connection to colonial domination, rather than solely from within Christian theology and the development of Science within Europe. In her view "it was in the context of the humanists' redescribing of the Christian definition of the human—in new, revalorizing, and (so to speak) propter nos homines and/or Man-centric terms—that the series of fifteenth-century voyages on whose basis the West began its global expansion voyages . . . were to initiate the rupture that would lead to the rise of the physical sciences."[56] By contrast, in Latour, the colonial enterprise is shaped by the Moderns' promise of civilization, as part of the cluster of transformations that emerged conjointly from within Europe. In our fourth section we will explain this dimension of Latour's genealogy of modernity as part of its Eurocentrism.

From "The West as Apocalypse" to Ecological Crisis and the Right of the Right

As natural resources are being depleted, Latour points out, the old common ideal of modernity—universalization as globalization—has proven to be impossible to achieve for everyone. New and old elites are creating alternative narratives that promise a haven from the threat of ecological disaster. Those on the right of the right do so by exteriorizing the threat in the form of an imaginary foreign threat: they promise to safeguard a "homeland" from the threats of (non-White) migrants, global hegemonic institutions, "uncivilized" cultures, and Islam. Latour suggests that we will not be able to explain this type of politics, and the politics of the last fifty years, if we do not recognize how the existential challenge posed by climate change, namely, the unsustainability of the modern way of life, evokes counterreactions of withdrawal, denial, and naïve self-assurance that are very exemplary for the narratives of the right of the right.

According to Latour, right-wing populist agendas should therefore be understood as part of a broader agenda of global elites to ensure for themselves an exclusive place on Earth, which is becoming increasingly uninhabitable for many people (as in the biblical story of Noah's ark):

> All of this is part of a single phenomenon: the elites have been so thoroughly convinced that there would be no future life for everyone that they have decided *to get rid of all the burdens of solidarity as fast as possible*—hence deregulation; they have decided that a sort of gilded fortress would have to be built for those (a small percentage) who would be able to make it through—hence the explosion of inequalities; and they have decided that, to conceal the crass selfishness of such a flight out of the shared world, they would have to reject absolutely the threat at the origin of this headlong flight—hence the denial of climate change.[57]

These phenomena all form part of a larger political agenda that is concerned with ensuring exclusive access to a certain piece of land and the way of life of a people that sees itself as belonging to that piece of land, in spite of international bonds, rights, treaties, and other forms of transnational solidarity. Drawing on this insight, we argue that the traditional exclusivist, conservative, and xenophobic stances of right-wing populist discourses should not be seen apart from the relatively new trend of climate skepticism. Indeed, these attitudes are symptoms of a broader and longer sentiment of aiming to protect a modern way of life, which is also essentially a White and capitalist way of life.

The spread of global capitalism through imperialism and globalization has, in Latour's view, led to an impulse of taking off from the Earth, which rather needs to be turned into one of Earthboundedness. The reconstruction of how "taking off" has emerged from the history of the Moderns in terms of a religious history and a failed secularization helps to fully understand what it means to come down to Earth, since becoming Earthbound is also theorized in terms of religion and secularism in Latour's elaboration. In the next section, we analyze what this specific approach entails, and show how the dynamics of religion and secularity, according to Latour, pushes into the direction of climate devastation and pulls into the direction of the right of the right.

EARTHBOUNDEDNESS

Earthboundedness is the central concept for Latour when he thinks of a livable future. It is opposite to the negligent modernism of the right of the right, but it is not immediately local, and does it romanticize the immediately local or the concepts often used to figure it, such as "nation," "community," and "identity." Earthboundedness is oriented toward a common ground, a shared horizon based on knowledge and the sciences, in which the Earth is accessible to and habitable for everyone, but local in the sense of not being construed as a globe to be objectified from a distance. To be Earthbound means to come to terms with the fact that it is not possible to "return to nature" as if one was ever apart from it, and instead it envisions humans as "on Earth" rather than "in nature."[58]

This enables us to think outside of modernist metaphysics, according to which "Nature" is ontologized in the form of passive objectivity and "Culture" as what transcends such determination (the nature/culture divide). For Latour, the problem of the Moderns is that they do not situate themselves within time. Because they are on the other side of the apocalypse, as Voegelin argued, they lack realism in the sense of understanding the time that they find themselves in: "They have never paid attention to the *direction* in which they are heading, obsessed as they have been by the idea of *escaping* their attachments to the old Earth."[59] This founding myth of modernity, according to which humans can overcome all uncertainty by controlling nature, has to be replaced, according to Latour, by the "secular figure of Gaia" in order for humans to be able to "face" Gaia, come "down to Earth," and become "Earthbound."

This can be effectuated through the work of the sciences in practice, because they carefully analyze the specific forms of agency of all things that in one way or the other act, signify, and, therefore, exist.[60] For Latour (in close connection to critical scholars in the life sciences, such as Donna Haraway, Lynn Margulis, Isabelle Stengers, and Vinciane Despret), the sciences in their (trans)disciplinary practices, in contrast to Science as a modern idea that conceives of Nature as governed by laws, exemplify such differentiated knowledge of the agency of all things: what they need to function, what they do, and therefore what they mean and how they exist. Scientific practices and cooperation thus give us access to Gaia as the secular figure for nature.

Science in practice and Earthboundedness are also implicitly religious if we follow the Serre's definition, as Latour does, according to which religion is the opposite of negligence.[61] Even one of the most popular concepts in Latour's work, "assemblage," has a Christian connotation, because the Greek word "ecclesia," which was translated as "the church" in the Christian tradition, translates as "assembly." Serres renders "to assemble" accordingly as the first meaning of "religion."[62] Religion is then also the assembling of connections, closely related to Haraway's "making kin."[63]

With the proposal for the "secular figure of Gaia," Latour means secular in the positive sense of "worldly," "earthly," in opposition to "irreligious" in the sense of "negligent," "careless." Still, he also goes out of his way to prevent anything religious from coming into the understanding of Gaia. He warns against animating nature and points out that Lovelock understands the Earth as active, but without "endowing it with a soul," or "taking Earth to be an already composed whole." Yet, Lovelock does consider all that "speaks," in the sense of having a meaning, a voice, an existence, an agency, because in some way or another it is active in relation to something else on the planet and forms part of Gaia. Latour writes:

> The paradox of the figure that we are attempting to confront is that the name of a proteiform, monstrous, shameless, primitive goddess has been given to what is probably the *least religious entity* produced by Western science. If the adjective "secular" signifies implying no external cause and no spiritual foundation, and thus "belonging wholly to this world," then Lovelock's intuition may be called *wholly secular*. Alas, "secular" invokes only the contrary of "religious."[64]

This positive and innovative way of being religious in Serres's sense is thus to be *wholly secular*, caring for and being attentive to, reading, knowing the things of this world as part of Earth, not a friendly Earth to be romanticized, but an active Earth that we can engage with. It is the opposite of being "religious" in the sense of "endowing something with a soul, an external cause, or a spiritual foundation," for this would drive you out of the worldly attendance.

That is also why the notion of "belief" is a misnomer for this way of being religious, as we have already seen with Serres's critique of this notion: believing drives us out of this world into the direction of some higher soul or cause or god. It leads to the contempt of matter. Religion *as belief* in a transcendent God is related to the scientific attitude toward the abstract globe of modernity, to outer space, and to counterreligion.

To summarize, whereas the idea of "Science/Nature" as a system of laws governing dead matter/objects has played a crucial role in the modernist negligence of the Earth (and the living beings on its outer crust), scientists in practice are closer to life/Gaia/Earth by differentiating the agencies that play their unique roles in the world. The fact that scientists are often still not able to find the political words/poetics to contradict climate skeptics and leave too much space for the right of the right is related to the modernist cling to "value-neutral Science," but not to the insights available in scientific practice. The sciences in their disciplinary and scholarly differentiation practices enable facing the "secular figure of Gaia" precisely when animals, rivers, bacteria, and all other natural agents can become known and heard in their differentiation and specific agency, which enables them to be cared for, and even politically defended.

The Power of Religion and the Religious Diplomacy of the Sciences

Latour thus revises the standard understanding of religion and secularity. By doing so, he might seem to break with religious traditions and invent something entirely new. However, his views more easily connect to recent trends in Catholicism than one might assume. For example, he regularly refers to Pope Francis's encyclical *Laudato si'*. The latter provides sources within Catholic Christianity, via the tradition of Saint Francis, that can be connected to the secular figure of Gaia: "Praise be to you, my Lord, through our Sister, Mother Earth, who sustains and governs us, and who produces various fruit with coloured flowers and herbs."[65] Pope Francis uses this reference to add his part in this vein: "This sister now cries out to us because of the harm we have inflicted on her. We have come to see ourselves as her lords and masters, entitled to plunder her at will. The violence present in our hearts, wounded by sin, is also reflected in the symptoms of sickness evident in the soil, in the water, in the air and in all forms of life. This is why the earth herself, burdened and laid waste, is among the most abandoned maltreated of our poor."[66] As Latour notes, concern for ecology had for long been seen as something New Age, and also pagan, but now motifs within Catholicism are being picked up that are connected to ecological thinking.[67]

Feminist critics point out the failures to link concerns with the environment and the need to redress colonial plunder and exploitative capitalism to feminist insights into how such exploitative practices were authorized through gendered metaphors grounded in Christian ontology. *Laudato si'*, in other words, may critically puncture exploitative capitalism by stressing the exploitation of the Earth, but the inability to confront patriarchal violence delimits its critical scope.[68]

In ways that echo *Laudato si'*, Latour notes an emptiness of European modern languages and philosophies to develop a cosmology at all, divided as they are between (Protestant-oriented) religion directed toward subjectivity as interiority, on the one hand, and secular science, directed toward objectivity as exteriority, on the other.

This modern division is the inheritance of the Cartesian divide between *res extensa* and *res cogitans*, which divides humans as "subjects" (psychological, ethical, political) from "nature" as the object of science. It explains why scientists are so often unable to express why their ecological knowledge is politically and socially relevant, instead of "value-free knowledge" based on neutral data or facts. Latour advocates instead for the exhortative power of religion, especially its transformative dimensions, as a source for a political ecology:

> Religion, in its Christian instantiation at least, presents itself as a rather plausible alternative to an ecological consciousness whose ethical and emotional drives do not seem to have enough petrol (or soybeans) to carry us through the tasks it has burdened upon us. In this respect, nothing is less conservative, and nothing is more down

to earth, than religion. . . . Whereas ecological consciousness has been unable to move us, the religious drive to renew the face of the earth just might.[69]

Religion, in his view, gives people stronger motivation than mere "science," because it speaks more to people than scientific scholarship.

What Latour does not mention here, however, an omission that in our view is connected to a closeness to the pope's religious language, is the power of literature, modern art, and journalism to move people, in comparison to what religion has been capable to do as far as ecology is concerned. In that sense, Latour seems moved by the debate about science and religion, which is one other branch of religio-secularism. And why "religion, in its Christian instantiation at least?" Perhaps this limitation is a sign of modesty, but it is also excluding non-Christian backgrounds, Indigenous in the first place, that can be said to be earthly in many ways, and that inspire ecological consciousness worldwide.

It is partly for what Latour calls "diplomatic" reasons that he appeals to religion and secularity, because religion captures for many peoples around the world "what they care for in this world." This is what he thinks is basically missing in both modern religion as a form of belief and in modern Science. Especially for scholars, it would be of great value if they were able to exchange diplomatically what they care for, and not just what they know objectively, with other peoples of the world.[70] Latour extends this meaning toward "becoming attentive to that to which others cling," hereby making the connection to diplomacy.[71] As irreligion means a lack of care and negligence, this also entails the refusal to take the effort to become diplomatic in the sense of listening to what others care for, and these others are not limited to humans but to all agents that, by acting, have a certain voice and meaning.

The notion of religious diplomacy may be of use to a philosopher who wants to move something "big" in the world, such as hypermodernist lifestyles and politics. The use of a religio-secular framework enables them to be in conversation with those for whom this religious distinction is relevant in a global political context. Thus, Latour's proposal is an explicit attempt to reach beyond the secular academic language to which ecologism is often connected (or confined) and to connect it with religious discourses. He proposes this not just for democratic reasons, but also because such discourses traditionally have been able to express meaning of and in the world, and therefore have cosmological and care dimensions.

Religion, religious transformation, and secularization are thus the root of the ecological problem for Latour, but they also form a complicated answer to it: *religio*, in Serres's sense, together with the "secular figure of Gaia" are the decisive elements of Earthboundedness. This implies a turn away from a belief-oriented and institutional conception of religion toward a care-oriented notion of religion. As such, there is no religious field in opposition to another, secular field. The whole idea of religious diplomacy as "what we care for" is that it can be translated into and compared with "what others care for" through diplomatic comparison (which is not possible with counterreligions). The secular figure is not "secularist" in the sense of nonreligious: it is about worldliness. The trick is to sense and locate meaning in the world, the cosmos, including the moving, living things on the planet, and its crust reacting to human presence, and therefore also to see the connections between semiosis and scientific practice.

Evaluating the Ecological and Political Scope of Latour's Religio-Secularism

We have seen that Latour analyzes the causes of the ecological crisis through a combined epistemological, ontological, and theological lens, tracing them to modern conceptions of nature and science and their theological basis in the Manichaean contempt of matter. This same contempt is also the basis of the pull to the right of the right as a defensive attitude spreading under populations increasingly at risk of losing the destructive habitus and the imperial way of life they would like to hold on to. With this approach Latour constructs a classical secularization narrative with a specifically eco-political twist. Thus, religious transformation and secularization in European history are not just the root causes of the pull to the right of the right and ecological devastation; religion and secularity differently conceived are not just the framework of analysis but also part of the solution. This is what we call the "religio-secularism" of Latour's analysis. By "religio-secularism," to recall, we mean the explanation of ontological and political-historical problems and dynamics through the lens of religion and secularism (or secularization) as its driving factors.[72] We can now evaluate the merit of religio-secularism for understanding the relation between climate devastation and the pull to the right of the right.

Is Earthboundedness Earthly Enough?

We have seen that, when talking about the religious causes of the ecological crisis, Latour uses the concepts of religion and secularity not as a familiar dyad, but in a way that demonstrates how they can be used as opposites that can also be intertwined with and reinforce each other. He does so by talking about Gaia as a "(finally secular) figure of nature," while also explaining contemporary scientific practice in terms of a Serresian conception of religion—the opposite of negligence. This perspective enables us, as we have seen, to understand how the pull to the right of the right and the ecological crisis both stem from the deep-seated modern *negligence* available in modern science and Christianity, and to see possible ways of countering these phenomena. Bringing religion and secularity together problematizes a certain conception of modernity. It helps us to see the broad connections across domains and fields that are usually opposed to each other and often implicitly lead to either the one or the other being made responsible (either religion or secularity) for deeper, underlying problems that modern secularity and religion share. Thus, addressing them together may help to address the problems at the root level, and to find new ways in which the contemporary sciences in practice and religions beyond modern Manichaeism can find each other.

However, if we want to fully understand the link between the ecological crisis and the pull to the right of the right, it is crucial to see the connections between the religious/modernist neglect and contempt of matter, and the *material conditions* that made this negligence attractive, normalized it, and fostered its global spreading. Working from within a religio-secularist framework, Latour in our view is not particularly well equipped to critically engage with these crucial material and practical aspects of the modernist contempt of matter.

When the right of the right aims to protect its religious, national, racial, or civilizational way of life, this is always also the protection of a capitalist and imperial way of life that has become normalized through modernization. Looking through a material, socioeconomic, and political-historical lens as a complement to a theological, epistemological, or ontological one, enables one to consider the history of capitalism, consumerism, urbanization, and the exploitation of the Earth and its inhabitants as a set of practices that are shared among peoples and populations of many different backgrounds and locations. Such differences *can* go along with a specific theological history, but not necessarily.

The politics of climate change denial and the pull to the right of the right exist broadly as a resistance to giving up a destructive way of life. This destructive way of life, on the one hand, interprets itself as the realization of the good life (as Latour emphasizes). On the other hand, however, it is also a way of life that the White Euro-settler populations have become habituated to, because of the promises and dreams connected to access to wealth and consumption, and the valorization of greed and profit. In accordance with Latour, we suggest that this way of life is a legacy of conceiving ourselves as modern, and of religious motives hinging on a conception of nature as distant, meaningless matter.

However, although Latour's valorization of scientific practice (in contrast to the modern idea of science) gives an important innovative perspective, he problematically remains firmly within the Eurocentric and secularization-oriented variant of the critique of modernity. As we have seen, he explains the connections between the pull to the right and climate ideology in terms of a secularization narrative that starts with the emergence of monotheism, and which he specifies in Assmann's terms, referring to the history of counter-religion. Thus, instead of seeing the rise of capitalism and colonialism as constitutive dimensions of modernity, Latour rather presents these processes as add-ons to immanent European processes, classically interpreted through the lens of the history of philosophy. In his interpretation one religious or philosophical scheme calls for reaction from another from within, instead of being understood as systematically related to technological and economic developments in connection with non-European actors.

In this sense, Latour takes a step back into the direction of theology in comparison to Sylvia Wynter, as we discussed above, but even in comparison to medieval historian Lynn White's analysis of the ecological crisis from 1967. Although Latour distances himself from White's analysis of the religious roots of the ecological crisis in *Facing Gaia*, in our view, some of the criticisms leveled at White's work in terms of its being too theologically oriented apply even more strongly to Latour's own analysis. White published his famous article in *Science* under the title "The Historical

Roots of Our Ecological Crisis," which thoroughly influenced ecological thinking.[73] Like Latour, White followed a religio-secular methodology, but one that makes an intrinsic connection to technology, and he thus steps out of religio-secularism more than Latour does in this respect.

White identified several crucial developments that together explain the ecological crisis. As a historian, he pointed out how medieval monastic communities in northern European regions were the first to adopt new technologies, such as the heavy plough, "to attack" the Earth and as such signify human mastery of nature. A further integration of technology and science took place in the nineteenth century, which caused this "attack" on the Earth to be strongly reinforced and spread all over the globe through empire. Thus, White traces a more intricate relation between ecology and technology than Latour does. However, like Latour, he ultimately follows a religio-secular narrative, only it's a different, even more encompassing one than Latour's: White traces the root cause of this development back to "Judeo-Christianity" in general. This is where Latour rejects his view in favor of one concentrated on the Renaissance transformation of Christianity.[74]

White emphasized how the Bible presents humans as an outstanding species, essentially distinct from nature, referring to Genesis 1:28, which reads: "And God blessed them, and God said to them, 'Be fruitful and multiply and fill the earth and subdue it; and have dominion over the fish of the sea and over the birds of the air and over every living thing that moves upon the earth.'" White understood Genesis as illustrating how "Judeo-Christianity," especially in connection to heavy technology that developed from the late Middle Ages onward, had brought about the idea that Man was meant to master (or "steward") the Earth and all its creatures, being created in the image of God and therefore being apart from nature from the beginning. White thus put forward a relatively technology-focused version of the secularization narrative in reconstructing European civilization, where secularization is seen as the root of modernity and the devastation of nature connected to it, and as coming from "within" Europe, (problematically) designated as "Judeo-Christian."[75]

Like Latour's, White's analysis does not introduce factors that may have arisen from European actors' connections with the world outside of Europe. As such, the material and sociopolitical way of life connected to capitalism, race, and gender hierarchy is, as a cause of the ecological problems, subordinated to a more general theological level. If we follow that path, the process seems to unfold by itself, from within Christianity and its secularization. This conceals the systematic link between modernity, coloniality, gendered racism, capitalism, and ecology, which we conversely regain when we reconstruct the emergence of ecological crisis as the result of interaction with the rest of the world through capitalist coloniality.[76] Both White's and Latour's analyses can therefore ultimately be read as versions of a narrative in which secularization lies at the root of modernity, and in which the devastation of nature develops in a systematic way from within Christianity (or Judeo-Christianity) and its secularization.

Already in 1970, again in *Science*, Lewis Moncrief had criticized White for overlooking the ways in which factors such as the spread of democratization, urbanization, and wealth played crucial roles in the ecological crisis, through his narrow focus on and simplification of the Judeo-Christian tradition. According to Moncrief, these factors did not develop separately from secularization, but they did have other, more sociological dimensions apart from specific religio-secular genealogies.[77] In our view, a similar criticism applies to Latour's analysis.

There is a crucial mediating factor at play in the modernist development that extends beyond the religio-secular dimension, and, with that, beyond the European history of secularization, and which drops out of Latour's analysis *as a systematic factor*, although he does mention it. We already discussed in the first main section how Sylvia Wynter analyzes the intricacy of the emergence of "Man" in relation to the colonial enterprise. Here, we would like to draw attention to the history of what geographer Jason Moore calls "cheap nature," which goes hand in hand with "cheap labor,"[78] and which shows the material and power dimension of the imperial mode of living that is so characteristic of modernity in its current state.

Moore emphasizes the importance of the capitalist dimension for the nature/culture divide, which one misses if one focuses solely on the place of the (hu)man vis-à-vis nature (Anthropocene/science). To belong to "nature" means to be regarded as savage, slave, woman, plantation soil, mineral resource, meat, fur, and so on, and as such it means to be "cheapened," to be transformed into exploitable labor or an extractable resource. From early modernity onward, this cheapening increasingly took the form of seeing those necessary for labor and profit as potential and exploitable raw material and capital. Moore points out that these are not merely analytical abstractions, but rather real abstractions, resulting from a praxis of domination and alienation making them "*practically* abstract."[79] Hence, the modernistic conception of "nature" as separate from society, and therefore from morality, value, and meaning, has contributed to a host of practices of extraction and exploitation that have spread globally. These practices have extended the scale of nature's exploitation throughout modernity, especially through capitalist/imperialist expansion.

Similarly, Brand and Wissen have reconstructed how the development of modernity, driving on the imperial impulses of capitalism, is founded on an exclusionary (White) privilege to colonize and appropriate land, extract its resources, and exhaust nature, animals, and laborers (successfully "cheapened," in Moore's sense). Like Latour, they point toward the externalizing logic that is inherent to this imperial mode of living, namely, the idea that the promise of modernity lies "elsewhere," albeit here on Earth: "By its nature, it implies disproportionate access to natural and human resources on a global scale—in other words: an 'elsewhere.' It also demands that others abstain from their own proportional share."[80] More strongly than Latour, however, they emphasize the material conditions that create the necessity of this "elsewhere." This "elsewhere" is the locus for the constant need to extract raw materials to sustain the mode of living that we call "modern" or "civilized" but that inherently demands the "worldwide exploitation of nature—and wage and non-wage labour—while simultaneously externalizing the social and ecological consequences arising from it."[81] Contempt, disregard, cheapening, and exclusion obviously go hand in hand here, but this logic does not stem merely from being driven "out of this world," but also from the very real and insatiable material demands of the imperial way of living.

Moreover, critical philosophies of modernity, capitalism, and alienation often have recognized a motive related to "negligence" as a root cause of these developments. According to this motive, the moral result of modernity's tendency toward abstraction can be understood, in Theodor Adorno's earlier terms, as *bürgerliche Kälte* ("bourgeois coldness"), closely related to negligence and contempt. This motive is close to Latour's irreligious modernity in terms of its carelessness, but it includes an immediate relation to capitalism (abstraction) that only comes after the religious motive in Latour, and it adds an extra layer to the idea of contempt in modernity.

An interpretation of such coldness immediately related to capitalism and modernity is missing in Latour's analysis, because it remains a story of secularization and modernity. A characteristic of the right of the right today, as it was of fascism, seems to be that it intensifies the bourgeois coldness toward "nature" from a passive "negligence," and turns it into an aggression toward everything associated with nature. Such a perspective can help to explain the typical aggression connected to the right of the right. Today, we see how such aggression is directed toward exploitable nature itself, for example, in the vehement support for fracking, or in projects such as the Dakota pipeline being defended not just from an economic, calculative perspective, but with a conviction, a boasting, that exceeds the "just economic," as in the rhetoric of Trumpism.[82] Nearly all far-right populists have their anti-ecological rhetoric and practices, however, whether it concerns the Amazon rainforest destruction or the destruction of the last forest close to Istanbul for the creation of Europe's largest airport. Famously, the relatively early far-right French populist Jean-Marie Le Pen already dismissed ecology in the 1990s as the "new religion of the bobo" (bohemian bourgeois). This hatred against ecology is difficult for Latour to theorize because of his insufficiently practice- and matter-oriented religio-secular perspective.[83]

An analysis in terms of a broad category of modernity is connected to a broad analysis of ecological destruction in terms of the "Anthropocene," but Moore and others propose that "Capitalocene" would be a more adequate concept.[84] If we conceive the causes of ecological destruction as the relatively independent process of the (imperial) expansion of capitalism in the form of a set of attitudes and practices—a way of life governed by laws of competition, exploitation, extraction, and consumption—we arrive at a different analysis than if we follow the theological/epistemological/history of the sciences methodology proposed by Latour. In other words, the contempt for matter should also be explained in terms of a motive of cheapening nature for capital "elsewhere" and protecting the exclusionary way of life that it sustains "here," hence the isolationist panic reactions of those pulling to the right of the right.[85]

In sum, Latour's methodological choices cause him to remain overly focused on the role of Euro-American-centered historiographies of modernity, and to overlook the link between the religio-secular and the undertheorization of exploitation and consumption practices. These methodological choices also matter politically. In our view, Latour's reconstruction is neither secular nor earthly enough. This is precisely because it remains within religio-secularism and does not sufficiently recognize the spread of consumer and wealth practices in connection to the (colonial) history of the imperial way of living. We stress the importance of bringing the externalizing logic of the imperial way of living into the analysis of the pull to the right of the right, and this logic cannot be sufficiently addressed from within a religio-secular framework.

Is Latour's Analysis Religiously Diplomatic and Pluralistic Enough?

We have analyzed how Latour's analysis of the "secular figure of Gaia" is related to *Laudato si'* and the Canticle of Saint Francis. Both Pope Francis and Saint Francis discuss the connections between creation and creatures, the Earth, and the poor, and so they combine attentiveness for nature with justice. Latour argues that the connection between care for the poor and care for the Earth is what is missing in left and green political programs, and that this connection urgently needs to become the direction today (*Down to Earth*). Thus, in Latour's proposed direction we have as a point of reference the secular, scientific figure of Gaia, referring us back to the Greece that Europeans at least since Kant have regarded as the *noeud*, where philosophy, science, and history, and with it "Europe" as an idea, took off. Latour also connects the figure of Gaia to the green, social justice-oriented program of Pope Francis,[86] and elsewhere we also find many references to Catholicism both in Latour and in Serres, not coincidentally the religious tradition that both authors were raised in.[87]

The right of the right imagines Europe mostly by referring to either Greek (pagan/philosophical) or Christian references, often implicitly or explicitly remembering elements of what has been called "Aryan Christianity" (which we would now call "White supremacist" or "White nationalist Christianity"). The right wing viewed historically placed Christianity, if accepted at all, within Europe, and at a distance the "Middle Eastern," "fanatical," Semitic, and monotheistic dimensions that it ascribed to Judaism and Islam.[88] Sometimes, for the right of the right, the Greek/European reference is mixed up with an even Whiter, either Celtic or polar, boreal, and explicitly anti-Christian reference, but antimonotheism and antisemitism are available both in the Aryan-Christian and the pagan (Greek, Celtic, Germanic, or polar) versions. In our view, Latour lacks reflection on this cultural-political imaginary by so strongly drawing from the Greek and

Christian sources for imagining the ecological crisis and particularly for the discursive and imaginary sources for countering it, even if he certainly does not support the right of the right, and even actively opposes it.

Tracing, as Latour does via Assmann, the genealogy of modernity's ecological troubles to the notion of counterreligion is bringing it close to a genealogy that quite one-sidedly associates modernity's troubles with the negative moment in religion. This moment has been reconstructed, again starting from the nineteenth century—when the secular disciplines were separated from theology and philosophy—as the "monotheistic" moment, and this was seen as historically associated with Judaism and Islam. Although there has been quite some discussion on these problematic aspects of Assmann's reconstruction, Latour incorporates reference to Assmann's work into his own reconstruction without even mentioning these critiques.[89]

The reference brings him close to Lynn White's overly generalizing dismissal of what he saw as "Judeo-Christianity." Notably, the earliest version of such a general critique of Judaism, Christianity (and Islam) as the basis of an anthropocentrism that elevates humanity above living nature is to be found in the work of the German evolutionary biologist Ernst Haeckel, who coined the term "anthropocentric" in 1868. Haeckel argued: "The anthropocentric dogma culminates in the idea that man is the preordained center and aim of all terrestrial life . . . and is intimately connected with the dogmas of the Mosaic, Christian and Mohammedan theologies."[90] Haeckel was one of the scientists who participated in the early stages of antireligious biologism that played its part in the development of European racism in the nineteenth century.[91] Connecting anthropocentrism to counterreligion in such broad historical terms brought Lynn White in proximity to a careless dismissal of Judaism, Islam, and Christianity as the ultimate causes of anthropocentrism today. Latour is critical of White's generalizing genealogy of anthropocentrism, but reintroduces its theological interpretation with his adoption of Assmann's problematic reconstruction of counterreligion. This brings us to the problem that Latour's analysis is perhaps not religiously pluralist enough, sticking as it does to a classically European reconstruction of secularization and the emergence of the sciences. He proposes a combination of Greek philosophy (secular, Gaia) and Christianity (self-reflexive, beyond modern Manichaeism) as an imagined alternative to strive toward. In our view, these references remain too classically European and are too dependent on, and participating in, the same Eurocentric civilizationism that we find among the right of the right, to inspire a fruitful diplomatic political-theological ecology.

We argue that these cultural references are not enough JewGreek, GreenDin, Eco-Judaic, Indigenous, feminist, queer, Indian, Chinese, and others, and, thus, not enough outside of the right-wing political imaginary, for today's world plagued by the pull to the right of the right.[92] The political stance that Latour rightly calls for requires the equal role and voice of non-European sources to counter the civilizational narrative about Europe, and to deconstruct the distinction between philosophical/scientific/secular and religious/theological/mythical more thoroughly than Latour can do from within religio-secularism.

Regretfully, these insensitivities occur in the figurative use of language too. Latour starts from the Greek female figure of Gaia to capture the premythical origins of a secular and scientific semiosis, and calls Gaia "a terrifying, chthonic power, dark-skinned, dark-haired and somber."[93] The implicit link here between skin color, temper, and gender would have deserved more critical attention.

As in Latour, a reflexivity toward the European archives is sometimes missing in Donna Haraway's *Staying with the Trouble*, which is otherwise an admirable model of critical and creative thinking. *Chthonos* is one of the root-words of the "Chthulucene" she introduces as an alternative to "Anthropocene." Here again ancient Greece becomes a model for a contemporary alternative: "chthonic" is a variation on *chthonos*, the Greek word for "earth."[94] The Chthulucene, for Haraway, is about compost, making kin, and thus about closeness to living beings. But *chthonos* is also the root of the damned words "allochthone" and "autochthone," separating those "of the Earth" from those "from elsewhere," and this would have deserved a more thorough attentiveness from within the turn toward Gaia, just like the reference to Gaia as a dark-skinned goddess.

Haraway also falls into the trap of the Lynn White legacy when she writes, in the first pages of her book: "Chthonic ones are monsters in the best sense: they demonstrate and perform the material meaningfulness of earth processes and critters. . . . No wonder the world's great monotheisms in both religious and secular guises have tried again and again to exterminate the chthonic ones. The scandals of times called the Anthropocene and the Capitalocene are the latest and most dangerous of these exterminating forces."[95]

In our view, it is simply too strong and one-sided to impute to "monotheism"—which as a concept is a complicated and problematic, mainly nineteenth-century Christian-secular construction in itself—an extermination of the chthonic monsters on which Haraway models Earthboundedness, where ancient Greece comes to represent again an archsource of scholarly knowledge, interest in the world, beauty, and philosophy.[96] Such a binary presentation reiterates the nineteenth-century tension of "Greece" with its classical "other," which did not get a similarly sympathetic treatment: "monotheism."[97] Ernest Renan's notion of a *race monothéiste* is one of the clearest examples of how the discussion of monotheistic religions has historically been inextricably bound up with racist categories in creation of Europe's "others."[98] In *De l'origine du langage*, Ernest Renan divides this "race" into two components, the one connected with Indo-European languages and the philosophical and scientific promise of Europe related to Greece, the other connected to the Semitic languages and theologies (Judaism and Islam), which he characterized as one-dimensional and unpromising.[99] The one-sided dismissal or at least suspicion of monotheism or counterreligion does not sufficiently recognize these complex historical entanglements and actually reiterates them.[100]

We have questioned the effectiveness of precisely this religio-secular European imaginary in the analysis of, but also the struggle against, the right of the right. The French dimension of Latour's work does not make these things better: in France, the right of the right has a long pagan tradition, and it is often anti-Christian, precisely because it is anti-Judaic and anti-Islamic. Some of the most important intellectuals in the *nouvelle droite*, such as Alain de Benoist, call themselves "pagan" with pride and are critical of (what they consider) monotheism.[101]

Latour and Haraway take a very different path: scholarly, scientific, and certainly not antisemitic. However, their imagined alternative does not leave enough room for rethinking ecological consciousness outside the European imagination, and especially not when associated with "monotheism."[102] Ecological consciousness can recognize a call for transcendence, justice, repair, and transformation as part of itself and of its own history, acknowledging such a call's more than religious dimensions, instead of being made into that "other," problematic tradition to which so much trouble is perhaps a bit negligently ascribed, counterreligious, Manichaeist, or monotheist. We just need to be more precise, more attentive to different agentic forces and actors. Lack of care in these matters can lead to the justification of some of the imaginative *commonplaces* in the archives of the right of the right, which are no other than the late eighteenth- and nineteenth-century Kantian, Hegelian, and Renanian colonial archives that constructed what came to be seen as European civilization.

In short, there is much work outside the specifically religio-secular, European, and Christian history laid out by Latour to draw Earthboundedness further away from the framework of the right of the right, and to respect and acknowledge the motivational power of other philosophies than the secular and/or Christian, European ones.[103]

To take this one step further, "religion" as a concept separate from the "secular," is itself a product of the history of secularization that Latour traces and has limited use outside of this history. Derrida introduced his concept of *mondialatinisation* to draw attention to how European imperialism imposed a religious framework on non–Latin Christian systems of signification that are not immediately accessible in terms of religion.[104] Latour acknowledges this and stretches the very use of "religion" to bring its European signification more in line with non-religio-secular systems of signification. He associates such forms of signification with ancient Greece, as we have seen, but he stresses that he is not focusing on the spiritual, sacred nature of things (soul), but rather on their worldly agency, traced through secular scientific work. We may ask, therefore: Why should we still work from within a religio-secular framework after *mondialatinisation*, and in light of the importance of taking the imperial mode of living, its externalizing logic, and its global spread into account?

Conclusion

Our discussion of Latour's philosophical contribution to the debate about political ecology and the right of the right brought us, first, to emphasize the importance of a framework in which the distinction between the religious and the secular becomes more systematically connected to race, civilizationism, and capitalism in the web of life (Moore) or "the imperial way of living" (Brand and Wissen), to give it a more critical scope; second, to a renewed philosophical attention on how proximity to the Earth could be brought further away from the ultimately Euro-colonial intellectual traditions that privilege the "secular" over the "religious," even if only slightly, as is the case in Latour's analysis, and thus make it better equipped for the global translational task that Latour foresees for "religion" within a political ecology. Staying with the European secularization story and methodological religio-secularism steers Latour's analysis toward a critique of "modernist globalization" that remains relatively Eurocentric. It presents the nexus between the ecological crisis, religion, and the pull to the right of the right as one that can be understood based on a critical reflection on what went wrong in modern European secularization, and in tandem with that, within Christianity. Latour presents this failed secularization as the main driver that dramatically altered European and colonial-European relations to nature, the world, and other peoples, into the direction of the ecological crisis, and he imagines Earthboundedness as a new alternative. Our approach takes Earthboundedness out of the European frameworks of Christianity and (Greek) philosophy (or religio-secularity as a myth about a specifically European trajectory). We argued in favor of a more open, decolonial, and practice-oriented approach, one which goes beyond the religio-secular framework, and takes the role of the imperial mode of living systematically into account.

NOTES

1. "Science" is capitalized in Latour's work in order to contrast the discourse of "Science," as an objective (and thus normative) discourse about universal "truths" and "laws," with the practices of "the sciences." The idea of Science in Latour's view politicizes the sciences through an epistemology that renders "ordinary political life impotent through the threat of an incontestable nature"; Bruno Latour, *Politics of Nature: How to Bring the Sciences into Democracy*, trans. Catherine Porter (Cambridge, MA: Harvard University Press, 2004), 10. As we will see, this critique of Science is closely related to his analysis of the religious origins of the ecological crisis and of the rise of the Far Right.

2. Bruno Latour, *Down to Earth: Politics in the New Climatic Regime*, trans. Catherine Porter (Cambridge: Polity Press, 2018).

3. Bruno Latour, *Facing Gaia: Eight Lectures on the New Climatic Regime*, trans. Catherine Porter (Malden, MA: Wiley, 2017); first published in French as *Face à Gaia: Huit conférences sur le Nouveau Régime Climatique* (Paris: La Découverte, 2015), and based on Latour's Gifford Lectures from 2013.

4. See further Yolande Jansen, "Beyond Comparing Secularisms: A Critique of Religio-Secularism," in *Oxford Handbook of Secularism*, ed. John Shook and Phil Zuckerman (Oxford: Oxford University Press, 2017), 369–86.

5. Latour, *Facing Gaia*, 86. "Gaia" is a figure in ancient Greek mythology designating "Earth." The early Earth systems scholar James Lovelock used this term to underline his discovery, as Latour interprets it, that "the Earth has a behavior," and is "endowed with a sensitive and perishable envelope," in short, that it will react to global warming.

6. Pope Francis, *Laudato si'*, May 24, 2015, https://www.vatican.va/content/francesco/en/encyclicals/documents/papa-francesco_20150524_enciclica-laudato-si.html.

7. Jason Moore, *Capitalism in the Web of Life: Ecology and the Accumulation of Capital* (New York: Verso, 2015). For the notion of "the imperial mode of living" (*imperiale Lebensweise*), see Ulrich Brand and Markus Wissen, *The Imperial Mode of Living: Everyday Life and the Ecological Crisis of Capitalism* (New York: Verso, 2021; German original 2017).

8. We use "Euro-colonial" to denote the historical realm of Europe and its legacies across the globe, including the colonial and settler-colonial extensions. For an elaboration on how Latour and others working in Euro-Atlantic universities often fail to acknowledge Indigenous traditions that informed their concepts (such as "Gaia"), see Zoe Todd, "An Indigenous Feminist's Take on the Ontological Turn: 'Ontology' Is Just Another Word for Colonialism," *Journal of Historical Sociology* 29, no. 1 (2016): 4–22.

9. This notion was introduced by the French author Renaud Camus in 2011.

10. See Thomas Chatterton Williams, "The French Origin of 'You Will Not Replace Us': The European Thinkers behind the White-Nationalist Rallying Cry," *The New Yorker*, December 4, 2017, https://www.newyorker.com/magazine/2017/12/04/the-french-origins-of-you-will-not-replace-us. See also Sarah Bracke and Luis Hernández Aguilar, "'They Love Death as We Love Life': The 'Muslim Question' and the Biopolitics of Replacement," *British Journal of Sociology* 71, no. 4 (2020): 680–701.

11. Roger Griffin, "Between Metapolitics and Apoliteia: The *Nouvelle Droite*'s Strategy for Conserving the Fascist Vision in the 'Interregnum,'" *Modern & Contemporary France* 8, no. 1 (2000): 35–53.

12. Arktos Media has published English translations of various authors from the *nouvelle droite*.

13. See Mark Sedgwick, ed., *Key Thinkers of the Radical Right: Behind the New Threat to Liberal Democracy* (Oxford: Oxford University Press, 2017). The term *nouvelle droite* is a matter for debate in view of the many links with fascism that remain hidden behind the "New" in the New Right. See Tamir Bar-On, *Where Have All the Fascists Gone?* (Aldershot: Ashgate, 2007).

14. Formulation by the French historian Nicholas Lebourg. See Lebourg, "Ce n'est Pas Une Interview: C'est Une Déclaration de Guerre de Jean-Marie Le Pen," *Slate France*, April 8, 2015, http://www.slate.fr/story/100111/fn-jean-marie-le-pen. Venner is the man who committed suicide in the Notre-Dame Cathedral in 2013 in protest against *marriage pour tous*. He is a hero of the far-right Bloc Identitaire. See Jean-Yves Camus, "Le Mouvement Identitaire ou la Construction d'un Mythe des Origines Européennes," May 1, 2018, https://www.revue-elements.com/wp-content/uploads/2019/07/le-mouvement-identitaire-ou-la-construction-d-un-mythe-des-origines-europeennes.pdf.

15. Rogers Brubaker, "Between Nationalism and Civilizationism: The European Populist Moment in Comparative Perspective," *Ethnic and Racial Studies* 40, no. 8 (2017): 1191–1226. See Blake Stewart, "The Rise of Far-Right Civilizationism," *Critical Sociology* 46, no. 7–8 (2020): 1207–20.

16. The notion "boréal" refers to the most northern and polar regions of Europe and is being used in far-right circles to express the idea that the "original" European population was White and came from the north and should try to return to that Whiteness, instead of succumbing to the "great replacement." Jean-Marie Le Pen used the notion in an interview in 2015 with the magazine *Rivarol*, entitled "We Must Save Europe and the White World." The Dutch politician Thierry Baudet, whose FvD Party came out second-biggest in provincial elections in the Netherlands in 2019 and has been represented in Parliament since March 2021 with eight seats, used the term in programmatic texts. See Stéphane François, *Au-delà des vents du Nord* (Lyon: Presses universitaires de Lyon, 2014).

17. Chetan Bhatt, "White Extinction: Metaphysical Elements of Contemporary Western Fascism," *Theory, Culture & Society* 38, no. 1 (2021): 27–52. Bhatt argues that the one general element in contemporary fascism is the "fear of white extinction."

18. Williams, "The French Origin of 'You Will Not Replace Us.'"

19. David Brody, "Secretary of State Pompeo to CBN News: God May Have Raised Up Trump Like He Raised Up Queen Esther," CBN News, March 22, 2019, https://www1.cbn.com/cbnnews/israel/2019/march/exclusive-secretary-of-state-pompeo-to-news-god-may-have-raised-up-trump-like-he-raised-up-queen-esther; Ishan Tharoor, "The Trump Administration's Obsession with an Ancient Persian Emperor," *Washington Post*, November 1, 2019, https://www.washingtonpost.com/world/2019/11/01/trump-administrations-obsession-with-an-ancient-persian-emperor/.

20. Michel Serres, *The Natural Contract*, trans. Elizabeth MacArthur and William Paulson (Ann Arbor: University of Michigan Press, 1995), 47–48.

21. Ibid., 47–48 (original emphasis). Serres uses *notre temps*, which not only means "our time" but also "our weather," and, by association, also "our climate."

22. *Ensauvagement* is another French term that originates in the discourse of the extreme Right but that has made its way into mainstream language.

23. Charles W. Mills, "Decolonizing Western Political Philosophy," *New Political Science* 37, no. 1 (2015): 1–24. Mills heavily criticizes the concept of "well-ordered societies" in John Rawls's *Theory of Justice* as hiding the deep racial inequalities in real American society. The metaphors of streaming and flooding connote the female body, especially in French literature (*mer/mère*). As ecofeminists have pointed out, the nature/culture divide has always gone together with a gender division and hierarchy, and is recognizable in the antifeminist rhetoric and practices of the right of the right.

24. Latour, *Down to Earth*, 3.

25. Latour, *Facing Gaia*, 208.

26. To give some telling examples: former president Trump stated that "the concept of global warming was created by and for the Chinese in order to make U.S. manufacturing non-competitive," in a Twitter announcement (2012, https://twitter.com/realDonaldTrump/status/265895292191248385?s=20); that he does not "believe" in climate change (BBC, November 28, 2018, https://www.bbc.com/news/world-us-canada-46351940); and that climate scientists have "a political agenda" (BBC, October 15, 2018, https://www.bbc.com/news/world-us-canada-45859325). In the Dutch context, far right-wing politician Thierry Baudet has mentioned that he regards climate science as "mystique" and that he regards climate activist Al Gore as a "religious fanatic" and a "high priest of the newest flood religion" (2018, https://twitter.com/thierrybaudet/status/948464423827632128?s=20).

27. Latour, *Down to Earth*, 10, 3, 11. Rogers Brubaker points out that European strands of populism have come to define themselves not so much in national, but more and more in civilizationist terms, with which he means "an identitarian 'Christianism,' a secularist posture, a philosemitic stance, and an ostensibly liberal defence of gender equality, gay rights, and freedom of speech" and which according to him stems from a preoccupation with Islam (Brubaker, "Between Nationalism and Civilizationism," 1193). With Latour, we argue that such European civilizationism, including the preoccupation with Islam, forms part of a wider and more general move to the right that stems from an existential fear of losing one's habitat because of the ecological crisis. However, in our third main section, we will explain why we think we should take another step and interpret this fear as a fear of having to abandon the "imperial mode of living."

28. Latour, *Down to Earth*, 21.

29. Brand and Wissen explain the authoritarian move in politics in a similar way when they write: "That reactionary forces are on the rise in many places is also due to their ability to present themselves as the better guarantors of the exclusivity of the imperial mode of living, an exclusivity that is now under threat" (Brand and Wissen, *The Imperial Mode of Living*, 7).

30. Like the term "Science," Latour capitalizes the notions "Local" and "Moderns" in order to denote the people connected to the particular beliefs and institutions of Modernity, which is closely connected to Science and its particular idea of the local.

31. Latour, *Down to Earth*, 26–27.

32. Ibid., 41 (emphasis in original).

33. Latour, *Facing Gaia*, from 196 onward.

34. In Aristotelian physics, the sublunar realm, referring to the sphere of change, of nature, and mortality, was distinguished from the superlunar realm, which denoted the sphere of eternity and universal laws.

35. Latour, *Facing Gaia*, 197.

36. Ibid., 198.

37. Ibid., 195, 199.

38. Ibid., 155–56.

39. Ibid., 201.

40. Ibid., 203.

41. Ibid., 208.

42. Ibid., 200.

43. Ibid., 211. Nature obviously did not just mean "objects" but also "primitive peoples," women, and nonhuman animals.

44. Carolyn Merchant, *The Death of Nature: Women, Ecology, and the Scientific Revolution* (New York: Harper & Row, 1989).

45. Latour, *Facing Gaia*, 200. An ironic example of such belief is summarized in an anecdote once told by a student of how, in a religious group she formerly belonged to, believers were exhorted to put their waste into the wrong basket (so plastic with bio-waste, bio-waste with glass, glass with paper, etc.) to speed up the apocalypse by their humble personal contribution.

46. Ibid., 208.

47. Ibid., 206 (original emphasis).

48. Ibid., 208 (original emphasis).

49. Ibid., 209.

50. Ibid., chap. 2.

51. Ibid., 204.

52. Ibid., 206.

53. J. Kameron Carter, *Race: A Theological Account* (Oxford: Oxford University Press, 2008).

54. In *Becoming Human*, Zakiyyah Iman Jackson meticulously traces and

analyzes the ways in which these categories have been inextricably intertwined with gender, the human/animal distinction, and antiblackness in the modern world. See Jackson, *Becoming Human: Matter and Meaning in an Antiblack World* (New York: New York University Press, 2020).

55. Sylvia Wynter, "Unsettling the Coloniality of Being/Power/Truth/Freedom: Towards the Human, after Man, Its Overrepresentation—an Argument," *New Centennial Review* 3, no. 3 (2003): 257–337, at 260–61.

56. Ibid., 280.

57. Latour, *Down to Earth*, 19 (emphasis in original).

58. Latour, *Facing Gaia*, 38.

59. Ibid., 243 (emphasis in original).

60. Ibid., 68.

61. Michel Serres, *The Natural Contract* (Ann Arbor: University of Michigan Press, 1995), 47.

62. Serres hereby also draws on the etymology of "religion," which stems from the Latin verb *religare*, "to bind, to connect."

63. Donna Haraway, *Staying with the Trouble: Making Kin in the Chthulucene* (Durham, NC: Duke University Press, 2015).

64. Latour, *Facing Gaia*, 86, 87 (emphasis in original.)

65. Pope Francis, *Laudato si'*. Here Pope Francis is quoting Saint Francis, *Canticle of the Creatures*, in *Francis of Assisi: Early Documents*, ed. Regis J. Armstrong, J. A. Wayne Hellmann, and William J. Short (New York: New City Press, 1999), 1:113–14.

66. Ibid.

67. Commented on by Bruno Latour, *La Grande Clameur par le Pape Francois*, September 2015, http://www.bruno-latour.fr/sites/default/files/P-176-LAUDATO%20SI.pdf.

68. See, for this line of critique, Nicole M. Flores, "'Our Sister, Mother Earth': Solidarity and Familial Ecology in *Laudato si'*," *Journal of Religious Ethics* 46, no. 3 (2018): 463–78.

69. Bruno Latour, "Will Non-Humans Be Saved? An Argument in Ecotheology," *Journal of the Royal Anthropological Institute* 15 (2009): 459–75, at 463.

70. Latour, *Facing Gaia*, 146–83.

71. Ibid., 152.

72. Without having the space to develop this further here, we think that religio-secularism is also traceable (and problematic) in Charles Taylor's *A Secular Age*, and other major works in contemporary philosophy, such as John Rawls's *Political Liberalism* and Jürgen Habermas's works on religion and postsecularism. See Rawls, *Political Liberalism* (New York: Columbia University Press, 1993); Habermas, *Between Naturalism and Religion: Philosophical Essays* (Cambridge: Polity Press, 2008); Habermas, "Notes on Post-Secular Society," *New Perspectives Quarterly* 25 (2008): 17–29.

73. Lynn White, "The Historical Roots of Our Ecological Crisis," *Science* 155 (1967): 1203–7. For Latour's distancing, see Latour, *Facing Gaia*, 210.

74. White, "The Historical Roots of Our Ecological Crisis," 1205.

75. For a problematization of the notion of "Judeo-Christianity," see, e.g., Anya Topolski, "The Dangerous Discourse of the 'Judeo-Christian' Myth: Masking the Race-Religion Constellation in Europe," *Patterns of Prejudice* 54, no. 1–2 (2020): 71–90.

76. See Wynter, "Unsettling the Coloniality of Being/Power/Truth/Freedom," and other scholars in the Caribbean and decolonial philosophical traditions. For a gendered account of coloniality/modernity, see Maria Lugones, "Heterosexualism and the Colonial/Modern Gender System," *Hypatia* 22, no. 1 (2007): 186–209.

77. In view of the recent Oxfam report asserting that the 1 percent richest people in the world produce more greenhouse gasses than the 50 percent poorest, this seems a sober way of putting things. See Tim Gore, "Confronting Carbon Inequality: Putting Climate Justice at the Heart of the COVID-19 Recovery," Oxfam, September 21, 2020, https://www.oxfam.org/en/research/confronting-carbon-inequality.

78. Jason W. Moore, "The Capitalocene, Part I: On the Nature and Origins of Our Ecological Crisis," *Journal of Peasant Studies* 44, no. 3 (2017): 594–630 (original emphasis).

79. Ibid., 601.

80. Brand and Wissen, *The Imperial Mode of Living*, 6.

81. Ibid., 4.

82. See Nick Estes, *Our History Is the Future: Standing Rock versus the Dakota Access Pipeline, and the Long Tradition of Indigenous Resistance* (London: Verso, 2019).

83. Clive Hamilton, *Requiem for a Species: Why We Resist the Truth about Climate Change* (London: Routledge, 2010), reconstructs how climate change denial was related to the rise of neoconservative think tanks funded by tobacco and fossil fuel industries from the 1990s onward.

84. Moore, "The Capitalocene, Part I," 596.

85. A decolonial argument for not coming up with one "central" cause of ecological crisis, also not in terms of "Capitalocene," is elaborated by Kathryn Yusoff, *A Billion Black Anthropocenes or None* (Minneapolis: University of Minnesota Press, 2018), 39–40.

86. The problem we'd like to address is related to how this program is bracketing or invisibilizing feminist, LGBTQI, and other margins and categories of dehumanization.

87. See Bruno Latour, *Rejoicing: Or the Torments of Religious Speech*, trans. Julie Rose (Cambridge: Polity, 2013).

88. See Susannah Heschel, *The Aryan Jesus: Christian Theologians and the Bible in Nazi Germany* (Princeton, NJ: Princeton University Press, 2010); and Maurice Olender, *Les Langues du Paradis: Semites et Aryens, un Couple Providentiel* (Paris: Gallimard, 1989); translated into English as *The Languages of Paradise: Race, Religion, and Philology in the Nineteenth Century*, trans. Arthur Goldhammer (Cambridge, MA: Harvard University Press, 2008).

89. See, e.g., Richard J. Bernstein, "Review of Jan Assmann, *Of God and Gods: Egypt, Israel, and the Rise of Monotheism* and J. Assmann, *Of God and Gods*," *Bryn Mawr Review of Comparative Literature* 8, no. 1 (2010): 1–8, https://repository.brynmawr.edu/bmrcl/vol8/iss1/3. Assmann reports about these debates himself and reacts to them in his later book, Jan Assmann, *The Price of Monotheism* (Stanford, CA: Stanford University Press, 2010).

90. Ernst Haeckel, *The Riddle of the Universe at the Close of the Nineteenth Century*, trans. Joseph McCabe (New York: Harper & Brothers, 1905), 12; retrieved from http://www.gutenberg.org.

91. For a critique of readings of Genesis in terms of anthropocentrism, see Ronald Simkins, "The Bible and Anthropocentrism: Putting Humans in their Place," *Dialectical Anthropology* 38, no. 4 (2014): 397–413.

92. We cannot explain these terms fully here. It suffices to note that JewGreek and GreekJew were introduced by James Joyce in *Ulysses* as figures of complicated self-reflection on Jewish and Christian entanglement in European history. This was picked up by Jacques Derrida, Hélène Cixous, and others in philosophy, and by the novelist Henri Raczymow in *Bloom & Bloch. Din* is connected to Islamic ecological thinking in the notion of *Green Din*.

93. Latour, *Facing Gaia*, 83.

94. Haraway explains that it derives from the Greek *khthon*, which means "earth," and relates to the mythological figures that were the *khthonios*, "of the earth" (*Staying With the Trouble*, 173–74n4).

95. Haraway, *Staying with the Trouble*, 2.

96. Olender, *Les Langues du Paradis*. See also Balibar Étienne, "Note sur l'origine et les Usages du Terme 'Monothéisme,'" *Critique* 1, no. 704–705 (2006): 19–45.

97. Concepts of "monotheism" and "counterreligion" thus keep being replicated despite having been thoroughly criticized in studies of the Hegelian legacies of nineteenth-century representations of religious history. See, e.g., Björn Wittrock, "The Axial Age in World History," in *The Cambridge World History*, ed. Craig Benjamin (Cambridge: Cambridge University Press, 2015), 101–19; and Dafydd Huw Rees, "Decolonizing Philosophy? Habermas and the Axial Age," *Constellations* 24, no. 2 (2017): 219–31. Assmann himself discusses these debates in his book on the *Price of Monotheism*, where he explains the "ambivalence" of the Mosaic distinction that he adapts from Freud's interpretation of Moses, enabling

the questioning of political authority by a very early de-deification of kings, and the emergence of an idea of justice and critique. Latour does not seem to pay much attention to that ambivalence. See also note 88, above.

98. Renan included Christianity in the *race monothéiste* to then distinguish between an "Indoeuropéan" linguistic variant (formed by Aryan Christianity and science, "European") from a "semitic" variant, including Judaism and Islam, which is one of the turns by which his orientalism was a source of antisemitism (and encompassed both Judaism and Islam). See Olender, *Les Langues du Paradis*, 51–81; Djamel Kouloughli, "Ernest Renan: Un Antisémite Savant," *Histoire Épistémologie Langage* 29, no. 2 (2007): 91–112. See also Yolande Jansen and Nasar Meer, "Genealogies of 'Jews' and 'Muslims: Social Imaginaries in the Race–Religion Nexus," *Patterns of Prejudice* 54, no. 1–2 (2020): 1–14.

99. Renan, *De l'origine du Langage*, cited in Kouloughli, "Ernest Renan: Un Antisémite Savant," 95–96.

100. See also Mohamad Amer Meziane, *Des Empires sous la terre: Histoire écologique et raciale de la sécularisation* (Paris: La Découverte), 343.

101. Stéphane François, "Les paganismes de la Nouvelle Droite (1980–2004)" (Thèse de doctorat, Université de Lille II Droit et Santé, 2005).

102. Apart from this, some of the theory of semiosis seems to have been developed partly in relation to Indigenous philosophy that has not been acknowledged as such. See Todd, "An Indigenous Feminist's Take on the Ontological Turn." See also Kyle Whyte, "Indigenous Climate Change Studies: Indigenizing Futures, Decolonizing the Anthropocene," *English Language Notes* 55, no. 1–2 (2017): 153–62; Deborah Bird Rose, *Wild Dog Dreaming: Love and Extinction* (Charlottesville: University of Virginia Press, 2011).

103. Apart from the theory and activism by Indigenous movements—for example, Leanne Betasamosake Simpson, *As We Have Always Done: Indigenous Freedom through Radical Resistance* (Minneapolis: University of Minnesota Press, 2021)—see the Green Din and eco-Judaism movements. See for example Ibrahim Abdul-Matin, *Green Deen: What Islam Teaches about Protecting the Planet* (San Francisco, CA: Berrett-Koehler, 2010).

104. Jacques Derrida, *"Foi et Savoir" suivi de "Le Siècle et le Pardon"* (Paris: Seuil, 2000).

CHAPTER 7

Which Populism, Which Christianity?

SINDRE BANGSTAD

Abstract

This chapter not only identifies and links key themes from some of the other chapters in this volume, but also raises important and enduring questions about the role of critique in "dark times." Since the vital interventions of anthropologist Talal Asad, genealogical critiques of modernity have explored the thoroughgoing co-constitution of modern discourses around the categories of "religion" and "secularism." Through a forceful defense of both the deconstructive and generative potentialities of such critical inquiry, this chapter brings the insights of these genealogical investigations into these interrelated aspects of modernity squarely into conversation with modern forms of nationalism. Weaving together the arguments from the volume's other contributions, the chapter underscores that there is no "outside" from which to assess the discursive construction of categories such as "religion" or the "secular," nor the frequently exclusionary identity categories constructed in and through the performance of these concepts within interlocking social, economic, and political systems. Placed into conversation with other case studies from this volume, examples from Norway help to further clarify

224 *Sindre Bangstad*

> *the extent to which right-wing populist constructions of particular ethnoreligious nationalist identities have gone global. In addition to noting the role of critical genealogies of modernity in explaining the emergence of these phenomena, the chapter closes with a call for ongoing interdisciplinary, multivariate, and intersectional forms of analysis that can better illuminate the most toxic contemporary manifestations of right-wing populism and religious nationalism.*

Beyond the Critical Turn?

As Atalia Omer and Joshua Lupo duly note in their introduction to this volume, ours is a dark time in which many scholars have come to think, like them, of the critical turn in scholarship on religion and modernity as "inhibiting."[1] They clearly identify this critical turn with Talal Asad's field-shaping work on Islam as a discursive tradition[2] and genealogies of religion and the secular,[3] and the rich and influential body of scholarship, not the least within the "anthropology of Islam" that Asad's work has inspired.[4] Omer and Lupo see this work as constraining "constructive engagements with 'religion' from their potentially emancipatory, prophetic, and subversive categories" by treating religion "solely as a category implicated in Euro- and Christian-centric visions of social and political life." Omer and Lupo instead call for retaining "the insights of genealogical accounts of the secular and the religious, while nonetheless pushing beyond them by also giving attention to the dynamic ways in which persons reinterpret these categories in particular social and political contexts."[5]

I am, for reasons having to do with my own prior critique of Asadian genealogical critique, bound to be sympathetic to this claim,[6] but it seems to me that the problem is not so much that this form of critique may have the practical effect of being politically and analytically "inhibiting." For, given that one may in fact equally well regard this form of critique as "enabling," even though the scholars involved in this turn have not (and cannot be held accountable for failing to) informed their readers about the alternative worlds they themselves would envision, "constraining" is a term I would refrain from applying in this context. It may therefore be more apt to describe Asadian genealogical critique as having reached an analytical and methodological impasse, an impasse in fact both illustrated and underlined by Asad's very own latest monograph.[7] For here, it seems to me that critique is reduced to a purely reactive rather than a productive and generative mode of approaching the world and our place in it, and that any attempt at mapping out an alternative vision of a worldly "ethics of care and repair" is simply abandoned.[8]

But we need to return to epistemological beginnings, and to the question of critique, and what it might mean in and for our time. A central starting point for any discussion of this would of course be the work of Michel Foucault. Foucault's essay "What Is Enlightenment?" provides a formulation of critique as nonreducible to the simplistic question of being "for" or "against" the Enlightenment or the conflation of the Enlightenment with humanism. For Foucault, "the thread that may connect us with the Enlightenment is not faithfulness to doctrinal elements, but rather the permanent reactivation of an attitude—that is, of a philosophical ethos that could be described as a permanent critique of our historical era."[9] In a series of lectures held toward the end of his life at the Collège de France in Paris and the University of California at Berkeley in 1983–1984, Foucault extends his work on critique by exploring the Greek concept of *parrhesia*.[10] Foucault notes therein that *parrhesia* is ordinarily rendered as "free speech" in English, but that it actually denotes "truth-telling," hence the rendering of his lectures on this under the title of "The Courage of Truth."[11] "The notion of *parrhesia* was first of all and fundamentally a political notion," Foucault argues.[12] "Etymologically, *parrhesia* is the activity that consists in saying everything: *pan rema. Parrhesiazesthai* is "telling all." The "*parrhestiastes* is the person who says everything." Foucault furthermore informs us that *parrhesia*, in being sharply demarcated and distinct from rhetoric, is tied to the truth, and that its expression in the public square "carries the risk of violence."[13] "So, in two words, *parrhesia* is the courage of truth in the person who speaks and who, regardless of everything, takes the risk of telling the whole truth that he thinks."[14] A recent body of scholarship does in fact set out to argue for the historical linkages between critique as an intellectual and epistemological stance and social and political action enabling concrete change in the world at large.[15] From Bernard E. Harcourt and Didier Fassin's inquiry into the conditions of critique of our time, we learn that "critical thinking cannot be apprehended as an isolated intellectual phenomenon"[16] and that "for critique," "contexts matter."[17] We also learn that "to be faithful to its core principle, critique must involve self-critique."[18] In the same volume, Linda Zerilli describes critique as "a practice of freedom, that is, of speaking and acting with citizens and strangers about matters of common concern." Zerilli also reminds us that Foucault in his writings on Kant and the Enlightenment defines "critique" as "the art of not being governed in a particular way and by particular people."[19] Fadi Bardawil's fascinating account of the small and long-defunct Arab Marxist organization Socialist Lebanon points to the fact that critique may not always and inevitably enable change in the world at large, and may not always and inevitably succeed in achieving anything but radical disenchantment among those involved, but it does open the vista toward a different and alternative view concerning what critique may be. Similarly, Achille Mbembe gestures toward an understanding of critique as "a form of care, healing and reparation."[20] Eve Kosofsky Sedgwick's notion of "reparative reading" provides other signposts in this regard.[21] Drawing upon the critical work of Hannah Arendt, Aimé Césaire, Frantz Fanon, and Edward Said, Bardawil in another context also makes the salient point that "one cannot in advance know the uses to which a critical work can be put" and cautions against a reductionistic "defensive theoretical anti-imperialism" and a "will to totality" "that is hard to square with the multiple political discourses, organizational forms and collective initiatives."[22] The "defensive theoretical anti-imperialism" about which Bardawil speaks has also been on full display in certain leftist responses to Russia's brutal and imperialist war on Ukraine in 2022. It represents a form of abstract reasoning that sees no inherent problem in reducing the lives of others to mere abstractions in the name of geopolitics, and to partaking in the silencing and marginalization of people faced with murderous atrocities.[23] In pointing to the fact that "capitalism's most common response to critique is not appropriation but marginalization" and the ways in which "external pressures" in the form of "neoliberalism" and its "market-oriented logics that infuse the whole higher education system," Fassin contributes to our analytical understanding of precisely why these alternative vistas about what critique is and may do have been rendered so obsolete in our time.

In making this detour into the terrain of critique, I simply want to make a point with which it seems to me that Omer and Lupo would readily concur, namely, that the intellectual task at hand is not so much to do away with as to seek to preserve the part of Asadian genealogical critique that merits preserving. For the distance between Omer and Lupo and the Asadians is perhaps not as great as one might be tempted to imagine: there being a crucial distinction between Asad's work itself and its multifarious deployments. But in spite of their different emphases, I read both Omer and Lupo and Asad as being ultimately concerned with analyzing and critiquing the exclusions of political modernity. "The focus on 'nation' and 'nationalism,' particularly in its contemporary exclusionary trends, sharpens our understanding of religion in modernity," Omer and Lupo argue.[24] Inspired by the work of scholars such as Anya Topolski, Yolande Jansen, and Nasar Meer, Omer and Lupo argue for a "genealogical approach to the analysis of modern nationalism," which they define as "an intellectual excavation that seeks to uncover the underlying antisemitic and anti-Muslim grammars of modernity, and their complex intersections with patterns of racialization."[25] The benefit of zoning in on political modernity as the central factor in ongoing processes of social and political exclusion is, as Omer and Lupo correctly intimate, that it prevents us from falling into stereotypical and reductionistic arguments concerning liberal and ethnic typologies of nationalism, where the former is assumed to represent "good nationalism" and the latter "bad nationalism," and prevents us from the all too facile assumption that right-wing populism as the latest iteration of exclusivist nationalism has little or nothing to do with the worlds wrought by racialized capitalism and neoliberalism over the past few decades.[26] For though its contemporary inflections in right-wing populism may be more radical and more brutal for the racialized minorities and the immigrants at the receiving end of its exclusions, the emphasis on the "religion" of others in the processes of "othering"[27] and the underlying currents of White supremacist and/or racist ideas at work in much right-wing populism will not in any way be novelties to citizens of and from the Global South hitherto more used to its once so triumphant liberal iterations.[28] The mode of analysis advanced by Omer and Lupo herein instead, and in Mahmood Mamdani's apt words, invites us to "attend . . . to the layers of exclusion—racial, ethnic, religious—that are a necessary outcome of the nation-state form shaped by political modernity."[29] Inasmuch as the conception of genealogical critique advanced by Omer and Lupo is more attentive to the question of what worlds we want to inhabit, and how one can move toward these worlds by an engagement with concrete and everyday struggles, theirs is a conception to both complement and expand on the Asadian conception of genealogical critique.

Who Are "The People" and What Is "Religion" in Right-Wing Populism?

I happen to have read and engaged with the contributions to this volume in the context of my reflecting on the run-up to the ten-year commemoration (July 22, 2021) of the worst terrorist attacks in modern Norwegian history. For though none of the contributions to this volume deal with Norway and the Far Right in Norway per se, they do provide informative entry points for anyone trying to think this through ten years on.

On July 22, 2011, an ordinarily very uneventful and peaceful Norway saw the worst terrorist attacks in modern Norwegian history, when a self-declared "Christian-conservative crusader," pumped up on years of exposure to online hatred of and conspiracy theories about Muslims in Norway and in wider Europe, set off a bomb at Government Headquarters in Oslo, and proceeded to massacre unarmed and defenseless Norwegian teenagers attending the annual summer camp of the then-governing social democratic Labor Party Youth camp at the small island of Utøya, sixty kilometers north of Oslo. The perpetrator, a White Norwegian right-wing extremist from Oslo West named Anders Behring Breivik wanted to set off a continent-wide war whose ultimate aim was the ethnic cleansing of Muslims from Norway and Europe.[30] In hindsight, Breivik has come to be something of a harbinger of right-wing extremist and White supremacist terrorism in Europe, Oceania, and the United States. Ten years on, and in spite of a plethora of books in various languages exploring from various angles the critical events of that fateful day during which eighty-one Norwegians lost their lives, silences abound. A wider societal and political confrontation with right-wing extremism and White supremacist ideologies was lost to concerns about forsaking "national unity" if one were to confront them.[31] A most central and recurrent silence is about Breivik's self-identification as a "conservative Christian." For true enough, in the public archive of these events, and in the archive of Breivik's life before and after his terror, there are very few indications of him ever being a practicing Christian. But as Omer and Lupo remind us in their introduction, "actual religious knowledge or literacy seems to be irrelevant to the realities shaped through ethnoreligious nationalist discourses."[32]

What this means is of course that we need to take these invocations of White "Christianity" and a "Judeo-Christian civilization" on the part of Breivik and other White nationalists that have emerged out of the scene of the far-right and right-wing populism in Europe and the United States in the past decade much more seriously than many Norwegian liberal theologians have hitherto seemed willing to do.[33] And this is where Richard Amesbury's important contribution to this volume (chapter 4) comes in. Given their different views about political violence and terrorism, it is not that right-wing extremism and right-wing populism are synonymous or analogous. But as anyone who has spent time familiarizing themselves with far-right ideological tracts over the past two decades can see, there is a far-right ideological continuum at work here where certain ideas about Muslims, immigrants, and racialized minorities circulate relatively freely across any right-wing extremist and right-wing populist demarcations. More than that, a genealogical account also tells us that ideas travel across time, spaces, and traditional demarcations: though this is missing from Amesbury's fine account, the very idea of Europe as a "Judeo-Christian civilization" now so ubiquitous in far-right circles across Europe first emerged in the work of liberal Protestant theologians in the United States in the 1930s who were attempting to mobilize political and intellectual resources for the struggle against fascism in Europe.[34] A similar point could of course readily have been made about the uses of the Italian Marxist Antonio Gramsci's ideas about *metapolitics* in far-right Identitarian circles in Europe in recent years.[35]

Taking aim at a central problem of much secular academic discourse about "religion," which is premised on a normative distinction or differentiation between "*genuine* or *authentic* religion on the one hand, and *politics*, on the other" (Amesbury's italics), Amesbury uses Olivier Roy, Nadia Marzouki, and Duncan McDonnell's *Saving The People: How Populists Hijack Religion* as a good example thereof.[36] For as Amesbury rightly notes, the very subtitle of that volume indicates a secular framing in which "*real* religion is *not* political, and its political 'uses' are merely strategic"[37] (Amesbury's italics). Amesbury is certainly not the first one to make this important point, but "the various ways in which *discourse about religion*, particularly about Islam and Christianity, functions and circulates" (Amesbury's italics) in right-wing populist movements and "how it is used to demarcate and legitimate the boundaries of 'the people,' and what this says about the anxieties of popular sovereignty and the larger Euro-American political-theological imagination" is at the crux of any attempt to analyze right-wing populism and its relationship to "religion." Amesbury is, however, careful in also noting that "religion" is far from "the only category in terms of which so-called populist movements articulate belonging, and that claims framed in terms of religion intersect with claims framed in other terms, for example, of race, gender, and sexuality."[38] To give but one concrete example: in my native Norway, there are long-standing and popular Islamophobic attitudes toward Norwegian-Somalis, who since the 1990s have found themselves at the bottom of ethnoracial hierarchies[39] in Norway and experience more overt racism, discrimination, and hate crimes than practically any other minority group in Norway,[40] often a very thin and instrumental veneer over racism anchored in biological ideas about "race."[41] Which is precisely why we require *intersectional approaches* and *multivariate analyses* in order to understand and analyze their experiences. It will be no news whatsoever to anyone familiar with the vast scholarly literature on the Far Right in Europe in particular that the discursive shift from an emphasis on "race" to an emphasis on "culture" and "religion" has also reflected a strategic move by sections of the Far Right concerned with a Gramscian "metapolitics of the right" to avoid being stigmatized as "racist." Though this strategic move first appeared in intellectual circles aligned with the so-called *nouvelle droite* or "New Right" in France in the 1970s, it was quickly adopted in far-right circles elsewhere in Europe.[42] And so much so, that in Norway and the Nordics, largely uneducated, marginalized, violent, and predominantly male neo-Nazis of the skinhead street Nazi variety that Norway saw throughout the 1990s, and until the racist and neo-Nazi murder of a fifteen-year-old Norwegian-African boy in Oslo in 2001,[43] avoided overt "race talk," preferring instead to coach their racism and White supremacist ideas in a language of ethnicity, "religion," and "culture."[44] None of this has rendered "race talk" a matter of the past, for as Yolande Jansen and Jasmijn Leeuwenkamp duly note in their contribution to this volume (chapter 6), "the civilizational markers" in the discursive "pull to the right of the right" have over the last decade "increasingly been complemented by explicitly racial references" entailed by the European New Right's turn "toward the vision of the 'great replacement' of White majorities by non-Whites, and the breeding of a 'fear of White extinction.'"[45]

Amesbury's chapter dismantles the popular scholarly myth that there is a space outside of politics in which terms such as "religion" or "the people" remain politically neutral and purely descriptive designators to be applied at will by scholars. It reminds us that such terms, whether used by "populists" themselves or by the scholars who purport to study them are "always already political" and that we are in a profound sense even as scholars "all populists."[46] On this view *"discourse about populism* is formally similar to *populist discourse*, demarcating boundaries of peoplehood and seeking to institutionalize certain claims to political authority"[47] (Amesbury's italics). One could go even further here and note with Jansen and Leeuwenkamp that much of modern liberal political theory, from Jürgen Habermas to Charles Taylor, and from John Rawls to Bruno Latour, is premised on a "religio-secularist framework" in which "religion and secularism (or secularization)" are seen as "driving factors" of political dynamics."[48]

For Amesbury, the central dimension of "theological language" that existing scholarship on populism and religion "tends to elide" then is summed up by the term "sovereignty." We should not conceive of the uses of this kind of language in populist discourses as being merely strategic: it is, in Amesbury's view, not its functional utility in "drawing in-group/out-group distinctions," but its function in "conferring legitimacy on these exclusions" that is central.[49]

Religious Nationalism, Racism, and White Supremacism

Following up on Amesbury's interpretations of right-wing populism, Philip Gorski in his contribution to this volume (chapter 1) takes Donald Trump's victory in the 2016 U.S. presidential election as a case in point for what he refers to as "the affinity between religious conservatism and right-wing populism" across the globe. To the general question as to why religious conservatives tend to support (right-wing?) populists, Gorski proposes the answer "religious nationalism," and declares them tending to be "White Christian nationalists" as the particular answer in the case of the United States.[50] Gorski is right to note that White Christian evangelicals voted overwhelmingly for Trump in 2016 and 2020. By doing so, they also served up a puzzle that one can duly expect to occupy literally thousands of political scientists and sociologists in the United States and elsewhere for years. For here was an "I, candidate for president" whose very background and lifestyle many would at the outset have thought sat uneasily with the worldviews of White Christian evangelicals. In his contribution, Gorski deftly analyzes the intimate linkages between White supremacism and religious nationalism in the United States. He argues that "Trumpism is best understood as a secularized version of White Christian nationalism," but as a version thereof that "has been evacuated of scriptural references and theological content."[51] Gorski sees Trumpism's mobilization of "central metaphors and tropes of White Christian nationalism, specifically blood metaphors and apocalyptic tropes" as the key to "why Trumpism still resonates with evangelicals, without being obviously evangelical."[52] Without entering the ongoing and in many respects futile scholarly debate about whether Trumpism should in fact be characterized as a late modern form of fascism or not,[53] one could arguably take this even further than Gorski seems willing to do, for "blood metaphors and apocalyptic tropes" are also historically central to fascism. In Norway, Breivik's cut-and-paste tract *2083: A European Declaration of Independence*, published online in the hours before his terrorist attacks, evidenced an obsession with Thomas Jefferson's oft-cited phrase to the effect that "the tree of liberty must be refreshed from time to time with the blood of patriots and tyrants," with the "patriots" here being identified with Breivik and other fascists, and the "tyrants" with Norwegian social democrats. In much fascist thought, long scientifically discredited ideas about biology, blood, and inheritance are also what ties particular peoples to particular territories, and the notion of bloody conflicts and wars with designed "enemies" of fascist will to power are the building blocks of the future society envisioned to emerge from the ruins of civilizational, cultural, and racial "decay." The White supremacist ideas inherent in political slogans such as "America First" and "Make America Great Again" do of course also have a demonstrably long historical genealogical lineage on the Far Right in the United States.[54]

As scholars such as Gorski know perfectly well, identities, whether ethnic or religious, are made and remade in and through human social processes. In the words of the late Stuart Hall (1932–2014), "Identity is always in the process of formation" and "always constructed through ambivalence."[55] What this means for Hall is furthermore that "all of us are composed of multiple social identities, not of one. That we are all complexly constructed through different categories, of different antagonisms, and these may have the effect of locating us socially in multiple positions of marginality and subordination, but positions that do not yet operate on us in exactly the same way." And that "because identifications change and shift, they can be worked on by political and economic forces outside of us, and they can be articulated in different ways." There is, in sum "absolutely no political guarantee already inscribed in an identity" and "we go to our pasts through history, through memory, through desire, not as a literal fact."[56] And though Gorski's remarks about Trumpism being "secular" and devoid of "scriptural references and theological content" certainly ring true, there is an inherent risk here in reinscribing the very distinctions between "real and authentic religion" and "inauthentic and strategic uses of religion" of certain secular discourses about religion and right-wing populism that Amesbury does well in cautioning us against in his contribution to this volume.

Gorski is surely also right to note that in the United States, "religious nationalism has always been entangled with White supremacism" and to note that White Christian nationalists "have usually defined American identity in terms of some ethnoreligious other" from Native Americans and African slaves, to Irish and Italian Catholics and Jews, to the Muslims and the Latinx of our time.[57]

But coming to this from the vantage point of the discipline of anthropology as I do, this leaves me wanting more empirical detail, of a contemporary rather than a historical kind. For if anything, the making of Trumpism's strong electoral constituency among White evangelical Christians is a multifaceted social and political phenomenon, one that requires multivariate analysis. Fixating on one facet of this phenomenon, namely, religious nationalism, can only bring us that far in the attempt to understand it. If we, like any sociologists of religion, happen to believe that citizens who identify as religious do not live worlds apart from the rest of us, and are affected by the same developments as any other citizens, analyses of the long-term social and political processes that created the very space of possibilities within which Trumpism could emerge successfully with its empty ritual promises of "making America great again" (for some Americans more than others for sure) in 2016 must surely include many other variables.

These are variables that would have to include the sheer devastation of the social fabric of many communities in the United States wrought by deindustrialization, unemployment, spiraling socioeconomic inequalities, and "deaths of despair" under conditions of neoliberalism since the Reagan era,[58] and include the "fear of falling from grace" that has become a virtual obsession in sections of the White middle class throughout the United States. They would also include the return to power and influence of the most virulent and unapologetic forms of White racism and White supremacism,[59] which on the back of the dog-whistle politics of U.S. Republicans after the civil rights struggle long preceded the Trump era.

Jason A. Springs's contribution in this volume (chapter 2) stands at a counterpoint to Gorski's, in that Springs emphasizes the continuities rather than the ruptures in the logics and patterns of the religious nationalism of White Christian evangelicals in the United States. Spring's main criticism is directed at Robert Jones's influential 2016 monograph *The End of White Christian America*,[60] whose claims about the waning social and political influence of White Christian evangelicals he finds overblown. More than the "Frankenstein's monster" of Jones's interpretation, Springs imagines White Christian evangelicalism to reflect a "zombie" form of nationalism. Though it has tended to be overused in much scholarship recently, the metaphor is good to think with, and has also been applied productively in the controversial work of the French sociologist Emmanuel Todd on "Zombie Catholicism" in contemporary France.[61] In emphasizing how central gender norms and sexual politics, from fury over "interracial marriage" in the 1960s to anger over public recognition of LGBT rights in the 1980s and 1990s, have in fact been to White evangelical Christians, Springs complements and adds to Amesbury and Gorski in important ways.[62] Springs also instructively notes the elements of fear and loss in the making of contemporary White Christian evangelical belief systems: U.S. White evangelical Christians conceptualize themselves as "an increasingly marginalized remnant in a society that (putatively) originally did, and that (allegedly) should still, reflect their central identity and values" and "perceive themselves to be perennially persecuted victims of an aggressively anti-Christian 'secular' society."[63] That these dynamics of perceived minoritization should engender forms of resentment leading to nihilism should not surprise us.

RIGHT-WING POPULISM, RELIGION, AND THE ECOLOGICAL CRISIS

In their contribution, Dutch scholars Yolande Jansen and Jasmijn Leeuwenkamp (chapter 6) take the analysis of right-wing populism and religion into a relatively original conceptual and analytical terrain. Preferring the broadening concept of a "pull to the right of the right" over more well-established terms originating in political science, such as "right-wing populism" or the "Far Right," they argue for the centrality of the current global ecological crisis and the "right-wing promise that we will not have to share the burden equally" in this "pull to the right of the right." In placing the global ecological crisis at the center of their analysis of "the pull to the right of the right," they follow the late French anthropologist Bruno Latour in his essayistic *Down to Earth: Politics in the New Climatic Regime*,[64] while departing from what they regard as the "religio-secularist" underpinnings of Latour's arguments. In their rendering, the notion of a "pull to the right of the right" "refers to a discursive process ('the pull to') whereby anti-egalitarian ideas, themes, and images about race, migration, the nation, Christianity, Whiteness, and gender and sexuality" that originated in nascent far-right movements in the 1970s gradually infused "more mainstream right-wing discourses and public imaginaries" and have since the 2000s spread even further "across the political spectrum and at a global scale."[65] It so happens that I agree with this contention: in the Nordic region, the once hegemonic social democratic parties, parties that in the proverbial "golden age of the European welfare state" stood for relatively inclusive and nonracial conceptions of citizenship, have under the influence of far-right discourses on immigration since the 1980s moved so far to the right that their policies and rhetoric are in many respects now quite indistinguishable from those of populist right-wing formations.[66] But in trying to understand the very political efficacy of these ideas across the political spectrum in the Nordic countries since the 1980s, one also has to understand that these were at the outset not ideas exclusive to the Far and populist Right. The key here is, in other words, not the Far and populist Right in and of itself, but modern state nationalism and more specifically welfare-state nationalism in the Nordic countries. In order to illustrate why this should be so, take for example the simple fact that it was a Norwegian social democratic Labor Party then in government power, and acting under the influence both of Norwegian social democratic–dominated labor unions—and social democratic–oriented state bureaucrats and academics—that in the face of the arrival of a few hundred male labor migrants from Pakistan, Morocco, Turkey, and India in Norway in the late 1960s and early 1970s created the very "moral panic" that led to introduction of the "Immigration Stop" in the Norwegian parliament in 1975. Though it would soon prove to fail to put a stop to nonwestern immigration to Norway in the years that followed, the "Immigration Stop" was intended to do precisely that, and was anchored in a racialized politics working at the very heart of Norwegian social democracy.[67] In Norway, as in many other European countries, the refugee crisis resulting from the brutal Russian war in Ukraine in 2022 has once more brought these racialized politics to the fore. For in the face of this refugee crisis, both Norwegian social democrats and Norwegian right-wing populists have suddenly fallen over themselves to appear to the electorate as the political party formations most welcoming to Ukrainian refugees, and offered up a politics of solidarity that was practically absent in their political platforms when the refugees happened to be Syrian, Afghan, or Somali.[68] These are empirical details I think may at least in part unsettle the historical teleology of Jansen and Leeuwenkamp's account of the "pull to the right of the right." What one would need to unthink—or "decolonize" as it were—is the very form that political modernity has assumed in taking modern state nationalism as its hegemonic form, and rendering a divide between "natives" and "nonnatives."[69]

Jansen and Leeuwenkamp's chapter is a very valuable attempt at broadening our intellectual horizon in thinking about the Far Right and right-wing populism.[70] For from Norway, a small and peripheral country that has long occupied a particular place in racialized, racist, and White supremacist imaginaries in the United States and Europe,[71] it has long been terrifyingly clear that ecological fears relating to having to share the land and the burdens of a global and planetary ecological crisis and demographic fears of White extinction and/or replacement by racialized others have been central factors in far-right imaginaries from Breivik to Manshaus. But as in the case of Gorski's contribution to this volume, one also has to enter the caveat that it is far from the only factor.

Right-Wing Populism and Civic Nationalism as Resistance

Geneviève Zubrzycki's ethnographically rich and informative account in this volume (chapter 5) of the struggles between religiously inflected forms of right-wing populism and liberal and secular civic nationalism over how to define postcommunist Poland serves as a reminder that the ascendancy of right-wing populism over the past two decades is something of a global phenomenon, and that the constitutive elements relating to "religion" therein need not necessarily be evangelical and Protestant Christianity. For there are few countries in which the hold of right-wing populism has seemed to be stronger, and the consequences for women, religious minorities, and LGBTQ+ people, indeed for the rule of law and for democracy, more dire than in predominantly Catholic Poland. So much so that the increasingly authoritarian turn of Poland raises the analytical question as to whether the government in power in Poland should not rather be characterized as a "far-right" government than as a "populist right-wing" government. As Zubrzycki argues, with reference to a term coined by the liberal former Solidarity activist and newspaper editor Adam Michnik, namely, "magical antisemitism," national identity in Poland "is primarily understood in ethnic terms," so that "Catholic" and "Polish" are often understood as synonymous, and "deviance from normative ethno-Catholic Polishness is ethnicized in such a way that individuals and groups that are not defending the prominent place of Catholicism and its symbols in the public sphere, and are advocating instead for a civic and secular Poland, are discursively turned into 'Jews' by the Right."[72] Zubrzycki vividly narrates how an appropriation of Jewish symbolic markers—whether ostensibly "religious" or "secular" for non-Jewish Poles—serves to "support a civic and secular vision of the nation" by separating Polishness from Catholicism and thereby "potentially *neutralizing* it."[73] But that response engenders its own conundrums, in that it uses Jewishness as a foil, and requires the Jew to remain "irremediably Other to achieve the goal of civic nationalism and multiculturalism."[74] And so we are, for better or for worse, back to Hall's dictum about identifications being worked upon by "social and economic forces outside of us"[75] —and entailing social and political consequences upon which we may exercise little or limited control. For social and political contexts such as exist in Poland, where a right-wing populism, which has proven quite virulent, is the hegemonic power and is underpinned by strong and popular links with conservative and even antisemitic factions of the Catholic Church, are contexts in which the necessary genealogical account and critique of secularism and the secular meets its limit. Opposition and resistance to those forms of hegemonic power can in all probability not but invoke a civic and "secular" discourse. But even that, as the Polish example also serves to illustrate, is hardly any guarantee for its success in the wider political and social arena. In reading Zubrzycki's account, I found myself wondering about a missing part of the puzzle, that is, how exactly other—and in comparison with Jews—rather small religious minorities in Poland that have also had a historical presence in the country feature in Polish populist right-wing imaginaries and in the imaginaries of their liberal, "secular," and civic-oriented left-leaning imaginaries. It is Poland's very small Muslim minority and the imaginaries relating to a supposed "threat of Muslim immigration" to Poland that seem to loom relatively large in the imaginaries of Polish labor migrants sympathetic to the government in their native Poland, but forced to work and live in other European countries, and the imaginaries of Poland's politicians in power I have in mind here.

In Lieu of a Conclusion

The history of the rise of the Far Right and right-wing populism in Euro-America and its relationship to "religion" over the past decades remains to be written. If ever it can be written. For as I have indicated in my comments on and reflections about the many fine contributions to this volume, this is an ongoing puzzle that requires a great deal of attention to empirical detail, and to multidisciplinary work and multivariate analysis. In a memorable reflection on the work of Stuart Hall, the anthropologist David Scott noted the following: "We live in Dark Times. . . . But Dark Times, as Hannah Arendt memorably said, need people who can give us illumination and call them forth into the public realm."[76]

NOTES

1. Atalia Omer and Joshua Lupo, "Introduction," herein.
2. Talal Asad, *Islam as a Discursive Tradition* (Washington, DC: Institute for Arab Studies, Georgetown University, 1986).
3. Talal Asad, *Genealogies of Religion: Discipline and Reasons of Power in Christianity and Islam* (Baltimore, MD: Johns Hopkins University Press, 1993); and Asad, *Formations of the Secular: Christianity, Islam, Modernity* (Stanford, CA: Stanford University Press, 2003).
4. Important work inspired by Asad includes Saba Mahmood, *Politics of Piety: The Islamic Revival and the Feminist Subject* (Princeton, NJ: Princeton

University Press, 2004); Mahmood, *Religious Difference in a Secular Age: A Minority Report* (Princeton, NJ: Princeton University Press, 2015); Charles Hirschkind, *The Ethical Soundscape: Cassette Sermons and Islamic Counterpublics* (New York: Columbia University Press, 2006); Winnifred Fallers Sullivan, *The Impossibility of Religious Freedom* (Princeton, NJ: Princeton University Press, 2005); Elizabeth Shakman Hurd, *The Politics of Secularism in International Relations* (Princeton, NJ: Princeton University Press, 2008); Hussein Ali Agrama, *Questioning Secularism: Islam, Sovereignty, and the Rule of Law in Modern Egypt* (Chicago: University of Chicago Press, 2012); Mayanthi Fernando, *The Republic Unsettled: Muslim French and the Contradictions of Secularism* (Durham, NC: Duke University Press, 2014).

5. Omer and Lupo, "Introduction."

6. Sindre Bangstad, "Contesting Secularism/s: Secularism and Islam in the Work of Talal Asad," *Anthropological Theory* 9, no. 2 (2009): 188–208; and Bangstad, "Saba Mahmood and Anthropological Feminism after Virtue," *Theory, Culture & Society* 28, no. 3 (2011): 28–54.

7. Talal Asad, *Secular Translations: Nation-State, Modern Self, and Calculative Reason* (New York: Columbia University Press, 2018).

8. See Achille Mbembe, *Out of the Dark Night: Essays on Decolonization* (New York: Columbia University Press, 2021), for these concepts.

9. Michel Foucault, "What Is Enlightenment?," in *The Foucault Reader: An Introduction to Foucault's Thought*, ed. Paul Rabinow, trans. Catherine Porter (London: Penguin, 1984), 32–50.

10. An early and very abbreviated version of these lectures appeared in English translation in Michel Foucault, *Fearless Speech*, ed. Joseph Pearson (Los Angeles: Semiotexte, 2001). My citations herein are from the full edited and annotated version of these lectures provided in Michel Foucault, *The Courage of Truth (The Government of Self and Others II): Lectures at the College de France 1983–1984*, ed. Frédéric Gros, trans. Graham Burchell (London: Palgrave Macmillan, 2011).

11. This section draws on Sindre Bangstad, *The Politics of Mediated Presence: Exploring the Voices of Muslims in Norway's Mediated Public Spheres* (Oslo: Scandinavian Academic Press, 2015), 231–32. Foucault's work on this is also put to good use in Lila Abu-Lughod, "The Courage of Truth: Making Anthropology Matter," Working Papers in Anthropology, September 7, 2019 (Leuven: KU Leuven, 2019), https://soc.kuleuven.be/immrc/paper_files/abu-lughod-wpa-2019-001.

12. Foucault, *The Courage of Truth*, 8.

13. Ibid., 10–11.

14. Ibid., 13.

15. See, e.g., Didier Fassin and Bernard E. Harcourt, eds., *A Time for Critique* (New York: Columbia University Press, 2019); Fadi A. Bardawil, *Revolution*

and Disenchantment: Arab Marxism and the Binds of Emancipation (Durham, NC: Duke University Press, 2020); and Bernard E. Harcourt, *Critique and Praxis* (New York: Columbia University Press, 2020).

16. Didier Fassin and Bernard E. Harcourt, "Introduction," in Fassin and Harcourt, eds., *A Time for Critique*, 1–12, at 3.

17. Didier Fassin, "How Is Critique?," in Fassin and Harcourt, eds., *A Time for Critique*, 13–35, at 16.

18. Fassin and Harcourt, "Introduction," 3.

19. Linda M. G. Zerilli, "Critique as a Political Practice of Freedom," in Fassin and Harcourt, eds., *A Time for Critique*, 36–51, at 36, 37.

20. "Interview: Achille Mbembe," *Chilperic*, November 9, 2020, https://www.chilperic.ch/interview/achille-mbembe-15.html?fbclid=IwAR1mzWZIUgKBShyNvucQpX_FUkNbkdpYXpDnO8oc_ToYZDcpBb0ak8J3xCY.

21. See Eve Kosofsky Sedgwick, "Paranoid Reading or Reparative Reading, or, You're so Paranoid, You Probably Think This Essay Is about You," in *Touching Feeling: Affect, Pedagogy, Performativity* (Durham, NC: Duke University Press, 2002), 123–51.

22. Fadi A. Bardawil, "Critical Theory in a Minor Key," in Fassin and Harcourt, eds., *A Time for Critique*, 174–92, at 175, 182, 181. It bears mentioning here that Bardawil's important intervention comes in the context of thinking and analyzing the ways in which certain strands of "leftist political critique and critical theory" among both "Arab and Euro-American leftists" have since 2011 led to "the calls of the men and women who risked everything in rising against the Assad dynastic rule [in Baathist Syria], [to remain] for the most part unheard, or deliberately shut out" (ibid., 176). For a superb account of the long-standing brutalities of the Assad regime in Syria, see Salwa Ismail, *The Rule of Violence: Subjectivity, Memory and Government in Syria* (Cambridge: Cambridge University Press, 2018).

23. For these points, see, e.g., Volodymyr Artiukh, "US-splaining Is Not Enough: To the Western Left, on Your and Our Mistakes," *Spilne/Commons*, March 1, 2022, https://commons.com.ua/en/us-plaining-not-enough-on-your-and-our-mistakes/; and Elisabeth Cullen Dunn, "When Western Anti-Imperialism Supports Imperialism," *Focaalblog*, March 3, 2022, https://www.focaalblog.com/2022/03/03/elizabeth-cullen-dunn-when-western-anti-imperialism-supports-imperialism/.

24. Omer and Lupo, "Introduction."

25. Ibid.

26. For a lucid critique of liberal readings of populism, see William Mazarella, "The Anthropology of Populism: Beyond the Liberal Settlement," *Annual Review of Anthropology* 48 (2019): 45–60.

27. It is all too often conveniently forgotten that scholarship on the history of racism in Europe has long informed us that European racism was never, ever purely based on assumptions about biology and race. So much so that in light of the fact

Which Populism, Which Christianity? 241

that historians of racism point to the racism faced by converts from Islam and Judaism during the Catholic Reconquista of the Iberian Peninsula from the twelfth century onward as the first demonstrable case of racism in European history, we may in fact argue that the contemporary emphasis on the "religion" of others in European racism is but a return to "origins" in an era of "racism without races." This is because the racism of the Catholic Reconquista preceded the invention of biological concepts of race. For this, see Francisco Bethencourt, *Racism: From the Crusades to the Twentieth Century* (Princeton, NJ: Princeton University Press, 2013); and Eduardo Bonilla-Silva, *Racism without Racists: Color-blind Racism and the Persistence of Racial Inequality in America*, 5th ed. (Lanham, MD: Rowman & Littlefield, 2018).

28. See, inter alia, Achille Mbembe, *Critique of Black Reason*, trans. Laurent Dubois (Durham, NC: Duke University Press, 2017).

29. Mahmood Mamdani, *Neither Settler nor Native: The Making and Unmaking of Permanent Minorities* (Cambridge, MA: Belknap Press of Harvard University Press, 2020), 339.

30. Sindre Bangstad, *Anders Breivik and the Rise of Islamophobia* (London: Zed Books, 2014).

31. For an analysis of the speeches of the then Labour Party prime minister and later NATO secretary-general Jens Stoltenberg, whose speeches played a central role in subsuming confrontation with right-wing extremism under the interests of "national unity," see Tore Rafoss, "Enemies of Freedom and Defenders of Democracy: The Metaphorical Response to Terrorism," *Acta Sociologica* 62, no. 3 (2019): 297–314.

32. Omer and Lupo, "Introduction."

33. Good exceptions to this from academic and theological points of view are, however, provided in Ulrich Schmiedel and Hannah Strømmen, *The Claim to Christianity: Responding to the Far Right* (London: SCM Press, 2020); and Kristin Graff-Kallevåg, Sven Thore Kloster, and Sturla J. Stålsett, eds., *Populisme og kristendom* (Oslo: Cappelen Damm, 2022).

34. For this point, see Mark Silk, "Notes on the Judeo-Christian Tradition in America," *American Quarterly* 36, no. 1 (1984): 65–85.

35. See José Pedro Zuqúete, *The Identitarians: The Movement against Globalism and Islam in Europe* (Notre Dame, IN: Notre Dame University Press, 2018). Amesbury also in this context references work by Rogers Brubaker on this in Brubaker, "Between Nationalism and Civilizationism: The European Populist Movement in Comparative Perspective," *Ethnic and Racial Studies* 40, no. 8 (2017): 1191–1226. The latter is another example of this much more widespread tendency.

36. Nadia Marzouki, Olivier Roy, and Duncan McDonnell, eds., *Saving the People: How Populists Hijack Religion* (New York: Oxford University Press, 2016).

37. Amesbury, chap. 4 herein.

38. Ibid.

39. I borrow the term "ethnoracial hierarchies" from the work of Eric Bleich. See Bleich, "Where Do Muslims Stand on Ethno-Racial Hierarchies in Britain and France? Evidence from Public Opinion Surveys, 1988–2008," *Patterns of Prejudice* 43, nos. 3–4 (2009): 379–400.

40. For this, see Christhard Hoffmann and Vibeke Moe, eds., *The Shifting Boundaries of Prejudice: Antisemitism and Islamophobia in Contemporary Norway* (Oslo: Scandinavian University Press, 2020).

41. Sindre Bangstad and Frode Helland, "The Rhetoric of Islamophobia: An Analysis of the Means of Persuasion in Hege Storhaug's Writings on Islam and Muslims," *Ethnic and Racial Studies* 42, no. 13 (2019): 2229–47.

42. Tamir Bar-On, "Transnationalism and the French Nouvelle Droite," *Patterns of Prejudice* 45, no. 3 (2011): 199–213.

43. Sindre Bangstad, "Remembering Benjamin," *Africa Is a Country*, January 26, 2021, https://africasacountry.com/2021/01/remembering-benjamin.

44. Katrine Fangen, "Right-Wing Skinheads: Nostalgia and Binary Oppositions," *Youth* 6, no. 3 (1998): 33–49.

45. Yolande Jansen and Jasmijn Leeuwenkamp, chap. 6 herein.

46. Amesbury, chap. 4 herein.

47. Ibid.

48. Jansen and Leeuwenkamp, chap. 6 herein.

49. Amesbury, chap. 4 herein.

50. Philip Gorski, chap. 1 herein.

51. Ibid.

52. Ibid.

53. Central advocates for the defense of the epithet of "fascism" in relation to Trump in the U.S. context include Jason Stanley, *How Fascism Works: The Politics of Us and Them* (New York: Random House, 2018); and Timothy Snyder, *On Tyranny: Twenty Lessons for the Twentieth Century* (New York: Tim Duggan Books, 2018). One central detractor includes Samuel Moyn, "The Fascism Question," *Chronicle of Higher Education*, January 11, 2021. Standard titles on fascism as a historical phenomenon in modern Europe include Stanley Payne, *A History of Fascism, 1913–1945* (Madison: University of Wisconsin Press, 1995); and Robert Paxton, *The Anatomy of Fascism* (New York: Vintage, 2005).

54. See Sarah Churchwell, *Behold, America: The Entangled History of "America First" and "The American Dream"* (New York: Basic Books, 2018); and Kathleen Belew, *Bring the War Home: The White Power Movement and Paramilitary America* (Cambridge, MA: Harvard University Press, 2018).

55. Stuart Hall, "Old and New Identities, Old and New Ethnicities," in *Essential Essays*, Vol 2, *Identity and Diaspora*, ed. David Morley (Durham, NC: Duke University Press, 2019), 63–82, at 69.

56. Ibid., 78, 79.

57. Gorski, chap 1. herein.

Which Populism, Which Christianity? 243

58. Some important titles here would include Tyler Stovell, *White Freedom: The Racial History of an Idea* (Princeton, NJ: Princeton University Press, 2021); Anne Case and Angus Deaton, *Deaths of Despair and the Future of Capitalism* (Princeton, NJ: Princeton University Press, 2020); Jonathan Metzl, *Dying of Whiteness: How the Politics of Racial Resentment Is Killing America's Heartland* (New York: Basic Books, 2019); Thomas Piketty, *Capital and Ideology* (Cambridge, MA: Belknap Press of Harvard University Press, 2019); Arlie Russel Hochschild, *Strangers in Their Own Land: Anger and Mourning on the American Right* (New York: The New Press, 2016); Robert Putnam, *Our Kids: The American Dream in Crisis* (New York: Simon and Schuster, 2016); Ian Haney López, *Dog Whistle Politics: How Coded Racial Appeals Have Reinvented Racism and Wrecked the Middle Class* (New York: Oxford University Press, 2015); and Katherine Newman, *Falling from Grace: Downward Mobility in the Age of Affluence* (Berkeley: University of California Press, 1999).

59. See, inter alia, Kathleen Belew, *Bring the War Home*); Cynthia Miller-Idriss, *Hate in the Homeland: The New Global Far Right* (Princeton, NJ: Princeton University Press, 2020); and Kathleen Belew and Ramón A. Gutiérrez, eds., *A Field Guide to White Supremacy* (Berkeley: University of California Press, 2022).

60. Robert Jones, *The End of White Christian America* (New York: Simon and Schuster, 2016).

61. Emmanuel Todd, *Who Is Charlie? Xenophobia and the New Middle Class* (London: Polity Press, 2015).

62. Jason Springs, chap. 2 herein.

63. Ibid.

64. Bruno Latour, *Down to Earth: Politics in the New Climatic Regime* (New York: Wiley, 2018).

65. Jansen and Leeuwenkamp, chap. 6 herein.

66. As a case in point, it is the female-led Social Democratic government of Prime Minister Mette Frederiksen in Denmark that has in a context of historically low numbers of asylum applicants arriving in Denmark declared for the first time in modern Danish history that the Danish government adheres to a vision of accepting "zero asylum seekers" on the pretext that "our social cohesion is already under threat." Such a move would obviously entail the Danish government violating international laws on the protection of refugees to an even greater extent than previous Danish governments that have since 2001 depended on the parliamentary support of Danish right-wing populists, which the current Danish government does not. See "Danish Prime Minister Wants Country to Accept 'Zero' Asylum Seekers," *The Local dk*, January 22, 2021, https://www.thelocal.dk/20210122/danish-prime-minister-wants-country-to-accept-zero-asylum-seekers/. See also Peter Hervik, *The Annoying Difference: The Emergence of Danish Neonationalism, Neoracism, and Populism in the Post-1989 World* (London: Berghahn Books,

2011), for an overview of the longue durée of the mainstreaming of the Far and populist Right in Denmark since the 1970s.

67. For more on this, see Bangstad, *Anders Breivik and the Rise of Islamophobia*, chap. 2.

68. For a very good critical analysis of the racial politics of European immigration, see Nicholas De Genova, "The 'Migrant Crisis' as Racial Crisis: Do Black Lives Matter in Europe?," *Ethnic and Racial Studies* 41, no. 10 (2018): 1756–82.

69. See Mamdani, *Neither Settler nor Native*.

70. It is for pragmatic reasons, and not out of any ill will, that I have here chosen to retain terms such as "far-right" and "right-wing populism" instead of adopting Jansen and Leeuwenkamp's alternative term wholesale. The former terms have for various reasons come to dominate the scholarly literature in this field, and there are also pragmatic reasons relating to the need to preserve some fundamental distinctions between historically variegated political phenomena in my choice of doing so. It is necessary to emphasize that terms such as these are above all heuristic devices, and as such may suffer from descriptive and analytical imperfections regardless of what choices one makes.

71. Note here that former president Trump's famous racist remarks about Haiti and "shithole countries" in Africa came in the context of a state visit of the Norwegian Conservative Party prime minister Erna Solberg to the White House in January 2018. And note the context of Trump contrasting immigrants from Haiti and supposedly "shithole countries" in Africa with immigrants from Norway, which he readily declared that the United States needed "more of." See Jen Kirby, "Trump Wants Fewer Immigrants from 'Shithole Countries' and More from Places Like Norway," *Vox*, January 11, 2018, https://www.vox.com/2018/1/11/16880750/trump-immigrants-shithole-countries-norway. The White supremacist idea of Norway and the Nordic countries as quintessentially "White spaces," which have long been rendered fictitious by the demographic shifts these countries have undergone since the 1960s, is of long standing in the far-right circles in the United States and in the Nordics. These ideas were arguably also central to the German Nazi obsession with Norway as a potential "breeding ground" for the future "Nordic" and "Aryan" race before and during the German Nazi occupation of Norway from 1940 to 1945. For this, see Despina Stratigakos, *Hitler's Northern Utopia: Building the New Order in Occupied Norway* (Princeton, NJ: Princeton University Press, 2020).

72. Geneviève Zubrzycki, chap. 5 herein.

73. Ibid. (emphasis original).

74. Ibid.

75. Hall, "Old and New Identities, Old and New Ethnicities," 78.

76. David Scott, "Stuart Hall's Ethics," *Small Axe* 17, no. 9 (2005): 2.

CHAPTER 8

Going Rogue on Islam

Derrida's Muslim Hauntology and Nationalism's Specters

EBRAHIM MOOSA

ABSTRACT

In response to the contributions in this volume, this chapter analyzes the continued haunting of the supposedly secular and democratic nation-state by exclusivist ideologies. The nation-state, it contends, continues to be plagued by an exclusionary ideology based on race, ethnicity, and religion. Rather than democratic polities where citizens can adjudicate their differences, nation-states, especially in the present populist moment, are political entities where difference is violently suppressed.

Jacques Derrida, it might seem, would be a natural ally for those who oppose essentialist and static visions of nation-states and seek to challenge oppressive structures within them. His philosophy of deconstruction breaks down the seeming naturalness of categories that have been used to oppress and marginalize. Yet, this chapter shows how Derrida's political theology remains indebted to an exclusivist model of the nation-state. This is most clear, the chapter contends, in his engagement with Islam and the question

> *of the political versus the theocratic. In uncritically accepting an account of Islam as theocratic and in its essence immutable, and Europe as secular and therefore open to change, Derrida replicates a division between Europe and Islam that both betrays his own philosophical program and obscures the violence necessary to maintaining this binary. Overcoming this exclusionary model of the nation-state, the author argues, requires a rethinking of the very meaning and structure of the nation-state in modernity.*

In the first decades of the twenty-first century, nationalism in all its ugly forms is rearing its head across multiple continents. Most disturbingly, a toxic version is rife in several democratic societies of the global North and South. This, however, is not the first time nationalism exploded. Roughly two decades ago, just after the fall of the Berlin Wall in 1989, historian Partha Chatterjee noted that political analysts were eager to claim that "the principal danger to world peace is now posed by the resurgence of nationalism in different parts of the world."[1] Chatterjee was critical of the predisposition of analysts to first deem something a "problem" before it could gain public and scholarly attention. Whether this early twenty-first-century wave of ethnocentric movements is an incarnation of older toxic and violent expressions of nationalism or something else, few would disagree that it disrupts global peace, and in some places it is the beginning of a dangerous moment in world history. This rather ominous form of nationalism now invades different shades of human bodies, ethnic and racial categories, religious traditions, and expressions of faith. Disentangling its myriad tentacles and dissecting its discursive and embodied expressions remains a challenge.

The reason dissecting nationalism is so challenging analytically is that in the twentieth century, nationalism was the feature of "victorious anticolonial struggles in Asia and Africa."[2] One of the many ironies of history is that during this period of emancipation from colonial rule "nationalism was generally considered one of Europe's most magnificent gifts to the rest of the world."[3] Anticolonial nationalist leaders of the global South adopted certain features of nationalism, but they also spoiled their records afterward when they undertook some of the most heinous and morally odious "ethnic politics" in distressing civil wars.[4] Today nationalist discourses in Europe, North America, and elsewhere similarly adopt some of the very toxic and dangerous features of nationalism's past. The new discursive practices of White nationalism are not shaped by "print-capitalism," as in Benedict Anderson's imagined communities, but rather fascist ideology. Social media and memes without any central editorial direction but clearly orchestrated as media campaigns are sponsored by a species of neoliberal capitalism that fuels these tendencies. Certain forms of White nationalism imagine the norms of the territory or earth they inhabit to be determined by a cosmology of Whiteness. Hence, when people of color cohabit or surge to become majorities, Whites or settlers view such a change as an alteration of the cosmic order, often inflected with religious overtones. Christian settler colonialists in South Africa and Jewish settlers in Israel exhibit a similar logic of combining territory and race or ethnicity, and then invert the negative appellation of "timeless natives" to themselves and thus deem themselves as "native" to their rhetorical advantage.[5]

This volume contains a cross section of ideas and analyses of nationalism in different contexts that are illuminating in multiple ways. I will try to build crosscutting conversations between some of the ideas shared by some contributors, especially in my engagement with the question of Islam in the context of western nationalism, since Islam is viewed as a major symbol that feeds raging White and other ethnocentric expressions of nationalism. Indeed, as I will show later, even ostensibly secular nationalist projects in the context of Europe and the United States rely on discrete theological disavowals that are in effect masked as "political disavowals" directed at the Muslim as "Other." The other feeder is, of course, race and the changing cultural and political demographics of North America and Europe. These shifts in effect exercise the anxieties of hegemonic White segments on both continents. Recent European and North American experiences have shown how once Jews were deemed the enemy, speedily the "Muslim problem," once the "Saracen problem," was added to that list of enemies.[6] It is thus unfortunate that avant-garde European intellectuals cultivate blind spots about these interrelated issues.

As a longtime reader of Derrida, I found elements of deconstructive modes of reading texts to be valuable. To go behind the veil of ideology and language was one useful way to understand how meaning is made by way of destabilizing orthodoxies and how politics animate texts. However, when I read Derrida's *Politics of Friendship*, there was something jarring in his warm and uncritical embrace of Carl Schmitt for me as a scholar of

Islam. Surprising was the absence of any demurral on the part of Derrida to Carl Schmitt's key portrayal of the Turk and Islam as the political enemy. In the light of Derrida's subsequent reflections in *Rogues* on Islam, the text of *Politics of Friendship* serves as a distant trace. Perhaps in defense of Derrida, though it does not insulate him from critique, the theologian David Tracy offers some insight: "All texts, theirs and mine, are saturated with the ideologies of particular societies, the history of ambiguous effects of particular traditions, and the hidden agendas of the unconscious."[7] So not even the most self-reflexive deconstructionist thinkers can claim they have freed themselves from the unconscious ideological saturations of history and society, since both elements engulf them too as they write and speak. So it is with Derrida.

Exploring the question of nationalism in the context of religion and political theology, the Algerian thinker Mustapha Chérif's conversation with Derrida on Islam and Algeria provides me with an opportunity to think through what I deem to be unventilated and contentious assumptions in Derrida's haunted readings of Islam and Muslims coupled with his neglect of a careful study of the phenomena he comments on, namely, Islam and Muslims. I begin with Chérif's conversation with Derrida on the question of Islam and the notion of the theological. I then draw on the critical insights of the political theorists Anne Norton, Wendy Brown, and prominent political philosopher Fred R. Dallmayr to leaven the conversation in a bid to propose a different way, one of coexistence for Muslims in Europe in a democratic idiom. Proleptically, I announce that Derrida makes a claim of the impossibility of democracy in conversation with "Islam" that is animated by his reading of developments in Algeria in 1992, and this constitutes Derrida's hauntology with respect to Islam. Some of the themes explored in this chapter, I am delighted to note, also resonate with the views of authors of select chapters in this volume.

Derrida in the Modern Political Context

In 2003, Derrida, the preeminent French philosopher, born in El-Biar, Algeria, left his Parisian hospital bed to speak at the final session of a colloquium, "Algeria-France: Tribute to the Great Figures of the Dialogue between Civilizations," held at the prestigious cultural site, the Institut du

Monde Arabe in Paris on May 26–27. Derrida, famous for his captivating philosophy of deconstruction, engaged in conversation with the Algerian philosopher and scholar of Islam Mustapha Chérif from the University of Algiers, who is also a sometime visiting professor at the Collège de France in Paris.

This exchange is one crucial thread in my reading of the book-length essay *Islam and the West: A Conversation with Jacques Derrida*. I later mediate this conversational essay through the lens of an essay in Derrida's *Politics of Friendship* and *Rogues* to complete the circle, so to speak. I explore what resources Derrida and Chérif can both offer to help us visualize pathways out of the rigid conceptualization of society as necessarily taking the form of nations and nation-states. I am not calling for the immediate abolition of the nation-state (such calls will not be heeded, even if made sincerely!). However, as with other contributors in this volume, my goal is to diagnose the current deficits of the nation-state and the dangers of nationalism that occur within it. There may very well be emancipatory possibilities that mark "the political" within the nation-state context. These might be brought about by asking specific questions as to how one might transform the nation-state so that it might reflect more humane political ideals. However, my aim here is primarily diagnostic rather than constructive.

What Derrida means by the idea of "the political" is to free political reason from any metaphysical and theological relationship, and therefore it is synonymous with the secular and the democratic.[8] For Derrida and his interpreters, the metaphysical assumes the disavowal of time by creating an opposition between the temporal and the eternal and in deeming knowledge to be absolute.[9] Arguing that there is no "front between responsibility and irresponsibility" in the context of Abraham's sacrifice, Derrida frames what remains as "different orders of responsibility, different other orders: the religious and the ethical, the religious and the ethico-political, the theological and the political, the theologico-political, the theocratic and the ethico-political, and so on."[10] One should be alert to these binary sets that frame "the political" in different instances where one dimension, often the nontheological, is privileged.

We should assess Derrida, to be fair, by his own standard, but the debate about the political has surpassed this metaphysical logic. Political reason in late modernity, Giorgio Agamben will tell us, is biopolitical. In other words, simple and natural life is now subject to the mechanisms and calculations of state power where the state is increasingly behaving in absolute ways or performing secular metaphysical gestures.[11] Many agree with Agamben and others that the neoliberal nation-state paradigm only increases impersonal and alienated relationships between citizens. Sometimes the idea of citizenship can become emptied of its values and be reduced to linguistic, racial, and/or identity markers denuded of community and meaningful coexistence. These are all valid observations and hence make the search beyond the nation-state framework more urgent. It is only by interrogating the secret link between "bare life" and the politics that govern modern political ideologies, which by my lights is a secular metaphysics, that the possibility of some form of emancipatory politics arises.

Democratic nation-states claim to preserve and enhance the freedom of the individual more than anything else. One of the central features of modernity is a new idea of freedom and a disenchanted relationship with nature, unknown to our predecessors in the annals of thought, where humans were embedded in a cosmic context. The modern notion of freedom promoted by democratic nation-states is a double-edged sword: we need it for our continued valuation of human life and yet it can also carry the bacilli of our undoing as a human community. A craving for freedom merely for the sake of resistance to government interference in one's life without an agenda for the common good often reveals freedom's ugly sides, as recent globalized conflicts, such as over the need to be vaccinated against the COVID-19 virus in the service of the public good, have demonstrated. Yet, democratic as well as autocratic nations have also invoked the concept of freedom to undertake imperial ventures and to vanquish political opponents. Here notions of individual freedom become entangled with the freedom of the nation-state on the international stage.

Agamben helpfully channels Foucault's sobering insight that the "modern Western state has integrated techniques of subjective individualization with procedures of objective totalization to an unprecedented degree."[12] For it was Foucault who drew attention to the totalization of the structures of modern power that occurred when a range of practices, including political practices, shifted from being subject to moral or legal judgments as good or bad (in terms of a law or a moral principle),[13] and instead were judged as "true or false." As Foucault put it, political practices became aligned to a "regime of truth" to form an "apparatus (*dispositif*) of knowledge-power that effectively marks out in reality that which does not exist and legitimately submits it to the division between true and false."[14] The modern political subject is placed in a political double-bind of both hyperindividualization and simultaneous subordination to modern biopower. The latter masquerades as truth and delegitimizes its antithesis as false.[15] I argue that we need to return to governmentality in politics where organized practices, inclusive of mentalities, rationalities (including practical reason), and a range of ethical and moral techniques in governing subjects ought to replace biopower.

Our disenchantment with aspects of modernity does, however, compel us to reach back to earlier knowledge resources where what we call "religion" was crucial to human social and political life. Democratic freedoms and democratic political orders proudly claim to host a new self that prizes exclusively the "human ego as the crucial and ultimately as the only secure and indubitable subject."[16] As Dallmayr notes, "Together with the stress on subjectivity, modern thought also relies centrally on human freedom—where freedom signifies no longer participation in a cosmic plan but rather independence from external bonds and autonomous authorship of all plans and initiatives."[17] In a cosmos-centered world, the "I" or "ego" was restricted to a surrounding context of disclosure. The cosmos or the heteronomous order to a large extent determined the measure of humans. Today we realize several problematic aspects of this heteronomous or cosmic order, but a context of entirely humanly constructed norms as the measure of humans also comes with its own challenges. In other words, political systems now are frameworks constructed by humans, and humans can also unmake those systems. Political orders in their nature and form are not sacrosanct. What is sacrosanct for moderns is to adhere to the order once sufficient agreement is reached so that the rules are uniformly applied and recognized. Politically modern humans invoke untrammeled notions of freedom, but there are more practical measures and matrices that decide the limits of what humans can do and might achieve. Religion and religious traditions have over time, and especially in the modern context, contested the political freedoms humans derived from secular philosophies, and often the two crossed swords. Still, the dialectical value that occurs when we engage both holds value. Foucault's and Agamben's critique of modernity and Dallmayr's reconstruction of the political serve as counterpoints or supplements to Derrida's very firm secular notion of the political.

Islam on the Mediterranean Stage

In his opening remarks, Chérif frames the image of Islam in the west as one of an ongoing and frustrating *ressentiment* or hostility. On his account, "Islam" as a synecdoche for a civilizational confrontation is fully entrapped by post-9/11 events, among them the invasions of Afghanistan and Iraq, the endless "war on terror" campaigns, and the securitization of the religion industry (especially of Islam and Muslims). These features, when coupled with the blithe disregard for human rights and civility in the policy postures of successive U.S. and European governments, make up the key elements of his framework. Chérif highlights the plight of Muslims in the world, but, specifically from his vantage point, those who live in the region of the Mediterranean where North Africa connects with southern Europe. He lists the plight of these communities as, first, resisting the injustice of the west, and second, resisting the "de-signification of the world."[18] By the latter he points to the fact that the symbolic and the spiritual in human life still retain their importance for these people. Since a range of Muslim majority societies offer "resistance to the decadence of modernity," the response of the west results in the stigmatization, as Chérif puts it, of "the eternal 'Saracen.'"[19] The "Saracen," which like the "eternal native" or "eternal Jew" in other contexts, is a stand-in for the "eternal Muslim" who becomes the target of western hate, both overt and covert, because he or she, it is alleged, opposes the very being of Euro-America's civilizational project and its standards of justice.[20] It is an opposition that inserts itself in every aspect of being in order to create an almost metaphysical otherness. The western media and some intellectuals, Chérif complains, "reject the right to be different, and claim to hold the truth in the name of scientific rationality and scientism."[21] To that Chérif insightfully adds: "One difficulty is the attitude of the West with entrenched ideas, which refuses to admit plurality, to really listen to the other, to recognize that there exist other, completely different ways to see the world—of a West that alarmingly seems to want to escape forward, while denying the deep crisis that is shaking it."[22] Chérif argues that it is not enough to question the dichotomy between east and west, to compare values, texts, and practices, or to create certain solidarity against the irrational.[23]

Derrida in his response confirms his rejection of categorizing cultures as developed versus undeveloped. "I agree with you," he addresses Chérif, "about the need to deconstruct the European intellectual construct of Islam." Then Derrida adds: "The so conventionally accepted contrast between Greeks, Jews, and Arabs must be challenged. We know very well that Arab thought and Greek thought intimately blended at a given historical moment and that one of the primary duties of our intellectual and philosophical memory is to rediscover that grafting, the reciprocal fertilization of the Greek, Arab, and the Jew. Spain comes to mind."[24] Derrida explains that his family probably came to North Africa from Spain where multiple modes of thinking blended. "One of our primary intellectual responsibilities today is to rediscover the sources and moments in which those currents, far from being in contrast, truly fertilized each other."[25] But all these words are perhaps a temporary reprieve since, as I will later show, Derrida's written (*écrit*) political philosophy in *Rogues* does not fully theorize this overtly compassionate and complex (phonocentric) voice of his; instead he had already gone in the opposite direction.

Chérif and Derrida share a commitment to "the principle of secularity" where, according to Chérif, it is "intrinsic to Islam, and this has been true since its origins."[26] Chérif projects secularity rather anachronistically onto the eighth-century birth of Islam as if the then notion of the "worldly" or the quotidian is the same as the modern idea of the secular today. To be charitable, he might have meant that the idea of the political in Islam is not theocratic, but rather value-centered, socially defined, and adaptive to change over time. This was the case for the caliphate model of governance, which demonstrated its adaptability over the centuries. Nevertheless, Chérif persists in critiquing the west for selectively applying the standard of democracy, and hence for being hypocritical when it comes to how it characterizes Arab/Muslim majority states and how it treats Muslim minorities in Europe. He uses the forum of dialogue with a distinguished French philosopher and an august audience to let them know that Arabs and Muslims especially are subject to double standards and "hypocritical political discourse." He highlights the deafening silence on the part of French intellectuals and the public alike when Arabs and Muslims discuss and contribute to the content and meaning of democracy. Often such efforts to expand the framework of an inclusive and blended form of democracy that includes the experiences of Muslim minorities are rebuffed. Chérif might possibly be speaking from his personal experiences in Europe. His is a more professorial complaint when compared to Houria Bouteldja's passionate plea and agenda for revolutionary love.[27]

In his opening remarks, Derrida wants the audience to know that he is speaking as an Algerian drawing on his personal history of being born in that country under French colonial rule, but he omits drawing attention to his Jewish Sephardi heritage that can be traced back to Muslim Spain or Andalus. The element of the protean and ambiguous cannot be suppressed in reading his text. "These are a few of the heartfelt things I want to tell you," Derrida says. "I want to speak here, today, as an Algerian, as an Algerian who became French at a given moment, lost his French citizenship, then recovered it. Of all the cultural wealth I have received, that I have inherited, my Algerian culture has sustained me the most. This is what I wanted to say in a testimony from the heart."[28] This is indeed a moving act of solidarity with his interlocutor, and one suspects the present and absent audiences whom he is addressing.

In response to Chérif's question about democracy Derrida asserts that as a political order it is a "model without a model, that accepts its own historicity . . . which accepts its self-criticism, which accepts its perfectibility."[29] As encouragement to Chérif and in agreement with him, Derrida adds: "To exist in a democracy is to agree to challenge, to be challenged, to challenge the status quo, which is called democratic, in the name of a democracy to come."[30] A dialogue about the nature of democracy, Derrida explains, can only occur "in the revelation of that democracy to come, whose occurrence and promise remain before us."[31] Ringing with messianic tones, Derrida proposes a new vision, that a democracy to come has to free itself from "the concept of autochthony, that is, the concept of being born on a land and belonging to it through birth, the concept of territory, the very concept of State."[32] This is all a very encouraging, if not an emancipatory, discourse. Derrida then advocates a democracy that is not simply tied to the nation-state and to citizenship. Cosmopolitanism is certainly respectable, but it is still associated with the notion of state and the *polis* as part of a nation-state and territoriality. The conversation Chérif hoped to pursue between east and west, Derrida suggests, can be explored through dialogue and exchange in discursive modalities that are not connected to the idea of a nation-state, citizenship, religion, language, and territoriality. Rather, it can be explored through something more ambitious, such as a democracy "to come," which is an expression that has become a hallmark of the philosophy of deconstruction. Language and religion can be recognized as part of the dialogue, but Derrida would concede that the task at hand that he advocates is somewhat different: translation. Translation of the language of the other in pursuit of a universal democracy. For this purpose, theorizing a new international law is Derrida's proposal to push the conversation beyond the limitations of the question of sovereignty and the nation-state.[33]

Regardless of the direction the dialogue takes, foremost on the mind of Chérif was modernity and secularization. For Chérif, though modernity is "inevitable," it is reasonable to have concerns about the direction of secularization. For this reason, he characterized it as "dehumanization, de-spiritualization, *de-signification*."[34] Chérif asked Derrida whether he shared a concern about the "*removal of religion from life* or at the very least the end of morality as it had been bequeathed by monotheism, a situation that destroys ethics and identity?"[35] Despite the institutions of the developed world and its attachment to human rights, Chérif claims that the quest for the "just, the beautiful and the true" seems increasingly elusive.[36] In this spirit he asks Derrida to share his reflections on scientism, secularism/laicism, and capitalism. And although these are all interesting questions, Derrida's remarks on the secular are the most relevant to my discussion.

Derrida, in his response to Chérif, articulates the democracy "to come" is part of his signature move of teleiopoeiesis, and assumes such a democratic future to be secular and embodied by secularism. What Derrida means by "secularism" is clear. He describes it as "both the detachment of the political from the theocratic and the theological, thus entailing a certain secularism of the political, while at the same time, encompassing freedom of worship in a completely consistent, coherent way, and absolute religious freedom guaranteed by the State, on the condition, obviously, that the secular space of the political and the religious space is not confused."[37] What is constructive in his response is his rare and implicit critique of the secular: "Today we need a concept of the secular that no longer has that sort of aggressive compulsion that it once had in France, in the moments of crisis between the State and religion. I believe the secular today must be more rigorous with itself, more tolerant toward religious cultures and toward the possibility for religious practices to exist freely, unequivocally, and without confusion."³⁸

His overtures to religion and religious culture are heartening, but his antipathy toward the "theocratic" and the "theological" is not entirely decipherable, especially from within a deconstructive perspective. From a deconstructive perspective, neither the theological nor the secular are self-sufficient or natural kinds of constructs. Against the shadow of the "theological," the proverbial elephant in the room is clearly the Muslim citizen of France. Among these is especially the female Muslim citizen, whose body has been subject to extraordinary legislative regulation when it comes to wearing the headcover in government institutions, such as schools, and where women are forbidden to don the facecover (*niqāb*) in public or don swimwear covering their bodies. Derrida does not name the female subject but does a fine pirouette around the issue. And based on Derrida's privileging of the secular, which I return to later, one must question whether he really differs substantively with radical secular French intellectuals and members of the public who take an uncompromising line against the veil and in favor of an uncompromising concept of French secularism (*laïcité*). Many of his views on Islam, as it will become evident later, stem from a sleight of hand where he implicitly casts Islam as a theocratic order or sometimes veils it as among the forces that are ranged against "the political," meaning the secular.

Many Muslim women express the decision to wear the veil as reflective of their commitment to the sharī'a (the legal and ethical aspects of Islamic life). The moral subject of the sharī'a is in part a heteronomous subject, obedient to the strictures of God, the Prophet, and the salvation or obedience practices (*dīn*) of Islam. To be fair, Derrida at different moments frames the individual as "autonomous" but also as one who "himself or herself [to] his or her law, [is] a sovereign subject" and where the freedom of such a subject also "presupposes a certain heteronomy, that is, a certain acceptance of the law of the other."³⁹ One could assume here that a veiling Muslim woman or any faith-adhering individual could be a sovereign subject. Furthermore, we can assume that the "other" in question mentioned by Derrida is the state or the divine. But we should note that this sovereignty of the subject is a qualified sovereignty on the grounds of what Derrida says next. This, in turn, betrays some of his less clear, if not problematic, liberal dispositions.

Continuing his reflections on the sovereign subject in relation to his or her law, presumably the law of the state or the law of religion, and whatever signified he meant should not really matter, he does, however, state a qualification: "But this heteronomy does not presuppose servitude or subjection, and the religious community can very well organize itself as a religious community, in a lay space, without invading the lay space and while respecting the freedom of the individual."[40] Here heteronomy to the other is qualified by the freedom of the individual. In other words, Derrida sees limitations in absolute heteronomy. It is a qualified surrender to the "other" that he advocates. Logically, this is a contradiction in terms, even though I am aware that deconstruction revels in defeating customary logic and contradiction. But the very idea of heteronomy is antithetical to freedom, and Derrida does not make clear the relationship he sees between the two. In other domains, separate or away from those prescribed by the heteronomous "other" such as the state, the law, or God, he seems to be saying that there is a limited kind of freedom or a nonheteronomous space, where a specific kind of freedom could be configured and imagined but that would not be the liberal freedom Derrida cherishes.

Derrida's difficulty with religion becomes clear when he writes: "I have always had the tendency to resist religious communitarianism, that is, any form of gregarious community that oppresses the individual, that prevents the individual from acting as a nonreligious citizen."[41] One might ask why Derrida found it necessary to privilege freeing the endangered species of the nonreligious citizen from the pressures of communitarianism when there are so many more powerful subliminal forces—such as advertising and marketing—that completely denude the person of any individuality. Derrida claims that he is keen to strike a peaceful "connection" between the individual and the religious community, provided that the religious community is not oppressive, overwhelming, or repressive.[42]

The presumption he makes of an entity known as the religious community that is oppressive and repressive deserves attention. Religious communities do have deficits, and repression might be one of them, but these cannot be totalized as a presumption fostered by the entire religious community or the leaders and caretakers of a tradition. Without devaluing the total system, these repressive aspects can be isolated and addressed just as they can be in secular systems. Yet, in Derrida's mind and in the minds of so many secular intellectuals, it is telling when the oppressive nature of the nation-state is not only naturalized but also excused as part of the necessity of "the political," while the theocratic is treated as dangerous or antithetical to life itself. More striking even is that the rhetoric of oppression only arises in the context of a conversation that centers around the elephant in the room, the practice of Islam in France and the contestation between the complex and diverse Muslim community, on the one hand, and the French state and legal system and Europe, on the other.

Derrida's transgressive reading of politics as displayed elsewhere in his more philosophical meditations on the political fades from view in this context where he explicitly deals with Islam. In the context of Arabs and Muslims, the situation inexplicably paves the way for him to take a more pragmatic approach to the state. One is tempted to say that he purchases into the "metaphysics of presence," which deconstruction with muscular effort disavows. In other works, Derrida critiques the metaphysics of presence—which is both explicitly and implicitly forwarded in many of the works of "western" philosophy—because it assumes an unmediated claim to truth. Despite his critique of the sovereign nation-state and the questions he asks about its origins, especially the theological character of state sovereignty following Carl Schmitt, he becomes emphatic in his promotion of the secular, a move that then surprisingly leads him to declare that he is *not* opposed to the state. Under certain circumstances, he asserts, the state "may be the guarantor of secularity, or of the life of religious communities."[43] Derrida repeatedly reminds his audience that one should simultaneously question the sovereignty of the state and at the same time maintain a complex concept of "the political," meaning the secular democratic. What is stunning is the notable absence on Derrida's part of his critical deconstructive posture when it applies to the nature and function of the French state vis-à-vis Muslims and Arabs! The only consolation is his theoretical allusion to the "democracy to come."

At the very instant of asserting the freedom or autonomy of the heteronomous subject, Derrida's rhetoric shifts from being an Algerian to being a European. How does he make this deft move? The "democracy to come" will allow us to question the sovereignty of the nation-state. But the outcome of this questioning will not be an ambivalent one, since it will surprisingly result in "the authentic secularization of the political, that is, the separation between the theocratic and the political."[44] Notice Derrida's constant use of the binary that pits the theocratic against the political. Sustaining binaries such as these is a cardinal sin in deconstruction, and Derrida's use of such a binary here is thus even more surprising. Here we need to observe that very subtly the naming of the "theocratic" is Derrida's reductionism and code word for Islam itself. Chérif is not alert to this move on the part of Derrida.

I am not alone in my observation of deconstruction's slippage in the wrong direction when it comes to engaging with Islam. Political theorist Wendy Brown has astutely questioned Derrida and other figures of the post-Marxist European Left in their identification of Islam with the theocratic: "How has the overtaking of Western political life by neoliberal rationality and by a figuring of Islam as theocratic produced a circling of the diverse wagons of this Left around an articulation of democracy that shores up the identification of the Euro-Atlantic world with civilization signified by individual freedom?"[45] I cannot improve on this eloquent and elegant encapsulation of the problem identified by Brown. I hope to have provided sufficient concrete examples to bolster her astute observation.

In dealing with the unnamed "Muslim question," one cannot help but notice that the founder of deconstruction, in this case, does less questioning and performs more decisively in favor of secularization. In Derrida's schema, secularization is deeply committed to sovereignty as the lynchpin of "the political." There are few instances where Derrida stakes out so unambiguous a claim as when he examines "the political." Contrary to his own theoretical strictures, Derrida has entrenched secularism's metaphysical suggestions while evacuating the metaphysics of theology. But the coup de grâce is in the very next line after he prophesizes that "the political" will be a more perfect secularization: "I believe that we must—here I am speaking as a Frenchman, a Westerner, a Western philosopher—I believe that what we must consider as our first task is to *ally* ourselves to that in the Arab and Muslim world which is trying to advance the idea of secularization of the idea of the political, the idea of a separation between the theocratic and the political—this both out of respect for the political and for democratization and out of respect for faith and religion."[46] The parallel respect for the political and the democratic, on the one hand, and the respect for faith and religion, on the other, is tautological at best, and either lacking in substance or a sleight of hand, at worst. Deconstruction's goal "to unsettle and shatter the original distinctions" as that unnamable play that challenges unitary structures and introduces heterodoxy sadly evaporates in the face of the theocratic/Islamic.[47]

Derrida would argue that deconstruction is not a set of rules and that the outcomes of deconstructive readings and possibilities take time and do not usher in instant solutions.[48] But Derrida has repeatedly stated that deconstruction is interested in the impossible. Yes, indeed, deconstruction asks us to face the impossible so that from that specific struggle and experience it is possible to encounter emancipatory horizons in thought and experience. My interrogation goes like this: Why is the theological not subject to the impossible new possibilities? Why are readings of Islam not subject to such generosity? Why, in an elaborate mystification and masking, does Derrida so aggressively and fundamentally set up the binary opposition between the theocratic and the political, Islam versus the secular? So, to be clear, I am seeking a certain "possibility" for the theological/theocratic/Islam against Derrida's claim that the only way the political cosmos can be definitively split is only and almost exclusively through "the authentic secularization of the political, that is, the separation between the theocratic and the political."

Derrida's most effective and powerful contribution to philosophical thought has been to combat what he calls "the metaphysics of presence." It is the Derridean antidote to the history of western metaphysics to say with Nietzsche that truth is actually the history of metaphors and metonymies.[49] In other words, all the names related to principles, fundamentals, and such have always designated the constancy of a presence in terms such as "essence," "existence," "substance," "subject," "consciousness," "conscience," "God," and "man," among other concepts subject to radical questioning in deconstruction.[50] Ordinary language philosophy assumes that when we do not have the thing present, then we use the detour of signs on the assumption that the thing is present and that we can reappropriate it through our searching.[51] Derrida's counterconception is that the sign or a word defers that falsely assumed presence and engages that sign continuously without us ever attaining absolute knowledge of the thing itself. Why, then, would Islam and theology be any different? Why does Derrida in this instance claim to have absolute knowledge of these categories? I would defer to Michel de Certeau, who so aptly invites us to contemplate his words: "Truth is what [the hu]man silences through the very practice of language. Communication is always the metaphor of what it hides."[52]

Derrida Reading Islam

Derrida's negative view of the theological and the theocratic stems from his view of theology as an essential component of logocentrism that enframes itself as an authoritative and final "book," as opposed to his notion of ongoing writing that reflexively disrupts all discursivities along the lines of *différance*. I am asking this: Why couldn't the endless signification of possibilities result in the possibility that the theological and the theocratic also reach new possibilities that are not necessarily secular? Derrida might well object and respond by saying that deconstruction is not about the *possible*; deconstruction represents a force and desire to experience the impossible and to reach the other as the invention of the impossible. This then prompts the question: Why is the invention of the impossibility of the theocratic not also thinkable or in the realm of desire? Why is the impossibility of a theocratic order yet to come, one that is different from past theocratic and theological orders, not thinkable?[53] Why not theological and theocratic (im)possibilities, yet to come, in true Derridean fashion? Derrida does not entertain these possibilities and is wedded to the political theology of French *laïcité*, albeit with a few qualifications, as mentioned above. Nonetheless, the underlying political ontology of the secular remains undisturbed. Deconstruction is about questioning metaphysics, but it has cultivated its own metaphysics, namely, the metaphysics or absolute knowledge of the secular.[54]

One common understanding of deconstruction is that it is an endless process of questioning ideas and concepts and is consistent with the endless signification of words and concepts. "The signified always already functions as the signifier," writes Derrida.[55] If we treat democracy and secularity as a medicine, as Derrida does in his reading of Plato, then they act "as both remedy and poison," and they are introduced into the body of discourse with all its ambivalence.[56] Just as the secular can be both remedy and poison, similarly the theological and theocratic should in theory hold the same potential.

Deconstruction turns into a profoundly prescriptive moment at the Institut de Monde Arabe in May 2003. It is as if Derrida did not hear Chérif's pleas for both the need for religious morals and a different form and modality of the secular. Derrida's opening gesture was that he speaks here as an "Algerian." That expression could be a nostalgic reflection on his youth in Algeria and possibly appropriate for what one assumes to be an audience that is largely from an Arab background of North African heritage. Can this space of Algerianness turn into a platitude when the person of Jacques Derrida articulates a vision that is a veiled *mission civilasatrice*, where he invokes his status as a "Frenchman," a "Westerner," and a "Western philosopher" to make certain prescriptive pronouncements about the need to strictly separate the theocratic from the political? Echoes of Moses Mendelssohn ring loud.

Deconstruction insists that we are always speaking under erasure where the winning term, in this instance, the idea of the secular, ought to be displaced and put under pressure. To speak under erasure means to say that finality is always deferred. Yet, this move seemingly disappears in Derrida's discourse, and the possibilities of being French resolve into concreteness at the very point when he makes muscular pronouncements about the future of the political as secular and the banishment of the theological. One cannot disguise the implication that the banished theological is code for Islam in the French public square. Yet, the theologically Catholic is not banished from the public square nor is it subject to public discourse. Anyone aware of the known legislative restrictions against Islam, especially against Muslim women, cannot reach a different conclusion. To spell it out, the Muslim is the "other" of modern Frenchness. The repeated rhetorical bifurcation between the theological (Islam) as the antithesis of the secular is startling. It is startling because Derrida himself admits that the secular is "fundamentally theological" or that "sovereignty" has a "theological heritage." Such a binary move is either a gross pratfall or a deconstructive smokescreen to privilege the secular. If in the basics of deconstruction we are taught that a fixed outcome cannot be predicted, then neither can the end of the endless signification of ideas, concepts, and history be predicted. It does appear that Derrida's idea of both the secular and the theological has not been subject to critical scrutiny with the help of a decolonial lens.[57]

What if a democratic society prefers a theological, or aspects of a theological, order to be part of the political? In places such as Tunisia,

Egypt, Sudan, and Pakistan it remains an aspiration. Why would an Indigenous African or Latin American polity that adopts a full-fledged pantheon of deities and a complex theocracy not be worth exploring rather than explaining away? The experiment with a version of Islamic democracy in post–Arab Spring Egypt in 2011 was quickly sundered by a military coup in 2013, and the surviving post–Arab Spring democratic experiment in Tunisia in 2021 suffered a setback. It is too early to judge Turkey's secular/Islamic hybrid experiment. Would such thought experiments, along with realized and materialized experiences, not be part of a democracy yet to come? Why is the European model of "the political" the only conceivable model?[58]

To further reinforce my case that Derrida insufficiently interrogates the secular and falls short of his own deconstructive prescriptions, let us examine his throwaway line about the 1992 elections in Algeria. Derrida briefly introduces the story of the aborted 1992 democratic elections in Algeria when the Islamists won the first round of the election and were poised to win the second round when the Algerian military capriciously canceled the elections. In his explanation Derrida takes a partisan line to a complex set of events. As Derrida put it, the military intervened on the pretext "of the threat of confiscation of democracy by the Islamist movement, when it was necessary, in Algeria, to suspend elections."[59] Most dispassionate observers will find Derrida's portrayal to be reductionist and deeply problematic. Upending a democratic process because of a predictable outcome of an Islamist victory made the military regime terminate the elections, and in the face of tremendous violence and upheaval, resulted in a seven-year civil war that claimed the lives of more than 200,000 Algerians, by conservative estimates. After touching this point, Derrida indicates that he does not wish to discuss this event further. But he was clearly willing to show his hand. Here the propping up of secular order brought the country no closer to a "democracy to come."

However, Derrida nevertheless continues to frame this tragic political event, and lesser ones that played out in France, as events that should be faced with knowledge, responsibility, and science. And in the very next move he turns to the Gnostic and mystificatory when he observes that the imperative to act during such overwhelming events takes place in the "moment of responsibility" and "does not come out of knowledge." He continues: "It is a leap that must be made by each person wherever he or she is and in the unique situation in which he or she happens to be. Between knowledge and responsibility there is an abyss . . . but there are also moments of faith, in which a leap is made."[60] To my ears this sounds more like providing a justification for the leap made by the Algerian military, yet the near Islamist victory does not qualify in Derrida's mind as a leap but rather appears as an ominous turn to the abyss.

These problematic philosophical insights are strewn alongside some real constructive ideas, such as his proposal for a new international alliance that goes beyond citizenship and states. In one posture, Derrida adopts the position of antiglobalization without much comment. Still, this is a constructive proposal. But in the same breath Derrida also redeems the German philosopher Immanuel Kant's comments on the French Revolution as almost an abject lesson we should apply in the context of the aborted 1992 Algerian elections. Kant, he tells us, favored the Republic spawned by the French Revolution of 1793 but decried the Terror that followed in its wake. In other words, Kant taught us that a failed enterprise can be worthy and noble because even a failure can foretell or anticipate that "progress is possible, that a perfectibility is coming."[61] This will hardly be solace for those killed in the Terror or be a balm for the survivors and families of those who perished in the Algerian civil war of 1992. But I can be persuaded that those complex political realities can force us into paradoxical and contradictory stone-cold political and philosophical dilemmas and aporias. In dealing with complex historical situations and their lessons, Derrida sees a silver lining in quite dim situations. Yet, these lessons only apply to one side of the equation, the allegedly authoritarian secular side of the Algerian civil war of the 1990s. Nor, I might add, is the complex issue of Muslims in French democracy subject to any complex understanding; only the secular side enjoys this privilege. In a less charitable mood, one can say that when it comes to Islam and the Arabs, all the sophisticated deconstructive possibilities can be sacrificed at the altar of the secular political, and the French nation-state in particular.

Haunting Saracen Phantoms

Derrida's reading of political events in the context of his dialogue with Chérif was preceded by his equally problematic reading of the political theory that was in vogue in the decades prior to 2003. "The Phantom Friend Returning (in the Name of 'Democracy')" is a meditation on friendship drawing on Aristotle, Montaigne, and Nietzsche. This is followed by Derrida's reading of Carl Schmitt's now-famous notion of the political-theological as constituted by the friend–enemy relationship. In short, the very idea of "the political," according to Schmitt, requires that you need to have an enemy. Friendship can be spectral and actual, and it is always haunted by the specter of the enemy and enmity. Like in all concepts, the binary logics constitute the mutual imprecation and the haunting at work in language, culture, and politics. Through his reading of Schmitt's friend–enemy dichotomy, Derrida grapples with some profound questions for our time. My question is this: Is the friend–enemy polarity about the *order of the political*? In other words, does the binary decide the system of governance itself, its rules and norms? Or is the friend–enemy figuration drawing the boundary at the very idea of *the political* itself in contrast to the theological?[62] To repeat, what Derrida means by the idea of "the political" is an appeal to secular political reason or democratic reason. The death of the political occurs, he explains, when "a political crime could no longer be defined or distinguished from other sorts of crimes." Then one's appeal to political reason becomes impossible.[63]

Derrida is enamored by Schmitt's insightful and philological reading of "the political," which is a kind of philological and philosophical deconstruction avant la lettre that the German jurist and Catholic thinker undertook. He endorses Schmitt's distinction that the enemy (*hostis*) is always a public enemy; the enemy is not a hated foe and is always encountered in the context of war, thereby eliminating any context of personal hatred. The example Schmitt provides for his illustration of the friend–enemy division is the Ottoman Empire, that is, the Turks or the more familiar medieval word to identify Muslims, "the Saracens." Schmitt writes: "Never in the thousand-year struggle between Christians and Moslems did it occur to a Christian to surrender rather than defend Europe out of love toward the Saracens or Turks. The enemy in the political sense need not be hated personally, and in the private sphere only does it make sense to love one's enemy, that is one's adversary."[64] Not absent is Schmitt's explanation that the public enemy is the enemy of a collectivity of people, particularly "a whole nation." On this account, one should not love the enemies of "one's own people."[65] Schmitt's analysis is historically flawed. One should immediately draw attention to the fact that the presence of a variety of Muslim political regimes and principalities prevailed in the Iberian Peninsula for nearly 700 years with instances of religious coexistence. This example should suffice to show that the enemy of Europe cannot be Muslim states, that is unless Schmitt does not consider Iberia to be part of Europe. Neither does Derrida, whose Jewish ancestors came from Muslim Spain to North Africa after the expulsion of both Jews in 1492 and Muslims in 1609–14, remember to remind Schmitt of his omission. Perhaps both Schmitt and Derrida betray their sense of what the "true Europe" is by not being alert to Europe as a complex historical space.

Derrida in his comment on Schmitt's above statement had this to say:

> We could say a great deal today.... Islam would remain an enemy even though we Europeans must love the Muslims as our neighbors. At a determining moment in the history of Europe, it was imperative not "to deliver Europe over to Islam" in the name of a universal Christianity. You are obliged, you will always have been obliged, to defend Europe against its other without confusing the genres, without confusing faith and politics, enmity and hostility, friendship and alliance or confusion.... *Indeed, strictly speaking, this would not be a war but a combat with the political at stake, a struggle for politics.... From then on the front of this opposition is difficult to place. It is no longer a thoroughly political front. In question would be a defensive operation destined to defend* the *political, beyond particular states or nations, beyond any geographical, ethnic or political continent. On the political side of this unusual front, the stakes would be saving the political as such, ensuring its survival in the face of another who would no longer even be a political enemy but an enemy of the political—more precisely, a being radically alien to the political as such, supposing at least that, in its purported purity, it is not Europeanized and shares nothing of the tradition of the juridical and the political called European.*[66] (italics mine)

The first part of Derrida's above comment is unremarkable in that it aligns with Schmitt's view of the need to love your enemy privately and Derrida's advocacy of loving the Muslim neighbor. But the latter part of Derrida's comment is deeply problematic. First, Derrida completely conflates the political with the secular, but in other instances deems it complex. And it also seems that he had completely internalized the modern idea of politics as a practice and regime of truth instead of an art of governing and governmental activity. Second, Derrida seems to pay little attention to the fact that since Schmitt's postwar Europe, Muslims are no longer just neighbors in Europe. Now they are citizens of multiple European states. They might be deserving of "love" as neighbors as Derrida states, but more importantly they are *entitled* to citizenship rights that ought to consider all their complex history and culture. And yet by endorsing Schmitt's discourse of love for the Muslim, not as citizen, neighbor, or migrant, Muslims are implicitly still treated as the Saracen "other." All cultural entities in Europe are complex, but Derrida's notion of the political as filtered through Schmitt is unable to account for this fact. Sovereignty, in the case of Catholic Poles, Geneviève Zubrzycki points out elsewhere in this volume (chapter 5), requires that Jews be defined as outside the boundaries of Polishness in a very similar way that Muslims are defined as outside the boundaries of Frenchness or Europeanness and, in all likelihood, outside of Whiteness.

Third, Schmitt's assumption that Derrida seems to endorse is that Europe will always have its other, and it seems that the father of deconstruction underwrites Schmitt's conception of the hostile Muslim other. Beyond that, Derrida reads Schmitt's friend–enemy polarity to signify a political combat over the very idea of "the political." In other words, the reasoning and rationality of politics that constitutes the political is war and hostility. "This is important for Schmitt," writes Derrida, "for whom war waged against a determinate enemy (*hostis*), a war or hostility that doesn't presuppose any hate, would be the condition of possibility of politics." Then he adds, that as Schmitt reminds us, "no Christian politics ever advised the West to love the Muslims who invaded Christian Europe."[67]

Furthermore, with respect to the political, why is the European model the only model worthy of consideration? Why is the idea of the political exclusively owned by Europe? Why would the Turks be such hostile foes? Is the implication that they have no sense of the political? For the sole reason of failing to own an idea of "the political," Islam falls outside the boundary of Europeanness, and here once again we can see resonances with Zubrzycki's discussion of similar features in the Polish context.

Fourth, Derrida and Schmitt lack the self-reflexivity that Arendt teaches us to adopt, namely, to look at history and the European experience in the aftermath of coloniality. If the Turks posed a threat to Europe historically, then did Europe not pose a threat to the rest of the world? Why is colonization seen as part of a privileged civilizing force? The Turks and multiple Muslim civilizations also viewed themselves as advancing some cause greater than themselves.

The stark absence of historical perspective on the part of both Schmitt and Derrida is breathtaking. For if anything, the Ottoman Empire, and the body of thought accumulated over centuries of Muslim intellectual and political history in other imperial forms, dedicated considerable effort and intellectual labor to the understanding of the political. Yet, even centuries of orientalist scholarship failed to edify Schmitt on Muslim political history, and Derrida makes no effort to familiarize himself with non-European political philosophies, least of all Islamic political philosophy. What Schmitt accomplishes more explicitly, and Derrida accomplishes via a mystifying political-theological reading, is this: a discursive move to effectively turn the "other" into a realm beyond the civilized. Once you can proclaim that the enemy has no political reason, only theological reason, then any kind of hostility can be legitimated, as post-9/11 Euro-American military adventures have demonstrated.[68] I do not believe Derrida ever contemplated this reading, but the inarticulate premises of his complex arguments amount to the charge I pose.[69]

This observation of mine finds resonance with Richard Amesbury's contribution to this volume (chapter 4), which identifies particular discursive registers of religion when it comes to marking out who is part of the political and who is not. As he shows, sovereignty, or the very foundation of the state, is often constructed on this fiction, as noted in Derrida's observations of the U.S. Constitution. As Amesbury demonstrates with regard to the cases of nationalism in the United States and Germany, I hope I have also convincingly shown how preeminent French intellectuals foster nationalism in a secular guise and in a broader Europe too, where the indigeneity of first peoples in North America and the Roma people in

Europe are completely erased from the idea of the political and the notion of sovereignty.

Countless Republican proponents of the antiveil laws in France defended their position on the grounds that such measures were necessary to protect civilization. To oppose the veil is to defend Europe. To endorse blaspheming Islam and Muslim sacred personages is to defend Europe. Schmitt has cast long shadows on Europe's political imagination, and the fascination of the European Left with his ideas in combat with liberalism remains a puzzle, especially in the light of his exclusivist ideology and flirtation with Nazism. One must thus conclude that to defend Europe is to defend *the* political as conceived by Schmitt and Derrida. Both have laid out the discursive means to defend France, and by implication Europe, against all others. Europe remains the Freudian "father" that haunts a good number of European intellectuals politically. Regrettably, it is hard to see how Derrida is not excluded from this group of intellectuals. His reading of Europe versus the Turks/Saracens remains as teleological and essentialist as Schmitt's.

There is some noteworthy rhetoric that follows Derrida's endorsement of Schmitt that requires further interrogation. After endorsing Schmitt's position that the Turks are Europe's enemies whereas one's Muslim neighbors are one's friends, Derrida provides an intriguing comment. He amplifies the friend–enemy polarity as *the* element that sublimates Islam and Muslims and requires the defense of Europe. One wonders why. Here he advocates not only the defense of territorial Europe, but also Europe itself as a synecdoche for "the political"! In a philosophical key, Europe now signifies the political universally. The exact words Derrida uses are telling:

> Today more than ever such a reading should take into account the fact that all the concepts of this theory of right and of politics are European, as Schmitt himself admits. Defending Europe against Islam, here considered a non-European invader of Europe, is then more than a war among wars, more than a political war. Indeed, strictly speaking, this would not be a war but a combat with the political at stake, a struggle for politics. And this holds even if it is not necessarily a struggle for democracy.... From then on, the front of this opposition is difficult to place. It is no longer a thoroughly political front. In question would be a

defensive operation destined to defend *the* political beyond particular states or nations, beyond any geographical, ethnic or political continent. On the political side of this unusual front, the stakes would be saving the political as such, ensuring its survival in the face of another who would no longer be a political enemy but an enemy of *the* political—more precisely, a being radically alien to the political as such.⁷⁰

Without disagreeing with Schmitt, Derrida effectively inscribes multiple ontological boundaries to show the difference between Islam and Europe. The combat with Islam is configured as a struggle over the "the political." And there is more than a hint that Islam will remain an alien enemy of the political unless it assimilates to some degree with the European juridical and political tradition. Assenting to the latter is the passport for inclusion and to becoming European. What this invitation betrays is also an astonishing ignorance of the political discourses current among European Muslims for the past several decades. But what Derrida's meditation also conveys is that Europe's leading philosopher can take the liberty to make serious judgments on a sensitive topic affecting the lives of millions without making any effort to understand what the nature and debate of the political is among the communities about whom he is pontificating. In collapsing the distinction between the political (democracy) and the secular altogether, Derrida in effect reduces the political to the secular. This was Derrida's predisposition before September 11, 2001, when the United States was attacked by al-Qaida.

In 2003, a year before he died, Derrida published *Voyous: Deux essais sur la raison*, which was published in English in 2005 as *Rogues: Two Essays on Reason*.⁷¹ Derrida says about the context of the 1992 Algerian elections: "The electoral process under way in Algeria risked giving power, in accordance with perfectly legal means, to a likely majority that presented itself as essentially Islamic and Islamist and to which one attributed the intention, no doubt with good reason, of wanting to change the constitution and abolish the normal functioning of democracy or the very democratization assumed to be in progress."⁷²

Derrida's summary conclusions on political Islam in Algeria resemble the views of the American political theorist Michael Walzer and his discussion of political Islam in that very country. Nader Hashemi's detailed analyses of Walzer's conclusions, I would argue, are equally applicable to Derrida, namely, that both of their conclusions are "ideologically biased, monochromatic, and distorted."[73] The opinions of the marginal extremist factions of Islamists were deployed and magnified to justify the actions of the Algerian military regime's cancellation of the democratic elections. The views of mainstream Islamist spokespersons were conveniently ignored. Derrida's summary analysis of the political developments in Algeria has all the hallmarks of the selective use of information and a pro-authoritarian-state bias despite the human cost to the Algerian people of at least 200,000 deaths, as Hashemi diagnosed the civil war in response to Walzer's claims. Both Derrida and Walzer prefer secular governance as the panacea for all political conflict, irrespective of history and culture. And they advocate the removal of religion or the theological from the political sphere. "The New World," writes Anne Norton in response to such narrow understanding of politics, "is not persuaded that people need to be stripped of their faith before they can govern themselves."[74]

Yet Derrida goes further. Algerian Islamism is "antidemocratic" and "this Islam, this particular one and not Islam in general (if such a thing exists)," he wrote, "would represent the only religious culture that would have resisted up until now a European (that is, Greco-Christian and globalatinizing) process of secularization, and thus of democratization, and thus, in the strict sense, of politicization."[75] The statement on its own with a dose of hermeneutic generosity would allow one to infer that he views Islamic cultures as resisting Greco-Christian notions of the political in a constructive observation, or otherwise that it is a muscular declamation and critique of Islam as perpetually manqué.

Even though Derrida strategically tries to bracket the Algerian event from Islam more generally, this distinction evaporates. In essentialist fashion, Derrida then attributes the failure of democracy or resistance to democracy in Islamic contexts to the fact that, historically, Islamic political philosophy did not know Aristotle's *Politics* and preferred Plato's philosopher-king or absolute monarch and "that goes hand in hand with the severe judgment brought against democracy."[76]

Norton, in her *On the Muslim Question*, relentlessly points out Derrida's utterly wrongheaded formulations on Islam and on the history of Muslim philosophy.[77] The pratfalls are embarrassing when Derrida says that it is a "rather troubling fact that Aristotle's *Politics*" was absent in the Muslim philosophical encounter with the Greek legacy.[78] Rebutting multiple claims, Norton writes: "Derrida managed three errors in one sentence: Aristotle was imported not to Islam from Europe, but to Europe from Islam in the period he cites; references to the *Politics* are present in Islamic philosophy of the period; and al-Farabi [an early Muslim political philosopher] not only takes more than the philosopher king from Plato, he moves Plato in a democratic direction. The substance of the errors here is less interesting than Derrida's willingness to construct Islam as antidemocratic based on what he himself calls his own ignorance."[79] Derrida's ejaculations on Islam here are a model display of chutzpah: writing about a crucial political-cultural phenomenon of contemporary life, namely, Islam and Muslims, without investing in any respectful scholarly labor, an observation that should make any fair and dispassionate reader cast a shadow on Derrida's judgment.

The specters that haunt Derrida are those figures whom he identifies as "the enemy of the political," "a being radically alien," those "not Europeanized" and who share nothing of the European political and juridical traditions. One reading suggests that Derrida's words are very categorical, and we should take him at his word. In other words, he is loading his discourse with ontological ballast, being and presence, the very antithesis of deconstruction. It seems that only the Muslims and the Arabs retain their authorizing presence as "substance/essence/existence (*ousia*)" contrary to everything we learned from grammatology.[80] In all other instances, Derrida challenges commanding fictions, such as the guiding notions of Platonic ideas and Hegelian teleology. Why does Derrida's revolutionary mode of reading and thinking remain active and compelling on matters related to one shore of the Mediterranean, but then allies with the metaphysics of presence at the shores on the African side of the Mediterranean, or in the slums of France that political scientist Gilles Kepel unflatteringly called the "Banlieue de la République"? Derrida's meditations on Islam remain, to my mind, inexplicable. Islam is the ghost, or the specter, that haunts deconstruction and resists the Greco-Christian notions of the political.[81]

If it is not clear by now, I am arguing that one of Europe's preeminent philosophers, Jacques Derrida, despite his other interventions of fragmenting sovereignty and softening secularity, is entirely committed to a secularized Christian political theology of Europe à la Schmitt on a universal scale. So, the question arises: Did Derrida the Algerian of Jewish heritage become assimilated to France to the extent that he has now colonized others with the weapons of French secularism, coded as "the political" in his theorization? If Algeria is emblematic of Arabs/Islam, then Derrida had for decades fostered ways to emasculate Algerians with his most stark ideological thinking.

If so, then one must also highlight the fact that the modern democratic order is not without boundaries, in other words, it is hosted in the nation-state. Democracy is captured and hosted within a political theology of Europeanness, meaning Christianness. Even if this Christianity is radically secularized, it nevertheless remains culturally Christian, as Zubrzycki points out. Given the ethnic nature of Polish identity, Zubrzycki adds, an abstract notion of civic identity or in my formulation as notions of governmentality, cannot be realized in such a nation-state since belonging itself is tied to a religious and ethnic identity that precludes others. Philosophically it remains within the European nationalist project. Here the nation represents the people, as Amesbury points out, and the people as White and culturally Christian/western. In the case of France, the idea of the people is symbolized by Europeanness ethnically and the idea of the political is symbolized by the secular. Hence, those who do not hail from European stock and are not committed to European ideas are in a lesser position. But it is Europeanness, a claim Derrida repeatedly makes, that forms the foundation of citizenship and belonging.

What French Republicans and the late pope Benedict at the time of the various controversies centered on Muslims in Europe all passionately share is a belief that Islam as a discursive political tradition must be prevented from any substantive participation in the existential and political order of Europe. This means not only by resisting the changing demographic complexion of Europe, but also by precluding Muslims from contributing to diversifying the epistemological and ontological dimensions of European life. Conversion to the secular and secularity is a prerequisite in the minds of many European leaders. In other words, the aim is to retain Europe, at any cost, as a secularized Christian space so that it does not become a multireligious and shared political and cultural space. Legal combat over the headcover and veil for Muslim women in France, the prohibition of the building of mosque minarets in Switzerland, and the struggles over multicultural education in the UK are all sublimations of the Battle of Lepanto of 1517, when the fleet of the Holy League defeated the Ottoman fleet and thus prevented the Ottomans from entering Italy. The acceptance of the headscarf, the veil, and minarets in the public space would have resulted in the acceptance of a difference, a Muslim difference, that would contaminate the ontology of the European space and complicate notions of Europeanness, all intolerable prospects to a good number of European intellectuals.

Conclusion

Dallmayr has engaged both Derrida and Schmitt in his scholarly writings and provided some of the most perceptive insights in countering Schmitt's notions of sovereignty and the friend–enemy distinction. His insights also carry implications for some of Derrida's political readings. For Schmitt "the primacy of sovereign power over all forms of public deliberation or civic cohesion," explains Dallmayr, is part of the twentieth century's neo-Hobbesianism.[82] Derrida too transposes the idea of sovereignty on the state and insists on its need, as both Wendy Brown and I show. For Derrida says: "And yet . . . it would be imprudent and hasty, in truth hardly reasonable, to oppose unconditionally, that is, head-on, a sovereignty that is itself unconditional and indivisible. One cannot combat, head-on, all sovereignty, sovereignty in general without threatening at the same time, beyond the nation-state figure of sovereignty, the classical principles of freedom and self-determination."[83] Here are dim echoes of Schmitt's overblown claim on sovereignty that beguiled so many twentieth-century and contemporary intellectuals: "Sovereign is he who decides on the exception."[84]

As Brown points out, Derrida wrests the unconditional from sovereignty, then channels the conditional to freedom, only to reinvent sovereignty as conditioned, divisible, and shared.[85] Unlike other European post-Marxists who think of sovereignty as outmoded and believe that it should be substituted with global justice, Derrida holds on to sovereignty. Brown reads Derrida as detaching freedom from the autonomous subject and detaching reason and faith from absolutism, but this is not the story Derrida tells in his conversation with Chérif with respect to the theological or theocratic subject. A certain amount of sovereignty underwrites his idea of individual freedom that lies at the heart of democracy, and hence Derrida's continuous rhetorical refrain that the religious subject must not be subordinate to the desires of the faith community, theological community, and those in authority. Yet, he does not edify us as to the limits of secular authority.

If Schmitt's friend–enemy distinction was not just a rhetorical formula but a criterion for war and peace, then, as Dallmayr puts it, "the enemy is someone who can be killed."[86] Political leaders and public intellectuals alike have deployed Schmitt for their own ends, as Dallmayr explains, and deepened the desire to "spread unlimited 'terror wars,'" by the upsurge of a Manichean division of the world into friends and enemies, into supporters of Western-style 'freedom' and devotees of an infernal 'axis of evil.'"[87]

Schmitt-inspired barriers divide friend from enemy and deem impermissible and impossible any kind of epistemic *métissage* (mixing), which might otherwise foster modes of living that include rich experiences from various communities. If philosophy is *not going to be a critical discipline*, then these mental and existential barriers will result in the exclusion of the unfamiliar or the alien. Philosophy will *contribute* to the fears and phobias fueled by death and terrorism, one among which Dallmayr lists as Islamophobia.[88] Fear of Islamic strangers becomes manifest in battles over veils, burqas, or minarets. Learned discourses of "the political" inform both left-wing and right-wing European governments' efforts to propose legislation to regulate immigration, especially Muslim immigration, to Europe. The "zombie nationalism" that Jason Springs (chapter 2 herein) identifies in the United States finds its counterpart on display in Europe as "zombie secularism."

Framing the theocratic as the antithesis of the political, Derrida exceeds Schmitt in proclaiming that the "other," the Muslim other, has no concept of the political or, at best, politics manqué. Derrida deprived himself of intimate knowledge of Islamic juridical and political systems, and he regrettably lumped all Islamdom in a mystified European philosophy that devalues the unconditional and the theocratic. European anxiety to preserve the Euro-Christian or the Greco-Christian secular is often sustained against the "other," which once was and remains the Jew, but now that list also includes Muslims, migrants, Romani peoples, and Black Africans. When Derrida, as a leading philosopher of deconstruction who had once scandalized the profession of philosophy with his subversive ideas, cannot unshackle himself from some of the more prejudicial elements of the European imaginary and instead lauds it as something profound and unique, the intellectual future of political philosophy itself looks bleak.

Deconstruction might have been subversive, but it did not sufficiently decontaminate or decolonize itself from the bacilli of European supremacy that generations of European thinkers have entrenched and universalized as knowledge. The hope itself lies in decolonizing and critically evaluating as well as provincializing the universalized western intellectual tradition to save it from its own demons. Even the most sophisticated forms of philosophical thinking continue to disguise ethnonationalism as the logic of "the political." "For French Muslims," the noted Marxist writer Tariq Ali wrote while observing developments in twenty-first-century France, "there is a stench of Vichy in the air, with pollution levels highest in cities and regions dominated by the far right. Few are searching for antidotes to this poison, but some exist."[89] Vichy was the collaboration of a section of France with Nazism between 1940 and 1944 under Marshal Philippe Pétain before the Allied liberation of France. One had hoped that deconstruction and Marxist thinking could have been part of this antidote and part of the emancipatory narrative, but alas. Instead, French secularism, *laïcité*, has become weaponized by a multitude of philosophies from positivism to Marxism, to deconstruction, and to even more seemingly avant-garde philosophies today.

NOTES

I would like to acknowledge the generous and detailed feedback from Atalia Omer, Josh Lupo, Sam Kigar, and Ali A. Mian in preparing this chapter. Any errors are mine alone.

1. Partha Chatterjee, *The Nation and Its Fragments: Colonial and Postcolonial Histories* (Princeton, NJ: Princeton University Press, 1993), 3.
2. Ibid.
3. Ibid., 4.
4. Ibid., 3.
5. See Mahmood Mamdani, *Neither Settler nor Native: The Making and Unmaking of Permanent Minorities* (Cambridge, MA: The Belknap Press of Harvard University Press, 2020), 150. I have borrowed the idea of timeless natives from Mamdani and applied it to White nationalism. The colonizing logic of timeless natives was deployed to subdue Indigenous people in Africa and North America.

6. Gil Anidjar, *The Jew, the Arab: A History of the Enemy* (Stanford, CA: Stanford University Press, 2003).

7. David Tracy, *Plurality and Ambiguity: Hermeneutics, Religion, Hope* (San Francisco: Harper & Row, 1987), 62.

8. Richard Beardsworth, *Derrida & the Political* (London: Routledge, 1996), xiii.

9. Ibid.; see also Jonathan Rée, "Metaphor and Metaphysics: The End of Philosophy and Derrida," *Radical Philosophy*, no. 38 (1984): 28–33.

10. Jacques Derrida, *The Gift of Death*, trans. David Wills (Chicago: University of Chicago Press, 1995), 70.

11. Giorgio Agamben, *Homo Sacer: Sovereign Power and Bare Life*, ed. Werner Hamacher and David E. Wellbery, trans. Daniel Heller-Roazen (Stanford, CA: Stanford University Press, 1998), 3.

12. Ibid., 5.

13. Michel Foucault, *The Birth of Biopolitics: Lectures at the Collège de France, 1978–1979*, trans. Graham Burchell (New York: Picador, 2010), 18.

14. Ibid., 19.

15. Agamben, *Homo Sacer*, 5.

16. Fred R. Dallmayr, "Farewell to Metaphysics: Nietzsche," in *Critical Encounters: Between Philosophy and Politics* (Notre Dame, IN: University of Notre Dame Press, 1987), 13–38, at 18.

17. Ibid., 14.

18. Jacques Derrida, Mustapha Chérif, and Giovanna Borradori, *Islam and the West: A Conversation with Jacques Derrida*, trans. Teresa Lavender Fagan (Chicago: University of Chicago Press, 2008), 4.

19. Ibid.

20. Ibid.

21. Ibid., 3.

22. Ibid., 10.

23. Ibid., 8. Chérif here grapples with the question of unreason in faith traditions and the range of challenges faith traditions encounter in the modern age. In his words: "We must try to understand the ineffable, to understand why and how reason, on the one hand, and faith, on the other, experience such difficulties in describing metamorphoses, in facing them, in accepting them. It is true that faith, as an intuition, sensation, conviction, lives and grasps the signs, risks, movements of the world in an easy, simple and natural way; from that, when it gives itself the Open for a horizon, it enables the human being to maintain a stand, a dignity, an ethics, even if nothing guarantees happiness" (ibid.). The insightful dilemmas and aporias he posed were not sustained in the conversation with Derrida.

24. Ibid., 39.

25. Ibid.

26. Ibid., 5, 13.

27. Houria Bouteldja, *Whites, Jews, and Us: Toward a Politics of Revolutionary Love*, trans. Rachel Valinsky (South Pasadena, CA: Semiotext(e), 2017).
28. Derrida, Chérif, and Borradori, *Islam & the West*, 30.
29. Ibid., 42.
30. Ibid.
31. Ibid., 43.
32. Ibid.
33. Ibid., 45.
34. Ibid., 49 (italics in original).
35. Ibid., 48 (italics in original).
36. Ibid., 49.
37. Ibid., 50.
38. Ibid., 50–51.
39. Ibid., 51.
40. Ibid.
41. Ibid.
42. Ibid., 51–52.
43. Ibid., 52.
44. Ibid., 53.
45. Wendy Brown, "Sovereign Hesitations," in *Derrida and the Time of the Political*, ed. Suzanne Guerlac and Pheng Cheah (Durham, NC: Duke University Press, 2009), 114–32, at 116.
46. Derrida, Chérif, and Borradori, *Islam & the West*, 53–54. Italics in original.
47. Madan Sarup, *An Introductory Guide to Post-Structuralism and Postmodernism*, 2nd ed. (New York: Harvester Wheatsheaf, 1993), 34–35.
48. Jacques Derrida, "Psyche: Inventions of the Other," in *Reading De Man Reading*, ed. Lindsay Waters and Wlad Godzich (Minneapolis: University of Minnesota Press, 1989), 25–65, at 36: "The most rigorous deconstruction has never claimed to be . . . nor above all to be *possible*. And I would say that deconstruction loses nothing from admitting that it is impossible; also, that those who would rush to delight in that admission lose nothing from having to wait. For a deconstructive possibility would rather be a danger, the danger of becoming an available set of rule-governed procedures, methods, accessible approaches. The interest of deconstruction, of such force and desire as it may have, is a certain experience of the impossible . . . the experience of the other as the invention of the impossible, in other words, as the only possible invention" (emphasis original).
49. Gayatri Chakravorty Spivak, "Translator's Preface," in Jacques Derrida, *Of Grammatology* (Baltimore: Johns Hopkins University Press, 1974), ix–lxxxvii, at xxi.
50. Ibid. "The formal essence of the signified is *presence*, and the privilege of its proximity to the logos as *phonè* is the privilege of presence" (Derrida, *Of Grammatology*, 18) (emphasis original).

51. Simon Glendinning, *Derrida: A Very Short Introduction* (Oxford: Oxford University Press, 2011), 76.

52. Michel de Certeau, *The Writing of History*, trans. Tom Conley (New York: Columbia University Press, 1988), 345.

53. Caputo among others sees a theological without the theocratic; see John D. Caputo, *The Prayers and Tears of Jacques Derrida: Religion without Religion* (Bloomington: Indiana University Press, 1997).

54. For the metaphysics of deconstruction, see Rée, "Metaphor and Metaphysics."

55. Derrida, *Of Grammatology*, 7.

56. Jacques Derrida, *Writing and Difference*, trans. Alan Bas (Chicago: University of Chicago Press, 1978), 70.

57. See Atalia Omer, "Decolonizing Religion and the Practice of Peace: Two Case Studies from the Postcolonial World," *Critical Research on Religion* 8, no. 3 (2020): 273–96; Santiago Slabodsky, "Not Every Radical Philosophy Is Decolonial," Contending Modernities, June 4, 2020, https://contendingmodernities.nd.edu/decoloniality/not-every-radical-philosophy-is-decolonial/.

58. See Michael Naas, "Derrida's *Laïcité*," *New Centennial Review* 7, no. 2 (2007): 21–42, at 38. Naas argues that Derrida has aligned himself with a notion of Europe that is both a space and a universalizing moment beyond space.

59. Derrida, Chérif, and Borradori, *Islam & the West*, 75.

60. Ibid., 75–76.

61. Ibid., 74.

62. Jacques Derrida, *Politics of Friendship*, trans. George Collins (London: Verso, 1997), 83.

63. Ibid.

64. Carl Schmitt, *The Concept of the Political*, exp. ed. (Chicago: University of Chicago Press, 2007), 29.

65. Ibid., 28 and 29.

66. Derrida, *Politics of Friendship*, 89. Parentheses surrounding quotations here and below are in the original.

67. Derrida, *The Gift of Death*, 103.

68. Ebrahim Moosa, "Post 9/11: America Agonizes over Islam," in *Cambridge History of Religions in America*, Vol. 3, *1945 to the Present*, ed. Stephen J. Stein (Cambridge: Cambridge University Press, 2009), 553–74.

69. I am not the only one to have observed Derrida's shortcomings in his analysis of Islam and Muslim culture; see Ahmad Achrati, "Deconstruction, Ethics and Islam," *Arabica* 53, no. 4 (October 2006): 472–510, at 504. Achrati writes: "For someone whose philosophy is about the rejection of the ethico-politics of ethnocentrism, Derrida's comments on the Arabo-Islamic hospitality surely come across as a postmodern variation on the very ethnocentrism which deconstruction is supposed to displace. In his treatment of the Arabo-Islamic hospitality, Derrida

remains as Eurocentric as can be, preoccupied with the civic, the urban, the cosmopolitan and the national" (ibid.). He adds in conclusion: "As to Derrida's perspective on Islam and the Arabo-Islamic culture, one can only regret that deconstruction has shown itself to be, in Heidegger's words, 'insufficiently original'" (507).

70. Derrida, *Politics of Friendship*, 89 (italics in original).

71. Jacques Derrida, *Rogues: Two Essays on Reason* (Stanford, CA.: Stanford University Press, 2005).

72. Ibid., 31.

73. Nader Hashemi, "The Secular Bias and the Study of Religious Politics: On Michael Walzer and Political Islam (with Insights from John Esposito)," in *Overcoming Orientalism: Essays in Honor of John L. Esposito*, ed. Tamara Sonn (New York: Oxford University Press, 2021), 80.

74. Anne Norton, *On the Muslim Question*, coursebook ed. (Princeton, NJ: Princeton University Press, 2013), 121.

75. Derrida, *Rogues*, 31.

76. Ibid., 32.

77. Norton, *On the Muslim Question*.

78. Derrida, *Rogues*, 31.

79. Norton, *On the Muslim Question*, 121.

80. Edward W. Said, "The Problem of Textuality: Two Exemplary Positions," *Critical Inquiry* 4, no. 4 (1978): 673–714, at 692.

81. Colin Davis, "Hauntology, Spectres and Phantoms," *French Studies* 59, no. 3 (2005): 373–79, at 378–79. See Alex Thomson, "Derrida's *Rogues*: Islam and the Futures of Deconstruction," in *Derrida: Negotiating the Legacy*, ed. Madeleine Fagan et al. (Edinburgh: Edinburgh University Press, 2007), 66–79, where the challenge of fitting Islam into existing models of the politico-theological is discussed.

82. Fred R. Dallmayr, *Being in the World: Dialogue and Cosmopolis* (Lexington: University Press of Kentucky, 2013), 88.

83. Derrida, *Rogues*, 158.

84. Carl Schmitt, *Political Theology: Four Chapters on the Concept of Sovereignty*, trans. George Schwab (Chicago: University of Chicago Press, 2005), 5.

85. Brown, "Sovereign Hesitations," 115.

86. Dallmayr, *Being in the World*, 89.

87. Ibid.

88. Ibid., 90.

89. Tariq Ali, "Winged Words," review of *Muhammad* by Maxime Rodinson, *London Review of Books* 43, no. 12 (2021): 14.

CONTRIBUTORS

RICHARD AMESBURY is professor of religious studies and of philosophy, and director of the School of Historical, Philosophical and Religious Studies at Arizona State University. He is a philosopher and scholar of religion with three main (occasionally overlapping) areas of interest: (1) religion and contemporary political thought, (2) Wittgenstein, and (3) the politics of the secular. Prior to joining ASU, he held the chair in theological ethics at the University of Zurich, Switzerland, and chaired the Philosophy and Religion Department at Clemson University, where he was professor of philosophy and of religious studies.

R. SCOTT APPLEBY is Marilyn Keough Dean of the Keough School of Global Affairs at the University of Notre Dame. Appleby's research examines the various ways in which religious movements and organizations shape and are shaped by national, regional, and global dynamics of governance, deadly conflict, international relations. and economic development. Appleby codirects, with Ebrahim Moosa and Atalia Omer, Contending Modernities, a major multiyear project to examine the interaction among Catholic, Muslim, and secular forces in the modern world. He is the author or editor of fifteen books, including the widely cited volumes *The Fundamentalism Project* (coedited with Martin E. Marty) and *The Ambivalence of the Sacred: Religion, Violence and Reconciliation* (1999). Most recently, Appleby coedited (with Atalia Omer) *The Oxford Handbook of Religion, Conflict and Peacebuilding* (2015).

Contributors

SINDRE BANGSTAD is a Norwegian social anthropologist and a research professor at KIFO (Institute for Church, Religion and Worldview Research) in Oslo, Norway. He is a 2022–23 Stanley Kelley Jr. Distinguished Visiting Professor in the Teaching of Anthropology at Princeton University. The author of seven books, Bangstad has ethnographic fieldwork experience from work on Muslims in Cape Town, South Africa, and Oslo, Norway. He is the author of, inter alia, *Anders Breivik and the Rise of Islamophobia* (2014), *The Politics of Mediated Presence* (2015), and *Anthropology of Our Times: An Edited Volume in Public Anthropology* (2017).

PHILIP GORSKI is the Frederick and Laura Goff Professor of Sociology and Religious Studies and chair of the Department of Sociology at Yale University. His research focuses primarily on religion and politics in early modern and modern Europe and the United States. Recent books include *American Covenant: A History of Civil Religion from the Puritans to the Present* (2017), and, with Samuel L. Perry, *The Flag and the Cross: White Christian Nationalism and the Threat to American Democracy* (2022). He is currently working on a Durkheimian alternative to secularization theory.

YOLANDE JANSEN is a professor by special appointment for the Socrates foundation at the Vrije Universiteit Amsterdam, where she holds the chair for humanism, religion, and secularity. In addition, Jansen is associate professor of social and political philosophy at the University of Amsterdam. She is the author of *Secularism, Assimilation and the Crisis of Multiculturalism: French Modernist Legacies* (2014), and co-editor, together with Joost de Bloois and Robin Celikates, of *The Irregularization of Migration in Contemporary Europe: Detention, Deportation, Drowning* (2015). With Nasar Meer, she edited a double special issue of the journal *Patterns of Prejudice* (February–May 2020), on "Genealogies of 'Jews' and 'Muslims': Social Imaginaries in the Race-Religion Nexus."

JASMIJN LEEUWENKAMP is a doctoral candidate in philosophy at the Amsterdam School of Cultural Analysis, University of Amsterdam. Her research focuses on anthropocentrism in human rights discourses and explores the interrelations between political philosophy, ecological concerns, social justice, and rights-based environmental protection strategies. She recently coauthored "Posthumanism and the 'Posterizing Impulse'" in the volume *Post-Everything: An Intellectual History of Post-Concepts* (2021).

JOSHUA LUPO is assistant director of the Contending Modernities research initiative at the Kroc Institute for International Peace Studies at the University of Notre Dame. He has published articles and reviews in *Soundings, Reading Religion, Sophia,* and *Religious Studies Review.* His current book project is titled *After Essentialism: A Critical Phenomenology for the Study of Religion.*

EBRAHIM MOOSA is Mirza Family Professor of Islamic Thought and Muslim Societies in the Keough School of Global Affairs at the University of Notre Dame. He codirects Contending Modernities, the global research and education initiative examining the interaction among faith traditions and secular forces in the world, with a special focus on traditional Islamic theological education. Moosa's interests span both classical and modern Islamic thought with a special focus on Islamic law, history, philosophy, ethics, and theology. His book *What Is a Madrasa?* was published in 2015. Moosa is also the author of *Ghazali and the Poetics of Imagination* (2006), winner of the American Academy of Religion's Best First Book in the History of Religions, and editor of the last manuscript of the late Fazlur Rahman, *Revival and Reform in Islam: A Study of Islamic Fundamentalism* (2000).

ATALIA OMER is professor of religion, conflict, and peace studies at the Kroc Institute for International Peace Studies and at the Keough School of Global Affairs at the University of Notre Dame. She is also the Dermot T. J. Dunphy Visiting Professor of Religion, Violence, and Peace Building at Harvard University, and a senior fellow at the Religion, Conflict, and Peace Initiative at Harvard University's Religion and Public Life program. Her research focuses on religion, violence, and peace-building with a particular focus on Palestine/Israel and on theories and methods in the study of religion. Omer was awarded an Andrew Carnegie Fellowship in 2017 to complete a manuscript titled *Decolonizing Religion and Peacebuilding.* Among other publications, Omer is the author of *When Peace Is Not Enough: How the Israeli Peace Camp Thinks about Religion, Nationalism, and Justice* (2015), and *Days of Awe: Reimagining Jewishness in Solidarity with Palestinians* (2019). She is also a coeditor of *The Oxford Handbook of Religion, Conflict, and Peacebuilding* (2015). Omer is codirector of Contending Modernities, a global research initiative.

JASON A. SPRINGS is professor of religion, ethics, and peace studies, Kroc Institute for International Peace Studies, Keough School for Global Affairs, University of Notre Dame. Springs is particularly interested in ethical, philosophical, and theological dimensions of restorative justice, attending specifically to its potential to intervene in racialized and class dimensions of the U.S. prison-industrial complex. He works on questions of structural and cultural violence, conceptions of religious toleration and the challenges posed by religious pluralism for transforming conflict, Islamophobia in Europe and North America, and democratic theories and practices as frameworks for peacebuilding. These concerns are oriented by his broader research interests in American pragmatist thought and postliberal theology. Springs's current book project studies the effectiveness of restorative justice initiatives in responding to structural forms of racism and injustice (e.g., the New Jim Crow). He is the author of *Healthy Conflict in Contemporary American Society: From Enemy to Adversary* (2018), *Toward a Generous Orthodoxy: Prospects for Hans Frei's Postliberal Theology* (2010), and coauthor (with Atalia Omer) of *Religious Nationalism: A Reference Handbook* (2013).

GENEVIÈVE ZUBRZYCKI is professor of sociology at the University of Michigan, where she directs the Weiser Center for Europe and Eurasia and the Copernicus Center for Polish Studies. A historical and cultural sociologist, her scholarship focuses on the relationship between national identity and religion, collective memory and national mythology, and the contested place of religious symbols in the public sphere. Her most recent book, *Resurrecting the Jew: Nationalism, Philosemitism and Poland's Jewish Revival* (2022), analyzes the current renewal of Jewish communal life in Poland and non-Jewish Poles' interest in all things Jewish. Her other works include the award-winning *The Crosses of Auschwitz: Nationalism and Religion in Post-Communist Poland* (2006), *Beheading the Saint: Nationalism, Religion, and Secularism in Quebec* (2016), and *National Matters: Materiality, Culture, and Nationalism* (2017). In 2021, Zubrzycki was the recipient of a Guggenheim fellowship and was awarded the Bronislaw Malinowski Prize in the Social Sciences from the Polish Institute of Arts and Sciences of America.

INDEX

Page numbers in italics refer to figures.

abortion rights
   Catholic stances on, 111, 115, 117–18
   opposition to, 42, 62, 72–73
   Roe v. Wade, 42, 72, 111, 117
   support for, 72–73, 95n79, 115
Achrati, Ahmad, 279n69
Adorno, Theodor, 207
AfD party. *See* Alternative for Germany (AfD) party
African Americans. *See* Black Americans
Agamben, Giorgio, 249–51
agape love, 82
aggiornamento, 110
Albertazzi, Daniele, 8
Algerian election (1992), 263–64, 270–71
Ali, Tariq, 276
Alinsky, Saul, 108
Alito, Samuel, 95n73
Alternative for Germany (AfD) party, 13, 132, 148–51, 158n51 manifesto, 146, 149–50, 157n35, 158n53
Alt-Right movement, 187
"America First" slogan, 232
American exceptionalism, 25, 59, 65
American Indians, 26, 28, 139–40
American Protective Association, 104
American Requiem (Carroll), 113
Anderson, Benedict, 7, 13, 157n35, 247
Anthropocene, 206, 208, 210–12
anti-Black racism, 8, 29, 120, 140, 155n20
   at Bob Jones University, 98n94
   toward Black Catholics, 104–6, 108–9, 111–12, 115–16, 125n6
   and civil rights, 97n88, 142
   and violence, 91n50, 107
   See also Black Americans; marriage, interracial; racism: structural; slavery

285

286   Index

anti-Catholic racism, 62, 102–4
  toward Black Catholics, 104–7, 109, 115–16, 125n6
  toward Latinx Catholics, 121–22
antifa, 87n26
anti-Muslim racism, 1, 3, 8–15, 146, 196
  American, 29, 33, 90n46, 155n20
  based on the concept of Judeo-Christian civilization, 158n53, 188
  by Buddhists and Hindus, 40
  compared to anti-Black and anti-Asian racism, 153n3
  exclusion of Muslims from European history, 209, 212
  and fears about Islamic terrorism, 33, 62, 90n46, 132, 275
  by feminists, 9
  French, 8, 15, 269, 273, 276
  —and Derrida, 256, 258, 261–64, 267
  —*laïcité*, 174, 256, 258, 261
  German, 13, 148–51, 158n53
  in the global South, 19n22
  history of, 240n27
  by Jerry Falwell, Jr., 131–32, 153
  Norwegian, 228–30
  othering of Muslims, 41, 132–33, 137, 157n44
  and philosemitism, 11, 158n53
  Polish, 238
  Trumpist, 53–54, 62, 132
  See also Islam; Muslim Americans
antisemitism, 3, 5, 8–15, 227, 275
  in American history, 28, 106, 126n9
  in antiquity, 32, 194
  and conspiracy theories, 57–58
  exclusion of Jews from European history, 209, 212, 222n98
  with Jews as elites, 158n53
  magical antisemitism, 158n54, 161–65, 237
  and Zionism, 15
  See also Jews; Judaism; philosemitism
antisemitism, without Jews, 159, 162
anti-Zionism, 176n3
apocalypse, the
  in Catholic nationalism, 116
  and Latour, 192–97, 218n45
  Marian apocalypticism, 128n35
  in pop culture, 27–28, 58–59
  in White evangelical nationalism, 30–32, 35, 39, 56–59, 232
  See also end-times, the
Arabs, 174, 240n22, 264
  and Derrida, 253, 258–59, 272–73, 279n69
Arab Spring, 263
Arendt, Hannah, 142, 145, 152, 238, 268
  On Revolution, 156n31
Aristotle, 265
  Aristotelian physics, 218n34
  Politics, 271–72
Asad, Talal, 7, 141, 223–27
Ashkenazi culture, 168
Asian Americans, 29, 93n59
  Catholic, 128n40
Assmann, Jan, 192, 210
  The Price of Monotheism, 221n89, 221n97
"Avoidance of Love, The" (Cavell), 131

Bardawil, Fadi, 226, 240n22
Barr, Juliana, 139
Battle of Lepanto (1517), 273–74
Baudet, Thierry, 216n16, 217n26

Becoming Human (Jackson), 218n54
behavioral psychology, 68
Bellah, Robert N., 145
belonging, 1, 9, 13, 15–16, 141–43
  by birth, 88n38, 254
  blood belonging, 28
  Catholic ways of, 106, 116
  land-based, 196, 206, 254
  by religious identity, 23–24, 133, 154n6, 273
  by various identities, 133, 230, 273
Bernardin, Joseph (cardinal), 117
Berrigan, Daniel (priest), 109–10, 113
Berrigan, Philip, 113
biblical literalism, 27, 29, 31–32
biblical prophecy, 27, 57–58, 80, 99n105, 99n107
Biden, Joe, 42, 84n8, 87n26, 112, 114–15. *See also* United States election (2020)
biopolitics, 249–51
birther conspiracy theory, 155n20
bisexual people. *See* lesbian, gay, bisexual, transgender, queer, and intersex (LGBTQI) people
Black Americans
  Catholic, 102, 104–12, 115–16, 125n6, 128n40
  conservative, 93n59
  See also anti-Black racism; marriage, interracial; racism: structural; slavery
Black Lives Matter (BLM), 53, 66
blood
  and antisemitism, 58
  metaphors in Catholic nationalism, 116
  metaphors in conservative traditions, 40
  metaphors in White evangelical nationalism, 23, 26–28, 30–31, 39, 232
  and Trump, 33
  uniting Christians, 11, 161
  uniting Jews, 11
Bob Jones University, 98n94
boreal civilization (racial concept), 188, 209, 216n16
born-again evangelicalism, 82, 93n59
bourgeois coldness, 207–8
Bouteldja, Houria, 254
Brand, Ulrich, 185, 189, 207, 214, 218n29
Breivik, Anders Behring, 228–29, 232
Brown, Wendy, 248, 259, 274
Brown v. Board of Education (1954), 98n94
Brubaker, Rogers, 133, 157n41, 157n44, 173, 217n27
Buchanan, Patrick J., 111–12, 114, 117
bürgerliche Kälte, 207

Camus, Renaud, 187
capitalism, 226
  associated with Polish Jews, 162
  Catholic resistance to, 107
  connected to ecological crisis, 185–86, 193, 196, 200, 203–8
  digital capitalism, 157n35
  print-capitalism, 247
Capitalocene, 208, 212. *See also* Anthropocene
Carroll, James, 111, 113–14
  American Requiem, 113
Carter, J. Kameron, 194
Cartesian divide, 200
"Catholic Church and the Negro Priest, The" 125n6

288   Index

Catholicism of continuity, 174n1
Catholic Reconquista, 241
Catholic sexual ethics, 108, 114, 118, 120
Catholic Worker Movement, 107–8
Cavell, Stanley, 131, 141–42
Chatterjee, Partha, 246
"cheap nature," 185, 206–7
Chérif, Mustapha, 248–49, 252–255, 259, 262, 274
  Islam and the West, 249
  on unreason and faith, 277n23
chosenness, 14
  national claims of, 24–25, 61, 76
  "new Israel," 25, 59
  Trump claims of, 33–34
Christian Front organizations, 106
Christianism, 13, 133, 217n27
Christian scripture, figural interpretation, 81, 99n107
chthonos, 211
Chthulucene, 211. *See also* Anthropocene
citizenship, 3, 5
  and Derrida, 254–55, 264, 267, 273
  and exclusion, 138, 140–42, 156n29, 160
  for gays and lesbians, 69
civic republicanism, 27
civilizationist populism, 157n41, 190, 217n27
civil religion, 89n41, 145, 153
civil rights, 75, 97n88
  civil rights movement, 107, 109–13
climate change. *See under* ecological crisis
climate denialism, 190, 196, 204
  by politicians, 217n26
Clinton, Hillary, 42, 115. *See also* United States election (2016)

colonialism, 3–4, 6–7, 10, 15–16
  and Bodin, 17n9
  and enslavement, 96n84, 127n19
  Euro-colonialism, 184, 186, 214, 215n8
  and Latour, 195, 204–6, 209
  themes and imagery of, 185–86
  western, 24–25, 213–14, 246–47
  and Wynter, 195, 205–6
  See also decolonialism
coloniality, 4, 6–7, 18n14, 206, 268
  and Christianity, 11, 13, 15–16
communism
  and antisemitism, 162, *163*, 174n1, 178n12
  associated with civic discourse, 170, 173
  godless Communism, 25, 30, 128n35
  post-communism, 160, 181n34
  as un-American, 160
communitas perfecta, 122
conspiracy theories
  appeal to evangelicals, 56–57, 86nn21–22, 87n26
  birther, 155n20
  Polish antisemitic, 161–64
  Protocols of the Elders of Zion, 57–58
  QAnon, 51, 56–59, 86nn21–24, 87n27
  stolen 2020 U.S. presidential election, 34, 57, 87n26
contempt for matter, 183, 189–94, 199, 202–3, 207–8
Contending Modernities (CM), 2
conversion therapy, 70, 95n73
cosmopolitanism, 159, 161–62, 254
Coughlin, Charles (reverend), 106, 126n9, 126n18

counterreligion, 192–94, 204, 210, 221n97. *See also* monotheism
COVID-19, 190, 250
cultural Marxism, 187
Cyrus the Great (king), 99n105
  compared to Donald Trump, 34, 80–81, 188

Dallmayr, Fred R., 248, 251, 274–75
"dark times," 223, 238
Dawn of the Dead (1978), 55–56
Day, Dorothy, 107–8, 112, 123, 126n14, 126n16
de Certeau, Michel, 260–61
Declaration of Independence, 139–40, 143–44, 152, 156n31
decolonialism, 6–8, 10–13, 276
  and Derrida, 262
  and ecology, 184, 220n85
  See also colonialism
deconstructive criticism, 247–49, 255–65, 272, 275–76, 278n48, 279n69
  overview of, 5
deep state, 57, 87n27
Defense of Marriage Act (1996), 71. *See also* marriage, same-sex
De l'origine du langage (Renan), 212
democracy, 140, 143, 145, 136–37
  Democracy in America (Tocqueville), 43
  and Derrida, 253–55, 258–61, 263–65, 269–71, 273, 275
  liberal democracy, 36, 136–37, 141
Democracy in America (Tocqueville), 43
"democracy to come" (Derrida), 254, 258, 263

Democratic Party (American), 57, 93n58, 115
demos, 130, 140, 142, 144–45
Derrida, Jacques, 139–40, 143–44, 152, 213
  Islam and the West, 249
  Politics of Friendship, 247–48
  Rogues, 248–49, 253, 270
Diagnostic and Statistical Manual of Mental Disorders (DSM), 68–69
digital capitalism, 157n35
Dionysus, 97n90
discursive traditions, 2, 186, 188, 230, 235, 246–47
  alternatives beyond the European framework, 5, 16, 254–55, 261, 268–69
  applied to the category of religion, 130, 134–35, 268
  and Islam, 174, 224, 273
  and Jews, 159, 161, 164–65, 237
Dobson, James, 70
Dolan, Jay P., 110
double critique, 7, 12, 19n19
Down to Earth (Latour), 184, 190, 209, 235
Drawing Hands (Escher), 138–39
Dred Scott v. Sandford (1857), 143

Earth, 189, 191–94, 200, 203–5, 207
  Earthboundedness, 183, 185–86, 196–99, 202–3, 212–14
  See also Gaia
ecological crisis, 10, 124, 234–36
  climate change, 66, 215n5, 217n26
elections. *See* Algerian election (1992); United States election (2012); United States election (2016); United States election (2020)

290   Index

elective affinities
  between American religious conservatism and right-wing populism, 14, 39–42
  binding White evangelicals to Trump, 80
  among ethnicity, religion, and nationalism, 53–54, 58, 60–61, 64–65, 88n38
  between Zionist antisemitism and Christian restorationist theologies, 15
Elgat, Guy, 93n63
elites, suspicion of, 8, 34, 36–38, 40, 135–36
  in America, 117, 132, 137
  and ecological disaster, 195–96
  in Europe, 148–49, 151
  Jews seen as elites, 158n53, 162
  by QAnon, 57–58, 87n27
  scientists seen as elites, 190
  by Trump, 34
Emerson, Michael, 30
End of White Christian America, The (Jones), 84n13, 234
end-times, the, 15, 28, 33, 56–58, 193. *See also* apocalypse, the
Enlightenment, the, 148, 225–26
ensauvagement, 189, 217n22
Ericksen, Adam, 97n90
eschatology, 27, 40, 80
ethno differentialisme, 187
ethnopluralisme, 187
ethnoracial hierarchies, 230, 242n39
Euro-colonialism, 184, 186, 214, 215n8
Europeanness, 267–68, 273–74
European New Right, 187–88, 230
  nouvelle droite (French New Right), 187, 212, 216n13, 230
European Union (EU), the

  opposition to, 146, 157n35, 174n1
  and Polish Jews, 160, 162, 178n13
"Europe We Can Believe In, A" 156n34
Exodus International ("gay conversion" organization), 70

Facing Gaia (Latour), 184, 191, 204
Falwell, Jerry, Jr., 131–32, 150, 153, 153n2, 155n20
Falwell, Jerry, Sr. (pastor), 146, 148
Far Right, the, 185–86, 214n1, 216n16, 235–36
  alternative nomenclature for, 185–86, 244n70
  in France, 208, 216n14, 276
  idealization of Nordic people and lands, 91n52, 244n71
  in the Netherlands, 216n16
  in Norway, 228
  in Poland, 162–64, 178n14, 237
  in Sweden, 187
  in the United States, 143, 232
  worldwide proliferation of, 182, 184–87, 229–30, 238
Farris, Sara, 9
fascism, 187, 216n13, 216n17, 232, 242n53
Fassin, Didier, 225–26
Fea, John, 71–72, 85n17, 98n94
Federated Colored Catholics, 109
feminism, 6
  Catholic, 108, 120
  ecofeminism, 200, 217n23
  femonationalism, 9
  Indigenous, 215n8
  Polish opposition to, 169, 177n7
  Polish support of, 171–72

pro-choice, 95n79
See also gender; women
Festival of Jewish Culture (Kraków), 166, 170
Flore, Joachim de (monk), 192
Focus on the Family ("gay conversion" organization), 70
Forum voor Democratie (Dutch party), 187
Foucault, Michel, 134, 225–26
  "regime of truth," 250–51, 267
Foundation for Freedom (Poland), 167
Francis (pope), 118–19, 200, 209
  Laudato si', 118, 185, 199–200, 209
Francis of Assisi (Saint), 199, 209
Frankenstein's monster, 54–55, 85n15
Fratelli tutti (Pope Francis), 119
Frederiksen, Mette, 243n66
freedom, 250–51
  American concepts of, 25, 27
  and Derrida, 256–59, 274–75
  of religion, 147, 154n15, 158n51, 255–56
  religious freedom as *ressentiment*, 67, 69–78, 95n73
  of speech, 95n73
French New Right. See *nouvelle droite*
French Revolution (1973), 43, 264
French secularism. *See* laicism
Friedland, Roger, 19n27, 84n12
friend–enemy relationship (Schmitt), 265–69, 274–75
Fuss, Peter, 165, 179n21

Gaia, 183, 191, 215n5
  secular figure of, 185, 197–99, 202–3, 209–11

See also Earth
Galtung, Johan, 91n50
Gauland, Alexander, 149
Gazeta Wyborcza, 162–63, 174n1
gender, 6, 9–10, 12–14
  biblical limits for marriage, 69, 71, 94n70
  and Catholicism, 102, 108, 119, 123, 177n7
  and the environment, 195, 200, 205–6, 211, 217n23
  norms, 53, 75, 96n81, 120–21, 256
See also feminism; women
genealogical critique, 2–7, 227, 229, 237
  and Asad, 223–27
  and Latour, 195–97, 210
  and Moncrief, 206
  and Serres, 188
Genealogy of Morals, The (Nietzsche), 65
Gibson, David, 115
Glemp, Józef (cardinal), 174n1
globalization, 184, 191, 196, 214, 264
global warming. *See* ecological crisis
Gnosticism, 183–84, 190–95, 263
Goldenberg, Naomi, 149
Gorka, Sebastian, 19n28
Graff, Agnieszka, 177n7
Gramsci, Antonio, 229–30
  Gramscism, 187–88
great replacement theory, 187–88, 216n16, 230
  grand remplacement, 187, 189
  White extinction, 188, 216n17, 230, 236
Greek civilization, 210, 215n5, 225, 253, 271–72

Greek civilization *(cont.)*
  influence on language, 198, 211, 221n94
  and White supremacy, 185, 209
GreekJew, 211, 221n92
Green Din, 211, 221n92, 222n103
Gregory XVI (pope), 127n19
gun control, opposition to, 35, 63, 131–32, 155n20
Gushee, David, 85n16

Haeckel, Ernst, 210
Hall, Stuart, 232, 237–38
Hamilton, Clive, 220n83
Haraway, Donna, 18n12, 198, 211–12, 221n94
Harcourt, Bernard E., 225
Harlem Renaissance, 104–5
Harlem Shadows (McKay), 105
Hart–Celler Immigration and Nationality Act of 1965, 65, 91n52
Hashemi, Nader, 270–71
Hegelian thought, 213, 221n97, 272
hermeneutics, 2–3, 14, 16–17, 122
  exclusionary, 13
  inclusionary, 12
  nihilistic, 12–13, 78–79, 81
Higham, John, 91n52
Hispanic Americans, 92n54, 92n56
  Catholic, 122, 128n40
  See also Latinx Americans
Hochschild, Arlie, 36
Hofstadter, Douglas R., 139
Holy Trinity. *See* Trinitarian doctrine
Home to Harlem (McKay), 105
Hughes, Langston, 140, 155n26
Humanae vitae (Pope Paul VI), 111, 114, 127n32
Hurd, Elizabeth Shakman, 150

Identitarianism, 133, 187, 217n27, 229
"imaginary Poles," 161
immigration to America
  by Asian immigrants, 26, 65
  by Catholic immigrants, 101–6, 110
  Catholic response to, 112, 114–15, 117, 120–22
  "century of immigration," 103
  Europeans as religious/racial others, 29
  Hart–Celler Immigration and Nationality Act of 1965, 65, 91n52
  by Hispanic immigrants, 128n40
  by Latinx immigrants, 29, 34, 65, 83n5
  nativist preference for northern and western Europeans, 91n52, 244n71
  opposition to, 36, 117, 143, 156n29
  reception by White vs. non-White evangelicals, 66
  Trump policies, 42, 52–53
  —at the Mexican border, 83n5, 83n7, 112
  —against Muslims, 53, 62
  —against "shithole countries," 244n71
immigration to Europe, 235–36, 238, 275
"imperial mode of living," 189, 202–4, 206–9, 213–14, 217n27, 218n29
Indigenous peoples, 6, 201, 236, 247, 276n5
  American Indians, 26, 28, 139–40

Church apology to, 118
erasure of, 215n8, 222n102, 268–69
and the theory of semiosis, 222n102
Indo-European civilization (racial concept), 188, 212
In supremo apostolatus (Pope Gregory XVI), 127n19
intersectionality, 7–9, 12, 16, 25, 230
Catholic, 122
intersex people. *See* lesbian, gay, bisexual, transgender, queer, and intersex (LGBTQI) people
Irish Catholic Americans, 28–29, 103–4
Islam
and Christianity, discourse about, 132, 137, 144, 147–51, 229
and critical Muslim Studies, 19n19
as a discursive tradition, 2, 224
and ecology, 210, 221n92, 222n103
evangelical Christian distancing from, 30
and Muslims as meaning-making agents, 2
populist preoccupation with, 217n27
"radical," 25, 30
See also anti-Muslim racism; Muslim Americans
Islam and the West (Derrida, Chérif, and Borradori), 249
Islamophobia. *See* anti-Muslim racism
Israel
contemporary culture of, 167–68, 180n23

Jerusalem, 80, 98n102
right-wing populist support of, 9–10, 24, 59
Italian Catholic Americans, 28–29, 103–4

Jackson, Zakiyyah Iman, 218n54
Jefferson, Thomas, 140, 152, 232
Jenkins, Jerry B., 27–28
Jerusalem, 80, 98n102
Jerusalem Embassy Act (1995), 80
Jesuits, 106
"Jesus Christ King of Poland" billboard, 165, 179n21
JewGreek, 211, 221n92
Jewish Americans. *See under* Jews
Jewish Community Center (JCC) (Kraków), 166–67, 169
Jews, 11, 16
and Derrida, 253–54, 266, 273
GreekJew, 211, 221n92
Israeli, 9, 80, 247
JewGreek, 211, 221n92
Jewish Americans, 23–24, 28–29, 106, 126n9
and Trump, 80, 188
as White, 10, 24, 29, 60
See also antisemitism; Judaism; philosemitism
Jim Crow laws, 76, 142
John Paul II (pope), 114, 158n54, 163–64, 172
Johnson, James Weldon, 104
Johnson–Reed Act (1924), 91n52
John XXIII (pope), 110
Joint Distribution Committee (JDC) (Warsaw), 168
Jones, Robert, 54–55
The End of White Christian America, 84n13, 234

294 Index

Judaism, 31, 210, 212, 222n98, 240n27. *See also* antisemitism; Jews; philosemitism
Judeo-Christian civilization, concept of, 10–11, 205–6, 210, 228–29
  as anti-Muslim, 158n53
  and Europe, 188
  and secularism, 150
  and the U.S., 29, 61, 65, 76, 85n17

Kant, Immanuel, 226, 264
Kepel, Gilles, 272
King, Martin Luther, Jr. (reverend), 110, 113–14
Kingdom of God, 27
Kingdom of the Spirit, 192
Klein, Ezra, 92n55
Know-Nothings, 104
Kowalski, Sergiusz, 161
Kruse, Kevin, 30
Ku Klux Klan (KKK), 104
Kwaśniewski, Aleksander, 162, *163*

Labor Party (Norwegian), 228, 235
LaFarge, John (pastor), 109–10, 126n18
LaHaye, Tim, 27–28
laicism (*laïcité*/French secularism), 150, 174, 255–56, 261, 276
Late Great Planet Earth, The (Lindsey), 58
Latinx Americans, 38, 93n59
  Catholic, 117, 121–23, 128n40
  Mexican, 29
  See also Hispanic Americans
Laudato si' (Pope Francis), 118, 185, 199–200, 209
Law and Justice Party (Poland), 160, 174n1
"Left Behind" series, 27–28, 58–59

Le Pen, Jean-Marie, 208, 216n16
lesbian, gay, bisexual, transgender, queer, and intersex (LGBTQI) people
  attempts to "cure," 68–70, 95n73
  employment discrimination against, 98n94
  as fashionable in Poland, 167–68
  Gay Pride, 71
  opposition to rights for, 9, 216n14
  Polish Catholic opposition to rights of, 169, 174n1, 177n7, 237
  rights in the U.S., 69
  seen as abominations, 68–69, 94n69
  and support for Jews in Poland, 172, 177n7
  See also marriage, same-sex
"Letter to a White Liberal" (Merton), 116
LGBTQI people. *See* lesbian, gay, bisexual, transgender, queer, and intersex (LGBTQI) people
liberal democracy, 36, 136–37, 141
Lienesch, Michael, 29
Lindsey, Hal, 58
line-cutting, 36, 117
Lloyd, Vincent W., 135
Lovelock, James, 198, 215n5
Loving v. Virginia (1967), 74, 98n94. *See also* marriage, interracial

MacWilliam, George Joseph, 125n6
mainstream media, 57, 87n27
Make America Great Again (MAGA) rhetoric, 42, 66, 142, 155n26, 232–33
Makuch, Janusz, 170

Mamdani, Mahmood, 227, 276n5
Manichaean religious perspectives, 39, 56, 190, 194, 202
Maritain, Jacques, 109
marriage, interracial, 12
  opposition to, 34, 72–79, 96n81, 96n84, 98n94
  support for, 78–79
marriage, same-sex, 12
  opposition to, 34, 68–79, 94n70, 95n73, 96n81, 98n94
  support for, 71, 81–82, 99n109
Marzouki, Nadia, 148
  Saving the People, 133, 229
Matovina, Timothy, 122
Maurin, Peter, 107, 113
Mbembe, Achille, 226
McCarthy, Cormac, 28
McCarthyism, 160
McDonnell, Duncan, 8, 148
  Saving the People, 133, 229
M. C. Escher, 138–39
McGreevy, John, 111, 119
  Parish Boundaries, 105
McIvor, Méadhbh, 154n15
McKay, Claude, 105
Merton, Thomas, 116
messianism
  in Catholic nationalism, 116
  in conservative traditions, 40–41
  and Trump, 33–34, 51, 56–58, 78, 80–82
  in White evangelical nationalism, 21, 30–34, 39, 58–59
metaphysics, 197, 249–50, 258–61, 272
metapolitics, 229–30
Mexican Americans, 29
Michalik, Józef (archbishop), 174n1
Michnik, Adam, 162
militarism
  Algerian, 263–64, 271
  American, 26–28, 35, 116
Mills, Charles W., 217n23
miscegenation. *See* marriage, interracial
Mit brennender Sorge (Pope Pius XI), 109
Mitchell, Clarence, 110
modernization, 77, 191, 193, 203
Moffitt, Benjamin, 38
Moncrief, Lewis, 206
mondialatinisation, 213
monotheism, 170, 255
  and *race monothéiste*, 212, 222n98
  and religious diplomatic limitations, 192, 204, 209–13, 221n97
  See also counterreligion
Moore, Brenna, 105
Moore, Diane, 18n12
Moore, Jason, 185, 206–8, 214
moral majority, 52, 146, 151
Moses, Robert, 109
multiculturalism, 148, 188, 273
  and philosemitism, 159, 166, 170–74, 237
multivariate analysis, 224, 230, 233, 238
Muslim Americans
  anti-Muslim rhetoric, 90n44, 131–33, 153, 155n20
  as other, 29, 40–41, 137, 153n3, 157n44
  policies against Muslim immigrants, 53, 62
  See also anti-Muslim racism; Islam

National Front (French party), 187
nationalism, Latin etymology of, 25, 88n38

nationalism, overview of, 3, 7–10
  religious nationalism, 22–26
nation-state, the (concept), 7, 245–46, 254–55
  in the AfD manifesto, 146, 157n35
  and American identity, 61, 76
  and ethnic exclusion, 169, 227, 273
  limitations of, 249–50, 258
  and religion, 135
  and sovereign legitimacy, 130, 141–42, 145–46, 150, 274
natural law, 72–75, 82, 96n85, 144
nature, environmental, 184–85, 189–91, 193–94, 197–200, 202–10
  "cheap nature," 185, 206–7
Nazis
  and Carl Schmitt, 269
  contemporary, 10, 230
  endorsement by Father Charles Coughlin, 9
  ideology of, 3, 244n71
  Nazi Germany, 109
  resistance against, 164
  and Vichy, 276
negligence (Serresian irreligiousness), 188–90, 198, 201, 203, 207–8
neoliberalism, 5, 12, 15, 186, 226, 259
  alienating qualities of, 250
  Catholic, 119
  and the devastation of U.S. social life, 233–34
  feminist, 9
  fueled by social media, 247
  and traditional conservative values, 42
Netanyahu, Benjamin, 10, 80

new Israel, 25, 59
New Right (French). See *nouvelle droite*
New York Catholic Interracial Council, 109
Nietzsche's Psychology of Ressentiment (Elgat), 93n63
Nietzsche, Friedrich, 13, 94n67, 97n90
  The Genealogy of Morals, 65
  and *ressentiment,* 54, 66–68, 77–78, 81, 93n63
nihilism, 12–13, 51–52, 65, 75, 234
  and *ressentiment,* 54, 68, 77–79, 81
9/11 terrorist attacks, 90n46, 160, 270
Noll, Mark, 29
"nones," religious (unaffiliated), 43, 117
Norton, Anne, 248
  On the Muslim Question, 271–72
nouvelle droite, 187, 212, 216n13, 230

Obama, Barack, 34, 112, 131, 155n20
  United States election (2012), 71
Obamacare, 160
Obergefell v. Hodges (2015), 71, 75, 95n73, 96n81. *See also* marriage, same-sex
On Revolution (Arendt), 156n31
On the Muslim Question (Norton), 271–72
Open Catholics (Polish group), 174n1
Ornstein, Jonathan, 167
Orozco, Romero, 121
Ottoman Empire, 40, 265, 268, 274

paganism, 188, 200
  and White supremacy, 209, 212
Palaver, Wolfgang, 154n6
Parish Boundaries (McGreevy), 105
"Paris Statement, The," 156n34
parrhesia, 225
passing (racist trope), 164
Paul VI (pope), 110–11, 113–14
  Humanae vitae, 111, 114, 127n32
People of God, 110, 114
Peretti, Frank, 58, 88n31
perfect community (Catholic), 122
perfect society (Catholic), 122
Perry, Samuel L., 34–35
persecution narratives. *See* victimization narratives
philosemitism, 10–11, 159–60, 172–73, 175n2
  as cover for anti-Islamicism, 158n53
  magical, 165–69
Philpott, Daniel, 94n70
Pius XI (pope), 109
Plato, 261, 271–72
Polak, Wojciech (cardinal), 174n1
Poland, Jewish revival, 165–72, 174, 181n34
Poland Fighting (symbol), 164
POLIN Museum of the History of Polish Jews, 166
Polish Catholic Americans, 104
Polish Catholics, 159–66, 168–69, 171–72, 174n1, 237
"political, the" (Derrida), 249–51, 256–59, 263–70, 273, 275–76
political theology, 3–4, 11–13, 101
  and Derrida, 245, 248, 261, 272–73

  and Schmitt, 17n8
  and Trump, 21, 23
Politics (Aristotle), 272–72
Politics of Friendship (Derrida), 247–48
Popper synagogue (Kraków), *167*
populism, overview of, 5, 35–36, 135–36, 228–31
postethnic identity, 101, 111–12, 121–23
postmillennialism, 27
premillennialism, 27, 116, 128n35
Price of Monotheism, The (Assmann), 221n89, 221n97
print-capitalism, 247
proof-texting, 81
Protocols of the Elders of Zion, 57–58
Puritans, 25, 103

QAnon conspiracy, 51, 56–59, 86nn21–24, 87n27
queer people. *See* lesbian, gay, bisexual, transgender, queer, and intersex (LGBTQI) people
Quijano, Aníbal, 18n14

Race: A Theological Account (Carter), 194
race monothéiste, 212, 222n98
racism, 1, 8–9, 52, 59, 231–34
  and American Catholics, 105–6, 108–23
  biological, 73–74, 210, 212, 230, 232, 240n27
  correlated with Christian nationalism, 34–35
  skepticism about, 64–65, 92n56, 98n96
  structural, 30, 63–64, 91n50, 104, 107, 140

Index

racism *(cont.)*
  and Trump, 244n71
  See also anti-Black racism; anti-Catholic racism; anti-Muslim racism; antisemitism; marriage, interracial; slavery
Radio Maryja, 163, 165, 172, 174n1, 178n16
Ramsey Colloquium, 96n81
Rassemblement National (French party), 187
Rawls, John, 217n23
Reagan, Ronald, 58, 103, 119
red scare, 160
refugees
  asylum seekers, 53, 243n66
  Central American, 42
  discrimination favoring Ukrainian, 236
  Jewish, 171
  opposition to, 42, 174–75, 236, 243n66
"regime of truth" (Foucault), 250–51, 267
religio-secularism, 185–86, 201–3, 205, 209–11, 214. *See also* "secular, the," episteme; secularism; secularity; secularization
religious diplomacy, 199–202, 209–13
religious freedom. *See under* freedom
religious literacy, 6, 18n12, 228
religious nationalist quadrilateral (RNQ), 39–40
Renan, Ernest, 212–13, 222n98
Reno, R. R., 156n29
Representing God (McIvor), 154n15
republicanism, 27, 43
Republican Party (American)
  and Catholics, 115, 118
  and conspiracy theories, 56, 87nn26–27
  and evangelicals, 44, 66, 82, 83n3, 83n7, 93nn58–59
  and White conservatives, 92n55
Requiem for a Species (Hamilton), 220n83
ressentiment, 52, 54, 93n63, 94n65, 95n73
  as ethnoreligious nationalism, 65–68
  and Islam, 252
  and religious freedom, 71–78
  and sexual politics, 68–71, 82
  See also victimization narratives
Revelation, book of, 27
reverse racism. *See* victimization narratives
Risk Oy clothing line, 167–68
Road, The (McCarthy), 28
Roberts, John, 96n81
Roe v. Wade (1973), 42, 72, 111, 117. *See also* abortion rights
Rogues (Derrida), 248–49, 253, 270
Romero, George, 55–56
Rousseau, Jean-Jacques, 156n31
Roy, Oliver, 148
  Saving the People, 133, 229
Ryan, John A. (monsignor), 126n18
Rydzyk, Tadeusz (priest), 178n16
Rykoszetem (Graff), 177n7

Saracens, 265, 267, 269
  "the eternal Saracen," 252
  "the Saracen problem," 247
Sartre, Jean-Paul, 162
Saving the People (Marzouki, Duncan, and Roy), 133, 229
Schmitt, Carl, 3, 17n8
  and Derrida, 247–48, 258, 265–70, 272, 274–75

Schudrich, Michael (rabbi), 180n22
science, 183–85, 190–91, 193–95, 197–206, 214n1, 217n26
Scott, David, 238
"secular, the," episteme, 97n93, 135, 137–38, 147, 150–52
    and Derrida, 255–56, 258, 260–64, 267, 270, 273
    See also religio-secularism
secularism, 185, 202
    as compatible with Christianity in Germany, 150–51, 158n51
    and Derrida, 255–56, 259, 273, 276
    Judeo-Christian, 150
    laicism (*laïcité*/French secularism), 150, 174, 255–56, 261, 276
    and Latour, 197
    Polish, 160, 171, 174, 237
    See also religio-secularism
secularity, 3, 41, 150, 185, 273
    and Derrida, 253, 258, 261, 272
    as an episteme, 147
    in Germany, 138, 148, 150
    and Latour, 190, 197, 199, 201–3
    in the U.S., 137–38, 146–47, 151
    See also religio-secularism
secularization
    and Derrida, 255, 258–60, 271
    and Latour, 184–85, 190, 197, 202, 213–14
    —limitations of, 185, 204, 208, 210–11
    and Moncrief, 206
    and White, 205–6
    See also religio-secularism
Sedgwick, Eve Kosofsky, 226
segregation, 29, 74, 77, 98n94, 106, 110
semiosis, 202, 211, 222n102

September 11, 2001, attacks, 90n46, 160, 270
Serres, Michel, 124, 199, 202–3, 209
    negligence (irreligiousness), 188–90, 198, 201, 203, 207–8
sexual minorities. *See* lesbian, gay, bisexual, transgender, queer, and intersex (LGBTQI) people
sexual orthodoxy, 69, 75
Shelley, Mary, 55–56, 85n15
"shining city upon a hill" metaphor, 103
Shohat, Ella, 18n14
situated knowledges, 18n12
Slabodsky, Santiago, 10
slavery, 26, 91n50, 96n84
    American amnesia toward, 139
    biblical justifications for, 29
    enslaved people as other, 28
    eventual condemnation by the Catholic Church, 109, 127n19
    and popular sovereignty, 142–43
    as practiced by Thomas Jefferson, 140
Smith, Christian, 30
Social Gospel, 29–30
socialism, 159–60, 162
Socialist Lebanon (organization), 226
social justice, 29, 107–10, 119, 209
Social Justice (newspaper), 126n9
societas perfecta, 122
Society of Jesus, the (Jesuits), 106
soft tyranny, 76, 94n70
Sokołowska, Karina, 168
sovereignty, 1, 13, 35–36, 229–31, 268–69
    and Derrida, 255–59, 262, 268, 272, 274
    of God, 82
    and Polish Jews, 173, 267

300   Index

sovereignty *(cont.)*
   and violence, 38
Spellman, Francis (cardinal), 109, 113
Środa, Magdalena, 177n7
Star of David, 162, *163*, 164, 167
storming of the U.S. Capitol (2021), 87n26, 88n29
"strange loop" metaphor, 139, 143, 152
Strangers in Their Own Land (Hochschild), 36
Swedish Far Right (party), 187

terrorism, 229
   Islamic, fears about, 33, 62, 132, 275
   9/11 attacks (U.S.), 90n46, 160, 270
   in Norway, 228–29, 232
   wars on terror, 1, 252, 275
theopolitics. *See* political theology
Theory of Justice (Rawls), 217n23
"timeless natives," 247, 276n5
Tocqueville, Alexis de, 43–44
Todd, Emmanuel, 234
toxic masculinity, 9, 12
Tracy, David, 248
transgender people. *See* lesbian, gay, bisexual, transgender, queer, and intersex (LGBTQI) people
transvaluation of values, 67–68, 70, 75–77, 81, 97n90. See also *ressentiment*
Traverso, Enzo, 162
Trinitarian doctrine, 30, 82, 99n109
Trump, Donald
   and the birther conspiracy, 155n20
   claims of stolen 2020 election, 57
   as Cyrus, 34, 80–81, 188
   disapproval of, 22, 42, 85n16, 86n19, 115
   as fascist, 232, 242n53
   on global warming, 217n26
   and immigration policies, 42, 52–53
   —at the Mexican border, 83n5, 83n7, 112
   —against Muslims, 54, 62
   —against "shithole countries," 244n71
   as messiah, 33–34, 57–58, 78
   and QAnon. 56–58, 87n27
   recognizing Jerusalem as the capital of Israel, 80
   rhetoric of, 33–34, 62
Trump, Donald, support of, 22, 42–44, 51–53, 80, 84n8, 231
   as abdication of the witness of Jesus, 85n16
   based on anti-Muslim rhetoric, 53, 62, 132
   based on messianic interpretations, 33–34, 58, 78
   based on quelling peaceful protests, 53
   by Catholics, 52, 112, 114–16
   correlated with church attendance, 83n7
   demographics of, 93n59
   driven by a sense of victimization, 71–72
   as repudiation of sexual politics, 71–72, 75, 79, 115
Trumpism, 14, 21, 55, 182
   and the ecological crisis, 184, 189, 208, 217n26
   as right-wing populism, 35–38, 62–63, 78, 79, 117
   as secularized White Christian nationalism, 23, 232–33

and White Christian nationalism, 22, 33–35, 64, 232–33
Tulli, Magdalena, 161
Turkey
 and Derrida, 248, 263, 265, 267–69
 right-wing populists of, 40
Turner, Thomas, 109
2083: A European Declaration of Independence (Breivik), 232
Tygodnik Powszechny, 163, 179n17, 179n20
typological interpretation. *See* Christian scripture, figural interpretation

"un-American" political beliefs, 160
United States election (2012), 71
United States election (2016), 21, 37–38, 65, 83n3, 84n13. *See also* Trump, Donald, support of
United States election (2020), 37, 65, 122
 conspiracy claims of stolen election, 34, 57, 87n26
 See also Trump, Donald, support of
United States v. Windsor (2013), 71. *See also* marriage, same-sex

Vatican, 110, 113, 126n18
Vatican II (1962–65), 110–12, 114, 122–23, 174n1
Venner, Dominique, 187, 216n14
victimization narratives, 39
 of Catholics, 112, 115–16
 and "polite persecution," 75–76, 94n70
 and Trump, 34

of White Christian nationalists, 21, 30–32, 56, 59, 234
 See also *ressentiment*
Vietnam War, 113
Voegelin, Eric, 189, 192, 197

Walzer, Michael, 270–71
Weber, Max, 60–61, 64, 88n38, 89nn39–40
welfare, 141
 American, 34
 European, 235
"We the people," 36, 143, 152
White, Lynn, 204–6, 210–11
White extinction, 188, 216n17, 230, 236. *See also* great replacement theory
Whitehead, Andrew L., 34–35
Whiteness, 36, 135, 140, 187, 195
 and Catholicism, 101, 121
 and Christianity, 14–16, 25–26, 29, 51–53, 62
 evangelical as ethnic identity, 92n56
 and geographic territory, 216n16, 247
whitening of marginalized ethnicities, 10, 29, 60, 104–6, 117
White privilege, 32, 36, 92n55, 111, 115, 207
White supremacy, 3–5, 227–28
 American, 25, 58, 65, 88n29, 91n52, 232–34
 —Catholic, 111, 117, 119–21
 European, 209, 230, 236, 244n71, 276
Williams, Thomas Chatterton, 188
Winthrop, John, 103
Wissen, Markus, 185, 189, 207, 214, 218n29
With Burning Concern (Pope Pius XI), 109

witness, Christian, 76, 81, 85n16, 94n70, 119
women
  and Catholicism, 107–9, 120–22, 125n6
  enslaved, 96n84
  Muslim, 256, 262, 273
  oppression of, 9, 97n88, 107, 174n1
  Polish, 168, 237
  and suffrage, 75, 97n88, 126n14, 143
  and Trump, 33, 42, 79
  women's rights, 75, 78, 97n88, 107–8
  See also feminism; gender
Women for Faith and Family (Catholic organization), 120
Wong, Janelle, 66, 83n3, 92n56, 93n59
Wynter, Sylvia, 152, 195

xenophobia, 8–9, 35, 91n52, 196
  anti-Catholic, 62
  practiced by Catholics, 101–2
X-Men: Apocalypse, 28

Yack, Bernard, 89n42
You Will Not Replace Us (Camus), 187

Zerilli, Linda, 226
Zionism, 9, 11, 15, 59, 162
zombie nationalism, 100, 102, 234, 275
  zombie Catholicism, 234

www.ingramcontent.com/pod-product-compliance
Lightning Source LLC
Chambersburg PA
CBHW071017240426
4366ICB00073B/2349